Also by William Fotheringham

Put Me Back on My Bike: In Search of Tom Simpson

Roule Britannia: A History of Britons in the Tour de France

Fallen Angel: The Passion of Fausto Coppi

A Century of Cycling

Fotheringham's Sporting Trivia

*Fotheringham's Sporting Trivia:
The Greatest Sporting Trivia Book Ever II*

CYCLOPEDIA

IT'S ALL ABOUT THE BIKE

WRITTEN BY
WILLIAM FOTHERINGHAM

CHICAGO REVIEW PRESS

Design and layout: www.carrstudio.co.uk

First published in the United Kingdom by Yellow Jersey Press in 2010
This substantially revised American edition published in 2011 by Chicago Review Press
Copyright © William Fotheringham 2010, 2011
Illustrations copyright © Telegramme Studio 2010

We are grateful to BBC *Focus* magazine for permission to use the pedal-power data first
published in the October 2009 issue.

Chicago Review Press Incorporated
814 North Franklin Street
Chicago IL 60637
ISBN 978-1-56976-817-4
Printed in the United States of America
5 4 3 2 1

PREFACE

The particular joy of cycling is in its infinite variety, its seemingly boundless history. Get on a bike and you can go anywhere, literally and metaphorically. Unlike a football or a tennis racket, a bike has multiple uses. It is simultaneously a piece of high-tech sports gear, a means of transportation to work or the store, a way of discovering the world, an escape to solitude and nature, a social network that beats any of the virtual variety, and a means of discovering your personal limits, whether by crawling up an Alpine pass or shredding your nerves downhill on a mountain bike. Over the last 150 years cycling has helped to change the world and it may yet help to save it from environmental catastrophe. Bikes have carried politicians, soldiers, explorers, suffragettes, socialists, artists, and artisans. Yet as cyclists we tend to exist in our own bubbles. We race, we ride to work, we may fret over whether to buy carbon fiber or titanium, we pedal off to picnics, we find new places. For whatever reason we ride our bikes, and whatever the depth of our personal passion, there will be sides of cycling, its history, its culture, that we don't even know exist. There isn't time to go everywhere and the signposts are not always there in the first place. And that is where this book may just be able to help, by giving some idea of the multiplicity of areas—social, technical, sporting, cultural, historical—to which two wheels can transport us.

There is one proviso. This book cannot help but reflect my personal views on a world in which I have been immersed for two-thirds of my life, over 30 years. No one will agree with everything they find here, but that is how it should be. The aim of this book is simply to offer some signposts toward what cycling has to offer, and some guidance through a world of never-ending possibilities. If, after reading it, you want to try something new, go to a race, or buy a book or DVD that you might not have known about, it will have served its purpose.

Enjoy the ride.

William Fotheringham,
July 2010

A

ABDUZHAPAROV, Djamolidin

(b. Uzbekistan, 1964)

Squat, tree-trunk thighed sprinter from Uzbekistan who was one of the biggest stars to emerge from the Eastern bloc after the fall of the Berlin Wall. Abdu' first came to prominence in the British MILK RACE, winning three stages in 1986, but it was in the 1991 TOUR DE FRANCE where his unique style grabbed world headlines: he put his head down low over the front wheel—a style later adopted to great effect by MARK CAVENDISH—and zigzagged up the finish straight, terrifying opponents and onlookers.

He took two stages in the 1991 Tour but came to grief in dramatic style as a third win beckoned on the Champs-Elysées: after colliding with an oversized cardboard Coke can standing against the barriers he somersaulted over the bars and rolled down the road. He had to be helped over the line, and was eventually awarded the points winner's green jersey three months later. This led to him being nicknamed the Terminator, because he got back up each time he was knocked down.

He went on to have a memorable feud with Italian sprinter Mario Cipollini—"send him back to Russia" was Cipo's line—and won a total of nine stages and three green points jerseys in the Tour. His career came to an end in 1997 after he tested positive for Bromantan, a drug used by Russian air force pilots; he retired to live on Lake Garda, where he tends pigeons.

(SEE **NICKNAMES** FOR OTHER BIZARRE CYCLING MONICKERS, AND **EASTERN EUROPE** FOR MORE INFO ON THE ORIGINS OF ABDU' AND HIS PEERS)

AERODYNAMICS If the strength of any cyclist is a given on a particular day, several key variables determine how fast he or she can travel: friction (resistance within the bearings and chain), the rolling resistance of the tires on the road, gravity, and air resistance. Of the four, air resistance is the hardest to overcome and has the greatest effect.

Air or wind resistance increases as a square of a cyclist's velocity; for every six miles per hour faster a cyclist travels, he must double his energy output. It is estimated that over 15 mph, overcoming wind resistance can account for up to 90 percent of energy output. Estimates vary as to how much a contrary wind can affect speed: some say it slows a cyclist down by half the windspeed (e.g., 2 mph for a 4 mph wind). Roughly a third of air resistance is encountered by the bike, roughly two-thirds by the rider.

The most obvious way to counter air resistance is by sheltering, be it merely by riding close to the hedge when the wind blows or choosing valley roads on a windy day. Riding in the slipstream of another cyclist uses up about 25 percent less energy depending on the size of the rider in front (team pursuit squads look for four cyclists about the same height and width to take advantage of this) and is the key to most of the tactical niceties of road and track racing. A bunch of cyclists riding together offers even greater shelter, as does a pacing motorbike such as a DERNY. Before motor vehicles got too quick, cyclists like FAUSTO COPPI

would go "truck-hunting" to get in speed training.

Changing handlebar position produces immediate results; riding with the hands on the "drops," not the brake levers, flattens the torso and increases speed by between 0.5 and 1.25 mph. Tucking in any loose clothing helps as well. Shaving the legs produces negligible benefits (see HAIR for other shaggy-cyclist stories), but wearing an aerodynamic teardrop-shaped helmet helps considerably, as does wearing a one-piece skinsuit rather than separate jersey and shorts, and putting covers over the shoes.

So much for the basics. Most recent aerodynamic developments can be traced back to FRANCESCO MOSER and his attempts on the HOUR RECORD in 1982. The Italian used a Lycra hat, shoe-covers, a plunging frame to lower the angle of his torso and reduce the profile of the bike, and solid disc wheels. All became widely accepted ways of reducing air resistance.

Tri-bars, so-called because they were first used by triathletes in the US in the 1980s, were the next major development. They provided the most dramatic recent illustration of the power of aerodynamics when GREG LEMOND used a pair to overturn a 50 second deficit in the final time trial of the 1989 TOUR DE FRANCE. The loser, LAURENT FIGNON, was not riding the extensions, which allow the user to flatten the torso and push the arms forward along the lines of a downhill skier's tuck.

Perhaps the ultimate tri-bar position was achieved by CHRIS BOARDMAN in the mid-1990s. He said of his work in the windtunnel at the Motor Industry Research Assocation in Birmingham, England: "They discovered that if I folded up my body position and tucked in my elbows the drag would be considerably reduced. What I learned was to reduce my frontal area. I have my handlebars about four or five centimeters lower than anybody else." As a result, if you drove behind Boardman when he was riding

Percentage of drag in the following:

BODY: 80%

WHEELS: 4%

FRAME: 5%

Ways to improve aerodynamics:

TRIATHLON BARS: 10%

    DEP. ON BODY SIZE + SHAPE

TEAR-DROP HELMET: 2%

ONE-PIECE SKINSUIT: 2%

SHOE COVERS: 1%

SMOOTHED OUT CARBON FRAME: 2%

DISC WHEELS: 2% DEP. ON WIND

    DIRECTION

a time trial, all that could be seen of him was his backside: his front end was completely flat, or pointing down slightly to minimize air resistance.

The boundaries were pushed further by GRAEME OBREE in the build-up to his Hour attempt in 1993, when the Scot experimented with a tuck position with his arms up close to his chest. Together with his coach Peter Keen, Boardman ran tests on the Manchester velodrome, riding in various positions and using POWER CRANKS to ensure his power output was relatively constant. Under these controlled conditions, Obree's tuck gave better airflow than either riding on the drops on a conventional bike or using triathlon handlebars. Obree later devised a stretched position known as "Superman"; both this and the tuck were eventually banned.

In the 1990 and 1991 Tours, LeMond rode Drop-In bars, which brought the tri-bar idea to road-racing bars; they had a lowered central section enabling him to get flatter and make his elbows more narrow than on conventional drops (they were also a handy location to put stickers advertising his bar-makers, Scott, for head-on television pictures); in the mid-1990s there was a brief craze for short triathlon-type extensions such as Cinelli's Spinaci bars, which could be fitted to the middle of road racing bars, again enabling the rider to lower his profile. They were banned from 1998 by the UCI; Cinelli are still campaigning for the ban to be lifted.

The wind and the drag coefficient of the cyclist and the bike are not the only factors affecting aerodynamics. Air resistance decreases as altitude is gained, because there are fewer molecules in the atmosphere for the cyclist to push through; traveling at 30 mph at 2,000 m above sea level should take about 20 percent less effort. Hence the choice of Mexico City and La Paz for record attempts by riders like CHRIS HOY and EDDY MERCKX.

Air temperature matters too, with air resistance reducing by about 1 percent for every increase of three degrees Celsius. It has been known for track meeting organizers to keep the doors closed before the home team rides a qualifier in an event such as the team pursuit, so they benefit from a higher temperature. They then open the doors shortly before their main rival goes to lower the temperature by a few degrees. Barometric pressure has an effect as well: the ideal weather conditions for recordbreaking are a high temperature combined with low pressure.

After tri-bars, the most efficient way to improve the aerodynamic profile of a bike is to fit disc wheels. These eliminate the drag produced by a conventional wheel with spokes, which have an uneven drag profile because as they come forward at the top of the wheel rotation they are going at twice the bike's forward speed.

Aerodynamic frame tubes also play a part: they should be teardrop-shaped, but three and a half times as long as they are round to be most efficient. "If a tube is too round, instead of flowing round the tube, the air bounces off it and creates mini vortexes that actually increase drag," says Boardman. Every part of the bike pulls on the air; hence the British Olympic team's return to the drawing board before the Beijing Games when their technicians—led by Boardman and the carbon frame specialist Dimitris Katsanis—assessed every last part of their carbon-fiber bikes. The result was smoothed-out handlebars, produced as a single element with the stem; even the wheelnuts were reconfigured to save an estimated 0.005 percent of drag coefficient.

(SEE BURROWS, RECUMBENTS, OLYMPIC GAMES)

AFRICA Cycling is a vital means of transport here and, in addition, cycle racing goes on in places and ways that few outside the continent know about. To take one example, in Eritrea the influence of Italian colonists from the early 20th century means that cycling is the national sport, with some 800 registered racers in the capital Asmara. The Giro di Eritrea was founded in 1946 and relaunched in 2001, eight years after the end of war with Ethiopia. There are said to be about 100 professionals in the country earning several times the average wage. An Eritrean cyclist, Daniel Teklehaimanot, finished 50th in the time trial in the 2009 world under-23 road race championships.

Italian and French colonial influence brought bike racing to the North African coast, and the sport is also strong in other former French colonies such as Burkina Faso and Mali. The Italian Marco Pastonesi interviewed Burkinabe cyclists for his 2007 book *The Craziest Race in the World*; they told him that cycling is the most popular sport in the country. The TOUR DE FRANCE organizers ASO recognize this by running the annual Tour du Faso each autumn. Cycle racing in Burkina Faso goes back to the postwar era, when FAUSTO COPPI came to race there in a series of criteriums in the capital, Ouagadougou, to celebrate the country's independence (it was then known as Upper Volta); after one of the races, Coppi caught the malaria which was to end his life.

Colonialism was also responsible for bringing the first African to the Tour de France: Abdel Kader Zaaf was an Algerian who became French national champion in 1942 and 1947, and rode the Tour in 1950 for a North Africa team. Zaaf was involved in a legendary episode when he was riding 16 minutes ahead of the bunch on a baking hot stage in the South of France and was given a bottle of wine by a spectator; the alcohol affected him so badly that he ended up riding the wrong way down the road.

More recently, in 2007, the South African team Barloworld became the first squad from the continent to race the Tour, when Robbie Hunter—already the first South African to start the Tour, in 2001—was the first stage winner from the country at Montpellier (see CAPE TOWN to read about the biggest bike race in Africa and the world). The best African races figure on the UCI's Africa Tour that includes events in Cameroon, Tunisia, Ivory Coast, Morocco, Gabon, Egypt, and Libya. The 2008–9 winner was Dan Craven, a Namibian riding with British squad Rapha-Condor.

In 2009, there were projects under way to turn cyclists in both Rwanda and Kenya into world-class roadmen. The Rwanda project was headed by Jonathan Boyer, the first American to finish the Tour de France. One of his riders,

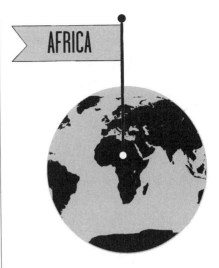

Leonard, was spotted when he kept pace with the team while carrying 150 pounds of potatoes on his bike. The project was set up by Tom Ritchey, one of the founding fathers of the MOUNTAIN BIKE, who set up a race, the Wooden Bike Classic, on which Rwandans could race the basic machines they used to carry coffee from the fields. The project in Kenya, backed by a French hedge fund, aims to transfer to cycling the endurance skills the Kenyans have shown in running.

ALPS   When the Alps were added to the TOUR DE FRANCE route in 1911, the idea of riding a bike over summits such as the 2,646 m high Col du Galibier seemed outlandish: such tracks connecting one mountain village with another were barely passable on foot, even in summer. When the Tour went over that July, the Galibier was still covered in vast snowdrifts and the road was a dirt track deeply rutted with streams of melt water. The road has been improved, but cycling to an altitude of nearly 9,000 ft remains an immense challenge.

Then, the Alps fitted perfectly with Tour founder HENRI DESGRANGE's aim of producing cycling supermen to captivate the readers of his paper *L'Auto*. Desgrange wanted to set his cyclists seemingly impossible tasks to perform amid epic backdrops, to make the most dramatic copy possible for his paper. Now, however, the mountains are accessible to ordinary cyclists thanks to better roads and the organization of a huge range of mass-participation events (see CYCLOSPORTIVES). In these events, the attraction lies in facing the same challenges as the stars of cycling, at a different speed.

The highest paved pass in the Alps is the Cime de la Bonette, sometimes known as the Bonette-Restefonds. It actually consists of two roads, one of which crosses the Col de Restefonds at an altitude just below that of the Col d'Iseran; to create the highest pass in Europe, the local council added a loop up around the black shale scree slopes of the Bonette peak, which is where the Tour goes.

Opinions vary, naturally, as to the toughest climb in the Alps: the north face of the Galibier, as climbed by the Tour in 1911, is a contender, because of the length of the ascent from Valloire over the Col du Télégraphe before the steepest part actually begins. Another contender is the Joux-Plane between Cluses and Morzine in the northern Alps, which is unremittingly steep, but toughest of all is probably

Mont Ventoux. This peak lies a little south of the main Alpine massif. It is longer than the Joux-Plane but almost as steep, with extreme conditions—heat or cold—occurring frequently on the summit. (see TOM SIMPSON to read the story of his death here).

The great Alpine climbs are used by CYCLOSPORTIVE events, of which the best-known is the Marmotte, which has been run for over 30 years. The 174 km course begins in Bourg d'Oisansand goes over the Croix de Fer and Galibier before finishing up l'Alpe d'Huez. La Ventoux ascends the Ventoux at the end of a 170 km loop. On some of the great climbs, local tourist offices run informal timed events up the climbs, so that amateurs can measure their times against the professionals—at l'Alpe d'Huez, for example, this takes place every Monday through the summer.

There are two Raids Alpines run along the lines of the better-known RAID PYRENEAN. These are informal challenges run by the cycling club in Thonon-les-Bains. One route takes cyclists from Lake Geneva to the Mediterranean Coast at Antibes over 43 passes with a total of 18,187 m climbing during the 740 km journey; the other travels from Thonon to Trieste, taking in 44 cols for a total of 22,131 m climbing in the 1,180 km route.

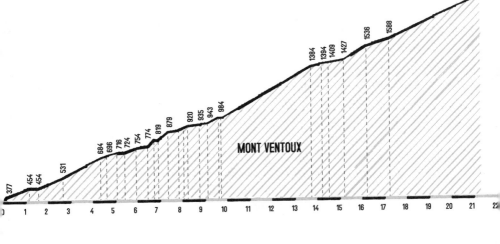

MONT VENTOUX

CLIMB	LENGTH	ALTITUDE	HEIGHT GAIN	NOTED FOR
Cime de la Bonette (from Jausiers)	23.8 km	2,802 m	1,582 m	Highest pass in Europe if you include the "loop to nowhere" at the top
Iseran (from Val d'Isère)	16 km	2,764 m	960 m	Vast glaciers and a wild summit in the Vanoise national park
Col Agnel (from Chateau Queyras)	20.5 km	2,744 m	1,384 m	In southern Alps, used by Tour for first time in 2008
Galibier (from Valloire)	18 km	2,646 m	1,216 m	Exposed scree slopes, a disused tunnel, memorial to Tour de France founder Henri Desgrange
Izoard (from Guillestre)	31.7 km	2,360 m	1,438 m	Death Valley–type pinnacles in the Casse Deserte, Tour de France museum at summit
Croix de Fer (from Rochetaille)	31.6 km	2,067 m	1,502 m	Massive lakes among epic glaciated rock formations, some downhill stretches
Madeleine (from La Chambre)	19.3 km	1,993 m	1,523 m	40 bends, 20 years construction work, stunning views through violet-filled meadows
Mont Ventoux (from Carpentras)	21 km	1,909 m	1,610 m	Bare moonscape at domed summit with observatory, Tom Simpson memorial
L'Alpe d'Huez (summit finish)	14.5 km	1,850 m	1,150 m	Winners' names on each of the 21 hairpins; timed climbs on Monday evenings
Joux-Plane (from Samoens)	11.8 km	1,691 m	988 m	Insanely steep climb with views of Mont Blanc

The passes in the south-eastern section of the Alps, over the Italian border from France, are a key element in the GIRO D'ITALIA, with their own cycling history: see DOLOMITES for more details.

Further reading: *Tour Climbs*, Chris Sidwells (Collins, 2008).

AMAURY SPORT ORGANISATION (ASO)

The world's leading cycle race organizer, responsible for the TOUR DE FRANCE, LIÈGE–BASTOGNE–LIÈGE and PARIS–ROUBAIX, and other races (see right) which make up the bulk of the French calendar. Based in Paris, the company also owns 49 percent of the Vuelta a España, and has partnerships with Tour of California. In early 2010 it took over the Dauphiné Libéré, giving it a near monopoly on French races.

ASO's lineage goes back to the newspaper *L'Auto*, which ran the first Tour de France. Under HENRI DESGRANGE and his successor Jacques Goddet, the paper organized the race until the outbreak of war in

The ASO Roster

◆

TOUR DE FRANCE

PARIS–ROUBAIX (PRO AND UNDER-23)

LIÈGE–BASTOGNE–LIÈGE

PARIS–TOURS (PRO AND UNDER-23)

FLÈCHE–WALLONNE (PRO AND WOMEN)

CRITÉRIUM INTERNATIONAL

PARIS–NICE

DAUPHINÉ LIBÉRÉ

TOUR DE PICARDIE

ÉTAPE DU TOUR

TOUR DE L'AVENIR

TOUR OF QATAR (PRO AND WOMEN)

TOUR DU FASO

PARIS–DAKAR MOTOR RACE

PARIS MARATHON

FRENCH GOLF OPEN

1940. During the war, Goddet continued to publish, which meant that after liberation, *L'Auto* could no longer appear as all publications that had printed under the Germans were shut down. After the war, the paper and its editor were charged with collaboration, but cleared, and Goddet was given charge of *L'Equipe*, a new paper that was in essence *L'Auto* under a different name. He then ran the race jointly with Émilien Amaury's *Le Parisien Libéré*, with Félix Lévitan as codirector. Amaury bought *L'Equipe* in 1965 and created a multimedia promotional and publishing empire that included venues such as the Parc des Princes stadium in Paris.

Later the group's cycling promotions were split off into a separate company, the Société du Tour de France; early in the 21st century this was merged into ASO, covering all Amaury's sports promotions. Goddet remained in charge of the STF's races until his retirement in 1989, when the former journalist Jean-Marie Leblanc took over. ASO grew rapidly during the 1990s, from less than 50 employees in 1992 to well over 200 in 2008, running 16 sports events including the Paris–Dakar rally, athletics, golf, and equestrianism.

After the 1998 doping scandal involving the Festina team, ASO became aware of the dangers that drugs posed to its races. The problem was that as race organizers, its options were limited: Leblanc tried refusing entry to those the race considered to be suspect, but he had limited support from the UCI, and in any case it was impossible to tell who was suspect and who wasn't. Leblanc retired in 2005; since then the Tour has been run by former television journalist Christian Prudhomme. (See section on the UCI for how ASO fell out with cycling's governing body between 2005 and 2008.)

The Tour is ASO's main source of income, estimated to bring in 70 percent of its profits.

ANDERSON, Phil (b. England, 1958)

Australian cycling's second great pioneer, after Sir HUBERT OPPERMAN. A whole new antipodean audience became aware of cycling thanks to Anderson's achievements in the 1980s, most notably his two stints in the Tour de France's yellow jersey in 1981 and 1982. Neither a truly great time triallist, sprinter, or climber, Anderson epitomized the battling Aussie, winning races through grit and racecraft.

An early member of the FOREIGN LEGION, he was a young pro with PEUGEOT when he hung on to BERNARD HINAULT at the Pla d'Adet climb in the 1981 Tour to become Australia's first wearer of the *maillot jaune*. Anderson went on to win two Tour stages (Nancy 1982, Quimper 1991) and finished in the Tour's top 10 five times, once while fighting the pain from a broken sternum. He also won two one-day CLASSICS (Amstel Gold 1985, Créteil–Chaville 1986); he was a member of two iconic teams, Peugeot and Panasonic, and together with GREG LEMOND helped to drag European cycling into the modern world.

Anderson was one of the first riders to arrive at a contractual meeting with a lawyer in tow ("I couldn't read French but that was the language of the contract so I turned up with a solicitor from Paris. He said it wasn't worth the paper it was written on," he said in Rupert Guinness's *Aussie Aussie Aussie Oui, Oui, Oui*). In addition, his relationship with 7-Eleven SOIGNEUR Shelley Verses in the late 1980s broke the long standing taboo over SEX in cycling. He was also a legendary hardman who late in his career suffered from a loose shoulder-joint that would dislocate when he crashed; Anderson would simply put it back in by the roadside and get back on his bike.

ANQUETIL, Jacques

Born: Mont-St-Aignan, France, January 8, 1934

Died: Rouen, November 18, 1987

Major wins: Tour de France 1957, 1961–64, 16 stage wins; Giro d'Italia 1960, 1964, six stage wins; Vuelta a España 1963, one stage win; Liège–Bastogne–Liège 1966; Ghent–Wevelgem 1964; Bordeaux–Paris 1965; GP des Nations 1953–58, 1961, 1965–66; world hour record 1956

Nickname: Master Jacques

Interests outside cycling: cards, alcohol, cigarettes, farming, women (especially close family members)

Further reading: *Sex, Lies and Handlebar Tape*, Paul Howard (Mainstream, 2008)

A single image of the Norman strawberry-grower's son is forever etched on France's national consciousness. The elbow-to-elbow battle between "Monsieur Jacques" and Raymond POULIDOR (nicknamed PouPou) on the Puy-de-Dôme mountaintop finish in the 1964 TOUR DE FRANCE remains French cycling's equivalent of the Stanley Matthews Cup Final. The RIVALRY between the pair was one of the greatest that French sports has ever seen.

Blond-haired and with chilly blue eyes, Anquetil made his name in 1956 aged only 22, by breaking the HOUR RECORD, which had been held by FAUSTO COPPI for 14 years; like the Italian, he won the Tour at his first attempt. Coppi was his early model in his approach to cycling, and like the CAMPIONISSIMO, he was a master of cycling style: always well dressed, with immaculately slicked-back hair, and with his glamorous wife, Jeanine, gracing his arm. He was respected rather than loved by French cycling fans, who found him clinical and unemotional; the less successful PouPou remains their favorite.

Anquetil was the first man to win five Tours, his best victories coming in 1963, when he took both major mountain stages, and in 1964, when his duel with Poulidor reached its climax on the extinct volcano in the Massif Central. There, knowing he had to gain time on Anquetil before the final time trial, PouPou attacked repeatedly and Monsieur Jacques hung on for grim death. Just before the finish, he cracked, but held the yellow jersey—and the psychological whiphand—by just 14 seconds.

Their rivalry was never personal, as Anquetil later said: "Of course I would like to see Poulidor win in my absence. I have beaten him so often that his victory would only add to my reputation."

Anquetil managed the Giro–Tour DOUBLE that year, but his most audacious feat came in 1965, when he took back-to-back wins in the Dauphiné Libéré stage race and the now defunct motorpaced Bordeaux–Paris (see CLASSICS for more on this event). The Dauphiné is eight days of racing through the Alps; the 560 km "Derby" lasted 15 hours. The stage race finished at 5 PM; Bordeaux–Paris began at two o'clock the following morning. Legend has it that Anquetil spent the time between the two races playing poker, but what is certain is that he was flown from the Alps to Bordeaux in a government jet with the blessing of General de Gaulle and then braved bone-chilling rain to win in Paris, having raced 2,500 km in nine days.

Anquetil was a supreme time triallist, winning 65 solo races in his career. He could churn massive gears in immaculate style, thanks to motorpaced training, and an efficient aerodynamic position. He made a point of ignoring conventional wisdom about diet— champagne, oysters, and whisky were among his favorites—posed for cigarette ads, and was notoriously open about his use of DRUGS, which he viewed as being no more than what it took to do the job he was paid to do. He refused a drug test after his second hour record— which was not ratified—and led a riders' strike against drug tests in 1966. His domestic life was also unconventional (see SEX).

A television commentator and gentleman farmer in retirement, as well as director of the Paris–Nice stage race, he died of stomach cancer in 1987 and is remembered with an ornate gravestone in the cemetery in his home village of Quincampoix, just outside Rouen. (SEE ALSO **MEMORIALS**)

ANTARCTICA Not the most hospitable of cycling environments, but during Sir Ernest Shackleton's abortive attempt to cross the continent in 1914–15 one of the more eccentric members of his crew, Thomas Orde-Lees, got on a bike and rode on the pack ice while the expedition's ship *Endurance* was frozen in the Weddell Sea.

APPAREL

Team apparel, a selection of the good, the bad, and the ugly:

Bic: gloriously simple, amazingly orange, to set off the brooding Hispanic looks of Luis Ocana, not to mention JACQUES ANQUETIL.

Brooklyn: Yankee stars and white stripes on a deep blue backdrop, and CLASSICS specialist ROGER DE VLAEMINCK to wear it.

Z: moldbreakingly bonkers comic-book "kapow splash" on a blue background. Crazy sponsor, crazy money for GREG LEMOND.

ONCE: dramatic yellow with "blind man" logo (or was it a lottery winner taking a leak?); the pink design for the Tour never worked that well.

EMI: one for the connoisseur, black diamond amid black and white hoops, worn by ace climber Charly Gaul, the "Angel of the Mountains."

St. Raphael: twirly lettering and the glamour of Jacques Anquetil and TOM SIMPSON.

La Vie Claire: groundbreaking Mondrian-style interlocking rectangles that took team jersey design away from the "name on colored background" template when BERNARD HINAULT began wearing it in 1984.

Saeco: the uniform itself was routine red, but the crazy variants created for wacky sprinter Mario Cipollini were unique, perhaps fortunately. Green with a peace symbol for Peace in Ireland, Julius Caesar's *"veni vidi vici,"* tiger stripes, "X-ray" showing internal organs, and so on. Impactful yes, tasteful no.

Carrera Jeans: basic blue-shoulders-on-white design that was simplicity itself and was fine in its first incarnation worn by STEPHEN ROCHE. But then the company decided to bring in "denim" shorts complete with fake pockets and rivets.

Le Groupement: a psychedelic nightmare of red, yellow, green, purple, and blue splotches worn inter alia by ROBERT MILLAR. A merciful deliverance when the pyramid sales group went bust in July 1995.

Great Britain, 1997: who can forget the green snot color that replaced good old blue with red shoulders. It certainly made the point that GB had broken with the past when lottery funding started (see GREAT BRITAIN).

Scotland, 1998: tartan shorts no less. Nationalists dreamed this one up, aesthetes just covered their eyes.

(SEE **SPONSORS** FOR A LIST OF WEIRD AND WONDERFUL CYCLING BACKERS; **TEAMS** FOR HOW THEY DEVELOPED PLUS SOME OF THE ICONIC NAMES AND THEIR COLORS)

ARMSTRONG, Lance

Born: Dallas, Texas, September, 18, 1971
Major wins: Tour de France 1999–2005,
22 stage wins; world road race
championship 1993; San Sebastian
Classic 1995, Flèche Wallonne 1996
Nicknames: Big Tex, Mellow Johnny, Le Boss
Further reading: *It's Not About the Bike*,
Lance Armstrong and Sally Jenkins,
Berkley Trade, 2000; *Lance Armstrong's
War*, Daniel Coyle, Harper Paperbacks,
2006; *Lance: The Making of the World's
Greatest Champion*, John Wilcockson, Da
Capo Press, 2010; *Comeback 2.0: Up
Close and Personal*, Lance Armstrong with
Elisabeth Kreutz, Touchstone, 2009

There are two sides to the record winner of the Tour de France: a hero to cancer survivors worldwide and a highly divisive figure within his sport. Armstrong will always be defined by his comeback from severe testicular cancer, diagnosed in September 1996 when he was only 25, but he had already won a world championship (1993), a brace of one-day CLASSICS, and a stage in the 1995 TOUR DE FRANCE. With lesions in his lungs, stomach, and brain as well as one testicle, he was told he had a 40 percent chance of survival but in fact the doctors did not expect him to come through.

Vicious courses of chemotherapy followed, but there was never any doubt about whether he would return to cycling, as his first thought when he was diagnosed had been for his sport. "When they told me about the cancer I can't remember which hit me first: I might die, or I might lose my cycling career." But while he was in remission, no team would gamble on signing him as they were worried his comeback would end in failure.

Armstrong eventually signed for the relatively small US Postal Team and remained bitterly angry with the European managers who had rejected him. By spring 1998 he was racing again, and in 1999 he won the Tour, sealing victory with a crushing mountaintop win at the Italian ski resort of Sestrière. Suddenly, he was cycling's biggest ever star: his autobiography *It's Not About the Bike* topped the bestseller lists, by 2002 his earnings were estimated at $7.5 million, and presidents Clinton and Bush jumped on the bandwagon.

To complete the dream story, Armstrong married his fiancée, Kristin Richards, and they had three children, conceived in vitro from sperm he had banked before his chemotherapy began. His cancer charity Livestrong was a rapid success, with its most successful promotion a distinctive yellow wristband launched in May 2004 and retailing at one dollar. Over 70 million have been snapped up to date, with up to 10,000 sold on a single day in the 2009 Tour de France.

Dominating the Tour in the early years of the new century, Armstrong took cycling to a new audience worldwide and particularly in the USA, popularizing the sport to the extent that a time trial up l'Alpe d'Huez in his seventh successive victorious Tour, 2005, was shown live on a big television screen in Times Square. By then, however, his private life had unraveled: he had divorced from Kristin in 2003 and would subsequently date rock singer Sheryl Crow and various Hollywood starlets before starting a second family with Anna Hansen in June 2009. His story brought the Tour onto the celebrity circuit:

as well as Crow, comedian Robin Williams and actor Jake Gyllenhaal came in Armstrong's wake. Damien Hirst customized a bike for him, while George W. Bush put him on a cancer commission.

For all the celebrity sheen, Armstrong can be vindictive toward anyone who crosses him: journalists, officials, former teammates, and other cyclists, as his exchanges with Alberto Contador after the 2009 Tour showed. During his run of seven Tour wins, a team press officer kept a blacklist of media "trolls," and he crossed swords regularly with the WADA head Dick Pound over the latter's views on doping. In the 2004 Tour the Texan waged a personal campaign against the Italian Filippo Simeoni, because he had testified against their trainer MICHELE FERRARI in a drugs trial.

Armstrong was accused of DOPING on several occasions. In his first Tour win, 1999, traces of corticosteroids were found in his urine, but a prescription indicated it came from a skin cream. In 2000, French police investigated packaging and bloodied compresses dumped by personnel from his team, but found nothing. When samples from the 1999 Tour de France were tested retroactively for EPO during research in 2005, several allegedly showed traces of the drug, but an inquiry concluded that no action should be taken. Questions were frequently asked about his close working relationship with Ferrari. He also won a case brought by the insurance company that guaranteed his win bonuses, alleging he had used banned practices to take his Tour wins. His response was consistently the same: he was the most tested athlete in the world and had nothing to hide. In 2005 on his retirement, standing on the winner's podium on the Champs-Elysées, he bitterly attacked those who had doubted his probity and that of his colleagues.

Armstrong returned to competition in 2009 after three seasons out. It was a lively year: a team of French drug testers claimed that Armstrong had breached protocol by taking a shower before a random test; the Texan boycotted the press during the Tour of Italy after falling out with the organizers, and when the equally combative five-times Tour winner BERNARD HINAULT questioned his comeback, the Texan responded on his Twitter feed that the Badger was a "wanker." In the background, as well, were constant doubts about the financial status of the backer Astana, a consortium of companies based in Kazakhstan. When money failed to turn up to pay the riders, Armstrong responded by riding in a jersey with none of the Kazakh sponsors' names visible on it. Shortly before the Tour, the team was within hours of being declared financially unviable.

The 2009 Tour was dominated by Armstrong's battle for leadership within Astana with Alberto Contador, the 2007 Tour winner. The Spaniard had the legs; Armstrong had the experience, the backing of team manager Johan Bruyneel, and the ability to wage psychological war. Although Contador ended up the winner, Armstrong became one of the oldest cyclists to get on the podium when he finished third. At the end of the season he and Bruyneel quit Astana to start their own team, sponsored by Radioshack.

Team Radioshack won the 2010 Tour de France team prize, although

Armstrong placed 23rd, in part due to a serious crash on stage 8. He announced that after the January 2011 Tour Down Under, he would confine his racing to the United States. In the meantime, the FDA is investigating whether Armstrong was involved in an organized doping operation as a member of the US Postal Service team between 1999 and 2004.

(SEE ALSO **UNITED STATES OF AMERICA, CHARITIES, LONGEVITY, RIVALRIES**)

ART FACTOID

At the end of 2009 six bikes decorated by contemporary artists for Lance Armstrong to ride during his comeback season were auctioned at Sotheby's in aid of the Texan's Livestrong charity. A Damien Hirst machine decorated with butterflies sold for $500,000.

ART The best-known cycling work of art is probably *La Chaine Simpson*, a poster produced by the cycling mad impressionist Henri de TOULOUSE-LAUTREC in 1896, while bikes are also featured in the work of Salvador Dali and Picasso. The Catalan impressionist painter Ramon Casas y Carbo (1866–1932) produced images similar to those of Toulouse-Lautrec. *The Repair* perfectly captures the moment when a cyclist bends down to his or her wheel to adjust a nut or a valve. *Woman on a bike* is a cartoon of a lady tricyclist;

The Tandem shows two hirsute, muscly men—a self-portrait of Casas and his fellow artist Pere Romeu—in full flight. Dali, for his part, produced an official postcard for the 1959 Tour de France—which no one seems able to locate today—and produced several works featuring cyclists, such as *Sentimental Conversation* (1944), in which a host of deathly figures on bikes ride across the canvas past a grand piano.

There are also a host of cycle specialist artists active today. For example, in the United

States, Brooklyn-based artist Taliah Lempert has been exhibiting since 1996 and is well known for her paintings, sketches, and prints of bicycles of all kinds: racers, shopping bikes, kids' playbikes, and classic Bianchis and Masis. Some of her work uses oils on large canvases containing a single bicycle against a semi-neutral background, with the emphasis on the machine as a work of art in itself, akin to a sculpture with its graded lines. Other works feature details of cut-out lugs and individual items such as waterbottles. In a 1999 interview, Lempert said she does not work from photographs or slides, but only from original bikes, which she rides in order to get a feel for the character of the machine: worn, shiny, pristine, etched with street grime. Lempert's work includes tangled piles of bikes such as might have been found outside a velodrome in the halcyon days of the sport, and "blind drawings," loosely drawn and impressionistic in style; she described these in an interview with thewashingmachinepost. net as an "explosion of color and lines, there's lots of movement."

In Great Britain, Cornish artist Peg Jarvis has produced a body of work featuring track cyclists including the award-winning etching *Pursuit 3.* "I particularly love the track; it reminds me of Roman chariot racing—the excitement, the sound, the fact that you can see everyone and everything. I need to see the cyclists at work, warming up, warming down. As an artist, you need to draw something 100 times before it sinks into the memory; on the road, they go past so quickly that they are no use to me."

Jarvis has moved from drawings to etching, in some cases manipulating photographic negatives and shining them onto light sensitive metal plates, in others simply sitting by the trackside and scratching onto huge metal plates. More recently she has used watercolors; she is particularly proud of a painting that used the photofinish image of Olympic cyclist Jason Kenny's crash in Manchester as its starting point. The photo was blown up, manipulated, and subdivided into sections that included artifacts such as parking tickets and stamps in order to illustrate its interaction with her own life.

Jarvis cites among her influences Italian and Russian futurists, for the way they attempted to capture speed and power: the best-known images of this kind include Umberto Boccioni's *Dynamism of a Cyclist* (1913) and *Au Velodrome* by the cubist Jean Metzinger, which includes cut-outs of words from newspapers glued onto the walls of the track.

The British artist Frank Patterson (1871–1952) has a devoted following for his pen-and-ink drawings of cyclists and the British landscape that appeared in the pages of *Cycling* magazine and the CTC journal *The Gazette* from 1893. Patterson was hugely prolific, working for other magazines owned by Temple Press, which published *Cycling*; his total number of drawings was estimated at about 26,000 in his 59-year career.

Pattersons are beautifully and precisely drawn, with an element of the draftsman to them. They are bucolic, romantic, occasionally humorous, and now look distinctly old-fashioned and even mannered, with their clubmen smoking pipes and wearing plus fours, bicycles leaning against a convenient tree while they admire the view. There is a timeless and very British charm about them.

ASO   See AMOURY SPORT ORGANISATION.

AUDAX   The term is used to denote long group rides covered in a set time in a single day and dates back to a group of Italian cyclists who rode from Rome to Naples—230 km—in June 1897.

The newspapers referred to those who completed the distance as *audace*—audacious—and when Neapolitan cyclists made the return trip they formed a club for riders who could do over 200 km in a day; the newspaper term was translated into Latin, *audax*, and the group called itself Audax Italiano. The rides are called Randonnées—a French term meaning an outing using any means of transport—and the riders *randonneurs*.

The notion of group rides within a certain time, halfway between leisure and pure competition, gained pace internationally when the TOUR DE FRANCE's father, HENRI DESGRANGE, founded a French body in 1904. Desgrange's paper *L'Auto*—organizer of the Tour—ran the first Audax event in which medals and certificates were awarded to finishers; yellow, the color of *L'Auto*'s pages and the leader's jersey in the Tour, remains the color of 200 km medals.

Audax rides differ from the more recently invented CYCLOSPORTIVES such as L'ÉTAPE DU TOUR in that in theory their events have to be ridden at a predetermined average speed—this was 18 kph until 1945—and there may be a "ride leader" who cannot be overtaken. The idea is to discourage racing. In practice there has been a rift in the movement and this is not universally followed. PARIS–BREST–PARIS, the largest and oldest Audax Randonnée, is not run on this basis; unlike cyclosportives, however, riders are set a minimum time, which means that superfast cyclists may have to wait for controls to open. Additionally, while some 'sportives have assistance cars and are fully signposted, Audaxes emphasise self-sufficiency.

Today, Audaxes are run over the set distances of 200, 400, and 600 km; qualification for major events such as Paris–Brest–Paris depends on completion of a certain number of distance rides, which is checked by reference to the rider's *brevet* book, which is stamped by the organizers. Events are thus sometimes also known as brevets.

AUSTRALIA   The bicycle has a long history here, beginning with its use in the 1880s by gold prospectors in the bush. Cycles were also used for early postal services and by groups of itinerant sheep-shearers. Track racing began early in Australia with the Austral run in 1887 by the Melbourne Bicycle Club at the MCG over two miles; the discipline would remain important for the next 120 years.

The first Australian cycling star was a SIX-DAY rider in the heyday of the American events, Reggie MacNamara, known as the Iron Man. He moved to the US in 1912 and rode 115 of the events. His was one of the longest pro careers ever: he did not retire until 1939 when he was 50 years old. By then he had made a fortune but he ended his days penniless, working as a doorkeeper at Madison Square Garden, his stomach so damaged by the lifestyle and the drugs that he could not keep food down for more than half an hour.

The first road race in the Southern Hemisphere was Warrnambool–Melbourne, first run in 1895 and now the longest one-day race in the world at 299 km, as well as the second oldest. By 1909, the Australasian road championship was drawing over 500 entries. But Australia enjoyed only a sporadic international presence, simply because it was so far from the European heartland. In 1920, for example, the sprinter Bob Spears, son of a sheep farmer, became world champion in the discipline and made headlines at French tracks for giving boomerang lessons in between races.

Professionals Don Kirkham and Snowy Munro did manage to finish the Tour in 1914, having spent the season racing in Europe as part of an Australian squad, riding classics such as Milan–San Remo and Paris–Roubaix. Kirkham and Munro rode the Tour as *domestiques* to the Frenchman Georges Passerieu; no Australian would again attempt the race until SIR HUBERT OPPERMAN made headlines in Europe and back home in the 1930s.

Australia continued to produce talented track riders such as Russell Mockridge, who won the Olympic kilometer title in 1952 and finished the Tour three years later, but internationally, the turning point came in the 1980s. In 1981 PHIL ANDERSON wore the yellow jersey briefly in the TOUR DE FRANCE, while in 1987 under the guidance of Charlie Walsh the Australian Institute of Sport began a cycling program that churned out droves of fine track racers—who dominated racing at the 2004 OLYMPIC GAMES— and guided their riders to the

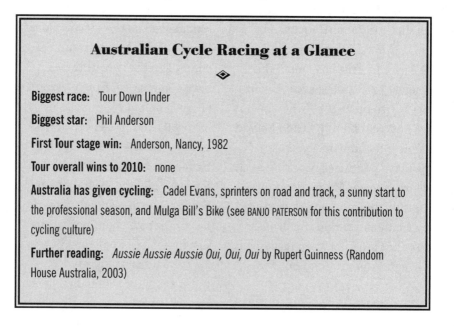

Australian Cycle Racing at a Glance

Biggest race: Tour Down Under

Biggest star: Phil Anderson

First Tour stage win: Anderson, Nancy, 1982

Tour overall wins to 2010: none

Australia has given cycling: Cadel Evans, sprinters on road and track, a sunny start to the professional season, and Mulga Bill's Bike (see BANJO PATERSON for this contribution to cycling culture)

Further reading: *Aussie Aussie Aussie Oui, Oui, Oui* by Rupert Guinness (Random House Australia, 2003)

road through the formation of a European academy in Tuscany, and a pro team sponsored by GIANT.

Anderson had already been followed to Europe by talented racers such as Allan Peiper (a member of the FOREIGN LEGION), Stephen Hodge, and Neil Stephens, but the AIS program produced so much talent that by the late 1990s and early years of the 21st century, Australia was a stronger presence—certainly in performance terms, and sometimes even numerically— in the Tour de France than traditional cycling nations such as Belgium and Holland.

Robbie McEwen twice won the Tour's most prestigious stage finish, on the Champs-Elysées (1999 and 2002) and won the green jersey in the latter year; Stuart O'Grady managed two spells in the yellow jersey (1998 and 2001), while Brad McGee landed the prologue time trial in 2003. An Australian event of truly international stature came onto the calendar in 2005 with the promotion of the Tour Down Under, which opens the UCI's ProTour calendar in January.

With Cadel Evans, meanwhile, Australia finally found a rider capable of challenging for overall titles in major Tours. Evans began racing as a mountain-biker, winning the World Cup in 1998 and 1999 before transferring to the road with Saeco and Mapei then T-Mobile.

He is a volatile character not exactly popular with the media, who were hardly charitable to him as he came close to winning both the 2007 and 2008 Tours de France: his moodiness earned him the nickname "Cuddles." Late 2009 saw him truly make history with a late solo attack to win Australia's first world title in the men's elite race at Mendrisio (see DOGS to learn how his love for his pet colored his relations with the media).

BAHAMONTES, Federico
(b. Spain, 1928)

Spain's first TOUR DE FRANCE winner, and one of the finest mountain climbers the sport has ever produced. The "Eagle of Toledo" was the first rider to be crowned King of the Mountains in all three major Tours, a feat emulated only by LUIS HERRERA of Colombia. He won the best-climber award in the Tour de France six times, a record that stood for 40 years. He is also one of the few cyclists to race the Vuelta, Giro, and Tour in the same year, finishing 6th, 17th, and 8th in the three events in 1958.

Bahamontes is celebrated as the rider who would race away from the field on the Tour's great passes, then would stop and eat an ice cream at the top. That's actually one of the race's great myths, a one-off incident, as Bahamontes explained in an interview: "one of my spokes broke on the way up [the Galibier], so I attacked so that the repair could be done at the top. But the team car with the spare was stuck behind the bunch, so I bought an ice cream to pass the time."

Bahamontes turned to cycling as a way of escaping starvation during the Spanish civil war, won his first race at 17, and was King of the Mountains in the Tour at his first attempt in 1954. He was received by the dictator General Franco after winning the Tour in 1959. His victory came partly thanks to a stalemate in the French team, which had two leaders, JACQUES ANQUETIL and Roger Rivière, neither of whom would work with the other. Bahamontes was a nervous, irrritable man who threw his bike into a ravine in the 1954 Tour because he was fed up and once chased a rival through the peloton brandishing a pump. After retirement he ran

a bike shop in his home town.

(SEE ALSO SPAIN, WAR, POLITICS)

BALLANTINE, Richard

Contender for the title of cycling's biggest-selling author, Ballantine introduced generations of Britons and Americans to cycling as a lifestyle through his million-selling *Richard's Bicycle Books* series, which have been market-leaders since the first one was launched in 1972. Ballantine was an adept trend reader, founding the UK's first glossy cycling magazine for the general market—*Bicycle Magazine* in 1981—and importing some of the first MOUNTAIN BIKES to the UK.

Prompted by the 1970s oil crisis, Ballantine was an early advocate of cycling as part of a green lifestyle, arguing strongly against the universal use of motor vehicles and suggesting that cycling was life-enhancing and liberating. *The Bicycle Book*, a practical guide to cycling for the novice, has been compared to Alex Comfort's *Joy of Sex* for the way it changed mindsets and established a whole new market. Its great strengths are the accessible way that essential cycling knowledge is presented and Ballantine's passion and humor about everything two-wheeled—one section in the Commuting chapter is simply labelled "Joy."

It also includes a robust section on dealing with DOGS, a guide to the dangers of cars, and argues strongly for DEFENSIVE CYCLING. Ballantine's latest work is *City Cycling*, which caters for the fast-growing cycle-commuter market.

BARTALI, Gino

Born: Ponte a Ema, Italy, July 18, 1914
Died: Ponte a Ema, Italy, May 5, 2000
Major wins: Tour de France 1938, 1948,
12 stage wins; Giro d'Italia 1936–7, 1946,
17 stage wins; Milan–San Remo 1939–40,
1947, 1950; Giro di Lombardia 1936,
1939–40; Championship of Zurich 1946,
1948; Tour of Switzerland 1946–7
Nicknames: the Pious One, the Iron Man,
the Old One

The Italian remains the oldest man
to win the TOUR DE FRANCE in the
postwar era, triumphing in 1948 at
the age of 34, 10 years after his first
victory in the event. His career was
one of cycling's longest, 19 years
spanning three decades; he won his
first Italian national title in 1935,
his last in 1952 (see LONGEVITY for
other durable cyclists).

Bartali was famed for his epic
RIVALRY with FAUSTO COPPI and
for his fervent CATHOLICISM—he
had a private chapel in his home
in Tuscany and famously attended
mass before stage starts in the Tour
and Giro. He was also said never
to have sworn once in seven years,
and to disapprove of fellow cyclists

urinating during races. Bartali
was courted by Benito Mussolini's
fascists—Il Duce put pressure on
him to ride the 1937 Tour—but he
refused to wear the party insignia.

Like Coppi he lost the best years
of his career to the Second World
War. During the conflict he carried
letters and forged documents
hidden in his bike; he appeared to
be merely training but was in fact
acting as a courier for a Catholic
network that was smuggling Jews
out of Italy. The material was used
to forge passports.

Postwar he became friendly with
the Christian Democrat Italian
prime minister Alcide de Gasperi.
Bartali's victory in the Tour in
1948 came as Italy descended into
chaos and near revolution following
the attempted murder of the
Communist party leader Palmiro
Togliatti. Before the critical stage
through the ALPS, de Gasperi called
Bartali at his hotel in Cannes and
asked him to win for his country.

He broke away through the Alps
to win the critical mountain stage,
and the revolution was averted.
Although historians contend that
the tumult in Italy might well have

died away whether or not Bartali had triumphed in the Tour, he has become celebrated as the man who prevented a revolution by winning it.

(SEE ALSO **WAR**, **POLITICS**)

BAUER, Steve (b. Canada, 1959)

While Alex Stieda has the honour of being the first Tour de France yellow jersey wearer from CANADA, Bauer blazed a lone trail as the country's Tour de France star through the late 1980s and early 1990s, spending a total 14 days in the *maillot jaune*, and achieving Canada's highest Tour finish of fourth in 1988. He was also Canada's first CLASSIC winner, taking the Championship of Zurich in 1989, and his career at the highest level lasted from his silver medal ride in the 1984 OLYMPIC GAMES road race at Los Angeles to the 1996 Games in Atlanta, the year he retired.

Bauer turned professional for the La Vie Claire team alongside BERNARD HINAULT in 1985, and won the first stage of the 1988 Tour de France riding for the Helvetia team run by Hinault's old manager Paul Koechli; he then wore the yellow jersey for five days. Later that year he was involved in one of the most controversial incidents seen in any WORLD CHAMPIONSHIPS, when he and Claude Criquielion of Belgium collided while sprinting for the finish of the pro road race in Ronsse, Belgium. Criquielion sued Bauer for assault and the case dragged on for three years before going Bauer's way.

In 1990 Bauer was on the wrong end of perhaps the closest finish to PARIS–ROUBAIX, coming second to Eddy Planckaert by a few millimeters, but later that year he was one of four riders who gained 10 minutes in the first stage of the Tour de France, and he ended up in the yellow jersey for nine days before eventually finishing 27th overall. In 1993, riding for Motorola, Bauer turned up at Paris–Roubaix on one of the strangest bikes ever seen there— an Eddy Merckx machine with a drastically relaxed seat angle nicknamed the stealth bike. It had a massively long wheelbase, a lengthened chain, and a special saddle with a raised back.

BBAR (British Best All Rounder)

The BBAR is the mainstay of British TIME TRIALLING, a season-long contest to decide the best endurance specialist of the year. The rankings are decided according to average speeds set over three disciplines—50 and 100 miles and 12 hours for men, and 25, 50, and 100 miles for women. Men who achieve an average of over 22 mph are given certificates; for women the cutoff is 20 mph. There are also team and veteran rankings and competitions for school-age boys and girls over shorter distances.

Individual clubs also run their own BBAR contests.

The BBAR was founded by the magazine *Cycling* in 1930, and the first winner was Frank Southall, who went on to win the contest four times in a row. After the war, the time trialling governing body, the Road Time Trials Council, took over the contest; until 1976, the average speed calculations were made by a Manchester cyclist named Tom Barlow using a slide rule. The women's contest was dominated for a quarter of a century by the late BERYL BURTON, a record that stands out in all sports.

BICYCLE

From the Latin "two wheels." Although there are claims that LEONARDO DA VINCI dreamed up a bike, the earliest

two-wheeled human-powered machines were produced at the start of the 19th century—first the DRAISIENNE or HOBBY HORSE, which didn't have any pedals, and later the BONESHAKER, which did. What followed was a constant search for improvement in any area where mechanics came into play, from industry to personal transport, and a wide variety of cycle designs were patented, many for tricycles and quadricycles, none of which caught on.

In the early 1840s KIRKPATRICK MACMILLAN and the Frenchman Alexandre Lefebvre both produced rear-wheel-driven machines that never became popular; instead the HIGH-WHEELER took over before the first SAFETY BICYCLES were produced in the 1880s, with the

definitive pattern set by JAMES
STARLEY's Rover in 1885.

Radical variations on this basic
bike design, truly established
at the end of the 19th century,
have been relatively rare. The
Moulton small-wheeler from the
1960s is one departure that has
enjoyed enduring popularity. The
BMX bike and rear-suspended
cross-country mountain bike are
others, while MIKE BURROWS's
Lotus monocoque and GRAEME
OBREE's cross-beamed frame are
reminders that we should never
be content with the status quo.

(SEE **MOULTON, OBREE, PEDERSEN** FOR
INVENTORS WHO TRIED TO BREAK THE
MOLD; **BRAKES, GEARS, WHEELS, TIRES,
FRAMES** FOR HOW THESE COMPONENTS
DEVELOPED)

BICYCLE LANES   Famously crap,
except in HOLLAND (go to that
country's section to find out why
this is the case). The first cycle
lane in Britain opened in 1934,
alongside the A40 in West London
and was two and a half miles long
and 2.5 m wide on either side
of the road. Even then cyclists
were complaining of a lack of

investment in facilities and things
have hardly improved since.
Every urban cyclist has their
own horror story of cars parked
where they shouldn't be, lanes
that lead onto main thoroughfares
and stop just when they are most
needed, and lanes that last, oh,
two meters if you are lucky. The
phenomenon was significant
enough that it generated its own
pocket novelty book, *Crap Cycle
Lanes*. We read it and wept.

BINDA, Alfredo

Born: Cittiglio, Italy, August 11, 1902
Died: March 30, 1986
Major wins: World road title 1927, 1930,
1932; Giro d'Italia 1925, 1927–9, 1933,
41 stages; Milan–San Remo 1929, 1931;
Giro di Lombardia 1925–7, 1931
Nickname: Mona Lisa

One of the CAMPIONISSIMO, the
first professional world champion,
a great team manager, and the only
man to be paid not to ride the Giro
d'Italia, because he was so good
that the organizers were worried
he would kill off any interest in the
race. By curious coincidence, he was

also the first man to be offered start money to ride the TOUR DE FRANCE.

Binda began working life as a bricklayer and developed his sprinting speed with track racing when he was young. From 1927 to 1930 he was almost unbeatable, taking the inaugural professional world road race title on the Nürburgring in Germany ahead of the other *campionissimo* of the time, Costanta Girardengo. He won the Giro in 1925 and from 1927 to 1929, with 12 stage wins in the 1929 race, but was discreetly requested not to start the 1930 race and given the equivalent of first prize, six stage wins, and the bonus he would have won. "My best Giro," he said later. "I consider I won it five and a half times."

At that year's Tour de France, on the other hand, HENRI DESGRANGE badly needed him to lend some luster to the event, being run for the first time with national rather than trade teams. Binda was paid a daily rate, won two stages, and quit so he could prepare to win a second world title. He was sworn to silence over the fee—Desgrange had been adamant he would never pay start money—and the secret emerged only in 1980.

After retirement in 1936, Binda became Italian national team manager, with the task of keeping FAUSTO COPPI and GINO BARTALI from falling out when their rivalry was at its height. He led the elaborate negotiations to ensure the pair would ride the 1949 Tour under Italian colors, then was responsible for persuading Coppi to stay in the race after he crashed on the stage to Saint-Malo and became convinced he should quit. He also had to deal with little matters like his deputy (Coppi's trade team manager) failing to provide Bartali with a feed bag, and the fact that on the decisive day in the ALPS, neither would cooperate with the other.

Binda also oversaw Coppi's second Tour win, in 1952, and guided Italy to world titles with Coppi and Ercole Baldini in 1953 and 1958. Later, he ran a company that made shoes, which was best known for producing toestraps, the universal way of attaching cycling shoes to pedals until ski-type bindings became popular in the late 1980s.

BMX   Bicycle motocross entered the mainstream in 2008 when it was part of the program at the Beijing OLYMPIC GAMES. The hackles of traditionalists were raised, because the event it ousted, the kilometer time trial, was one of the classic disciplines. But the appeal was obvious. Run over short obstacle courses using scaled-down bikes, BMX is accessible, spectator friendly, and spectacular for television viewers. It's also indelibly imprinted in the minds of anyone who watched the science fiction film *E.T.* "It's a power sport that calls for skills and nerve as well," says the British world champion Shanaze Reade. "You get a real rush of adrenaline when the start gate drops because you have only got 45 seconds to get everything out."

BMX began in the 1970s in California when kids used to mess around on dirt tracks, inspired by the skill and speed of motocross racers. Today, races consist of heats for up to eight riders over a short purpose-built course (300–400m) including banked curves (berms), humps, and jumps. The riders line up with their wheels against a start gate that drops to launch them down a start ramp. Usually this ramp is only a few meters high,

SADDLE
SEAT POST
HANDLEBARS
FRONT FORK
PEDAL AND CRANK
CHAIN
FAT TIRES

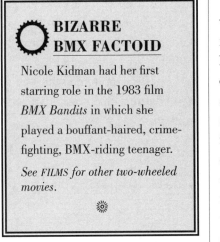

BIZARRE BMX FACTOID

Nicole Kidman had her first starring role in the 1983 film *BMX Bandits* in which she played a bouffant-haired, crime-fighting, BMX-riding teenager.

See FILMS for other two-wheeled movies.

Basic techniques include wheelies, bunnyhops, and manualing—when the rider lifts the front wheel of the bike over a jump with the back wheel still on the ground—as well as slide braking, in which the bike is pushed sideways around the corner, with the rider on the very edge of losing control. Contact is important as well, because on track the riders fight for position going into and out of the bends.

World championships have been held in BMX since 1982, while Freestyle BMX—doing tricks on the bike along the lines of skateboarding or snowboarding—is a staple at the annual extreme sports X Games. But the sport really gained credibility when it became part of the Olympic program in 2008. To assist Reade in her build-up for gold, the GREAT BRITAIN team built her a course in Manchester that included an extremely steep Olympic standard start ramp. Unfortunately she crashed out when going for gold; the inaugural Olympic champions were Anne-Caroline Chausson,

but at the Olympic Games, to make it a livelier spectacle for television, riders flew down a vertiginous eight-meter-high ramp with a slope of 33 percent. That meant the riders hit the course at over 30 mph, enabling them to get up to five meters into the air over the jumps.

Crashing is an ever-present risk so the riders wear loose-fit clothing and full motorcycle-style helmets. Bikes are small-wheeled—20 or 24 inches—with one brake and fat tires, and are small-framed with a huge amount of clearance between seat and saddle so that the riders can throw the bike about more easily.

a former MOUNTAIN-BIKE downhiller from France, and Maris Strombergs of Latvia.

Former BMX champions who have made it in other disciplines include: Robbie McEwen, Australian road sprinter who won the green jersey at the 2002 Tour de France; CHRIS HOY, Scottish track sprinter who took three gold medals at the 2008 Olympics; and Jamie Staff, BMX world champion who won Olympic gold on the track in 2008.

BOARDMAN, Chris

Born: Hoylake, England, August 26, 1968
Major wins: Olympic pursuit gold 1992; Olympic time trial bronze 1996; world time trial gold 1994; world pursuit champion 1994, 1996; world hour records 1993, 1996; three stage wins in Tour de France; MBE 1992
Further reading/viewing: *Chris Boardman, the Complete Book of Cycling*, Partridge Press, 2000; DVDs: *Battle of the Bikes; The Final Hour*

The first British Olympic cycling gold medalist of the modern era and one of the men behind the sport's great revival in GREAT BRITAIN in the 21st century, Boardman is mildly dyslexic, with an investigative brain and amazing mind for detail. His interest in cycling stemmed purely from a love of competition rather than the act of riding a bike. "I'm not a cyclist," he said. "I rode bikes. Ninety percent of me said 'I don't believe I'm here,' 10 percent said I had to do it. I was a visitor, which was a shame because [cycling] is a lovely sport."

Boardman began his career as a British TIME-TRIALLING champion— winning the 25-mile and hill-climb titles—then targeted the individual pursuit at the Barcelona Olympics, where his gold was the first by a British cyclist since 1920. To some extent, the feat was overshadowed by the fact that he won the pursuit on a radical aerodynamic bike with a carbon-fiber monocoque frame made by Lotus and designed by MIKE BURROWS; Boardman won the race, but the bike grabbed the headlines.

While his time-trialling RIVALRY with GRAEME OBREE made news in Britain he and his trainer, Peter Keen, turned their attention to the HOUR RECORD, which he broke in 1993, earning a professional contract with the French team GAN. In his first Tour de France, in 1994, his time-trialling skill secured him the yellow jersey when he won the prologue time trial. He also took the opening stage in 1997 and 1998, but crashed out of the Tour four times in six starts.

In 1994 Boardman won the inaugural time trial world championship and in 1996 he won an Olympic bronze medal at the discipline, then set what is now the definitive distance at the hour with 56.375 km. After the rules governing the hour record were changed, he decided to end his career with an attempt under the new system and managed to beat EDDY MERCKX's 1972 distance of 49.431 km by a mere 10 m.

Boardman was unlucky to race at a time when DOPING was rampant;

he found out late in his career that he suffered from a hormone deficiency that causes osteoporosis and that it could only be treated with injections of testosterone, a banned drug. Following the Festina doping scandal of 1998 the authorities did not feel they could let him use the drug, so he could only take up the treatment after retirement. He is perhaps the only cyclist to quit racing in order to use banned drugs.

Boardman and Keen had been highly inventive in their approach to training, using a treadmill to simulate mountain climbs and focusing on quality not volume.

After a few years in retirement, Boardman went to work on the British Lottery-funded Olympic track racing program founded by Keen. When not devoting time to extreme scuba diving—his personal obsession—and his large family, Boardman mentored gold medalists such as BRADLEY WIGGINS, devised coach management systems, became one of the program's core management quartet, and was one of the "secret squirrels" who researched aerodynamic uniforms in the run-up to the Beijing Games of 2008.

(SEE ALSO **AERODYNAMICS, GREAT BRITAIN, OLYMPIC GAMES**)

BOBET, Louison

Born: St Méen le Grand, France, March 12, 1925

Died: Biarritz, France, March 13, 1983

Major wins: World road race, 1954; Tour de France 1953–55, 11 stage wins; King of the Mountains 1950; Milan–San Remo 1951; Tour of Flanders 1955; Paris–Roubaix 1956; Giro di Lombardia 1951; Bordeaux–Paris 1959

Nickname: the Baker of St. Meen

Further reading: *Tomorrow We Ride*, Jean Bobet, Cordee, 2008

First man to win the TOUR DE FRANCE in three consecutive years (1953–55); the Breton was a tenacious cyclist who learned his trade alongside FAUSTO COPPI in Italy and was also capable of major one-day wins such as MILAN–

SAN REMO (1951), the TOUR OF LOMBARDY (1951), PARIS–ROUBAIX (1956), and the world road title (1954).

Bobet is also famous for a curious episode in the 1955 Tour when he refused to put on the yellow jersey because it was made of synthetic material; he was worried it might irritate his skin. Perhaps his nerves were understandable: he completed the Tour with a severe saddle boil, which was operated on after the race; he came back to competition too soon and was never the same again (see SADDLE SORES for other nether nasties).

Bobet was celebrated for his determination and ended his career with perhaps the bravest final act cycling has seen. In the 1959 Tour he was ill and suffering but forced himself to complete much of the race, finally riding to the top of the highest pass in the event, the Col de l'Iséran (see ALPS to find out how high and hard this one is relative to other *cols*). There he climbed off his bike, never to race again.

BONESHAKER   Generic term for early front-wheel bicycle similar to the machines invented in 1861 by the Frenchman Pierre Michaux and his son Ernest, not dissimilar to the DRAISIENNE, but it was powered by pedals on the axle of the front wheel, "like the crank handle of a grindstone" as Pierre put it; in 1865 his company turned out 400 of the things in their workshop near the Champs-Elysées. They were unforgiving and hard to steer, but they were also simple to use and speedy compared to walking.

Michaux understood the value of publicity; he supplied a bike to the French head of state Napoleon III and supplied JAMES MOORE with one for the first official cycle race in 1868. With some outside investment from Olivier Brothers, his company pushed up production to 200 a day; there were by now 60 other boneshaker makers in the capital and upmarket models were being made with steel frames, ebony wheels, and ivory grips on the handlebars.

In November 1869 the first cycling magazine, *Le Vélocipede Illustré*, and Olivier Brothers ran the Paris–Rouen race, won by Moore (see ROAD RACING) using the machines. By now race meetings were drawing up to 300 competitors, including women, and as many as 10,000 spectators. The vogue for the machines spread rapidly, to Switzerland, Belgium, Holland, Germany, Britain, and the US. In France, however, velocipede use stuttered with the onset of the Franco–Prussian war in 1870, and the political turmoil that followed.

In Britain the Midlands, and Coventry in particular, rapidly became the center for velocipede production. Gradually, the design changed: the unpowered back wheel of the Michaux-type machines was shrunk, to save weight, frames became more nimble, and the front wheel grew, to a limit set by the inside leg of the rider. The boneshaker disappeared, and the HIGH-WHEELER was born.

BOOKS—FICTION

A subjective selection in no particular order

The Wheels of Chance, H.G. Wells

Hard-to-find turn-of-the-century novel in which Wells's hero, Hoopdriver, undertakes a 10-day cycle tour of Britain's South Coast and falls in love with a fellow cyclist, one of many women given freedom by their newfound mobility. Beautiful portrait of cycling in the formative years of the pastime, with acute observation of the blurring of class distinctions the bicycle brought with it.

Cat, Freya North

Since its publication in 1999 this chick-lit tale of bedhopping on the Tour (as the author puts it, "big egos and bigger bulges in the lycra shorts") is probably the biggest selling cycling fiction work ever: 10 years later, almost every British thrift store and teenage female babysitter seem to have a copy. Tour journos who were on the 1998 race when La

North was researching the work are known to scrutinize the book closely trying to figure who is who. Trivia lovers note: there is a William Fotheringham in the pages, but he's sports editor of the *Guardian*. We emphasize that it is fiction.

Bad to the Bone, James Waddington

Surreal novel published by happy coincidence in 1998, the year of the Festina scandal, in which top cyclists in the TOUR DE FRANCE are offered a Faustian pact by a sports doctor: a wonder drug which will make them unbeatable, but which has horrendous side effects. It's fiction. Honest. Pro cyclists would never go so far—would they?

The Rider, Tim Krabbe

Cult novella with a popular English translation from 2002. Goes inside one rider's mind during a fictional race somewhere hilly in the South of France—the only issue being that if any cyclist actually thought that much he'd be too distracted to compete. Totally compulsive: you either love it or it leaves you cold.

The Yellow Jersey, Ralph Hurne
Possibly the least politically correct cycling work ever, what with the big-breasted, topless lady (alongside the Condor bike) on the Pan paperback, and the constant references to potential sexual partners as "it." Get past that and this 1973 novel is a hilarious, racy, suspenseful gem: you can't help but get drawn in as Terry Davenport, jaded ex-pro and womanizer, gears up for one last Tour and suffers like hell in the process. The bit where the top five riders in the race all test positive is amusingly prescient. Written with two endings, one for the British market, one for the US.

The Big Loop, Claire Huchet Bishop
Published in 1955, offering a Parisian teenager's view of a cycling career from aspirant without a bike to Tour winner. It has a certain charm as a portrait of French cycling in the glory days of Bobet and Robic, but is unlikely to cut much ice with the PlayStation generation.

BOOKS—NONFICTION

The Great Bike Race, Geoff Nicholson
Masterly history of the Tour de France crafted around the 1976 race, oozing humor and glorious detail without a hint of self.

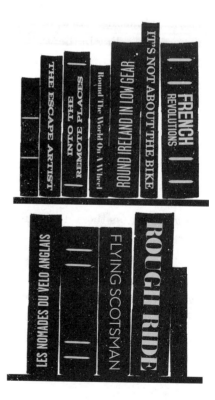

Nicholson, God rest his soul, was a writer who topped the Galibier while the others were toiling up the Télégraphe. His sequel, *Le Tour*, did not quite hit these heights.

Wide-Eyed and Legless, Jeff Connor

No journalist will ever get as close to a team as Connor got to ANC-Halfords in the 1987 Tour de France, and no squad will want them to, given the stuff he picked up thanks to his inimitable eye for detail. The gradual implosion of the first British trade team to ride the Tour is dissected in all its quarrelsome, anarchic glory. Connor's attempt to ride a Tour stage is the hilarious high point.

Lance Armstrong's War, Daniel Coyle

The best way to learn about LANCE ARMSTRONG and 21st century pro cycling, through the eyes of a wry outsider given inside access to Planet Lance. Brilliantly observed, hilariously written, but above all dispassionate, neither for nor against the controversial Texan.

Read and judge Le Boss for yourself.

Major Taylor, Andrew Ritchie

Ritchie set the standard for cycling biography with this account of the life of one of America's first nonwhite sports stars. Impeccable research and a lively re-creation of cycling's HEROIC ERA.

Kings of the Road, Robin Magowan and Graham Watson

This 1985 opus is the best integrated words-and-pictures book about professional cycle racing. Some of the content is dated but GRAHAM WATSON's photos and the pen-portraits of ROBERT MILLAR, SEAN KELLY, PHIL ANDERSON, and GREG LEMOND are timeless.

Kings of the Mountains, Matt Rendell

Exhaustive and intense investigation into cycling in COLOMBIA. Like Ritchie's *Major Taylor*, it extends way beyond things two-wheeled and offers a superb insight into a controversial, colorful nation.

Greg Lemond: The Incredible Comeback, Samuel Abt

The best work from one of the great cycling writers of the last quarter-century. This 1990 account of LeMond's return from near-death to win the best Tour de France ever is as good at it gets.

Sean Kelly: A Man for All Seasons, David Walsh

The definitive account of the great man's rise in the early 1980s; Walsh is superbly observant, can work out the deals his fellow Irishman is striking, and benefits from unlimited access. Those were the days.

BOOKS—MEMOIRS/ AUTOBIOGRAPHY

It's Not About the Bike, Lance Armstrong

Love or loathe Lance Armstrong, you can't ignore one of the biggest-selling cycling books ever, because of the visceral emotions it brings. The detail is telling, most notably the scene where Armstrong has to masturbate into a cup so that he can bank sperm before his testicular cancer operation. A key element in the Big-Tex myth.

Flying Scotsman, Graeme Obree

For my money the rawest and best cycling autobiography. Graeme Obree tells his story uncut, without the intermediary of a ghost writer, and tells of sexual abuse and attempted suicide with not a hint of self-pity. Alongside this the film of the same name is distinctly insipid.

Rough Ride, Paul Kimmage

As with Armstrong, you swoon or swear at this up and (let's face it, mainly) down account of

Paul Kimmage's career as a pro in the mid-1980s. Great inside stuff, but his drug "revelations" seem timid now, though at the time they were scandalous. No one describes suffering on a bike quite so well; brutally debunked the "glamour" of pro life, even if it is a bit Gone with a Whinge.

The Escape Artist, Matt Seaton
Elegiac telling of Matt Seaton's discovery of cycling against a background of serious "stuff of life," namely his wife's death of cancer. Beautifully written, elegantly crafted, tugs at the heartstrings, and sums up why we all ride bikes.

A Dog in a Hat, Joe Parkin
The life and times of a mediocre American pro in Belgium is one of the most compelling memoirs of its time, mainly because of Parkin's sheer love of Flandrian cycling culture and the pure weirdness of pro racing. The high point comes early on, when Parkin reads the lyrics to "Jumping Jack Flash" handwritten on Bob Roll's tires.

MEMOIRS   A brief selection:

For the Love of Jacques	Sophie Anquetil	2004
Glory Without the Yellow Jersey	Raymond Poulidor	1977
Boy Racer	Mark Cavendish	2009
Cycling Is my Life	Tom Simpson	1966, 2009
The Fastest Bicycle Racer in the World	Major Taylor	1928
In Pursuit of Glory	Bradley Wiggins	2008
Personal Best	Beryl Burton	reiss. 2008
Le Peloton des Souvenirs	Bernard Hinault	1988
We Were Young and Carefree	Laurent Fignon	2010
The Autobiography	Chris Hoy	2009

The spate of drug scandals since 1998 has given rise to a small and highly profitable genre: confessional memoirs by a drug taker or provider. First came *Secret High* by the almost unknown Erwann Mentheour, followed by *Massacre à la Chain* (translated as *Breaking the Chain*, Yellow Jersey, 2000) by the soigneur Willy Voet of Festina, which sold over 300,000 copies. Others to tell their stories in print included Jerome Chiotti, a mountain-bike world champion who returned his gold medal after confessing to drug use, the Cofidis professional Philippe Gaumont, the Festina manager Bruno Roussel and the team's leader Richard Virenque. The latter's book, *My Truth*, explained how he had not taken drugs, and was published before he changed his mind and confessed. Christophe Bassons, an anti-drugs campaigner and former Festina professional, wrote the ironically titled *Positif*.

BOOKS—TRAVEL

French Revolutions, Tim Moore
A cycling novice takes on a bonkers task: riding around France, loosely based on the 2000 Tour route. Moore has no inhibitions about his own failings and, unlike others who use the "I" word to destruction, he gets away with it because his sense of humor never flags. Probably the best constructed ending among all the fine tomes listed here.

Round Ireland in Low Gear, Eric Newby
Pretty eccentric tale, as the travel-writing great sets off in the depths of winter with wife Wanda to contend with Irish weather, Irish signposts, and their shared lack of cycling experience.

Round the World on a Wheel, John Foster-Fraser
Kipling or Baden Powell should have written this account of one of the first around-the-world trips. If you want to get an idea

of the mindset that made the British Empire what it was—in the best and worst senses—it's all there in this book, reissued in 1982. An excellent *Boys' Own-* style caper at the time, now a period piece.

Into the Remote Places, Ian Hibell

One of the original and best "ridden there" books. Hibell cannot match Moore for humor, or Newby for observation, but no holds are barred, from bust-ups with his (male) companions, to his love affair with a (female) companion, not to mention the extreme experience of crossing the Darien Gap, slashing the jungle, bike on his back, with a

septic leg oozing pus. You won't complain about riding your bike to the store again.

Full Tilt: Dunkirk to Delhi by Bicycle, Dervla Murphy

Setting off in the depths of Britain's hardest winter of the 20th century, 1963, Murphy made it all the way to India with her bike, producing an epic account of cycling through Iran, Afghanistan, Pakistan, and Kashmir that offers much food for thought given the current political situation.

(SEE **LITERATURE** FOR HOW CYCLING FITS INTO THE LITERARY WORLD OF HENRY MILLER, FLANN O'BRIEN, AND ALFRED JARRY)

BORYSEWICZ, Eddie (b. Poland, 1939)

Groundbreaking US national coach who masterminded the medal-winning performances at the Los Angeles Olympics, furthered the careers of GREG LEMOND and LANCE ARMSTRONG, and initially managed the team

that eventually became US Postal Service. Borysewicz was born in Poland, where he was a national junior champion before moving to coaching after a tuberculosis infection. He was on the Polish team staff at the 1976 Olympic Games in Montreal and joined the US Cycling Federation as head coach the following year, thanks to a chance meeting in a bike shop with the USCF's competition head Mike Fraysse.

Borysewicz spoke no English and initially relied on the 12-year-old son of Polish friends for translation. The riders nicknamed him Eddie B because they could not pronounce his surname. He bought his own desk at the Olympic Training Center in Squaw Valley and booted out most of the established national team, telling many of the riders they were too fat. Compared to established practices in EASTERN EUROPE, however, this was standard procedure. His first season in command was marked by silver medals on track and road for Sue Novara and CONNIE CARPENTER, but another big breakthrough came with LeMond's junior world road title in 1979. Four years later, Borysewicz guided the US team to a clean sweep of all the medals at the Panamerican Games, and in 1984 to its first Olympic medals since 1912, with the squad taking five golds in L.A. That triumph was, however, marred by the subsequent revelation that some of the team had used blood doping, a practice that was not illegal at the time but was later banned. Borysewicz denied involvement.

He left the US team in 1987 and founded an amateur team backed by Montgomery Securities that included Lance Armstrong among its members. Subaru-Montgomery raced the European circuit in 1993 without great success, but the Montgomery head Thomas Weisl stuck with the squad and it acquired backing from the US Postal Service in 1996. After quitting professional cycling, Eddie B coached the Polish national team in the run-up to the 2008 Beijing Olympics. Borysewicz was inducted into the US Bicycling Hall of Fame in 1996.

BOYER, Jonathan (b. Moab, Utah, 1955)

First American to finish the Tour de France and one of the first to forge a career in Continental Europe. Boyer was born in Utah, raised in Monterey, and moved to France in 1973 to join the ACBB cycling club in Paris, an outfit that had hosted Irish pioneer Shay Elliott in the 1950s and would subsequently become celebrated for producing many of the FOREIGN LEGION of British, Irish, and Australian pros. Boyer turned pro for the Lejeune-BP squad in 1977 but was subsequently hired by the Renault-Elf squad to assist Greg LeMond on his entry to European racing. He completed his first Tour in 1981, wearing a jersey with a stars and stripes design that suggested he was US national champion, but was actually a marketing ploy by the race organizers. In 1982 he was in contention for a medal at the world road race championships in Goodwood, England, but LeMond rode past en route to the silver medal. In 1983 he rode to his best Tour placing, 12th overall; his only major win in Europe was a stage of the Tour of Switzerland in 1984. Later, Boyer was a member of the 7-Eleven team managed by JIM OCHOWICZ in its early years racing the European circuit.

In November 2002 he was convicted of lewd behavior with a minor and served a year in jail and five years probation. Since his release, Boyer has completed the Race Across America—which he won in 1990—and has been active with mountain bike guru Tom Ritchey in promoting cycling in Rwanda.

BRAKES

Early bicycles had crude braking devices consisting of rod-operated spoons or rollers that pushed onto their solid tires, sometimes with a lever pushed by the foot. Pneumatic tires, invented in the 1890s, were more fragile, so rim brakes were developed, still powered by levers and rods; at the same time, the development of early free wheels resulted in the invention of the coaster brake, which meant the cyclist could brake by backpedalling. On a fixed-wheel bike, the rider can use inertia to slow down—the passive resistance of the legs as the pedals push them around—or for more rapid braking can try to slow down the pedals by pushing against the motion.

Rim brakes operated by various designs of calliper have been in use since 1879, when JAMES STARLEY patented the Grip with brass brake shoes; the stirrup brake, using levers and rods to pull the stirrup mounting for the shoes, came in early in the 20th century. Cantilever brakes—in which small callipers and brake shoes are attached to braze-on bosses on either side of the rim—have been used since the 1890s, and have always been popular on CYCLO-CROSS machines because of their great stopping power and the clearance they

offer; they were used on early mountain bikes.

Until the end of the 1970s, road racers chose between side-pull callipers, as made by CAMPAGNOLO from 1968, and center-pulls, in which the callipers crossed in a shallow X, of which the best were made by British company GB and

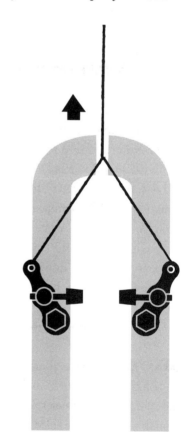

French firm Mafac. In the end, side-pulls became universal, mainly because of their greater simplicity, although Campagnolo's elegant, if heavy, Delta brake of the 1990s was in essence a center-pull with a parallelogram-shaped linkage.

The MOUNTAIN BIKE brought innovation in this area as well as others. First came powerful hydraulic brakes—the best made by French firm Magura—where the cables were replaced with fluid-filled control lines; these sat on the same bosses that would have taken cantilever brakes and produced such power that seat-stays could be seen bending under the strain. To counter this, they were sometimes backed up with metal bridging plates.

Drum brakes had been used on the very first mountain bikes, but their weight was a handicap; the best design has proved to be lightweight hydraulic disc brakes refined from motorbike models, offering one great advantage over rim brakes: they do not lose any efficiency in the wet, when it is estimated that water flowing over the rim can cause the loss of up to 60 percent of braking power.

BRIGHTON   Finish point for one of the world's largest mass bike rides, the London to Brighton, one of the first events of its kind. The ride was founded in 1975 as a demonstration of pedal power; 34 cyclists covered the 54-mile route. From 1980 it was run officially in aid of the British Heart Foundation. Now about 27,000 cyclists, of all ages and on all kinds of bikes, struggle up the final climb over the South Down's Ditchling Beacon just before the final swoop to the finish on Madeira Drive. Since 1980 almost 40 million dollars has been raised for the BHF, while an estimated 650,000 cyclists have taken part.

It's not clear who was the first cyclist to ride to the South Coast resort, but one of the first was John Mayal, who set out in

February 1869 on an old ordinary to get there in a day. It took him approximately 20 hours. London to Brighton and back remains one of the British RECORDS officially listed by the Road Records Association; the current record for a bike dates back to 1977 (Phil Griffiths, 4 hours 15 minutes 8 seconds).

Brighton was the venue for a British stage finish in the 1994 Tour de France, when the peloton rode over Ditchling, and the resort hosted a World Cup Classic for several years (see HEIN VERBRUGGEN'S entry for the history of the World Cup).

BURROWS, Mike (b. England, 1943)

Groundbreaking English bike designer who produced two definitive designs: the carbon-fiber monocoque engineered by the Lotus car company on

which CHRIS BOARDMAN rode to an Olympic gold medal in 1992, and the early TCR compact bike for GIANT, with a sloping top tube, which set the tone for most top-end road bikes in the early 21st century. Burrows is also a stalwart of the RECUMBENT bike movement, producing one of the most popular designs, the Windcheetah (see END TO END for one of the most surprising feats achieved on the machine).

Burrows began experimenting with smoothed out steel and carbon-fiber frames for TIME TRIALLING in the 1980s but the Lotus was the definitive design: a cross-shaped frame based on a single colossal smoothed-out strut running from the head tube to the rear hub, with extensions for the bottom bracket and saddle, and monoblade forks at front and rear. When Boardman won the gold medal, the bike received more attention than he did; it was estimated that Lotus gained about £100 million worth of free advertising. A road version was produced in 1994, and Boardman used it to win the prologue time trial of the TOUR DE FRANCE at record speed. On the downside, he went through a dozen of the frames; they were, he said, "neither robust nor reliable." In 1993, Burrows also produced a bike for Boardman's big rival GRAEME OBREE, but the Scot preferred to stick to his own machine.

Burrows has also produced a folding bike, the Giant Halfway, which uses his trademark one-piece forks to make the bike flatter when it is folded, and a super-thin bike, the 2D, that is intended to be stored in a narrow hallway. He stopped working for Giant in 2001.

Burrows now builds his own recumbent bikes such as the Ratracer, and also makes a freight bike for courier companies:

the 8Freight has an eight-foot wheelbase and thin profile so that it can be ridden down bike lanes. He has raced successfully on the Windcheetah, twice winning the European Human Powered Vehicle championships.

(TO READ ABOUT ANOTHER BIKE DESIGNER WHO BROKE THE MOLD, SEE **SIR ALEX MOULTON**; TO READ ABOUT ANOTHER RECUMBENT FAN, SEE **RICHARD BALLANTINE**)

BURTON, Beryl

Born: Halton, England, May 12, 1937

Died: Yorkshire, England, May 8, 1996

Major wins: World road race champion 1960, 1967; world pursuit champion 1959–60, 1962–63, 1966; 72 British time trial titles; 25 British Best All-Rounder titles; 26 national pursuit and road titles; national record (men and women) 12 hours 1967, MBE 1964, OBE 1968

Further reading: *Personal Best*, autobiography reissued by Mercian Manuals 2009

A fixture in women's racing for 30 years and a multiple world champion, the West Yorkshire racer was one of many cyclists done a disservice by the exclusion of women from the OLYMPIC GAMES until 1984. Born Beryl Charnock and introduced to cycling by her husband Charlie in 1955, Burton was a fearsome presence on the international stage, taking two world titles in the road race (1960, 1967) and 10 medals in the individual pursuit, including five golds. Her feats were recognized in France at least, where she was invited to ride the Grand Prix des Nations—a Classic normally limited to the best male professionals—in 1968. Riding before the professional field, Burton was some 11 minutes 30 seconds slower than the great Italian Felice Gimondi over the 45-mile course.

She combined her racing with various jobs including laboring on a fruit farm run by her Morley CC clubmate Nim Carline. No cosseted professional, when taking her first world title in Liege in 1959 she contributed expenses from her own pocket, and on returning home to Yorkshire she had to hitch a lift to her house from Leeds station. She dominated women's racing in Britain for 30 years, but her finest exploit came in 1967 when she broke the British record for 12 hours, beating the men's distance with 277.25 miles and overtaking the men's champion Mike McNamara along the way.

"Mac" had started two minutes ahead of Burton; she overhauled him in the final hour, and she later recalled the moment in her autobiography *Personal Best*: "'I'll have to pass him,' I thought. 'Poor Mac, it doesn't seem fair.'. . . 'Mac raised his head slightly and looked at me. Goodness knows what was going on in his mind but I thought some gesture was required on my part. I was carrying a bag of liquorice allsorts in the pocket of my jersey and on impulse I groped into the bag and pulled one out. It was one of those swiss-roll shaped ones, white with a coating of black liquorice. 'Liquorice allsort, Mac?' I shouted and held it towards him. He gave a wan smile. I put my head down and drew away."

That year, she was awarded an OBE and was elected British Sportswoman of the year. Burton's daughter Denise also competed, and mother and daughter both rode the world road race championships in Gap in 1972.

CAMPAGNOLO, Tullio (b. Italy, 1901, d. 1983)

Founder of cycling's most celebrated component makers and the man behind a host of innovations that are now universal in cycling, most notably the quick-release hub and a parallelogram rear derailleur that was not the first but was copied worldwide. During Campagnolo's 50-year manufacturing career he patented 135 inventions and bikes were transformed: from lumpen machines that had barely moved on since the invention of the safety bike, they became jewel-like, finely crafted pieces of lightweight engineering. The company remains highly secretive: for example, no one outside its factory knows what goes into its legendary off-white grease.

"When we saw a good-looking girl at the roadside, we'd say she was Campag," recalled the 1950s champion Raphael Geminiani. "Why is the name the most mythical in cycling? It's simple: Tullio changed the lives of cycling greats by producing cutting-edge components, and ordinary cyclists want to be like the greats."

All this dates back to one day, and one snow-hit race. Campagnolo was an amateur racing cyclist who was riding the Gran Premio della Vittoria over the Croce d'Aune pass in the Dolomites on November 4, 1924, when he had to change gears. This involved undoing the wingnuts on his back wheel and moving the chain to a different sprocket. The wingnuts had frozen up and his hands were too cold to turn them; he was unable to change gear and was deprived of the win.

Tullio's father owned an iron-monger's in Vicenza, northern Italy, where Campagnolo began experimenting. Over the next six years, he came up with the quick release mechanism, in which a hinged lever is turned inward against the wheel drop-out to hold the wheel spindle. The spindle is hollow, and when the lever is undone, springs on either side push the holding mechanism outward so the spindle remains centerd.

Next Tullio came up with various DERAILLEUR mechanisms, culminating in the radical Gran Sport (see time line on page 60). After the Second World War Campagnolo was carried along by the massive industrial growth that transformed Italy from a nation devastated by war to a dynamic modern society based on specialist manufacturing. The company worked with sports car makers Alfa, Ferrari, and Maserati at various times; the company's rapid expansion— from 1 employee in 1940 to 123 by 1950—and constant innovation was a key element in Italian cycling's golden years, when the rivalry between FAUSTO COPPI and GINO BARTALI was at its height. Both men raced on Campagnolo products, and Tullio was in constant contact with them and their mechanics to use their experience in the field to drive the manufacturing process forward. "The key one was the saddle fixing," said Geminiani. "Tullio brought in a two-pin cradle which meant everything, how far back the saddle was, how it sloped, could be adjusted to the millimeter." The Gran

Sport derailleur, and the 1956 racing pedal and seatpost, all became classic designs copied by many other manufacturers.

By the start of the 1970s, Campagnolo had diversified into motor parts, mainly wheels and brakes. In cycling, thanks to the constant consultation with the best racers and their mechanics—whose comments were recorded in Tullio's notebook—Campagnolo had become preeminent, constantly pushing forward with greats such as EDDY MERCKX using the components. "When I raced, 15 was the smallest sprocket," recalled Geminiani. "Tullio brought out the 13 for Anquetil, and the 12 for Merckx." In a similar vein, in 1996 Tullio's son Valentino traveled to the TOUR DE FRANCE with the first nine-speed gear for eventual winner Bjarne Riis.

In the 1970s, however, serious competition emerged in the form of Japanese companies SunTour and SHIMANO, leading to battles on the road between Merckx and Shimano-sponsored

rivals. Tullio Campagnolo died in 1983 just as his company was celebrating its 50th anniversary; a groupset specially produced for the occasion was presented to the pope. By then, the company's range was becoming unwieldy, and the advent of MOUNTAIN-BIKING in the US meant that road racing was no longer the cutting edge of componentry: progress was now driven by mountain-bike makers, and production of all but high-end equipment was moving to the Far East.

By the 1980s the most radical road developments no longer came from Campagnolo. Shimano raced ahead, first with indexed shifting, in which the derailleur clicked into predetermined positions so that shifting was no long a matter of guesswork; that in turn led to gear changers that were integrated into brake levers, the Shimano STI. Clipless pedals were produced by the French companies Look and Time, while Shimano and SunTour dominated the mountain-bike

Campagnolo Time Line

❖

1930—Tullio Campagnolo patents quick release hub.

1933—Campagnolo srl founded, first derailleur patented.

1943—Campagnolo logo featuring winged wheel appears for first time.

1948—Gino Bartali wins Tour de France using a *cambio corsa* derailleur.

1949—Parallelogram Gran Sport derailleur appears at Milan trade show; the definitive design appears in 1951.

1953—Fausto Coppi wins world championship using Gran Sport derailleur. Range now includes four rear derailleurs and two front, bar-end and down-tube shifters, hubs, dropouts, and various tools.

1958—Record name appears on five-pin cotterless crankset and hubs; soon features on track and road component groups. The range expands through the 1960s.

1966—Self-centring wine bottle opener patented.

1974—Super Record road and track groups appear, with titanium beginning to feature.

1980—Tullio Campagnolo oversees his last project, the Campagnolo freewheel.

1982—Range now includes Super Record, Nuovo Record, and Gran Sport, plus BMX componentry and promotional items including corkscrew and nutcracker.

1984—Seven-speed freewheel introduced.

1987—Last year Super Record produced until 2008.

1989—Mountain-bike groupset appears.

1992—Ergopower handlebar shifters introduced.

1994—Campagnolo leaves mountain-bike business.

1997—Nine-speed shifting brought in.

2000—Ten-speed shifting appears.

2004—Compact drivetrain brought in, featuring small chainrings, for cyclosportive events.

2008—Top-end groupsets now feature 11 sprockets.

market. It took several years for the Italian company to catch up, and in the meantime it brought out abortive products such as various unwieldy mountain-bike groupsets, the bizarre Delta parallelogram brakes, and heavy clipless pedals.

Campagnolo was revitalized in the early 1990s by the invention of the Ergopower handlebar/brake lever gear changers that took Shimano head-on. The rise of CYCLOSPORTIVE events in that decade also put the focus back on the road; in 1994 Campagnolo abandoned mountain-biking. Since then it has not attempted to take on Shimano in a straight fight, but has carved out its own niche, pushing road racing technology forward with the extensive use of carbon fiber, a move to 11-speed gearing, and compact gearing, which enables very low gears to be used in sportive events.

Campagnolo initiated the move to factory-built wheels with its groundbreaking Shamal although it appears to have fallen behind Shimano on electric gear-shifting. Its core value, however, remains its relationship with professional cyclists; one company insider estimated that 50 had been consulted before new 11-speed Ergopower changers were produced in 2008.

CAMPIONISSIMO   Italian term meaning champion of champions, coined in 1919 when Costante Girardengo won the GIRO D'ITALIA, taking 7 stages out of 10. The runner-up commented, "I'll never be a *campionissimo* but the names of a few pretty girls are etched on my heart." The second *campionissimo* was ALFREDO BINDA—five times a Giro winner, with a record 12 stages in 1927—but most often the term is used to refer to FAUSTO COPPI, although Italians would also use it when talking about EDDY MERCKX.

CANADA While all of Canada is not wilderness perpetually blanketed under ice and snow, there are good reasons why ice hockey is the country's dominant sport. Nevertheless, for much of cycling's history, it was arguably more robust in many parts of Canada, particularly Quebec, than it was in the United States.

TRACK in particular dominated cycling's early history in Canada. The biggest draw at SIX-DAY races was William Peden. Known as Torchy for his red hair, Peden won 38 six-days between 1929 and 1948, including 10 in 1932 alone.

Like many leading Canadian riders, Peden's bikes came from the Canadian Cycle and Motor Co., or CCM as it was better known. Canada's five largest bicycle makers merged operations to form CCM in 1899 when the initial bicycle boom waned. Although the company struggled initially, high import tariffs eventually enabled it to dominate the Canadian market. In 1950, for example, 130,413 bicycles were made in Canada, mostly by CCM, while just 29,354 bicycles were imported.

After World War II, time trialling and road racing developed in many parts of Canada largely thanks to a wave of immigrants from Britain and Italy. But cycling never regained the mass popularity it enjoyed during the height of the six-day era.

As is often the case with Canadian matters, the predominately French-speaking province of Quebec remained an exception. Racing there experienced much less of a decline between the end of the war and the second great bicycle boom of the 1970s. From the mid-1950s through the 1960s, Yvon Guillou organized the Tour du Saint Laurent, a stage race that attracted a variety of European amateur teams. It was briefly succeeded by a pro stage race, the Tour de la Nouvelle France, in the 1970s, which again featured European teams and prominent riders.

Since the 1980s, Serge Arsenault has continued to bring

pro racing to Quebec primarily with one-day races on a taxing circuit in downtown Montreal, a city that hosted the world championships in 1899 and 1974.

Perhaps surprisingly, however, the best known Canadian cyclists have not been from Quebec. Both STEVE BAUER, Canada's most successful road rider, and Gord Singleton, the first Canadian world champion (KEIRIN, 1982), come from near Niagara Falls. Bauer was initially coached by Colin Hearth, who also guided Singleton on the track.

Jocelyn Lovell was as irascible as he was successful, winning four gold medals in track events at the COMMONWEALTH GAMES in the 1970s. During a training ride in 1983, however, he was hit by a truck; the accident left him a quadriplegic.

Canadians have also been prominent in MOUNTAIN BIKING, most notably British Columbia's Alison Sydor, a three-time world champion in cross country and the winner of 17 World Cup races.

Clara Hughes found cycling fame in an unusual, and very Canadian, way. After winning, among many other titles, bronze medals in the road race and time trial at the 1996 Olympics, she switched back to speed skating, her first sport. She subsequently won gold, silver, and bronze Olympic medals on ice, making her the first Canadian to win medals at both the summer and winter games.

CAPE TOWN Site of the biggest competitive bike ride in the world: the Argus Pick'n'Pay Tour, which has about 40,000 participants. It usually takes place on the second Saturday in March and covers a 109-kilometer course starting and finishing in Cape Town, South Africa. Celebrity participants have included MIGUEL INDURAIN, GREG LEMOND, the Rugby World Cup-winning Springbok captain François

Pienaar, and EDDY MERCKX. The course record was set by South African Robbie Hunter in 2008 with 2 hours 27 minutes.

The Cape Argus was the first event outside Europe to be part of the UCI's Golden Bike series (see CYCLOSPORTIVES to read about the others). It is the centerpiece of a week of cycle events on the Cape including a mountain-bike challenge, a five-day professional stage race, and children's events.

The event has its roots in late 1978 when cycle activists staged a mass ride as part of a campaign for cycle paths in Cape Town. By the mid-1980s the event had become the Argus Cycle Tour and the field was up to several thousand, passing 20,000 by 1994. In 2002 the event was stopped due to extreme heat, while the toughest climb on the course, Chapman's, has been ruled out on occasion due to landslides. The 2009 event was run off in winds up to 60 mph.

(SEE **AFRICA** TO READ ABOUT CYCLING IN OTHER PARTS OF THE CONTINENT)

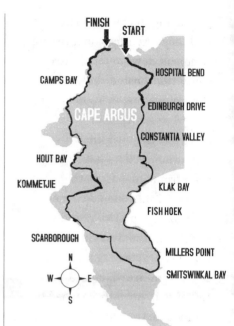

CARPENTER, Connie (b. Madison, Wisconsin, 1957)

Winner of the first Olympic Games road race gold medal for women in 1984, Carpenter was one of a group of US cycling team members who sparked the revival in the sport in the early 1980s and is arguably the greatest US women's bike racer to date. The former speed skater is also one of a rare breed: an athlete who has competed at both Summer and Winter Olympic Games. Carpenter was one of a bunch of US athletes who excelled at both speed skating and cycling (see the UNITED STATES entry for more on these), finishing seventh in the 1,500 m at the 1972 Winter Games at the age of 14. Carpenter moved to cycling after an ankle injury cut short her skating career in 1976; the following year she raced to a silver medal in the world road race championships. She became a multiple US champion on road and track and in 1978 and 1979 competed prominently in varsity rowing for the University of California. In 1983 she became the world 3 km track pursuit champion, following that up in 1984 with the road world title and the Olympic road title in a two-up sprint with her fellow American Rebecca Twigg. Carpenter retired two days later. She had earlier married her fellow Olympian Davis Phinney, who was to win a stage of the Tour de France in 1987. Their son Taylor Phinney is a strong

time triallist and track racer, was world pursuit champion in 2009 and 2010, and turned professional in 2011 for the BMC team run by JIM OCHOWICZ.

CARTOONISTS   There is a rich vein of cycling cartoons, dating back to the pioneering era, when cycling was just another social phenomenon lampooned affectionately in the pages of magazines such as *Punch*. That tradition is maintained today by a string of cartoonists of whom the best known is probably Frenchman Jean-Jacques Sempé, whose beautifully detailed and frequently poignant work has appeared on the cover of the *New Yorker* magazine since 1978, and has also been regularly featured in *Paris-Match* and *l'Equipe* magazines. Bikes are prominent subjects in Sempé's cartoons of French life, such as the couple on a bike that forms the cover for his collection *Displays of Affection*. While Sempé's best-known creation is *Le Petit Nicolas*, among his work is the graphic novel *Raoul Taburin Keeps a Secret* (published in France in 1995 as *Raoul Taburin: une bicyclette à propos de son père*), the story of the great Ralph Sprockett, an expert bike mechanic who knows all there is to know about bikes apart from how to ride one. Four volumes of his work are available in English, and there is also a range of stationery based on his collection *A Simple Question of Balance*. The US cycling scene has produced its own cartoonists, with Patrick O'Grady being one of the leaders. An avid cyclist himself who has been writing as well as drawing for *VeloNews* magazine since 1989, O'Grady regularly pokes subversive, merciless fun at his fellows. His work includes the collection *The Season Starts When?* (1999, Velopress). Bikes are also important subjects, if in more surreal style, in the work of US illustrator Neal Skorpen, and, frequently with an environmental slant, in the drawings of the British illustrator Brick.

Further back, the best-known European cycle racing cartoonist was the Swiss-domiciled French artist Pellos, who enjoys a similar place in French cycling culture to the writer Antoine Blondin. Both were key parts of the sport's heyday in the 1950s and 1960s. His caricatures of the greats appeared in French magazines such as *Match, Miroir Sprint*, and *Miroir du Cyclisme* from 1931 to 1982. Pellos was the pen name of Rene Pellarin (b. 1900, d. 1988), who competed in the 1924 Olympic Games in the javelin, 800 m, and shot put before taking up drawing full-time.

Pellarin also drew rugby and boxing, and was one of the most successful French 20th-century cartoon artists, producing definitive strips including *Les pieds nickelés* (which roughly translates to *Silver Feet*), about three youths who are constantly involved in various crazy schemes, which ran for 30 years. For cycling, he could produce evocative line illustration, but most often his work evokes the characteristics journalists and fans saw in the stars and the sport's backdrops: Tom Simpson is depicted as a beatnik, Jacques Anquetil sitting on a bottle of champagne, Mont Ventoux as a monstrous torturer compared to the benign smiling Alps.

British cycling has produced two longstanding cartoon strips that epitomize two radically different eras and cultures. *Honk*, drawn by the club rider Johnny Helms for *Cycling* magazine from the 1940s to the 1980s, was a whimsical character of the kind that could only appear in England. Honk has adventures with wayward dogs and punctures and curious things happen to him in cafés and on tandem bikes with smiling clubgirls. Helms continued to produce cartoons for *Cycling* until his death in November 2009 at the age of 85, by which time he had been working for the magazine for 63 years, and his drawings looked somewhat outdated.

On the other hand, the other notable British cartoon, *Mint Sauce*, which stars a mountain-

biking sheep, is quite relevant to its time. *Mint* was created in 1988 by the Brighton cartoonist Jo Burt, initially for *Bicycle Action* magazine, and has appeared in *Mountain Biking UK* for over 20 years. Burt cites *Krazy Kat* and *Calvin & Hobbes* among his influences; there is a strong mystical Celtic flavor to the strips, which incorporate rock lyrics for added effect. *Mint* also stars Coleman, a mountain-biking cow, Mint's girlfriend Oonagh Herdwick, and a black sheep with horns named Chipko. There's a dreamy babe named Summer—this being a British cartoon, she is a fickle creature—and a Grim Reaper figure who is always out to get Mint, but never quite manages to.

CATHOLICISM Is cycling the religion's official sport, or is Catholicism cycling's semi-official religion?

- The pope frequently receives the peloton in the GIRO D'ITALIA, most notably before the 2000 start, when among the blessed was MARCO PANTANI, fresh from being thrown off the 1999 race due to a failed blood test.

- The finish climb at the Flèche Wallonne CLASSIC has the stations of the cross at each hairpin.
- The Euskaltel team from Spain would receive a priest's blessing before traveling to major races.
- Pope Pius XII designated the Madonna del Ghisallo the cyclists' CHAPEL; it has since been visited by Paul VI and John Paul II.

- The Catholic church attempted to force FAUSTO COPPI to return to his wife during his divorce in 1954.
- Cycling writers use religious imagery: a painful race is a Calvary; Coppi has been compared to Piero della Francesco's tortured Christ.
- GINO BARTALI had a chapel in his house and went to Mass each morning before he raced.
- Most of the greats of cycling have donated jerseys, bikes, or both to the chapels at Ghisallo and Labastide d'Armagnac.

CAVENDISH, Mark

Born: Isle of Man, May 21, 1985

Major wins: World Madison champion 2005, 2008; Milan–San Remo 2009; 10 stage wins in Tour de France to 2009; five stage wins in Giro d'Italia

Interests outside cycling: design, ballroom dancing, FIAT 500s

Further reading: *Boy Racer*, Mark Cavendish, Velo Press, 2010

Highly talented and volatile sprinter from the Isle of Man who spearheaded the cycling renaissance in GREAT BRITAIN in 2008–9 and was set to dominate the finish straight for years to come. By 2009 Cavendish had set a new British record for TOUR DE FRANCE stage wins—10 in just two Tours— and had become, together with Tom Simpson, the only Briton to win a cycling MONUMENT in the modern era; he was also the first British cyclist to take victory on the Champs-Elysées in the Tour de France. He notched up over 50 pro wins in 2007, 2008, and 2009, a prolific record that bore comparison with the likes of EDDY MERCKX and Freddy Maertens.

Cavendish came out of the British Olympic program's academy for under-23 riders, where he was initially considered underpowered. He worked in a bank on the Isle of Man to finance his racing trips to the "mainland" and credited the academy's founder Rod Ellingworth with turning him from a "fat banker into a world champion." By 2005 he had become Madison world champion (see TRACK RACING for more details of this event) and in 2007 he turned professional for T-Mobile and started the Tour de France, crashing heavily twice before pulling out in the Alps.

His breakthrough year was 2008, with two stage wins at the GIRO D'ITALIA and four at the Tour, although he was bitterly disappointed not to win a medal

in the OLYMPIC GAMES. In 2009 he surprised many continental followers with a last-gasp victory in the sprint that decided MILAN–SAN REMO; it was, however, the fruit of detailed planning together with Ellingworth. At that year's Tour, he was more dominant than any sprinter since Maertens in 1976 and 1981, winning stages by huge margins. He also wrote a MEMOIR, *Boy Racer,* which detailed his adventures at the academy and pulled no punches when it came to former coaches and adversaries.

There are various reasons for Cavendish's success. One is his background in track racing, which means he can spin the pedals faster than the opposition. Another is his small size, which enables him to get lower on the bike; he has worked with his coaches to get so far forward over the front wheel that his handlebars and front forks have to be reinforced. This gives him a 4 percent AERODYNAMIC advantage over his rivals. His Columbia team has put in a huge amount of work to give him a perfect "lead-out" train—something Cav acknowledges after every win—while Cavendish himself prepares every race in detail with Ellingworth.

Outside cycling, Cavendish has a collection of iconic Italian design items that includes vintage Fiat 500s and Lambrettas. He lives in an apartment near the British base in Quarrata, Tuscany.

CHAPELS   Not surprisingly for a sport that has close links to CATHOLICISM, there are several cyclists' chapels across Europe. The best known is at Madonna del Ghisallo above Lake Como in Italy, which stands next to a spacious, modern museum of cycling and has a fine statue of FAUSTO COPPI outside its front door. Inside the chapel are bikes and jerseys donated by many of the greats of the sport, and a panel on the wall bearing photographs of cyclists, professional and amateur, who have died on the roads of Europe, going back to the 1930s; GINO BARTALI's brother Giulio is among them. The bikes on display include Bartali's 1948 Tour-

winning Legnano and a futuristic machine used by FRANCESCO MOSER for an hour record. The cyclists who have donated jerseys include BERNARD HINAULT, Mario Cipollini, MIGUEL INDURAIN, and MARCO PANTANI.

The Madonna del Ghisallo was known as a patroness of travelers; in the 1940s the local priest, Don Ermelindo Vigano, suggested that his church should be the site of a cyclists' shrine, as the climb up from the lakeside was the decisive point in the Tour of Lombardy. Leading cyclists including Coppi signed a petition, and the Madonna was designated the patroness of cyclists in 1949 by Pope Pius XII, who also blessed the GIRO D'ITALIA and received Coppi and Bartali at the Vatican. The "race of the falling leaves" still passes the Ghisallo, where the bell rings as the racers toil up the hill.

In southwest France, a similar chapel at Labastide-d'Armagnac dating back to the 12th century has been known as Notre Dame des Cyclistes since Pope

John XXIII made the church a National Sanctuary for Cycling and Cyclists in 1959. Like the Ghisallo, Notre Dame includes a cycling museum including jerseys donated by Hinault, EDDY MERCKX, JACQUES ANQUETIL, RAYMOND POULIDOR, and TOM SIMPSON. There is also a stained-glass window donated by the 1964 world champion Henri Anglade. The Tour de France began a stage in the village in 1989.

In Spain, the patroness of cycling is the Virgin of Dorleta; one sanctuary of Our Lady of Dorleta is in the Basque Country village of Leintz-Gatzaga (Salinas de Léniz in Spanish). There are shrines to the Dorleta virgin across Spain, including one in Andalucia on the Suspiro del Moro pass south of Granada, where the inscription reads:

Our Lady of Dorleta, patron of Spanish cyclists. Maria, queen of the world, protect earthly roads in all ways for cyclists who love nature's great works created by our Lord.

CHARITIES While the Livestrong charity founded by LANCE ARMSTRONG is the best-known fundraising body linked to the sport, there are several others. The **Amy Gillett Foundation** was launched after the Australian rower-turned-cyclist was knocked down by a car and killed in Germany in 2005 while out training with the national team. It has as its main goal to "reduce the incidence of injury and death caused by the interaction between cyclists and motorists." Patrons include Tour de France stars Phil Anderson and Cadel Evans and the Formula One driver Mark Webber, and it funds two scholarships, one to support talented young cyclists and the other to research cycle safety.

The **Fabio Casartelli Foundation** was formed after the death of the 1992 Olympic champion from head injuries in the 1995 Tour de France and has goals that include supporting ex-cyclists and emerging talent. It runs a Gran Fondo every year.

MARCO PANTANI, the Tour winner who died of drug addiction in 2004, has also inspired a *fondazione*, which variously supports the disabled, has funded a school for partially sighted cyclists, runs youth training camps, and donates money to a team in the war-hit city of Vinkovci in Croatia. It also runs a Gran Fondo and supports another two, all named after Pantani.

In Yorkshire, meanwhile, the **Dave Rayner Fund** was begun in 1993 after the death of this talented young cyclist; it raises money to help talented young cyclists who wish to race abroad and supported 25 of them in 2009. Among its activities is a fundraising dinner attended by various celebrities and the organization of the Étape du Dales Sportive.

The **Braveheart Fund** plays a similar role in Scotland; as with the Rayner Fund, its dinner is one of the highlights of the British winter cycling calendar, with CHRIS HOY and MARK CAVENDISH among the 2008 diners—Hoy, indeed, went to the dinner rather than the British Cycling function, in the year of his Olympic triumph. Braveheart invested over £35,000 in Scottish cycling in 2009, with cash going to 13 cyclists aged 15 to 23, and to another 3 with a chance of riding at the Commonwealth Games in 2010.

Livestrong, however, is the daddy of all cycling-based charities. Founded in 1998 after LANCE ARMSTRONG's recovery from cancer, it invested $21 million dollars in research in its first 10 years of existence and relies heavily on Armstrong's leverage with politicians and business people. Armstrong has worked on cancer panels at national level and is renowned worldwide as a cancer campaigner. The charity turned the yellow Livestrong wristband into a must-have item for celebrities and politicians; they sell at one dollar each and were developed by Nike and their ad agency. They have sparked controversy over pirating and profiteering through eBay, have spawned hundreds of multicolored imitators, and were even spoofed by comedian Stephen Colbert.

(SEE **POLITICS** FOR A LIST OF LEADERS WHO HAVE JUMPED ON THE BANDWAGON)

CLASSICS   The term used for the sport's major one-day races including the five MONUMENTS: Milan–San Remo, Tour of Flanders, Paris–Roubaix, Liège–Bastogne–Liège and the Tour of Lombardy (see their separate entries; see COBBLES for Classics that include this nasty road surface).

Major one-day races come and go but other Classics include:

- **Het Volk** (founded 1945): Held in Belgium in early March using many of the climbs from the Tour of Flanders.
- **Ghent–Wevelgem** (f. 1934): Another Flandrian race, it goes over the steep Kemmelberg, with its First World War ossuary.
- **Flèche Wallonne** (f. 1936): On the other side of Belgium in

the French-speaking area of Wallonia. Finishes at the town of Huy on top of the steep climb up the "Wall."
- **Amstel Gold** (f. 1966): A complex series of many loops around the Dutch province of Limburg crossing a multitude of tiny climbs.
- **Paris–Tours** (f. 1896): A long, flat, autumn event known as the "sprinters' classic" that until 2009 had the longest finish straight in cycling: 2.5 km up Avenue de Grammont. In 2010 the finish was changed as a streetcar route is constructed.
- **GP Ouest France** (f. 1931): Held in Brittany in August at the bike-mad village of Plouay.
- **Milan–Turin** (f. 1876): The oldest one-day race still on the calendar, although not run continuously since that date: culminates with a climb to the Superga monastery.
- **Giro del Piemonte** (f. 1906): A race through the Alpine foothills around western Italy, also finishing in Turin.
- **Giro del Lazio** (f. 1935): A loop around Rome.

- **Scheldeprijs** (f. 1907): The oldest cycle race in FLANDERS, held around Antwerp.
- **GP Frankfurt** (f. 1962): Known for many years as the Henninger Tower, after a vast grain silo owned by the brewery that backed the race until 2008.
- **GP San Sebastian** (f. 1981): Spain's main one-day race, on a hilly course in the Basque Country.
- **Paris–Brussels** (f. 1893): Actually starts 90 km north of Paris at the town of Soissons.
- **Philadelphia GP** (f. 1985): Run under various names and sponsors over a course in the city that includes the 17 percent grade Manayunk Wall.
- **Lincoln GP** (f. 1956 as Witham GP): The oldest extant one-day race in Britain, it features the 25 percent climb through the medieval city, up to the cathedral.

Most of the great Classics have CYCLOSPORTIVES run along all or part of their route: PARIS–ROUBAIX, the Tour of FLANDERS, the Tour of Lombardy, and MILAN–SAN REMO are among the most popular.

CLASSICS—DEFUNCT

There are several Classics that were prestigious in their time but which are no longer run. The best example is **Bordeaux–Paris**, the Derby of the Road, which dated back to the origins of cycling in the 19th century. It lasted 14 hours and was unique in that the riders were paced by small motorbikes known as DERNYS for the second half; it survived until 1988.

The **Grand Prix des Nations** time trial was founded in 1932 by the journalists Gaston Benac and Albert Baker d'Isy and witnessed some of JACQUES ANQUETIL's greatest rides. It was upstaged by the inception of the world time trial championships in 1994 and was last run in 2005.

The **Championship of Zurich** enjoyed the longest uninterrupted run of any Classic (1917–2006) because it was kept going through both world wars thanks to Swiss neutrality, but it eventually succumbed to a lack of sponsorship.

GREAT BRITAIN was awarded a round of the UCI's World Cup series, a race which always carried the suffix "Classic"—although it had no tradition and was a manufactured event—and this ran from 1989 to 1996 at Newcastle, Brighton, Leeds, and Rochester.

CLASSICS GREATS

The greatest Classic cyclist of them all, by a huge margin, was EDDY MERCKX, who took 33 wins in major one-day races. The other great all-around specialists include: RIK VAN LOOY (17), ROGER DE VLAEMINCK (16), Jan Raas (14), and FAUSTO COPPI (12). During the 1980s and 1990s, one-day racing was dominated by SEAN KELLY (11) and Johan Museeuw (12); today, however, most cyclists specialize in either the hillier Classics or the flatter cobbled events. Some cyclists achieved particular dominance in a single event: JACQUES ANQUETIL, for example, won the GP des Nations nine times—but only took three other Classics, while Merckx managed seven victories in Milan–San Remo.

RIDER	MAJOR ONE-DAY RACE WINS
EDDY MERCKX	33
RIK VAN LOOY	17
ROGER DE VLAEMINCK	16
JAN RAAS	14
JACQUES ANQUETIL	12
FAUSTO COPPI	12
JOHAN MUSEEUW	12
SEAN KELLY	11

CLUBS Cycling clubs were born as the world discovered the bicycle, and their history in the United States runs parallel with that of the sport: massive early growth, later decline following the development of the automobile, and a depression before a phase of rebirth later in the 20th century. The term "wheelmen" was commonly used, and the clubs' umbrella body, the League of American Wheelmen, was founded in 1880. Its membership peaked at 103,000 in 1898, but it folded in 1902 with under 9,000 members. After several attempts, it was reformed in 1955.

To take just one example of the height cycling clubs reached in the late 19th century, the Detroit Bicycle Club, formed in 1879 and renamed the Detroit Wheelmen in 1890, boasted 450 members by 1896 and had sufficient resources to build an elaborate, elegantly designed clubhouse costing $40,000 that contained an auditorium, card tables, bowling alley, baths, library, and kitchen. The building remained standing in the center of Detroit until the 1970s. Another more notable Detroit club was the Wolverine Wheelmen, founded in 1888 and eventually—after folding and being reformed in 1937—morphing into a club that also catered for cross-country skiers and speedskaters. Thanks to the cross-fertilization between skating and cycling, Wolverine members such as Sue Novara-Reber, Sheila Young, and Connie Paraskevin played a key role in the development of US cycling in the 1970s and 1980s. LANCE ARMSTRONG's teammate Frankie Andreu was also a member.

Perhaps the strongest club the US has produced to date is New York squad GS Mengoni, founded in 1981 by a former Italian racer Fred Mengoni. In the 1980s Mengoni's squad included racers such as Alexi Grewal, Steve Bauer, Matt Eaton, Leonard "Harvey" Nitz, and Doug Shapiro and was able to give the pros of 7-Eleven a run for their money. The stand-out result was Bauer's silver medal in the 1984 OLYMPIC GAMES as a Mengoni amateur, followed a month later by bronze in his first World's as a pro. Mengoni tried, and failed, to get the young GREG LEMOND to race for him, but a later incarnation of the team included George Hincapie, an Olympian for Mengoni and later a Tour de France stage winner. Mengoni was a cofounder of USPRO, the first real governing body for professional racing in the US.

Some of the more curious cycling clubs are to be found in GREAT BRITAIN. The A5 Rangers were named after the road they used for their runs up Watling Street; the North Road and Bath Road followed the same principle. South London's San Fairy Ann, on the other hand, comes from a misliteration of the French *Ça ne fait rien* —"it doesn't matter at all." In the Welsh capital Cardiff, the Jif club was set up as a rival to the Ajax and was named after a competing washing powder. The Comical Cycling Club of Penshurst (in Sussex) was founded solely so that they could wear jerseys bearing the cyrillic initials of the old Soviet Union.

The Pickwick Bicycle Club claims to be the oldest cycling club in the world; founded on June 22, 1870—and given the name because this date coincided with the death of Charles Dickens— it is now largely a dining club but keeps to the founding rule that members must display a knowledge of Dickens's Pickwick Papers. Equally arcane is the 300,000 Mile Club, founded in 1962, with entry restricted to the 70 or so cyclists who have covered more than that distance in their lifetime, with every mile officially logged. In the same vein, the Ordre des Cols Durs is a French club for "pass-bashers"—cyclists who record the heights of the mountain passes around they world they ride each season— while the Cape Wrath Fellowship is open to cyclists who have braved the ferry ride and dead-end road that lead to this remote headland in northern Scotland.

COBBLES   Synonymous with two of the sport's MONUMENTS (see FLANDERS, PARIS–ROUBAIX) and other one-day CLASSICS such as Ghent–Wevelgem, stone-paved roads are now a throwback to cycling's earliest days. In French they are known as *pavé*, in Flemish *kinderkopje* (children's heads). Racing cyclists fear them because in the wet they can be virtually impossible to ride on safely.

The threat from any sort of cobble depends on the stone it is made of: blue slate is extra slippery, while granite is a greater puncture threat. Cobbled sections included in Paris–Roubaix are occasionally put in the TOUR DE FRANCE, most recently in the 1983 and 2004 races, as well as in 2010.

The three most notorious cobbled roads in cycling are:

The Trouée d'Arenberg in Paris–Roubaix, a 2.5 km long dead-straight road laid in the time of Napoleon that undulates due to mining subsidence and has massive holes between the stones. The riders used to switch—at speeds of about 35 mph—between the grass verge and the *pavé* until the organizers erected barriers. It is often tackled in a downhill direction, hence the high speeds and horrendous crashes. The most celebrated victim of Arenberg was the Belgian champion Johan Museeuw, who nearly died after crashing there in 1999; in 2001 the French cyclist Philippe Gaumont suffered an open fracture of the femur, which cost him six weeks in bed.

The Koppenberg in the Tour of Flanders, a climb that is only 400 m long but has a gradient of 25 percent. It's not always in the route, being so narrow that crashes are a certainty; the most famous happened in 1987 when the Dane Jesper Skibby was inches from being run over by the race organizer as he lay on the cobbles strapped in to his bike. A series of photos by GRAHAM WATSON captured the moment.

The Kemmelberg in Ghent–Wevelgem is as steep as the Koppenberg, but wider and longer, so less conducive to crashes as the riders climb up. It was a focal point for fighting in the First World War, and has a vast ossuary on the top. There is also a fine restaurant in the final meters, where fans gather to munch steak and fries and applaud the riders. What is truly fearsome is the descent: vertiginously steep, over massive paving stones, and virtually unridable in the wet.

Another major race that includes cobbles is the Four Days of Dunkirk, which has a stage over the fearsome Mont Cassel, while the Scheldeprijs at Antwerp has seven cobbled sections. But cobbles are not restricted to French and Belgian Flanders. In Great Britain the Lincoln Grand Prix has a cobbled climb to match either of the latter: a half-mile long 25 percent ascent through the heart of the ancient city to the Norman cathedral. In the US, the Philadelphia Grand Prix includes cobbles on Cresson Street on the fearsome Manayunk Wall climb.

CODES As police forces in Europe investigated DOPING in the early 21st century, tapping phone calls and intercepting e-mails, drug-takers in cycling and their doctors and suppliers began to use cyphers to refer to certain drugs and practices. In one Belgian case, "wasp" referred to the blood booster Aranesp, a "wasps' nest" to a course of the drug, while a "washing machine" was a centrifuge used to measure blood levels and "strawberry jam" meant EPO. In the Operación Puerto blood-doping operation, the riders whose blood was stored for reinjection were referred to by coded names, not all of which have been deciphered. "Bella" was the German Jorg Jaksche; Ivan Basso of Italy was called "Birillo" after his dog; there is still speculation over the identity of "Hijo de Birillo" (Son of Birillo).

Codes were also used by FAUSTO COPPI and GINO BARTALI at the height of their rivalry to pass on instructions to their *gregari*: Coppi would tell Sandrino Carrea to "slow down" when he wanted him to set a furious pace, while Bartali had a teammate look at Coppi's legs and shout "the vein" when a vein on his calf began pulsating, a sign that Coppi might be struggling.

Lance Armstrong refers to himself as Juan Pelota, most notably on Twitter, the pun being that *pelota* is Spanish for *ball*, and Armstrong had one testicle removed during testicular cancer treatment.

In Great Britain, meanwhile, after road racing was banned at the turn of the century, TIME TRIALLING was carried out on courses referred to by coded names to keep the events secret. Courses are still known by their code today, although they are deciphered in the governing body's handbook and website: the most famous of all was probably E72/25: E stands for the region, East, while 25 is the distance and 72 referred to a course starting on the A12 Colchester Bypass, where many British records were broken.

COLOMBIA Ranks with FLANDERS, northern ITALY, and the Basque Country (see SPAIN) as a nation where cycling is part of the fabric; like the KEIRIN racers of Japan, however, Colombian cyclists are now largely out of the international mainstream. There was, however, a brief interlude in the 1980s and 1990s when they burst on to the pro-cycling scene and performed far better than cyclists from richer nations where cycling was far better resourced.

Cycling's place in Colombian culture is explored in depth in one of the finest cycle-racing BOOKS of recent years, Matt Rendell's *Kings of the Mountains* (Aurum, 2002). High altitude, poverty, and poor roads made Colombia inhospitable cycling country, but even so, the first races were held, as in many other nations, before the end of the 19th century. The first Vuelta a Colombia was held in 1951; insanely tough due to the high mountains and abominable roads, 1,154 km and 10 stages long, it was won by Ephraim Forero Triviño, known simply as "the Zipa," amid massive popular support.

A brief racing visit by FAUSTO COPPI lent new momentum to the sport in 1957, although whether Coppi was ever paid for his efforts remains unclear. In the 1960s the arrival of the first Colombian to succeed outside his own borders, Cochise Rodriguez, did change things, and by the 1970s, Colombians were dominant in South American racing; Cochise, meanwhile, took the world amateur HOUR RECORD in 1970, and added the pursuit world gold medal in Italy a year later, Colombia's first cycling world title.

Controversially, he was refused entry to the 1972 Olympics on the grounds that he had broken amateur rules on sponsorship. Instead, he turned pro with Bianchi in Italy, won two stages in the Giro, and became the first Colombian to finish the Tour.

In the 1980s the Colombians had begun to perform consistently in the mountains in world-level amateur races. When the Tour went open to amateurs in 1983 Colombia was the only nation to take up the challenge, with sponsorship from battery company Varta. The little climbers suffered on the flat stages but performed well enough in the Alps and Pyrenées, with Patrocinio Jimenez spending five days in the polka-dot King of the Mountain jersey.

Varta's sponsorship was a sound move as most Colombians followed the Tour on radio and the gabbling commentators declaiming down phone lines were a distinctive presence on the race for a decade. The following year the country's best racer, LUIS HERRERA, returned with a squad sponsored by Café de Colombia and took the prestigious finish at l'Alpe d'Huez ahead of LAURENT FIGNON and BERNARD HINAULT. In 1985

Herrera, "the little gardener," won two more stages and was King of the Mountains; an estimated one million people turned out to welcome him home. He took Colombia's biggest win, the Vuelta a España, in 1987; the finish date, May 15, was declared a national holiday.

Others came to Europe with Herrera, mainly racing for Spanish teams, including Oliverio Rincon—winner of a Tour stage at Andorra in 1993—and the accident prone Fabio Parra, cruelly nicknamed "Parra-chute." In 1995 the world road championships traveled to Colombia, held on an extremely hard circuit at the town of Duitama, with Abraham Olano winning the pro road race. In 2000 Santiago Botero ground out an improbable victory in the Tour's King of the Mountains title.

Since then, Colombian cycling has been off the world stage. Rendell puts it down variously to the rise of the national soccer team, the economic decline and migration that has accompanied the country's narco-war, and the UCI's inability to boost cycling in poorer, marginal countries. As a footnote, cycling has had links with Colombia's drugs syndicates; down-on-their-luck pros traveling to Europe were employed as couriers, while in one of the most dramatic passages in Rendell's *Kings of the Mountains* he interviews Roberto Escobar, brother of the notorious drug king Pablo. Roberto, a fine cyclist, watched Coppi and Koblet on their racing trip to Colombia and ended up making bikes and running teams. His brother, meanwhile, had a velodrome built in his hometown of Medellin so he could bet on the races held there.

COMMONWEALTH GAMES

There was no cycling in the inaugural British Empire Games of 1930; bike races appeared four years later. The Games take place on a four-year cycle which alternates with the Olympics. It was not until 1974, after various name changes, that the name Commonwealth Games was settled upon. Women's cycling did not appear until 1990, while the 1998 Games in Kuala Lumpur saw the introduction of team events, and in 2002, in Manchester, events for athletes with disability were introduced. Alongside the senior Games, the Youth Games for athletes under 18 is run.

Since the advent of lottery funding (see GREAT BRITAIN) the British cycling team has sent large numbers of athletes to compete under their various national banners, but with management and logistics back-up from within the Great Britain Olympic team set-up. Years of Australian domination in the cycling disiplines came to an end at the Games in 2002 in Manchester.

COOKE, Nicole

Born: Swansea, Wales, April 13, 1983

Major wins: Olympic road race champion 2008; world road race champion 2008; Commonwealth Games road race champion 2002; women's World Cup 2003, 2006; Giro d'Italia 2004; 10 times GB national champion between 1999 and 2009; MBE 2009

Further reading: *Cycle for Life*, Nicole Cooke, Abbeville Press, 2009

The Welsh woman was the flag carrier for British women's cycling throughout the early 2000s, from her unique triple junior world titles (road, time trial, mountain bike) in 2001 to her unprecedented double of world and Olympic road race titles in 2008, when she was elected *Sunday Times* Sportswoman of the Year.

Even while attending Brynteg Comprehensive in south Wales— where rugby star Gavin Henson was a fellow pupil—Cooke was a precocious talent, the youngest rider ever to win the senior women's national title, which she achieved at 16. She is known for her total determination and consistency in major title races, taking two bronze and a silver medal in world road titles between 2003 and 2006.

Her career has been disrupted by the economic difficulties that beset women's racing—several of her teams have suffered financial problems. She has also had to contend with injury, mainly to her left knee, which has twice required surgery. After a second operation, in late 2007—which deprived her of a third title in the women's World Cup—she contemplated quitting the sport.

Cooke truly bounced back the following year. Her victory in Beijing came on a soaking wet day after her teammate Emma Pooley split the field with a searing attack. It set up the GB cycling team for an unprecedented medal rush. In Varese six weeks later, Cooke rode the perfect tactical race to triumph in a sprint finish from the Dutchwoman Marianne Vos, so often her nemesis in previous seasons. She now spends most of her time in her adopted home near Lugano, Switzerland

(SEE **DAVE BRAILSFORD**, **CHRIS HOY**, **BRADLEY WIGGINS** FOR MORE ON GB'S SUCCESS IN 2008)

COPPI, Fausto

Born: Castellania, Italy, September 15, 1919

Died: Tortona, Italy, January 2, 1960

Major wins: World road race champion 1953; Tour de France 1949, 1952, 9 stage wins; Giro d'Italia 1940, 1947, 1949, 1952, 1953, 22 stage wins; Milan–San Remo 1946, 1948–9; Giro di Lombardia, 1946–9, 1954; Paris–Roubaix 1950; Flèche Wallonne 1950; GP des Nations 1946–7, world pursuit champion 1947, 1949; world hour record 1942

Nicknames: Faustino, *il Campionissimo*, the Heron

Interests outside cycling: football, shooting

Further reading/viewing: *Fallen Angel, the Passion of Fausto Coppi*, by William Fotheringham, Random House UK, 2010; *Coppi's Angel*, Ugo Riccarelli, trs Michael McDermott, Middlesex University Press, 2009; DVD, *Il Vero Fausto*

Voted Italy's greatest sportsman of the 20th century, the CAMPIONISSIMO is famed for becoming the first man to manage the apparently impossible Giro-Tour DOUBLE, in 1949, with a repeat in 1952. Coppi's story, "a novel" said his good friend Raphael Geminiani, includes love, war, scandal, phenomenal success, and personal tragedy and ended with his bizarre death in 1960 when he caught malaria and the doctors did not diagnose it. The cocktail of emotions he arouses among fans in his native Italy has made

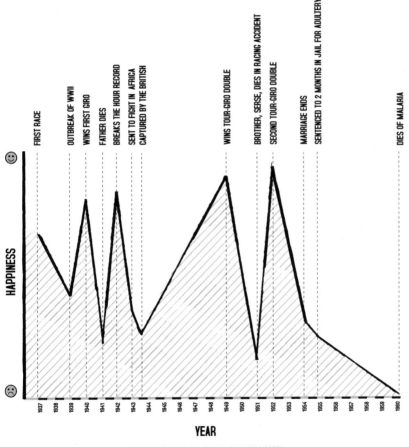

GRADIENT PROFILE OF THE LIFE OF FAUSTO COPPI

him an inspirational figure, with
his tale retold in biopics, television
documentaries, novels, plays, and
even an opera. There are numerous
Coppi memorials across Europe
as well as sculptures, paintings,
and lyrical descriptions such as
this, from the Tour winner turned
journalist André Leducq: "He
seems to caress the handlebars,
while his torso seems fixed by
screws in the saddle. His long legs
stretch to the pedals like the limbs
of a gazelle, All the moving parts
turn as if in oil. His long face is like
a knifeblade as he climbs without
apparent effort, like a great artist
painting a watercolor."

Born into a peasant farming
family in Liguria, Coppi won his first
GIRO D'ITALIA at 20 with the help
of the SOIGNEUR Biagio Cavanna,
who was to remain a key influence.
He broke the world HOUR RECORD
in 1942 as Allied bombs fell on
Milan and was sent to fight in North
Africa, where he was captured by the
British. After the war he relaunched
his career together with his brother
Serse. As Italy rebuilt its economy
and society, Coppi forged his greatest
wins in the Giro and MILAN–SAN

REMO. He also managed a record
five wins in the GIRO DI LOMBARDIA.
For all Italians, his RIVALRY with
GINO BARTALI symbolizes a golden
era when the country emerged from
the war and classic designs such as
the Fiat 500 and the Vespa left the
drawing board. Coppi's 1949 TOUR
DE FRANCE win included overturning
a 37-minute deficit on the early
leader Jacques Marinelli; it came
after he had taken his third Giro with
a crushing stage win over Bartali on
an Alpine loop between Cuneo and
Pinerolo. In 1952 as he rode to his
second Giro-Tour double, Coppi's
form was so devastating that the
organizers doubled the prize money
for second place in an attempt to
restore a little interest in the race.

Tragedy stalked Coppi as he
raced: his father Domenico died
not long after his first Giro win
in 1940, and Serse was killed in
a seemingly innocuous racing
accident in 1951. In 1953 and 1954
he scandalized Italy by ending
his marriage and beginning a
relationship with a doctor's wife,
Giulia Occhini, immortalized as
"the white lady." Both were married
at a time when adultery was illegal:

they ended up in court and Giulia was taken briefly to jail. Coppi's career never recovered, but when he died after catching malaria at a criterium in Africa, his country was overwhelmed with grief. His name lives on in Coppi bikes and in the Giro d'Italia, where a special prize is awarded each year on the "Coppi summit," the highest pass crossed by the race.

Coppi's enduring popularity can be seen by the plethora of memorials to the man all over Italy: at the Madonna del Ghisallo chapel, in his home village of Castellania and the nearby town of Novi Ligure, outside the cycle track in Turin, on the Pordoi and Stelvio passes, on the Bocchetta pass near Genova and the Macerola near Amalfi, on the Col d'Izoard in the French Alps, the summit of the Puy-de-Dôme mountain in central France, and at the Milan–San Remo monument on the Capo Berta.

(SEE **MEMORIALS** FOR MORE PLACES WHERE CYCLING GREATS ARE REMEMBERED; **POETRY** FOR ANOTHER WAY IN WHICH COPPI IS CELEBRATED)

COURIERS   Funny hair, scruffy faces, big bags on their backs, the way they annoy car drivers and pedestrians as they swoop in and out of the traffic: that may be how outsiders see cycle couriers, but in fact they are part of a long-standing tradition of deliveries by bike. That goes back to the 1890s, when Western Union delivery boys began zipping around New York City. Cycle courier races might seem a novelty, but in Paris, the hordes of newspaper delivery boys—some of them half-decent amateur cyclists— raced criteriums for over 50 years, enjoying massive popular support.

The peak days for couriering were the 1980s and early 1990s, before fax and e-mail enabled documents to be sent reliably by wire. At one point in the 1980s there were 7,000 couriers in New York; among them was Nelson Vails, who made the jump from messaging to become Olympic sprint champion at Los Angeles in 1984. Vails reckoned he was in the top 10 of couriers, carrying out 35 to 60 drops a day, giving 40 percent of his earnings to his dispatch company.

In London in 2003 there were an estimated 400 bicycle messengers: that figure is understood to have contracted during the recession of 2008–9 so there are probably between 300 and 350. Earnings are about the mininum wage, unlikely to exceed $400 per week without taking equipment costs into account. It is also a dangerous job: a 2002 Harvard School of Public Health report into couriers in Boston estimated that the rate of injury requiring time off work was 13 times the US average.

Couriers use personally adapted bikes. Gear has to be as indestructible as possible, and easy to service and replace. So couriers often ride fixed-wheel for the added control it gives in city riding. Additionally, a single gear has no cables to rust up, even if it is used in all weathers (see FIXED-WHEEL to learn how courier-type bikes became trendy in the early 2000s). Frames may be taken from mountain bikes or track machines, with bars anything from "cowhorn" time trial bars to radically cut down straight off-road bars.

The first courier world championships were held in 1993 in Berlin, testing messenger skills such as speed, navigation, and the ability to work under pressure. The annual gathering led to an awareness of the courier subculture worldwide; informal courier races known as "alleycats" became more common.

Further information: movingtargetzine.com

CRITICAL MASS   Widely perceived as mass protests by cyclists in major cities worldwide, Critical Mass rides are informal, leaderless events that participants insist are celebrations and spontaneous gatherings, which means they fall outside rules that may require organized protests to be notified to local police. The aim is simply to reclaim road space from motorists, if only for a while. Critical Mass rides are usually held on the last Friday of every month and have a nonhierarchical structure: the routes may simply be decided by whoever happens to lead the group or by a vote from a variety of routes handed out to each participant. All that matters is that enough cyclists turn up and ride together so that they can "occupy" the road.

The first Critical Mass ride was held in San Francisco in 1992 with a couple of dozen cyclists. Now over 300 cities worldwide host Critical Mass rides, with a biennial event in Budapest drawing over 80,000 cyclists. Sometimes as the cyclists roll along small groups will block traffic on side roads for a few moments to enable the others to pass through junctions without stopping, a practice known as "corking."

There are now variants on Critical Mass including Critical Manners rides in the US, which aim to encourage cyclists to observe road laws; Critical Sass is an all-women ride in Louisiana; NUDE CYCLING campaigning rides have adopted the names Critical Ass and Critical Tits.

CURSE   Cycling lore has it that the rainbow jersey of professional road world champion carries a hex, a belief based on the number of pro road world champions who have suffered a poor season immediately after taking the title.

The list begins with FAUSTO COPPI, 1953 world champion and never again a major winner after a spate of crashes and illness. The notion of the curse started with the 1955 world champion Stan Ockers of Belgium, who died the winter after winning the title; he crashed and cracked his skull while track racing, throwing Belgium into a state of mourning. The 1987 winner STEPHEN ROCHE barely raced in 1988 due to a knee injury that he said flared up the morning after his victory; he was never the same athlete again.

TOM SIMPSON, 1965 champion, broke his leg skiing over the winter and missed most of 1966. The 1997 rainbow jersey Laurent Brochard was embroiled in the Festina DOPING scandal, while the 1970 title winner Jean-Pierre Monsere died in a racing crash in 1971.

The 1981 world champion Freddy Maertens slumped into obscurity after that win, the 1990 winner Rudy Dhaenens was barely seen in action again after contracting a virus, and the 1994 rainbow jersey winner Luc Leblanc's sponsor went bust the next season. The 1969 world champion Harm Ottenbros was unknown when he won and quickly went back that way.

The 1996 champion Johan Museeuw was plagued by troubles that included an infected scratch in his knee, tangling his wheel in another rider's quick-release mechanism, punctures, and a urinary infection. More recently, Romans Vainsteins (2000) and Igor Astarloa (2003) disappeared without trace, while 2003 time trial world champion David Millar was busted for drugs the following year.

There are some exceptions, however. Being a world champion did not seem to affect EDDY MERCKX adversely, while GREG LEMOND won the TOUR DE FRANCE a year after taking the world title in 1989, and 1980 world champion BERNARD HINAULT won the Tour de France and Paris–Roubaix in the next season. Perhaps the curse applies only to mere mortals.

CYCLE SPEEDWAY Cycling discipline run along the same lines as motorized speedway, with short, sharp races run counterclockwise on an oval track, with a standing start. It developed in the 1940s when the motorized version was at its zenith, when kids began racing on British bombsites using discarded bikes, with bars made of copper piping to imitate motorbike handebars. Now, races are held on outdoor dirt tracks between 65 and 90 meters in length. As in TRACK RACING, bikes have single speed gears and no brakes, but the gear is a freewheel not a fixed and is far lower than that used for track racing, spun at up to 200 pedal revs per minute. The races are usually between four riders over four laps, most often between two pairs of riders from opposing teams; first over the line is the winner, with points awarded over an evening's racing. The riders draw for grid position, which can be a critical factor as overtaking is difficult—inside grid is best. All the tracks are subtly different, so previous knowledge of what lines to adopt around the curves can be important. Physical contact is permitted—jostling and barging for corners—but the referees have tightened up on it in recent years. The best riders are explosive sprinters but stamina is needed for up to 10 races in a meeting, while cornering, overtaking, and physical contact mean that high skill levels and decent upper body strength are called for.

There are about 40 clubs in Britain, with regional leagues, and also clubs in Australia, the US, Sweden, Holland, and Poland. Among the major names, the first rider to take the "Grand Slam" of national junior, under-21, senior, Australian, and world titles was Jim Varnish of Great Britain. The 2009 British champion was Gavin Wheeler, while the 2009 world champion was Daniel Pudney (Australia).

(SEE **BMX** AND **GRASS TRACK RACING** FOR OTHER BRANCHES OF CYCLING INVOLVING SHORT RACES ON STRIPPED-DOWN BIKES ON OUTDOOR CIRCUITS)

CYCLO-CROSS The oldest form of off-road racing has been upstaged by brash newcomer MOUNTAIN-BIKING, but remains popular at a grassroots level in Europe, particularly in Belgium, Holland, and Switzerland, and is gaining popularity in North America. Cyclo-cross racers use adapted road-racing bikes on circuits that are usually short and include obstacles: ditches, steps, tree roots, logs, mud, sand, ice; one famous course used the steps leading up to Montmartre in Paris in the 1940s.

Most cyclo-cross circuits require the rider to run with the bike, meaning that the ability to dismount and remount smoothly is paramount. Bike changes are permitted; on muddy courses, racers will switch bikes as their machines become clogged up.

Compared to road and track, cyclo-cross is a latecomer: the sport was in existence in the 1900s, and a French national championship was run in 1902, but the first world championships were only held in 1950. In Britain, the toughest 'cross race

in the world, the THREE PEAKS, was founded in 1961.

Traditionally, continental cyclo-cross was a way for road racers to keep fit in winter—the first man to put a bike over his shoulder 'cross style is said to be Octave Lapize, 1910 Tour winner, and another star of the HEROIC ERA, Eugène Christophe, was seven-times French champion.

The first world champion, Jean Robic, had won the TOUR DE FRANCE in 1947. BERNARD HINAULT was a regular cyclo-cross racer, and his final race was a 'cross in his home village in Brittany in 1986, but the most successful 'cross and road racer was ROGER DE VLAEMINCK of Belgium, a multiple CLASSIC winner in the 1970s and also world cyclo-cross champion in 1975. De Vlaeminck's elder brother Eric (b. 1945) won the world 'cross title seven times, and also took a stage in the Tour de France. In the 1980s, Adri Van Der Poel of Holland won a world cyclo-cross title and several Classics. Recently, however, 'cross has been dominated by specialists, some of whom double up with mountain-bike racing in the summer.

Cyclo-cross bikes now use a mix of road- and mountain-bike technology with the emphasis on two factors: coping with mud and with a variety of other surfaces. Clipless mountain-bike pedals are ubiquitous, while CAMPAGNOLO Ergopower and SHIMANO STI gear-changers are common, with a few die-hards sticking to old-style handlebar-end gear-changers.

Most cyclo-cross bikes now have double front chain rings rather than the traditional single, with mountain-bike rear derailleur and cassette for a wide range of gears. Frames are specially built with larger clearances and fittings for cantilever brakes. Tires are specially made high pressures or tubulars, much wider than usual (34 mm rather than 23 mm for the road), with studs. Top riders will choose tires for a particular course or conditions. For years the whole pedal issue was a nightmare, with riders fitting double toeclips for extra strength and customizing toestraps to eliminate mud build up. Then Shimano invented the SPD pedal for the mountain bike and 'crossers immediately latched on.

CYCLOSPORTIVES   Offering a challenge midway between racing and touring, cyclosportives have been run in Europe since the start of the 20th century. Since the 1990s they have been cycling's biggest growth area, with events proliferating across Europe—many of them oversubscribed—and a field of 35,000 turning out for the most popular event worldwide, the Cape Argus Pick'n'Pay Tour in South Africa.

They are to cycling what the great marathon events are to

runners. The key attraction is that riders can choose their pace: whether that means going with the best or pedaling gently. The huge fields mean you never lack company. The best follow the format of the ÉTAPE DU TOUR, founded in 1993, which itself drew partly from major mountain-bike events where completing the course and having a good time was what mattered, and partly from the more spartan AUDAX and *randonneur* events such as Flèche Velocio and Paris–

Brest–Paris. Sportives are hugely popular in Great Britain and France, and in Italy, where they have a long history and are known as *Gran Fondo*, or "long distance."

A Sportif route is tough and if possible linked to a major professional race or at least including climbs that are a little out of the ordinary. Most offer a variety of route lengths so that all abilities are catered for, with a well signposted course In the best events the riders are timed accurately, so that even

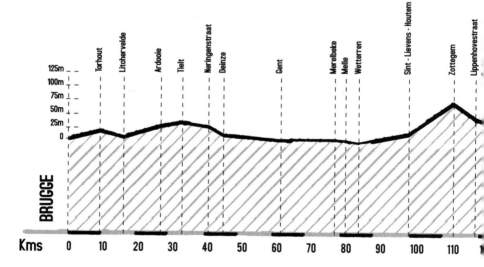

GRADIENT PROFILE FOR TOUR

though they are not—officially—competitive events, all starters have something for posterity and to compare with their friends. There may be medals for finishing within a certain time for certain age categories. Support is provided, with feeding stations, a broom wagon to pick up stragglers, and sometimes service vehicles. There is usually a prerace pasta party, possibly a "village" of sponsors' stands where the riders can spend their money, and everyone is given a goody bag containing free gifts

from sponsors. In many cases, sportives are run by or on behalf of former pros in their local area; media stars such as PHIL LIGGETT also have their own events.

Recognizing the popularity of the events, the UCI created the Golden Bike series of seven long-established sportives around the world. In 2009, they were:

- The **Cape Argus Pick'n'Pay Tour**, starting in Cape Town. See separate entry for CAPE TOWN.

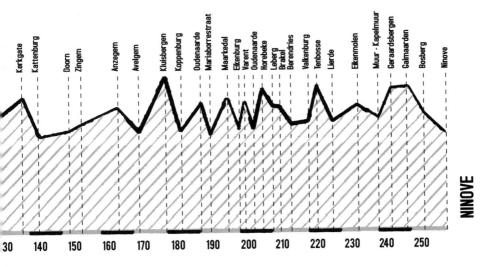

NDERS CYCLOSPORTIF

- The **Tour of Flanders,** over the same course and cobbled climbs used for the professional CLASSIC, with options from 74 to 257 km, and mountain-bike events as well. It's run the day before the pro event, starting and finishing in the town of Ninove.
- **L'Ariegoise,** uses relatively unknown but tough climbs through the Pyrenées, finishing at the Plateau de Deille ski station, which has hosted Tour de France finishes.
- **Gran Fondo Internazionale Felice Gimondi,** starts and finishes in Bergamo and takes in the Dolomite foothills. The Giro winner and world champion uses his connections to bring a bevy of former stars along.
- **Quebrantahuesos,** starts and finishes in the northwest Spanish town of Sabinanigo and takes in some of the classic Pyrenean climbs such as the Col de Marie Blanque, the Portalet and the Somport.
- **Gruyere Cycling Tour,** around the lake where Switzerland's famous cheese comes from, with a host of climbs in the hills around Lausanne.
- **Wattyl Lake Taupo Cycle Challenge,** another lake, but on the other side of the world in New Zealand. The course is 160 km, and can be covered in relays of 40 km for those who want to share the challenge, or as a 320 or 640 km event for true masochists.

Other great sportives include:

- **The Autumn Epic,** a 90-mile event through the hilly Welsh borders, voted best sportif in the UK.
- **Étape Caledonia,** 80 miles through the Scottish Highlands from the town of Pitlochry, the only UK event offering closed roads. In 2009, it was hit by saboteurs who strewed tacks on the road, causing over 50 punctures.
- **The Fred Whitton Challenge,** in the Lake District, a 112-mile event starting and finishing at Coniston and including the

climbs of Kirkstone, Honister, Whinlatter, Hardknott, and Wrynose passes.

- **Northern Rock Cyclone**, the British round of Golden Bike, starting and finishing on the north side of Newcastle and taking in the moors of North East England.
- **Gran Fondo Nove Colli Marco Pantani**, starting and finishing in Pantani's birthplace of Cesenatico on the Adriatic Coast, and taking in nine tough ascents in the Apennines. The field is up to 11,000.
- **The Ardechoise**, is a hugely popular and often overlooked series of events in the tough hills of Central France. 14,000 people took part in 2007; they offer a big range of distances, up to 654 km in three days, with 11,255 m of climbing.

The cyclo-sportive phenomenon of the 1990s drew heavily from mountain biking, and there are many well-established off-road sportives such as the Rough Ride in Britain's Welsh Borders and the Hell of the North Cotswolds.

(SEE **ALPS**, **PYRENÉES**, AND **DOLOMITES** FOR EVENTS THAT TAKE IN THESE LEGENDARY MOUNTAIN RANGES; SEE **MOUNTAIN BIKES** FOR THE BEST OFF-ROAD SPORTIVES)

DA VINCI, Leonardo

Learned and heated debate has raged for three decades among a small group of art historians about Leonardo's "bicycle." The issue is whether, at the very end of the 15th century, the Italian artist and inventor, or one of his pupils, actually drew what appears to be a sketch for a bicycle, or whether the image is a fake added in the 1960s by patriotic restorers who were keen to claim the bike's parentage for Italy.

Scholars believe the bike may have been drawn around 1493; the drawing is on the back of papers later used for architectural sketches. About this time, Leonardo was developing chain and cog wheel devices. There is much discussion of ink types and lost manuscript sheets, but no one knows the answer.

(SEE **DRAISIENNE** AND **HOBBY HORSE** TO LEARN HOW THE BIKE WAS BORN)

DE VLAEMINCK, Roger

Born: Eeklo, Belgium, August 4, 1947

Major wins: Milan–San Remo 1973, 1978–9; Tour of Flanders 1977; Paris–Roubaix 1972, 1974–5, 1977; Liège–Bastogne–Liège 1970; Giro di Lombardia 1974, 1976; Het Volk 1969, 1979; Flèche Wallonne, 1971; Championship of Zurich 1975, Paris-Brussels 1981; Tour of Switzerland 1975; world cyclo-cross champion 1975

Nicknames: the Beast of Eeklo, the Gypsy

Possessor of the finest pair of sideburns cycling has ever seen, more importantly De Vlaeminck was the best CLASSIC rider of the 1970s after EDDY MERCKX. Between 1972 and 1977 he won PARIS–ROUBAIX four times, which is still the record. He rode the race every year bar one between 1969 and 1982, never finishing lower than seventh. The one major single-day race to elude him was the world road championship.

He remains one of FLANDERS' and cycling's great characters: after retirement he was to be found living on a farm outside his home village along with a vast menagerie of animals that included ducks and deer, and he was still trying to outride professionals and amateurs a third his age as he entered his 60s. De Vlaeminck's training rides over the border into Holland are legendary: each rider spends 1 km on the front, single file is maintained, and not a word spoken.

De Vlaeminck was born into a family of traveling clothiers and thus acquired the nickname "the Gypsy" at school. He never attained Merckx's popularity and avoided the TOUR DE FRANCE once it became clear that he would not match Merckx in the event. The pair had a bitter rivalry early in the 1970s, whipped up by the national press. "When a Belgian daily paper ran a photograph of Merckx entertaining De Vlaeminck at his breakfast table, it was as if the Pope had been caught supping with the Devil," wrote Geoffrey Nicholson. (See RIVALRIES for other great cycling head-to-heads.)

Later, however, the two Belgians buried the hatchet and formed an alliance against another Classics specialist, Freddy Maertens; De Vlaeminck's son is named after

Merckx. While never a Tour de France star, he was one of the few cyclists capable of winning any one of the Classics, be it in the steep hills of the Ardennes, the sprint finish of Milan–San Remo, or the cobbles of Paris–Roubaix. He was also a winner of the CYCLO-CROSS world championship and took a massive 22 stage wins in the Giro d'Italia.

DEFEATS Unfairly, some cyclists are better known for losing than for winning. LAURENT FIGNON has gone down in cycling history for being just 8 seconds adrift of victory in the 1989 TOUR DE FRANCE, a record margin estimated at about 100 m in a race lasting 3,285 km and 87.5 hours. As Fignon said, "Eight seconds, 20 seconds, a minute, what's the difference?" Not all notable runners-up have said similar things. A year after Fignon's defeat, the Canadian Steve Bauer came within a millimeter or two of winning PARIS–ROUBAIX, only for the photofinish to be awarded to Eddy Planckaert of Belgium. "Second in Roubaix is OK I guess," was his reaction.

The most famous and popular loser of all was RAYMOND POULIDOR of France, the first man to be nicknamed the "Eternal second" after finishing second or third in the Tour eight times. Poulidor lost the 1964 Tour by 55 seconds—an astonishingly small margin at a time when margins of 5 to 10 minutes were not uncommon— yet lost a minute when he sprinted for a 60 second time bonus on the wrong lap at a stage finish. The second "Eternal second" was Joop Zoetemelk, a Dutchman who made a fine comeback from a life-threatening head injury to finish runner-up in the Tour six times between 1971 and 1982. Jan Ullrich, who managed five second places in six starts to one win between 1996 and 2003, was the third.

Unlucky losers are everywhere in cycling, but few are as

unfortunate as the French sprinter Lucien Michard, who was given second place in the 1931 world championship in spite of photofinish evidence and even though his opponent Falk Hansen of Denmark declared that he had definitely lost. Officials simply pointed at the rule book that said their decision was final and gave Hansen the gold medal.

DEFENSIVE CYCLING   Term used to describe the tactics cyclists adopt to protect themselves from motorists on busy modern roads. Cyclists view this as defensive assertion of their right to space in order to avoid injury or worse; motorists may not share that view.

Defensive tactics include:

- Looking over the shoulder at cars approaching from the rear to alert the driver to the fact that the thing in front is a human being. Riding out of the saddle and wobbling slightly works as well, as this gives the cyclist a bigger profile, encouraging the car driver to give the cyclist more road space.
- Pulling out a little to prevent drivers overtaking on blind bends, indicating if necessary that the driver is to stay behind.
- Pulling out before a left-hand junction to prevent a car from overtaking and then cutting in to turn left.
- Riding a little further out from the gutter than might be expected to create "escape space" if a truck overtakes or a car comes too close.
- Allowing space when riding down a line of parked cars for the one driver in a hundred who hasn't seen you coming and opens his door on your fast-moving knee.

DERAILLEUR see GEARS

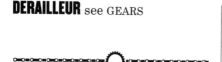

DERNY Small motorbike with a gas tank across the handlebars used in TRACK RACING. Dernys have a 98 cc two-stroke engine backed up by the driver pedaling a large fixed gear, typically 70 × 11, giving smooth acceleration and deceleration. They have to be bump-started, and their top speed is about 50 mph.

Dernys take the field up to speed in the opening laps of international KEIRIN races, are used to pace riders in MOTORPACE races at track meetings, and can be seen making the pace in training and warming up. They were also used for many years in the Bordeaux–Paris motorpaced CLASSIC.

They are named after the firm that first made them in 1938, Roger Derny et Fils in Ave St. Mande, Paris. Derny et Fils shut down in 1957, and most of the machines are now made in Neerpelt, Belgium. The term is listed in the French dictionary *Larousse* as a generic description for a small pacing motorbike. Contrary to popular belief, there is no contractual obligation for the drivers to be overweight, to have bizarre facial hair, and to wear obscure Belgian cycle club jerseys. It's just coincidence.

DESGRANGE, Henri

(b. France, 1865, d. 1940)

The father of two of the sport's premier events: the TOUR DE FRANCE and the HOUR RECORD, and also a founder of the leisure cyclists' AUDAX movement. An austere figure who began working life as a lawyer's clerk but was caught up in the 1890s passion for cycling, Desgrange lost his job for riding bare-legged. He turned to record-breaking, setting the first hour record at the Buffalo velodrome (see TRACK RACING) in Paris on May 11, 1893, and new standards at distances from 1 kilometer to 100 miles. He then became manager of the Parc des Princes velodrome and later the track that was known as the VELODROME D'HIVER. In 1900, Desgrange was appointed editor of the fledgling newspaper *L'Auto*, but he did not manage to break the market stranglehold of its rival, *Le Vélo*. In December 1902 at a crisis meeting to devise ways to give the paper new impetus, he took up the suggestion of his assistant Géo Lefèvre, a writer on rugby and cycling, for a novel publicity stunt: a bike race longer than any other run before, along the lines of *Le Vélo*'s PARIS–BREST–PARIS but that circumnavigated France in five stages. The initial plan was for a race that would take 35 days, but after protests from the professional cyclists who would make up the field this was amended to a six-stage event taking 19 days.

The race was announced in the paper on January 19, 1903. Desgrange was not confident of its success and stayed away from the first Tour when it began on July 1, 1903 at the Réveil-Matin Café in the Paris suburb of Montgeron (the centenary Tour of 2003 also began from the Réveil-Matin, still in situ but by then a Wild-West themed restaurant). It was Lefèvre who followed the race from start to finish, traveling by train and bike and providing a page of reports every day. His son described his role like this: "lost all alone in the night, he would stand on the edge of the road, a storm lantern in his hand, searching the shadows for riders who surged out of the dark from time to time, yelled their name and disappeared into the distance. He alone was the 'organisation' of the Tour de France."

The first Tour was an unqualified success: *L'Auto*'s circulation jumped from 25,000 to 65,000, and *Le Vélo* went bust. By the second running of the Tour, however, the field had worked out ways of getting around the rudimentary rules and there was a wave of cheating, which led Desgrange to announce that "The Tour de France is finished." But in 1905 he personally took over the running of the race and brought in numerous changes, most importantly shorter stages that meant the riders would not be out on lonely French country roads at night.

Under Desgrange, the Tour was run dictatorially but also with a constant search for novelty and timeliness, which remains part of the organizers' ethos today. It was, wrote Geoffrey Nicholson, "established as a battle against fearful odds often fought in inhospitable regions which the readers of newspaper reports could only imagine." He took the event into the disputed territory of Alsace-Lorraine in 1906, ran the first mountain stages, experimented with team time trials and attempted to limit the influence of the cycle manufacturers by making the riders use identical machines issued by the race organizers. He also brought in the advance caravan of advertising vehicles that draws spectators today.

A believer that exercise and suffering led to moral improvement, he was uncompromising in his merciless attitude to the riders, giving rise to some of the Tour's most legendary episodes (see HEROIC ERA; PELISSIER for examples). During the First World War, Desgrange enrolled as an infantryman and won the Croix de Guerre; he returned to his paper in 1919 when he conceived his masterstroke: the introduction of a distinctive jersey as a way of recognizing the race leader. The jersey was yellow, the same color as the pages of *L'Auto*; the jersey bears his initials even today, and every stage race in the world has a leader's jersey, usually yellow.

Desgrange began the tradition that the Tour organizer should also be a journalist. As a writer, he modeled himself on Émile Zola. His style was florid and crammed with imagery and is still imitated by color-writers on *L'Auto*'s successor *L'Equipe* today. His essay in *L'Auto* introducing the Tour was entitled "The Sowers" and begins: "With the broad and powerful swing of the hand which Zola gave to his ploughman in *The Earth, L'Auto,* a paper of ideas and action, is going to fling across France today those reckless and uncouth sowers of energy, the great professional road racers. . . . From Paris to the blue waves of the Mediterranean, along the rosy, dreaming roads sleeping under the sun, across the calm of the fields of the Vendée, following the still and silently flowing Loire, our men are going to race madly and tirelessly." He described Henri Pelissier's win in 1923 as having "the classicism of a work by Racine, the value of a perfect statue, a faultless classic or a piece of music destined to stay in everyone's minds."

Desgrange cohabited for much of his life with the avant-garde artist Jeanne (Jane) Deley. In 1936, after a prostate operation, he gave up the running of the Tour de France to Jacques Goddet—the son of the *L'Auto* treasurer Victor Goddet—and after he died in 1940 a MEMORIAL was put up in his honor on top of the Col du Galibier. A street off Quai de Bercy next to the Seine, on the southeast side of Paris (post code 75012) is named after him.

DOGS Man's best friend, a cyclist's worst enemy* (and occasional training aid as you sprint to get away from those snapping teeth). Victorian cyclists carried heavyweight small-caliber pistols to deal with

threatening mutts—presumably on a high-wheel Old Ordinary there was a serious risk of losing control during a dog attack. The Germans made gunpowder-filled anti-dog grenades, while US cyclists could buy ammonia sprays and some still carry mace or pepper spray. One US study estimated that 8 percent of cycle accidents were caused by Fido and friends.

While matches between cyclists and HORSES go back over a century, races between cyclists and canines are more recent. In 2009, the Spanish champion Alejandro Valverde lost a circuit race in Valencia against a team of six huskies drawing a wheeled sleigh. A rematch was called for, with two cyclists taking on the huskies, but halfway through the animals decided it was time for a nap.

Dogs sometimes intervene in major bike races, for example in two stages in the 2007 TOUR DE FRANCE, where pooch-bike interface resulted in injuries to, firstly, the German Marcus Burghardt, and, later, Frenchman Sandy Casar, who won a stage after being brought down by a dog early on.

The best-known dog in pro racing belongs to the 2009 world champion Cadel Evans of Australia. In a media crush at the 2008 Tour, Evans shouted at one journalist, "If you stand on my dog I'll cut your head off." His website later sold T-shirts with the motto: "Don't stand on my dog."

In the 1950s, the cycling cartoonist Johnny Helms perfectly depicted the cyclist's nightmare: a mischievous breed of hound with sharklike teeth and gaping grin, often with a scrap of cycling shorts in its mouth. The bestselling bike bible *Richard's Bicycle Book* by RICHARD BALLANTINE offers a grimly detailed guide on dealing with vicious dogs. He recommends using pepper sprays, ramming the pump down the dog's throat, kicking its genitals. He concludes: "If worst comes to worst and you are forced down to the ground by a dog, ram your entire arm down his throat. He will choke and die. Better your arm than your throat."

* THIS IS TAKING "ENEMY" AS REFERRING TO AN ANIMATE ENTITY; THE GREATEST DANGER, OBVIOUSLY, COMES FROM INANIMATE OBJECTS WITH FOUR WHEELS OR MORE AND AN ENGINE.

DOLOMITES   It was not until the 1930s that the GIRO D'ITALIA visited the passes through the section of the ALPS that dominates northern Italy. However, they are now decisive in the race, which also uses the climbs of the southeastern Alps and the shorter, less testing ascents in the Apennines. Geographically, Dolomites refers to the mountains between the Adige river in the west and the Piave valley to the east. Dolomite climbs frequently have spectacular backdrops such as the rock pinnacles on the Pordoi pass. They are shorter and steeper than the Alpine climbs that figure in the TOUR DE FRANCE.

The Giro tackles the Dolomites in early summer and is vulnerable to extreme weather. The most legendary example was in 1988 on the Gavia Pass, which lies in the west of the range between Sondrio and Brescia. This was the springboard for the first win in the Giro for the UNITED STATES as Andy Hampsten took over the pink leader's jersey on a notorious day when heavy snow fell unexpectedly on this high pass with its unmetaled roads. There were dramatic scenes as shivering riders stopped on the descent to urinate on their frozen hands.

The most notorious Dolomite passes are shown below.

Numerous CYCLOSPORTIVES take in the great passes of the Dolomites, most notably the **Maratona dles Dolomites**, founded in 1987 and now so popular that 5,000 of the 9,000 places are designated by a lottery; the event draws around 20,000 applications. The event is subdivided into three courses of varying severity, all starting and finishing in the town of Corvara in the Badia valley: the toughest, over 86 miles, includes

CLIMB	LENGTH	ALTITUDE	HEIGHT GAIN	NOTED FOR
Mortirolo (from Mazzo Valtellina)	12.4 km	1,885 m	1,315 m	Marco Pantani memorial and gradients that reach nearly 20 percent
Pordoi (from Canazei)	13 km	2,239 m	786 m	Fausto Coppi memorial
Gavia (from Ponte di Legno)	17.3 km	2,621 m	1,363 m	Steep and long and narrow, and famously snowy in the 1988 Giro
Sella (from Canazei)	11.4 km	2,244 m	758 m	Superb panorama of the Torri di Sella at the summit

(See STELVIO for a climb that is not geographically part of the Dolomites but has a whole history of its own.)

the climbs of Campolongo (twice), Pordoi, Sella, Gardena, Giau, and Falzarego. None of the passes is over seven miles long but their steepness means the total amount of climbing is 13,747 feet.

The Granfondo Sportful, (previously known as GF Campagnolo, but now with new sponsor) is held on the third Sunday in June, based in the town of Feltre, and covers six Dolomite passes, including the Croce d'Aune (see CAMPAGNOLO for the significance of this climb in cycling history).

The Granfondo Marco Pantani includes the Gavia and Mortirolo, starting and finishing in the town of Aprica.

The great Dolomite climbs feature in the RAID Alpine route from Thonon les Bains to Trieste.

DOPING   See DRUGS

DOUBLE   Cycle racing has two legendary "doubles": most prestigious is the GIRO D'ITALIA followed by the TOUR DE FRANCE in the same year, a rare feat achieved only by the greats: FAUSTO COPPI (1949 and 1952), JACQUES ANQUETIL (1964), EDDY MERCKX (1970, 1972, 1974), BERNARD HINAULT (1982, 1985), STEPHEN ROCHE (1987), and MARCO PANTANI (1998). MIGUEL INDURAIN of Spain achieved a "double double" by winning Giro and Tour two years running, 1992 and 1993, while in 1974 and 1987 respectively Merckx and Roche achieved a legendary triple: Giro, Tour, and world championships.

The other "double" is the Ardennes double: victories in Flèche Wallonne and Liège–Bastogne–Liège in the same year (see CLASSICS). Cyclists who have managed this are: Ferdi Kubler (Switzerland) 1951–2; Stan Ockers (Belgium) 1955; Eddy Merckx (Belgium) 1972; Moreno Argentin (Italy) 1991; Davide Rebellin (Italy) 2004; Alejandro Valverde (Spain) 2006.

DOWNHILL   The original form of MOUNTAIN-BIKING, and still the most traditional variant of the sport, with its principles unchanged since the days of the REPACK downhill in California in the late 1970s. It is simply a downhill time trial on a short course—usually lasting between two and six minutes. Competitors wear full-face helmets and sometimes body armor. Downhill has become a natural summer sport for ski resorts, many of which now have marked, graded runs and open ski lifts to transport the bikers to the top of the runs. The UCI runs a season-long World Cup and a world championship.

The Repack riders used the "clunkers" that evolved into the mountain bike, and later downhillers rode either conventional mountain bikes or customized variants. It was not until the 1990s that specialist downhill machines became widespread. These have large-diameter disc brakes, front and rear suspension with far more travel than machines used for cross-country and touring, and more laid-back frame design so that the rider can get his or her weight further back. More lightweight dual suspension and discs are now ubiquitious on all top-end mountain bikes; in these areas downhill has pushed development forward.

Downhill was included in the first UCI mountain-bike world championships at Durango, Colorado, in 1990: the winners were Greg Herbold of the US and Cindy Devine of Canada. The bike-handling element and

---

Variants on mountain-bike downhill include **Super-D**, a mix of cross-country and downhill with uphill sections that discourage the use of downhill machines; **Freeride**, a test of riding skill scored for riding style, selection of trajectory, tricks, and time; **Dual-Slalom**, a knock-out event with two riders side by side on identical courses; **Four-Cross**, four riders starting together like BMX with an initial timed solo round for seeding, followed by knock-out rounds.

need for upper-body strength has meant there has always been crossover with BMX, with one early champion the former BMX racer John Tomac. GREAT BRITAIN is surprisingly strong in the discipline. Steve Peat was world champion in 2009, while the union jack is flown by the Atherton family from Wales: Rachel, Gee—the 2008 world champion—and Dan.

Downhill venues include some of the same French Alpine resorts that host Tour de France stages, including l'Alpe d'Huez and Morzine, Italian ski resorts such as Bardonnechia and Pila, while in Liguria there are downhill courses that end by the Mediterranean. In Great Britain, most downhill courses are in Wales and Scotland, with a World Cup and world championship venue at Ben Nevis.

There are few comparable events in road cycling, although there is the Red Bull Descent, a

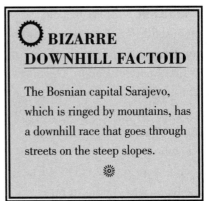

BIZARRE DOWNHILL FACTOID

The Bosnian capital Sarajevo, which is ringed by mountains, has a downhill race that goes through streets on the steep slopes.

timed downhill challenge using the hairpins that wind down from the Pyrenéan ski resort of Pla d'Adet. The 2009 winner was the Frenchman Fred Moncassin, a former stage winner in both the mountain-bike and road Tours de France.

There is a curious subculture to downhill, in which speed record attempts are made on frozen ski-slopes by heavily protected downhillers, a fashion that caught on in the late 1990s inspired by Frenchman Fabrice Taillefer. These are fear-inspiring and very quick: the record is over 130 mph.

DRAISIENNE Early bicycle, invented in 1817 by Baron Karl von Drais, Master of the Forests in the duchy of Baden, Germany, whose other inventions included a typewriter and a meat grinder. Made of wood, it consisted of two wheels joined by a frame with a seat for the rider, with the front wheel able to rotate freely so the machine could be steered. There were no pedals. It included a seat, luggage rack, and a "balancing board" on which the rider placed his elbows. The speeds attained by the Draisienne depended on the road surface and gradient, but it was found to be four times faster than post-coaches.

The Draisienne was patented at the start of 1818 and launched in France later that year; by then there were four companies making similar machines in Germany, and others across Europe began copying the model.

In December 1818 a patent was registered in London by a carriage maker named Denis Johnson, for a "pedestrian curricle" made largely of iron and selling at 8 or 10 guineas, and based on the Draisienne design. The "hobby horse" was born and was rapidly taken up by Regency London; the wealthy would turn up at his two schools to be instructed in riding the machine. A drop-frame version was made for ladies to accommodate long skirts. So many people rode the hobby horses that they were banned from pavements in London; the craze spread to America, pushed by Johnson, but eventually died out.

(SEE **BONESHAKER** FOR THE NEXT STAGE IN CYCLE DEVELOPMENT; **HIGH-WHEELER** AND **SAFETY BICYCLE** FOR LATER VARIANTS; **BICYCLE** FOR A SUMMARY OF THE MACHINE'S DEVELOPMENT; **LEONARDO DA VINCI** FOR THE DEBATE OVER A POSSIBLE EARLY MACHINE)

DRUGS Cycle racing is one of the toughest endurance disciplines in sport, and a variety of illegal substances have been used over the years as cyclists have attempted to go farther and faster. Doping began with the marathon events of the 1890s, particularly the SIX-DAY races, where riders would use caffeine, strychnine, and arsenic. By the 1930s, drug-taking in cycling was so institutionalized that the rider contracts in the TOUR DE FRANCE stated that the cost of "stimulants, tonics and doping" had to be paid by the riders themselves, according to historian Benjo Maso.

Ironically in view of the mythology that surrounds drug-taking, the effects have often been counterproductive rather than performance enhancing. Cyclists have ended up with long-term injuries and mental problems through drug taking— not to mention the deaths— while recent developments in professional cycling suggest that winning the biggest events "clean" thanks to proper training is probably more straightforward.

Alcohol was often used up to the 1970s for its painkilling and euphoric effects. TOM SIMPSON was seen drinking brandy shortly before his death in the 1967 Tour de France.

Amphetamines became popular during the 1950s after large amounts of Benzedrine produced for the airmen of the Second World War came onto the market. Its euphoric effect enabled a cyclist to ignore the pain, but it is highly addictive so regular users ended up taking more and more to get the same effect. In addition, the feeling of invincibility reported by amphetamine users could lead to crashes and bizarrely timed attacks that resulted in defeat. After Simpson's death, testing was brought in and the use of amphetamines in major events declined, although the Irish pro Paul Kimmage wrote that it was widespread in lesser races as late as the 1980s.

Anabolic agents were most used in the 1970s and 1980s.

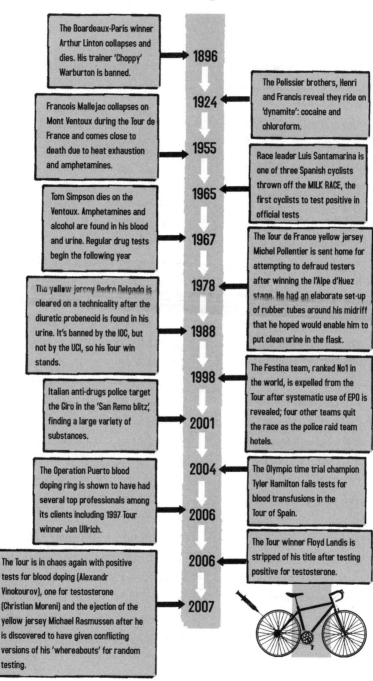

The Boardeaux-Paris winner Arthur Linton collapses and dies. His trainer 'Choppy' Warburton is banned.

1896

The Pelissier brothers, Henri and Francis reveal they ride on 'dynamite': cocaine and chloroform.

1924

Francois Mallejac collapses on Mont Ventoux during the Tour de France and comes close to death due to heat exhaustion and amphetamines.

1955

Race leader Luis Santamarina is one of three Spanish cyclists thrown off the MILK RACE, the first cyclists to test positive in official tests

1965

Tom Simpson dies on the Ventoux. Amphetamines and alcohol are found in his blood and urine. Regular drug tests begin the following year

1967

The Tour de France yellow jersey Michel Pollentier is sent home for attempting to defraud testers after winning the l'Alpe d'Huez stage. He had an elaborate set-up of rubber tubes around his midriff that he hoped would enable him to put clean urine in the flask.

1978

The yellow jersey Pedro Delgado is cleared on a technicality after the diuretic probenecid is found in his urine. It's banned by the IOC, but not by the UCI, so his Tour win stands.

1988

The Festina team, ranked No1 in the world, is expelled from the Tour after systematic use of EPO is revealed; four other teams quit the race as the police raid team hotels.

1998

Italian anti-drugs police target the Giro in the 'San Remo blitz', finding a large variety of substances.

2001

The Olympic time trial champion Tyler Hamilton fails tests for blood transfusions in the Tour of Spain.

2004

The Operation Puerto blood doping ring is shown to have had several top professionals among its clients including 1997 Tour winner Jan Ullrich.

2006

The Tour winner Floyd Landis is stripped of his title after testing positive for testosterone.

2006

The Tour is in chaos again with positive tests for blood doping (Alexandr Vinokourov), one for testosterone (Christian Moreni) and the ejection of the yellow jersey Michael Rasmussen after he is discovered to have given conflicting versions of his 'whereabouts' for random testing.

2007

Whereas amphetamines act in the short term on a cyclist's nervous system, anabolic agents alter the body's physical state in the medium term, increasing muscle mass and in theory assisting recovery after training. Given that cyclists don't want muscle mass, their use may often be counterproductive. Gradually the testers caught up with these, although the male hormone testosterone was still being used into the 21st century, according to the Scot David Millar.

Avoiding drug-tests was something of an art, according to the SOIGNEUR Willy Voet, the lead protagonist in the Festina scandal of 1998. Initially, riders simply didn't show up, but after JACQUES ANQUETIL's hour record was refused in 1968 because he didn't give a sample, that stopped. The most famous case of attempted evasion was that of the Tour de France leader Michel Pollentier, shopped in 1978 (see page 114). Voet describes how a rider would stick a condom filled with clean urine up his anus and how urine samples might

---

"Not me, guv"—the best excuses for doping/possession from cyclists

❖

Franck Vandenbroucke: "The steroids and EPO were for my dog."

Raimondas Rumsas: "The 40 diffferent drugs in the back of my wife's car were for my mother-in-law."

Tyler Hamilton: "I was one of twins, one of which died in the womb, that's why I had two different types of blood."

Ivan Basso: "I had blood removed and saved for reinjection but it was 'just in case' and I never used it."

Floyd Landis: "I got drunk after a bad day in the mountains, hence my high testosterone levels."

Richard Virenque: "I had no idea what I was being given. If I was given drugs it was without my knowledge."

---

be switched by distracting the tester. More recently, it's said that the EPO test can be avoided by urinating over fingers that have been dipped in laundry detergent.

Belgian mix was a cocktail of drugs that might include heroin, morphine, amphetamine, and cocaine. It was used mainly for training in bad weather, for partying, and to help stay awake while driving between races. It was either sold by dealers or produced by a group of cyclists who would all put a different drug in the pot; as a result, its effects would vary depending on which drug was there in the greatest quantity.

Blood boosters became popular in the late 1980s and early 1990s. The first and most popular was erythropoietin, or EPO, a synthetic version of the hormone that stimulates the body to produce more red blood cells, thus increasing its capacity to supply oxygen to the muscles; this in turn enabled more power to be produced. This was a variant on **blood doping**, used in the 1970s and early 1980s, where blood would be removed from an athlete and reinjected just before competition. That eventually evolved into using someone else's blood, leading to rumors that some teams hired staff according to their blood group. After the introduction of an EPO test in 2000, the practice came back into vogue, along with sophisticated EPO variants such as CERA.

Blood tests were introduced by the UCI in 1997 and have become more and more sophisticated over the years. Initially they were intended to limit EPO use, but now they are used more to discover cyclists who are suspect—these are put on the UCI's red list and they are then targeted for testing. In 2009 the UCI brought in the **blood passport** system, which draws up a detailed picture of each pro rider's blood parameters; anomalies can result in a ban or in highly targeted testing.

Cortisone, the painkiller the body produces during exercise, was frequently injected in artificial form during the 1980s and 1990s for its euphoric effects, but can now be detected.

Insulin was found occasionally at races in the early 21st century and was assumed to be used to speed up sugar intake to aid recovery after tough stages.

Legal Drugs have also been commonly used, most notably caffeine, which was once banned above a certain limit but is now permitted. Most riders drink coffee before a race, and Coke or Red Bull in the final phase, but suppositories and tablets are also used.

Out-of-competition testing is carried out all year round, with cyclists declaring their where-abouts for set periods each week.

Painkillers were popular in cycling's early days, with morphine and heroin used in the late 19th century to help riders complete six-day races. They were also taken in the 1950s as part of the Anquetil cocktail: analgesic to take away pain in the legs, amphetamine to counter the drowsiness these induced, sleeping pills to bring the rider down at night.

Police raids on races in search of banned substances became more common after the Festina scandal of 1998. The Italian police were the most enthusiastic, but the country's slow-moving legal system meant convictions were rare; French customs men also became active, most notably in 2002, with the detention of Edita Rumsas, the wife of Raimondas, who finished third in the Tour. Her car was crammed with drugs.

Recreational drugs are not commonly found in cycling, although there is evidence of a cocaine problem. The 1998 Tour winner MARCO PANTANI died of a cocaine overdose, as did the top Spanish climber Jose-Maria Jimenez, while the Belgian champion Tom Boonen was found to have taken the drug on two occasions.

Sleeping pills have been used for recreational purposes (the Cofidis scandal of 2004 involving Millar revealed this) but were also used to counter all that caffeine, and, in the past, other uppers. As one Tour rider said, "You can tell which week of the Tour you are in by the number of sleepers you take: one in the first week, two in the second, three in the third."

DRUGS; SLANG

One illustration of the depth of doping culture in cycling is the fact that French, cycling's lingua franca, has an almost endless repertoire of slang referring to drug use. Some selected highlights:

PHRASE	ENGLISH MEANING	ACTUAL MEANING
Charger la chaudière	Warm up the heater	Use amphetamines
Allumer les phares	Put on the headlights	Use amphetamines
Saler la moutarde	Salt the mustard	General use of drugs
Pisser violet	Piss violet	General use of drugs
Avoir la valise magique	Have a magic suitcase	General use of drugs
Dîner chez Virenque	Dine with Virenque	Use drugs (refers to the Festina drug scandal of 1998)
La flèche	Arrow	Needle or adapted syringe
Tonton, tintin, fifi		Various kinds of amphetamine.
La topette	Small bottle with a stimulant	English racing slang refers to this as a "charge bottle"

Spain has the following:

Marker pen = cortisone
Oil change = blood transfusion
Pelas (slang for pesetas) = units of EPO

EASTERN EUROPE Sports were an important way in which the communist nations of Eastern Europe asserted themselves during the Cold War, and cycling was one of the key disciplines. The value of international victories as propaganda—at home as evidence of the system's power, abroad to show it could compete on equal terms—had been rapidly appreciated, and entire sports infrastructures were built, with the finest talent creamed off into academies based in the biggest cities: most legendary was the Russian pursuit school in Leningrad (now St. Petersburg) run by the hyper-tough Alexandr Kuznetsov.

Training regimes were draconian, the demands on personal life and health were considerable, but the rewards were tangible: privileges, apartments, cars, and, above all, foreign travel and the chance to earn hard currency. Cycles produced in Eastern Europe were often crude and poorly made, however, so the Soviet team rode Italian bikes made by Ernesto Colnago. The clubs tended to get the hand-me-downs. Western gear of any kind had high black-market value into the early 1990s, as did Western cycling magazines and posters.

By the 1970s Poland, the Soviet Union, and East Germany all boasted "amateur" cycling teams that were not far off the standard of pro squads in Western Europe, with full-time cyclists whose "jobs" were often military. The East Europeans were almost unbeatable in their own events. The biggest of these was the Berlin–Warsaw–Prague Peace Race, founded in 1948 and sponsored by newspapers in East Germany, Poland, and Czechoslovakia. A blue jersey with a white dove on the front was worn by the leading team, and in its heyday the route covered 2,000 km in front of crowds numbering in the millions.

East-bloc racers were just as fearsome abroad, dominating major amateur events and walking off with many of the medals in world track and road championships. "We were like amateurs against pros," said Bob Downs, a British cyclist who was one of the elite few who had the legs to put up a decent fight against the Russians and Poles in the MILK RACE in the 1970s. "The whole Russian team used to get on the front and not let anyone else in. The only way you could stand a chance was to ride as near as possible to them and wait for them to make a mistake."

"Every time an East German climbed on to the rostrum, win or lose, there was the same unsmiling solemn glare. There is no getting away from it, [they] are consistently phenomenal, technically brilliant athletes," wrote Les Woodland in the 1981 *International Cycling Guide.* The East Europeans were often impenetrable for the media but had a love of shopping, selling anything they could—most often tubular tires—to get currency.

The system was comprehensive and sophisticated, recalls the former East German trainer Heiko Salzwedel. At the bottom of the pyramid was a network of sports clubs attached to major enterprises such as the police or railways. At the top were the half-dozen national cycling centers across East Germany, each with about 10 trainers, dealing with up to 100 athletes. Children were selected from an early age, partly through biometric tests that assessed their capacity for various sports, partly through their parents' background, partly through selection races.

There were official guidelines, but coaches had a fair degree of flexibility in setting their own criteria; riders' Stasi files would be checked—to see whether a potential athlete had West German connections, for example—but coaches might push better athletes with undesirable backgrounds higher up selection lists to ensure they got in the team anyway. The screening systems were later adapted for use by the cycling teams of Australia and GREAT BRITAIN.

The sudden collapse of the Berlin Wall in 1989 left the sports centers across Eastern Europe short of money, and a vast number of talented amateurs came on the market: they flooded into cycling. The sprinter DJAMOLIDIN ABDUZHAPAROV made the biggest impact alongside Olaf Ludwig, Andrei Tchmil, and Zenon Jaskuta, who in 1993 was the first Pole to make it to the Tour podium. Jan Ullrich was the first product of the Eastern system to win the Tour in 1997.

The legacy of the old Eastern Europe is obvious now. Individual nations from the former Soviet Union such as Ukraine and Belarus punch above their weight on the international stage, while almost every professional cycling team in the world has at least one "Goombah."

This term was coined by LANCE ARMSTRONG's biographer Dan Coyle, who wrote that Viatcheslav Ekimov, Alexandr Vinokourov, and Jens Voigt "had been selected as children, their growth plates and femurs measured against that of a 'superior child' and [had been] whisked away to . . . sports schools throughout the former Soviet empire. Once there their life became an endless series of training exercises, the governing philosophy of which was summed up by a former coach: 'you throw a carton of eggs against the wall, then keep the ones that do not break.'"

Six Great Unbreakable Eggs

◆

Olaf Ludwig: Ludwig's sprint win in Besançon in the 1990 Tour de France was the first and last for East Germany, as unification came not long afterwards. Prior to that the rider from Gera had won the Olympic road race in 1988, two overall victories in the Peace Race and a record 38 stages, and two East German Sportsman of the Year awards. As a pro he landed the World Cup in 1992, the green jersey in the 1990 Tour, and the Amstel Gold Race.

Sergei Soukhouroutchenkov: 1980 Moscow Olympic games road race winner, dominant in amateur racing from 1979 to 1981, with two wins in the Tour de l'Avenir, two in the Giro delle Regioni, and one in the Peace Race. Turned pro briefly in 1989–90 but by then his best days were gone.

Gustave-Adolf "Täve" Schur: East German double world amateur champion (1958–9), gave up his chance of a third title by helping his friend Bernhard Eckstein. He was also a double Peace Race winner (1955 and 1959). He later became a parliamentiary deputy; his son Jan rode briefly as a professional in the early 1990s. His 1955 biography sold 100,000 copies, such was his popularity.

Viktor Kapitonov: Russian who won the Olympic road race in Rome in 1960, sprinting twice—with a lap to go because he misread the lapboard, then for real a lap later. He became national trainer, masterminding all those dollar-winning trips to the west in the 1970s.

Viatcheslav Ekimov: Took four world pursuit titles (three as an amateur, one as a pro), and two Olympic gold medals, the first in the team pursuit in 1988, the second in the time trial in 2000. He was the finest product of the Kuznetsov cycling school. "Eki" went on to ride and finish 15 Tours de France. He was a key *domestique* to Lance Armstrong and went on to work with the Texan at the RadioShack team.

Andrei Tchmil: Turned pro with the first batch of Russians in 1989, and went on to take victories in PARIS–ROUBAIX (1994), Paris–Tours (1997), MILAN–SAN REMO (1999), and the Tour of FLANDERS (2000). He changed nationality several times, riding for Russia, Ukraine, Moldova, and Belgium, and went on to be minister of sport in his native Moldova before founding the Katyusha pro team.

END TO END The 850-plus miles from Land's End to John O'Groats—from one end of Great Britain to the other—is one of the most evocative long-distance rides, tackled for charity or simply for the sense of achievement it engenders. It is also the most prestigious British long-distance record. Most End-to-Enders start in Cornwall, to take advantage of the prevailing southwesterly winds. The toughest sections are early on, over the constantly climbing roads of Cornwall and Devon, and in the final quarter through the Scotttish highlands.

The first End-to-Enders were H. Blackwell and C. A. Harmon of the Canonbury Bicycle Club who did it on old ordinaries in 1880, taking 13 days. The first name on the Road Record Association record sheets is G. P. Mills—also a winner of the Bordeaux–Paris Classic—with a time of 5 days, 1 hour, 45 minutes, on a penny farthing with a 52-inch front wheel. Mills was paced by other cyclists, as was customary in those days; the first unpaced record was set in 1903 by C. J. Mather, in 5 days, 5 hours, 12 minutes.

The first man to achieve the distance inside two days was Dick Poole, in 1965. Poole then went on to attempt the 1,000-mile record; frustratingly, he covered 1,010 miles (enough to allow for error, so his timekeeper

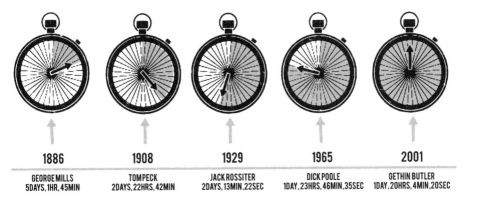

1886	1908	1929	1965	2001
GEORGE MILLS	TOM PECK	JACK ROSSITER	DICK POOLE	GETHIN BUTLER
5 DAYS, 1 HR, 45 MIN	2 DAYS, 22 HRS, 42 MIN	2 DAYS, 13 MIN, 22 SEC	1 DAY, 23 HRS, 46 MIN, 35 SEC	1 DAY, 20 HRS, 4 MIN, 20 SEC

thought) but was still found to be a few yards short so the record was not ratified. Attempts on the record have led to extreme feats of endurance, partly because the only way to break it is to go without sleep as far as possible, but also because the wind can change over the 48 hours from a helpful southerly to a northerly headwind. In 1980 the Viking Cycles professional Paul Carbutt benefited from the opening of the Forth Bridge which cut 13 miles off the distance to break Poole's record but collapsed due to heatstroke southwest of Edinburgh. He was unconscious for about 25 minutes but was put back on his bike to continue with a damp facecloth under his racing hat.

The record set by Andy Wilkinson using the highly aerodynamic Windcheetah RECUMBENT was unofficial but was as extreme as any of the others. Because of the temperatures building up inside the enclosed bike, Wilkinson needed about two liters of fluid an hour to avoid dehydration, so

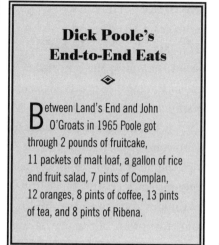

Dick Poole's End-to-End Eats

◈

Between Land's End and John O'Groats in 1965 Poole got through 2 pounds of fruitcake, 11 packets of malt loaf, a gallon of rice and fruit salad, 7 pints of Complan, 12 oranges, 8 pints of coffee, 13 pints of tea, and 8 pints of Ribena.

it took a 20-strong support team to give him a bottle every half-hour, collect discarded bottles, and then overtake him to hand up new ones. His fluid output was also high: "We rigged up a special condom connected to a metre-long tube to provide relief without having to stop. The tube exited the Windcheetah at the back of the fairing," says the Windcheetah website. Wilkinson reached close to 80 mph on long descents, and covered the distance in 41 hours, 4 minutes, 22 seconds including a stop of almost an hour to replace a rear axle.

ENVIRONMENT Cycling is now a recognized means of lowering one's carbon footprint. The figures speak for themselves—100 calories takes a cyclist 3 miles, a car all of 280 feet. In 2009 research indicated that if cycling use in cities doubles from 4 percent of journeys to 8 percent, there would be a total drop of 1.1 percent in carbon emissions. If those journeys are intermodal (public transport + bike), the figure can go up to 1.8 percent because greater distances can be covered.

On the other hand, cycling as a pastime rather than a means of transport is by no means carbon friendly. Driving from London to the south of France with a bike on the roofrack creates 360 kgm of CO_2; taking the train and hiring a bike creates 100 kgm; flying with the bike in the hold creates 850 kgm, more than heating the average house for a year.

Few studies exist into the carbon footprint of bike races but the number of vehicle miles involved suggest that it is horrendous. That is borne out by a study from the International Institute for Sport Science and Technology, which calculated that the Tour of Romandie, a six-day stage race for pros, produced 138 tons of CO_2, which is just under the amount of CO_2 emissions produced by Nauru, an island state in the South Pacific.

ÉTAPE DU TOUR The most celebrated CYCLOSPORTIVE event, and the first with the now universal format of prerace party, classic route, accurate timing, well-filled goody bag, and ample technical support. Founded by the *Vélo* magazine editor Claude Droussent in 1993 the Étape is run each year on one of the rest days (usually a Monday) during the TOUR DE FRANCE and covers one of the Tour's mountain stages with only the tiniest variations. In itself, the Étape is rarely tougher than other sportives such as the Marmotte or the Nove Colli, but it is by far the hardest to get into, even though 7,000 places are available.

Cyclists outside France have no option but to enter through one of the companies that sell places. Its popularity comes down to two things: the road closure is total, unlike in many other sportives, and riding the Étape feels like riding the Tour. The same motorcycle outriders from the Garde Republicaine are used to ensure roads are totally free of traffic.

The Étape is also a fertile celebrity spotting ground. The winner tends to be a pro who hasn't got into the Tour, while Alain Prost, LAURENT FIGNON, MIGUEL INDURAIN, and British Olympian CHRIS HOY have all been spotted riding in the past.

F

FERRARI, Michele

The most celebrated and controversial trainer in modern-day cycling; a miracle-worker to his disciples who included the seven times TOUR DE FRANCE winner LANCE ARMSTRONG, but tainted with doping allegations according to his adversaries.

Ferrari comes from Emilia-Romagna in Italy and came to prominence as one of the coaches who guided FRANCESCO MOSER to his HOUR RECORD successes in 1984. He was Moser's team doctor in the 1984 season when the Italian won MILAN–SAN REMO and the GIRO D'ITALIA; in the early 1990s he worked with the Swiss star Tony Rominger, a triple winner of the Tour of Spain, and by 1994 he was doctor at the Gewiss team, which was, briefly, spectacularly successful, winning that year's Giro with Evgeni Berzin and several CLASSICS—including a clean sweep of the first three placings at the 1994 Flèche Wallonne. He was thrown off Gewiss after he told reporters that the banned blood booster EPO was no more dangerous than orange juice unless it was abused. In 1995, he was introduced to Armstrong by the American's friend EDDY MERCKX.

Armstrong's biographer Dan Coyle (see BOOKS) described him as "dark-haired and darty-eyed," adding that he was nicknamed Dr. Evil because of his notoriety. Coyle related an episode in which Ferrari jokingly said that Parmesan cheese should be banned because it was good for those who ate it, thus giving them an unfair advantage. Ferrari said that he and Armstrong had been in close contact since the early stages of his comeback from cancer in 1998, even though their relationship did not become public until 2000.

The Italian estimated that he spent one week a month in the cycling season with Armstrong. The Italian tested Armstrong to assess his power-to-weight ratio and lactate tolerance and worked to make him climb mountains using a higher, more efficient cadence. During some stages of the Tour, and most famously in the 2000 race, Ferrari would be in touch with Armstrong via a mobile phone to his team car to advise him on tactics at key moments. The partnership drew fierce criticism from Armstrong's fellow American, triple Tour winner GREG LEMOND.

Armstrong officially ended their collaboration in October 2004 when Ferrari was found guilty of unlawful distribution of medicines and sporting fraud, after a trial that had lasted several years. Subsequently the sentence would be rescinded on appeal. The main witness was Italian professional Filippo Simeoni, who alleged that Ferrari had advised him to use drugs: other witnesses disputed this, as did the trainer himself. There were no allegations concerning Ferrari's work with the Texan.

FIGNON, Laurent (b. France, 1960, d. 2010)

After retirement, the bespectacled, blond-haired double TOUR DE FRANCE winner ran motivational courses for industrialists. At his first meeting, he was greeted with the words "Aren't you the guy who lost the Tour de France by eight seconds?" Fignon replied solemnly that he preferred to be remembered as a man who won the race twice and also took back-to-back wins in the MILAN–SAN REMO classic (1988 and 1989).

Part of the legendary Renault

squad (see TEAMS), Fignon was one of the few cyclists to win the Tour at their first attempt (EDDY MERCKX and FAUSTO COPPI are two others). He followed up that 1983 win with an epic victory in the 1984 Tour, when he won five stages along the way and completely dominated four-time winner BERNARD HINAULT. He was also unlucky to lose the 1984 GIRO D'ITALIA to FRANCESCO MOSER.

His dramatic defeat by GREG LEMOND after a ding-dong battle throughout the 1989 race is what has stuck in most minds, however: it concluded what many saw as the finest Tour ever. Fignon began the 25 km final time trial stage from Versailles to the Champs-Elysées wearing the yellow jersey, with a 50 second lead on LeMond and victory seemingly in the bag.

Unfortunately he had a sore on his backside that made pedaling a penance, and, in addition, LeMond, a better time triallist at the time, was using radical new triathlon handlebars that gave him an advantage estimated at 1 second per kilometer (see AERODYNAMICS for other tricks). Fignon was at another disadvantage: he started three minutes after LeMond, and the crowd along the route could see he was behind the American. Their shouts of "25 seconds" and "you are behind" played on his mind.

Fignon was never the same after that defeat, although he won a stage in the 1992 Tour. He retired and ran the Paris–Nice race for a while and worked for French television. His memoir, *Nous Étions Jeunes et Insouciants* (*We Were Young and Carefree*), was published in 2009 and included a confession that he had used the drugs cortisone and amphetamine; the book was sympathetically received as before publication it was revealed that Fignon was suffering advanced cancer of the intestine and pancreas. He finally succumbed in August 2010. (See also DEFEATS.)

FILMS

The best cycling films of all time: a subjective list.

Breaking Away (1979, dir. Peter Yates)
A growing-up movie, wistful and hilarious by turns, written by Steve Tesich and starring Dennis Christopher as an Italian-cycling obsessed lad in middle America. Dennis Quaid and Daniel Stern costar. Dave Stoller's cycling passion is a framework for exploring his and his friends' fraught relations with the local college boys and the exhilaration and disillusion of their entering the adult world. The best scene, for me, is where Dave attempts to talk Italian to a group of professionals who visit for a local race; they respond by putting a pump in his front wheel. The film is based on a real-life race, the Little 500 race in Indianapolis; Dave Stoller is named after a legendary rider Dave Blasé (like the film Dave an Italian enthusiast) and his manager Bob Stoller.

American Flyers (1985, dir. Steve Badham)
Stars David Grant as Marcus, a young cyclist who dreams of winning a prestigious bike race in Colorado, with a young Kevin Costner (sporting a cheesy 1980s moustache) supporting as his elder brother, a failed international. Also written by Tesich, this one uses cycling to explore the tensions within Marcus's family following the death of his father. Great '80s soundtrack, the most fearsome beard in cycling (see HAIR for other tonsorial nasties), and fine location footage from the Coors Classic (see UNITED STATES OF AMERICA for more on this race). Badham was also responsible for the iconic disco film *Saturday Night Fever*.

Bicycle Thieves (Ladri di Biciclette)
(1948, dir. Vittorio De Sica)
Iconic black-and-white Italian film about the economic deprivation that followed the Second World War. The central character is a man dependent on his bike to earn a living: it is stolen, and he and his son desperately try to recover it. Finally he faces a dilemma: should he become a thief as well?

Sunday in Hell (1977, dir. JØRGEN LETH)
Probably the greatest cycling
documentary ever, based on the
1976 PARIS–ROUBAIX race, seen
from different viewpoints—
riders, spectators, mechanics,
protesters who stop the race—
and including stars of the
time such as EDDY MERCKX
and Freddy Maertens. The
slow-motion footage of cyclists
bouncing over the cobbles is
spinechilling. (See Leth's entry
for his other documentaries.)

Less Well-Known Cycling-Based Films

❖

Beijing Bicycle (2001):
Similar plot to *The Bicycle Thieves* and *Pee Wee's Big Adventure* but with a backdrop of the
economic boom in urban China.

Un Affaire d'Hommes (1981):
Stars Jean-Louis Trintignant as a member of a group of bike racers who uses cycling to cover
up the murder of his wife, with the final showdown involving bikes rather than guns.

Six Day Bike Racer (1934):
US comedy with SIX-DAY RACING as its backdrop.

The Flying Scotsman (2005):
Based on the life of GRAEME OBREE starring Jonny Lee Miller but not quite living up to the strength
of the book.

Les Bicyclettes de Belsize (1969):
Swinging '60s romance in which a shopowner finds love through his MOULTON folding bike.

Jour de Fête (1949):
Comedy starring Jacques Tati as a village postman who delivers mail on his bike but has to
come to terms with the modern world.

Death on the Mountain (2005):
Award-winning BBC documentary on the life and death of TOM SIMPSON.

La Course en Tête (1974, dir. Joel Santoni)
Follows Merckx in the 1973
Vuelta and Giro, shot in the
style of French *cinema-vérité*,
including the iconic scene in
which the Cannibal rides the
rollers in his garage with the
sound constantly increasing.
Combines live and archive
footage to a bizarre baroque
soundtrack.

Le Vélo de Ghislain Lambert
(2001, dir. Philippe Harel)
Belgian comedy narrated by
Antoine de Caunes, starring
Benoît Poelvoorde as a cyclist
who wants to be a great but can't
quite make it. Includes a
defining scene in which two
cyclists try to inject amphetamines in each others' buttocks in
a very small toilet cubicle.

⚙ BIZARRE CYCLING FILM FACTOIDS:

- A Bollywood film *Jo Jeeta Wohi Sikandar* was inspired by *Breaking Away*.

- *Ladri di Biciclette* is partly based on a real episode in which a cycle thief was lynched by a mob in postwar Italy.

- Ridley Scott's first feature was a short cycling film, *Boy & Bicycle*, which depicted his brother Tony playing truant from school to explore the coast of North East England.

- Diana Dors starred in a 1949 English rom-com, *A Boy, A Girl and a Bike*, with Jimmy Savile making a brief appearance as an extra.

- The 1948 Italian comedy *Toto Al Giro* included the finest lineup of cycling stars ever to figure in a single film: Fausto Coppi, GINO BARTALI, Fiorenzo Magni, LOUISON BOBET, and Ferdi Kubler all appear as themselves.

Les Triplettes de Belleville—
Eng: Belleville Rendezvous
(2003, dir. Sylvain Chomet)

Hilarious, poignant, and beautifully drawn cartoon parable. It stars a cyclist with a distinct resemblance to FAUSTO COPPI, his unfeasibly supportive grandmother, and their loyal if depressed-looking dog Bruno, set against a backdrop that can only be the Tour in the 1950s. The cyclist is kidnapped by villains who make him race continually on a stationary bike to recreate the Tour for gambling. Granny and dog set out to rescue him.

FISHER, Gary (b. 1950)

Together with his college roommate Charlie Kelly and frame-builder Tom Ritchey, Fisher is considered one of the founding fathers of MOUNTAIN-BIKING. Fisher was a CYCLO-CROSS rider, initially a road racer, but was suspended for a time because officials considered that his hair was too long.

By the mid-1970s he had begun modifying a 1930s SCHWINN Excelsior X bike for off-road use, fitting salvaged drum-brakes, motorcycle brake levers, and triple chainrings. Such "clunkers" were the prototype for today's mountain bikes.

Fisher was one of the participants in the REPACK downhill race run by Kelly, who began using the term "mountain bike" in 1979 to describe the fat-tired, multi-geared, and—in those days—extremely heavy bikes the Repack crew were using: in that year he and Fisher founded MountainBikes, the first company to make the off-road bikes. Ritchey was their frame-builder and later founded his own brand, an industry-leader to this day.

The first year's production was just 160 bikes, retailing at $1,300 each. With no cashflow

Fisher, Kelly, and Ritchie relied on trusting customers to pay up front. MountainBikes ceased trading in 1983, and Fisher then formed his own company, which is now owned by Trek and still makes bikes bearing his name.

FIXED-WHEEL   Curiously, even as cycle component makers pushed the number of gears available on most road-racing bikes into the 20s and 30s, London and some other major cities worldwide were hit by a new craze: fixed-gear bikes that were based on the stripped-down models used by cycle COURIERS and by HILL CLIMB specialists.

Top London shop Condor Cycles, which produced the first new-era "fixie" in 2002, estimated that it had sold several thousand of the bikes in their first seven years. Relatively few were visible on the streets, implying that they were retained for weekend use or simply to be admired.

Fixie adherents were happy to crunch up hills in an over-large gear and rev out downhill, because the machines were stylish and minimalist. They were also retro—hinting at the halcyon club cycling days between the 1920s and the 1950s when virtually every clubman would turn out on fixed for racing and social rides.

"The bike is a blank canvas on which riders express an individuality or a community . . . an aesthetic reference point shared with designers and artists who have helped shape fashion and street culture," said the intro to *Fixed*, a glossy book about the bikes.

(SEE **GEARS** FOR HOW BIKES BEGAN TO MOVE BEYOND THE FIXED-WHEEL BACK IN THE 1890S)

FLANDERS   A small chunk of Europe that has an influence on bike racing out of proportion to its area or population. There are more bike races held in the Flemish-speaking area of Belgium than anywhere else in the world; the local people are simply obsessed with the sport, and above all with "their" CLASSIC, the Tour of Flanders, founded in 1913 and now the climax of a series of gritty races in late March and early April.

One episode sums up the local mania with cycling and "De Ronde": in 1984 a farmer who lived on the race route grew jealous of all the attention given to the race's most notorious climb, the Koppenberg, which was situated on his neighbor's fields (see COBBLES for more on this ascent). He announced in the papers that he was going to create his own climb. Within 18 months a strip of cobbles had been laid up his fields: the Patersberg has been part of the race since 1986.

The Koppenberg itself shows the depth of the Flemish obsession. It was removed from the race in 1987, and 10 years later a local paper ran an April Fool's story that it was to be paved over. Two thousand people turned up for a demonstration in support of the climb: as a result it was then restored at a cost of $325,000 using cobbles imported from Poland. The importance of cycling in Belgium was summed up by the presence of the minister of culture at the official reopening.

Situated between the North Sea, the French border, and the French-speaking area of Wallonia to the south, Flanders has been fought over by invading armies for years. Local identity is passionately asserted—the lion flag is flown by nationalists at most major races—and it dominates Belgian cycling as south Wales dominates Welsh rugby. The cultural divide between French- and Flemish-speaking areas is strongly felt: neither likes the other much and the cycling rivalry is an assertion of that feeling.

Even within Flanders itself there are local rivalries even down to the papers that run the bike races: the Tour of Flanders, organized by *Het Niewsblad*, was the only classic to be run in occupied Europe during the Second World War, with the Germans helping to police the route. A second newspaper, *Het Volk*, started its own event, also called the Tour of Flanders, on a similar course after liberation, to make the point

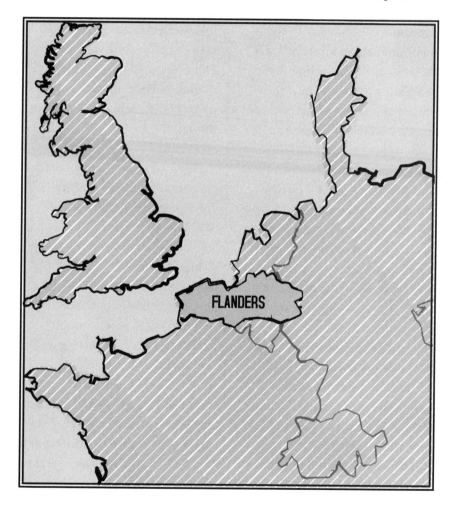

that its rival had been accused of collaboration. It was later ruled that the name should be changed (see CLASSICS for more on this race and other major one-dayers).

The wind and rain and bad roads breed a species of hard men who live to an almost monastic canon of hard work and self-sacrifice. Every village seems to boast a Classic winner, who usually runs a bike shop or café. Flandrian cycling is

---

The Key Flandrian Climbs:

❖

Old Kwaremont: 2.2 km long, 11% steepest, approx 95 km from the finish

Patersberg: 360 m long, 13% steepest, approx 90 km from finish

Koppenberg: 600 m long, 25% steepest, approx 85 km from finish*

Kapelmuur: 475 m long, 20% steepest, approx 25 km from finish

Bosberg: 980 m long, 11% steepest, approx 20 km from finish

*not always included in route

---

essentially nostalgic: the heroes of today never quite live up to those of yesteryear. Several cyclists, including the top Classic rider Johan Museeuw, have been dubbed the "last of the Flandrians," another of whom was the evocatively named Alberic "Brick" Schotte. Schotte was brought out of his first communion to watch the Tour of Flanders go past in 1930 and as an amateur he would get up at 3:30 AM to go to work to ensure that he could start training at 1 PM. He rode the Classic 20 times and was a strong influence on another cycling hardman, the Irishman SEAN KELLY, who spent most of his career based in Belgium.

Few foreigners break through in Flanders but those who do become adopted sons, such as Kelly and the Italian Fiorenzo Magni, who won the Classic three times in a row from 1949–51. So too the Moldovan Andrei Tchmil, who led Belgian's biggest team, Lotto, for nine years, and was naturalized as Belgian in 2000. Home greats include RIK VAN LOOY, ROGER DE VLAEMINCK, Museeuw—10 times a Classic winner—and Rik Van Steenbergen, a hulking brute known as Rik I so he would not be confused with Van Looy (Rik II). In spite of a legendary Flanders win in 1969, EDDY MERCKX never quite fitted in to this culture because he was a French-speaker from Brussels: his big rivals Walter Godefroot and Freddy Maertens were more popular.

What might be called "Tour of Flanders country" is an area of little hills along the Scheldt and Deinze rivers known as the Flemish Ardennes; the race began coming here in the 1950s, when it needed to be made tougher but the roads were generally being improved, so the organizers had to seek out small lanes and steep hills.

The race loops up and down onto the hills, starting with the Old Kwaremont, a windswept stretch of cobbles up a bleak hillside with a café at the top, and culminating with the "Chapel wall"—Kapelmuur—at Geraardsbergen, which twists upward at 20 percent to a chapel by a grassy bank where the fans congregate.

FOLDING BIKES   These aim to provide a solution to a perennial bike problem: getting the thing in a small car, putting it in a house or office where space is at a premium, or fitting on a train where the operator doesn't want to carry them. It's not always been that way; an early folder, made by MIKAEL PEDERSEN, was used in the Boer War by the British Army, and in the Second World War British paratroopers used folders made by BSA, which were full-sized bikes that could be carried when jumping out of aircraft.

Folding bikes compromise on performance: they either hinge at the mid-point of the frame or have a flip-round rear triangle. They usually have small wheels, and the wheelbase may be shorter than usual, all to save space. Tires may be fatter than usual, and the frame tubes may well be more substantial than on a

conventional road bike; however, the aluminium Bickerton, made in the 1970s and 1980s, weighed in at just 18 lb.

Among the best models are those from British company Brompton, whose top of the range bike weighs in at less than 10 kg and has 16-inch wheels and rear suspension. Small wheel bikes made by MOULTON qualify as folders, because they can be "split" for storage or transport. At the radical end of the spectrum, the Strida has drum brakes and a rubber drive belt and futuristic looks. Aficionados also swear by the Pocket Rocket, which fits in a suitcase 22 × 29 × 10 inches yet turns into a replica racing bike.

An annual Brompton world championship is run in which the riders wear suit jackets, cycle shorts, and cycle helmets and have a Le Mans–type start, running to unfold their bikes. Bizarrely, a regular contestant is the Spaniard Roberto Heras, disqualified from first place in the 2004 VUELTA A ESPAÑA for doping.

FOREIGN LEGION A term coined by the Australian journalist Rupert Guinness. It was the title for his book published in 1993, which traced the fortunes of the group of English-speaking professional cyclists who opened up the European-dominated sport during the 1980s. In essence they made cycling truly international. The bulk of legionnaires passed through the elite Parisian amateur club Association Cycliste de Boulogne-Billancourt (ACBB), which was sponsored by PEUGEOT as a feeder club to their professional team. PHIL ANDERSON, Graham Jones, ROBERT MILLAR, SEAN YATES, and STEPHEN ROCHE all took this route between 1979 and 1983.

While Jones's career never took off in spite of his undoubted class, Anderson was the first Australian to wear the yellow jersey in the Tour de France, the first to win a CLASSIC, and the first to win a Tour stage. Millar was the first Briton to win a major award in the Tour, taking the mountains jersey in 1984 while Roche achieved the golden triple in 1987: GIRO D'ITALIA, TOUR DE FRANCE, and world championship.

Of the non-ACBB riders, SEAN KELLY won the points jersey of the Tour a record four times between 1983 and 1989 and was world number one for five years, while GREG LEMOND pioneered the sport in America with his Tour win in 1986. Between them they paved the way for the first American team to start the Tour, 7-Eleven in 1986, and the first British squad, ANC-Halfords in 1987. Together with the arrival of cyclists from COLOMBIA at the Tour in 1983, their influence helped to transform the sport within a decade.

(SEE ALSO AUSTRALIA, IRELAND, GREAT BRITAIN, ROAD RACING, UNITED STATES)

FOSTER FRASER, John

(b. England, 1868, d. 1936)

One of the first round-the-world cyclists, who set off with two friends, Edward Lunn and F. H. Lowe, to circumnavigate the globe between 1896 and 1898. Their route took in Persia, the Indian sub-continent from Karachi to Calcutta, through Burma to China and Shanghai, thence to Japan, San Francisco, and across the United States, a total of 19,237 miles.

Foster Fraser's account of the trip, *Round the World on a Wheel*, was published in 1899 and reissued in 1982; it is one of the first and one of the finest cycle travelogues. It features encounters with Russian officials straight out of Tolstoy, riotous arguments with Cossacks in the Caucasus, a trip to a medieval dungeon and the Shah's palace in Iran, not to mention near-death from hypothermia in the Hindu Kush.

The tone is smugly Victorian—"The Georgians are a lazy race, much addicted to gourmandising," "being Europeans and strangers we of course ran the gauntlet of all the halt, lame and blind in Teheran"—but there is an exquisite irony in the fact that international conflicts, officialdom, and terrorism would make such a journey far more risky in the 21st century.

(SEE **BOOKS—TRAVEL** FOR OTHER INTREPID CYCLISTS WHO HAVE WRITTEN ABOUT THEIR ADVENTURES)

FRAMES—DESIGN   Frame
size is usually expressed by measuring the seat tube—either center to center, from the middle of the bottom bracket to the middle of the seat lug, or center to top. The advent of smaller frames with sloping top tubes means that a more important measurement now is the distance between the center of the bottom bracket and the top of the saddle.

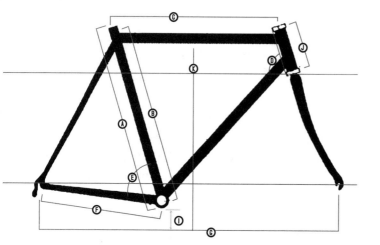

A - Size
B - Seat Tube, Center of BB to to
C - Effective Top Tube length
D - Head Tube Angle
E - Seat Tube Angle
F - Chainstay
G - Wheelbase
I - Bottom Bracket Height
J - Head Tube
K - Standover

Another complication is that bottom bracket height can vary, particularly with cyclo-cross machines and children's bikes, affecting the "stand-over" height.

Frame performance depends on several factors. Handling stability depends mainly on the amount of "trail"—the distance between a notional line taken down the steerer tube and the point where the front tire makes contact with the road. The extent of trail depends on the angle of the head tube, and the rake of the forks, which may be curved or bent at the fork crown—the shallower the head angle and the longer the rake, the greater the trail. More trail equals more stability, which in riding terms translates into whether a bike can be ridden safely with hands off the bars, and for how far, and the degree of comfort over bumps.

Another key element is seat-tube angle, usually measured compared to a notional horizontal line, in some cases to the top tube. The usual range is between 69 and 74 degrees; the lower the number, the shallower the angle, and the less upright the seat tube. Bikes with shallower angles are usually more stable and comfortable, and may well have longer seat- and chain-stays to give a longer wheelbase and greater comfort;

bikes with tighter angles and a shorter rear triangle are more responsive, but are less forgiving on bumpy roads.

The forward reach of the bike—the distance between the tip of the saddle and the center of the handlebars—is a key factor in determining comfort, whether the rider is hunched up or stretched out, and aerodynamics, the extent to which the torso is flat or upright. Forward reach depends on top tube length and seat angle, the degree to which the saddle is pushed forward or back, and the length of the stem.

FRAMES—MAKERS

The refinement of steel tubing meant that the handbuilt road-racing or track frame eventually became a mini art form. The lugs that hold the tubes together and provide a surface for bonding to take place were cut into forms that varied from basic curves to the elaborate filigree that was the trademark of the East London firm Hetchins.

In Great Britain and Northern Italy, artisan frame makers turning out a few hundred bikes a year for the racing and high-end touring markets were relatively widespread until the 1990s, when the nature of the cycle trade changed with the arrival of carbon-fiber and aluminum—which were less suited to small producers— and compact frames that, the manufacturers claimed, offered equal performance for lower price and less hassle. Some makers now cater for both, offering a number of custom-made machines but relying on off-the-rack bikes for most of their trade.

Best-known North American makers include:

Richard Sachs, Chester, Connecticut. The ultimate in the United States; served his apprenticeship at Witcomb Cycles in London almost 40 years ago. "At Richard Sachs

Cycles, I am the work force," says his website.

Mariposa, Toronto. Canada's most prominent framebuilder. Their mainstay Mike Barry is now retired so production is limited to a few special projects.

Spectrum Cycles, LeHigh Valley, Pennsylvania. Two-man operation run by Tom Kellogg and Mike Duser; Kellogg has been building since 1976. Collaborated in late 1980s with titanium makers Merlin, with whom the company still works.

Moots Cycles, Steamboat Springs, Colorado. Founded by Kent Eriksen in 1981, one of the early mountain bike makers, now produces a wide variety of handbuilt titanium frames. Logo is a distinctive, lovable, crocodile.

Roland Della Santa, Reno, Nevada. Another builder with over 35 years experience, Della Santa most notably made frames for GREG LEMOND.

Independent Fabrication, Somerville, Massachusetts. Founded 1995, employee-owned, and best known for its steel frames; the crowned IF logo is one of the most distinctive in the world.

Best-known British makers include:

Hetchins (Tottenham, London; then Southend). Produced frames with delicately curved seat stays, seat tubes, and S-shaped chainstays— the legendary "Curly." Their machines were given Latin names such as Nulli Secundus and Magnum Bonum and are now collectors' items. The original makers ran from the 1920s to the late 1980s, but the frames are still made under license.

Bates (East London). Another now defunct maker, who produced a bent fork design known as the Diadrant and used "Cantiflex" frame tubing, which featured an oversized central section to reduce frame flex. Founded by brothers Eddie and Horace, with a bat as the logo, they were one of London's leading makers from the 1930s through the 1950s, although the brothers eventually went their separate ways. Like Hetchins, they are now made under license.

Mercian Cycles (Derby). One of the last remaining companies to make hand-built frames in any volume. Opened in 1946, and known for their fine finishes, they keep frame design records dating to the 1970s so their customers can refer back if they want a new frame.

Bob Jackson (Leeds). Variously marketed under the names JRJ and Merlin; produced frames under license for Hetchins in the 1980s and is still producing them today after over 70 years. Like Mercian, fine finishes are a specialty.

Chas Roberts (Croydon). London's leading custom-made frame builder, set up in the early 1960s by Charlie, the father of the current owner, Chas, who had to train as a frame maker for 10 years before he met the standard the company demanded.

FRAMES—MATERIALS Early
cycle frames were built of wood or iron; the key development came in 1897 when Alfred Reynolds patented double-butted tubing in which the ends of the tubes had thicker walls than the middle, improving the strength-to-weight ratio.

Thirty-eight years later Reynolds would go on to produce the definitive steel frame tube, initially for lightweight motorcycles. Reynolds 531 was named after the ratio of the other materials used in the steel alloy: manganese, molybdenum, and silica. The British company dominated the tubing market for many years: 27 out of 31 TOUR DE

⚙ **FRAME FACTOID**

In 2007, to coincide with the Tour de France start in London, top designer Paul Smith produced a range of jeans branded 531, taking the name from Reynolds' iconic tubing. Smith was a racing cyclist in the 1960s before a crash curtailed his career, but he remained intensely interested in the sport.

✺

FRANCE winners between 1958 and 1989 rode on steel tubes such as 531 and the much thinner and lighter 753. By the golden jubilee of 531 in 1985, Reynolds estimated that the tubing had gone into 20 million frame sets worldwide. The other major steel tubing name came from Italy, where Angelo Colombo began making steel cycle tubing in 1919 and produced butted tubes from 1930.

Aluminium frames were produced as early as the 1890s, but it took the best part of 80 years for frame makers to master the process of joining the tubes. In the 1970s, Italian firm ALAN (from the acronym ALuminium ANodised) made attractive, light, lugged frames which remain popular with cyclo-cross riders today. But steel remained the material of choice until the advent of the MOUNTAIN BIKE and the perfection of welding processes in the 1980s. Oversize aluminium—stronger, yet lighter tubes, in spite of the increased size—came from mountain-biking and was popularized initially by the Cannondale company from the US, who sponsored the Italian sprinter Mario Cipollini in the early 1990s.

Titanium frames appeared in the mid-1950s and were used in the Tour de France by the Spaniard Luis Ocana in the 1970s, but they were sloppy and fragile; again the mountain-bike boom was the spur for the perfection of the product. Again, the initial boost came from the US, where Merlin and Litespeed were turning out jewel-like products by the early 1990s.

Carbon-fiber composite frames appeared in the 1980s, when companies like Vitus made frames of carbon tubes with aluminium lugs, and have been gaining in popularity since the 1990s, spurred on by the arrival of companies like Giant, Specialised, and Trek in professional cycling; in the early 1990s GREG LEMOND's bike company produced carbon frames with web-like joins. The process sounds simple—sheets of the fibers are bonded with epoxy resin and then baked—but it has taken time to perfect. Much of the impetus has come from military technology, where carbon fibers are used for lightweight armoring, for example bullet-proof pads for helicopters.

Monocoques, solid one-piece carbon-fiber frames, were permitted by the UCI between 1990 and 2000. MIKE BURROWS began working on carbon monocoques in the early 1980s and his Lotus, used by CHRIS BOARDMAN in the 1992 Olympics and 1994 Tour de France, opened minds. MIGUEL INDURAIN used a futuristic carbon Pinarello, the Espada (Spanish for sword), to beat the HOUR RECORD in 1994, while Boardman switched from the Lotus to a Corima monocoque for his 1993 record. French firm Look's KG196 from the early 1990s was equally radical. It had a flattened carbon-kevlar frame with an early, crude-looking

adjustable stem.

The GREAT BRITAIN Olympic team use UKSI bikes with sleek black carbon-fiber frames, in which the carbon fibers run in different directions depending on the forces exerted by the cyclist in the various parts of the frame. Most of the carbon-fiber parts are made at Advanced Components Group on an anonymous-looking industrial estate in Heanor in the East Midlands.

The company has an exotic client list: every car on a Formula One starting grid will include something made here, while other products include ejector seats for fighter aircraft. The cost of the frames is kept down by using a modular system: different lengths of stem joined with different bars to produce a one-piece item; different models for the front end of a frame combined with a standard back end.

⚙

FRANCE Together with GREAT BRITAIN, one of cycling's founding nations: home of

the BONESHAKER, the clipless pedal and the first derailleur GEAR, the world's greatest bike race, the HOUR RECORD, and organized cycle touring events. French cycling has two fathers, TOUR DE FRANCE founder HENRI DESGRANGE and the journalist Paul de Viviès (see VÉLOCIO), who had a more open-minded, less monastic attitude and campaigned for cycling as enjoyment, coining the term *cyclotourisme*.

Cycling was hugely popular in the velocipede era, with 120 races organized in June and July 1869, according to the world's first cycling magazine, *Le Vélocipède Illustré*. ITALY and Britain were where the initial growth came in the 1870s as France coped with the aftermath of the Franco–Prussian war, but in the early 1890s, growth was rapid as the notion of long-distance events was adopted from Britain; and in the mid-1890s a host of cycle tracks were built to cater to the fans, with the Buffalo Vélodrome one of three to open in Paris in 1893 alone.

Among the early short-distance stars was one Henri Farman, who later built pioneering airplanes with his brother Maurice. The top endurance specialists were Constant Huret and Charles Terront. The latter famously won one 1,000 km event—2,500 laps of the VÉLODROME D'HIVER—by not taking any toilet stops, but instead urinating into an inner-tube.

The magazines and papers continued to develop long-distance events culminating in the founding of the Tour de France in 1903. As Henri Desgrange expanded his race, De Viviès pushed *cyclotourisme* through his magazine *Le Cycliste*. A whole world of mass events was born—the Diagonal rides from one corner of France to another, the RAID PYRENEAN, AUDAX, and other *randonneur* marathons.

Alongside the commercial razzmatazz of the Tour, there is now nostalgia for a golden era: when RAYMOND POULIDOR and JACQUES ANQUETIL fought elbow to elbow, when the accordionist Yvette Horner provided the soundtrack to July each year, when each village in Brittany and Normandy had at least one circuit race organized to coincide with the annual fête, and every *pays* had a son of its own in one of four or five French regional teams in the great bike race. It is the Tour captured on film by Louis Malle and in words by Antoine Blondin.

The golden era of French cycling can be accurately dated: it began when Henri Desgrange brought national teams into the Tour in 1930, opening the way for riders like André Leducq, Antonin Magne, and Jean Robic, and it closed with BERNARD HINAULT's fifth win in 1986. What ended it? The Tour grew quickly in the 1980s and 1990s, and French cyclists couldn't

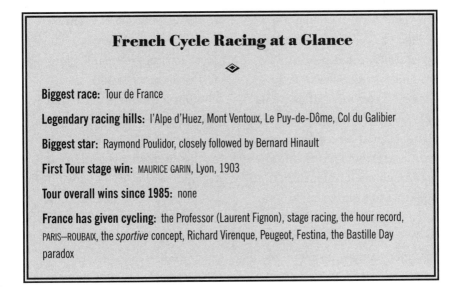

French Cycle Racing at a Glance

Biggest race: Tour de France

Legendary racing hills: l'Alpe d'Huez, Mont Ventoux, Le Puy-de-Dôme, Col du Galibier

Biggest star: Raymond Poulidor, closely followed by Bernard Hinault

First Tour stage win: MAURICE GARIN, Lyon, 1903

Tour overall wins since 1985: none

France has given cycling: the Professor (Laurent Fignon), stage racing, the hour record, PARIS–ROUBAIX, the *sportive* concept, Richard Virenque, Peugeot, Festina, the Bastille Day paradox keep up. With the talent of the entire cycling world eligible to ride the race after the arrival of Australians and Americans and the collapse of the Berlin Wall, there was less room for the home riders. Hence the fact that there has been no young star to succeed Hinault or LAURENT FIGNON, both men of the 1980s.

French cycling was traumatized by the Festina DRUG scandal of 1998 that centered on the nation's leading team and its national hero, Richard Virenque, but also hit other teams including Casino and Française des Jeux; a more stringent attitude to doping gained ground and the Tour came under greater scrutiny from newspapers such as *Le Monde*. There were allegations of two-speed cycling, with the French at a disadvantage because they stayed clean. There was an element of truth in that, but it wasn't quite that simple.

Post Festina, cycle racing in France has suffered, even though cycling is probably more popular than ever due to the growth of CYCLOSPORTIVES. But the structure has changed: village races are dying out as organizers become older and traffic increases even in the regions; the criteriums, which used to be a cottage industry in themselves after the Tour, are declining due to a lack of French stars. Fewer young people come into bike racing because of its tarnished reputation, along with competition from other sports.

The French cycle-component industry was once one of the largest in the world boasting names such as Mafac (brakes), Simplex (gears), and TA (bottle cages), not to mention manufacturers like PEUGEOT. However, the companies largely failed to compete with the Japanese when SHIMANO and SunTour moved into Europe in the 1970s. There was a big shakeout during the 1980s and the industry is now headed by pedal makers Look and Time, and wheelmakers Mavic. Once market leaders, Peugeot no longer make many bikes.

Sponsors are still drawn to

the top end of the sport, because the Tour organizers' need for a strong French element guarantees them a place in the field, but no Frenchman has looked a likely winner since Fignon in 1989; the last French world road champion was Laurent Brochard in 1997 but he was subsequently disgraced in the Festina scandal.

FREESTYLE   Most BMX riders like to do fancy moves to test their bikehandling; push that to the limit and you end up with a cross between skateboarding and cycling.

Freestyle kicked off in the 1970s in San Diego, not long after the BMX boom started in the USA. One of the founders was a teenager named Bob Haro, who now builds most of the bikes used by freestylers. The first public demonstrations began in 1980.

Straightforward flat surfaces are used (Flatland) but so too are street obstacles, purpose-built skate or BMX parks or trails, and large ramps known as "Verts," which have two semicircular ramps facing each other so that the riders can continually go up one and down the other, using the top of each ramp to perform tricks on vertical extensions, hence the name. The biggest ramp used is a 27-footer at the X Games. The unofficial record for a jump is over 15 meters from the ground.

The bikes are subtly adapted from BMX machines, using heavier-duty tubing if necessary, and with three- to five-inch pegs at the front and rear hubs to give additional contact points for doing grinds. Some riders have pegs on one side only; street riders often have no brakes, while dirt riders have knobbly tires. The bikes often have two-piece brake-cable detanglers (a gyro, or rotor) on ball-bearings, so that the bars can be spun time and time again.

One of the earliest tricks was the Rock Walk, in which the bike is stationary and first the rear then the front tire is pulled through 180 degrees so the bike does a 360-degree turn. Others include: grinds, where the bike slides along a surface (e.g., the lip of a ramp) on a part of the bike other than the wheels, for example the rear and front axle pegs or a pedal, and air tricks such as back and front flips and spins and the CanCan, in which one foot is taken from one side of the bike to the other.

Flatland tricks are closer to conventional BMX moves: wheelies, manuals—in which the bike is ridden over a hump with the front wheel in the air—and bunny hops. These are given twists such as the nose manual, in which only the front wheel is on the ground, and the cherry picker, in which the bike is hopped on only the rear wheel.

FRENCH The lingua franca of international cycle sports since its inception, certain French terms are now universal in cycling (see also SLANG). Often they are simply anglicized in pronunciation.

bidon: term for waterbottle now used by most English-speaking cyclists. French pronunciation is bee-daw(n); it's anglicised as bidden.

bonification: time bonus, used in stage racing, when seconds may be deducted from the overall time of riders who place in the first three in the stage, or at intermediate sprints.

casquette: cotton racing hat.

classement general: overall classification.

commissaire: race referee even in events outside France.

contre la montre: time trial.

critérium: race on a short circuit around a town.

directeur sportif: team manager.

domestique (cf British water-carrier, Italian *gregario*): lesser rider in a team who works for the leader.

dossard: race number.

echelon: diagonal formation for combating sidewind in which the cyclists ride through and off.

lanterne rouge: last man in a stage race, so called because he was awarded a red lantern such as might be put on the back of a freight train.

maillot jaune: yellow jersey worn by leader of a stage race (cf *à pois*, *vert*, *blanc*).

musette: cloth bag (literally "nosebag") handed up at feed station (*ravitaillement*) containing *bidons* and race food.

neutralisation: spell in a race when the riders are on their bikes but not actually racing. Most stages of the Tour de France are "neutralised" from the formal start in a town center to the actual start on the outskirts of town; track races may be "neutralised" after a crash.

nocturne: a criterium run at night. In smaller venues this means at least one stretch in the dark.

peloton: main group in a race, in English "the bunch."

prime: intermediate prize of any kind, also a bonus given for performance by a team or club.

prologue: brief opening time trial in a stage race.

ravitaillement (abbr. ravito): feed zone where *musettes* are handed up by *soigneurs*.

rouleur: a racing cyclist with stamina who can mix it with the best all day and be in there at the finish.

signature: where the riders register and receive numbers, the English term is sign-on.

soigneur: team assistant who provides race food and massage. Anglicized as swanee, also carer.

speaker: announcer at major races who introduces the riders at the sign-on. (See MANGEAS to read more about the voice of French racing.)

voiture balai: vehicle that drives at back of race convoy to "sweep up" riders who drop out. Anglicized as broom wagon.

G

GARIN, Maurice

Born: Aosta, Italy, March 23, 1871
Died: Lens, France, February 18, 1957
Major wins: Tour de France 1903, 3 stage wins; Paris–Roubaix 1897–8; Paris–Brest–Paris 1901; Bordeaux–Paris 1902
Nicknames: the White Dulldog, the Chimney Sweep

The winner of the first TOUR DE FRANCE in 1903, and the main protagonist in its first great scandal, was one of tens of thousands of boys from the Alps who trekked up to Paris in the late 19th century to earn a living cleaning the capital's chimneys.

Born on the Italian side of the border in Aosta, Garin was one of the best distance racers of the time: he won two early editions of the PARIS–ROUBAIX classic—which finished in the town where he ran a cycle shop—as well as 24-hour races

in Paris and Liège, Bordeaux–Paris and PARIS–BREST–PARIS in 1901. He also set a record for 500 km in 1895. Garin won the first stage of the Tour, the 467 km from Paris to Lyon, at an average speed of 26 kph, and led the race throughout, losing two and a half kilograms over the three weeks.

Garin was also winner of the Tour de France in 1904, but was disqualified after a four-month investigation by the Union Vélocepédique Française that led to 29 of the field being sanctioned. The report was never published but the riders' offences included holding onto cars, taking shortcuts, swapping race numbers to avoid controls, colluding with fellow competitors, and catching trains. The scandal led Tour organizer HENRI DESGRANGE to write that his race had been destroyed.

Such charges were common in races of the HEROIC ERA, in which the riders spent long periods out in the countryside meaning it was impossible for officials to keep tabs on them. In the 1903 race, Garin avoided being beaten up by a rival's supporter in the depths of night only by pretending he was someone else. Ironically, he was a victim of the worst episode of the 1904 race, when a mob held up the riders near St-Étienne, demanding that the local rider André Fauré be allowed to win. He was hit on the head with a bottle, and the mob dispersed only when the race organizer Géo Lefèvre turned up and fired pistol shots into the air.

Garin was banned for two years and raced again only once, in the 1911 Paris–Brest–Paris. But he had time to invest the prize money from the 1904 Tour win in a garage in the northern France town of Lens, where he worked until his death. Historian Les Woodland described him as "an old man, a bit stooped" but still with the enormous handlebar moustache of his youth.

He is buried in section F3 of the Cimetière Est off rue Constant Darras between Lens and Sallaumines; there is no formal memorial. The assistant gravedigger there, Maurice Vernaldé, told Woodland that Garin admitted cheating in the 1904 Tour: "He used to laugh and say 'Well I was young . . .' Maybe at the time he said he didn't but when he got older and it didn't matter so much."

GEARS   Although experimentation with multiple gears began in the days of the velocipede, the first bicycles used single fixed gears, in which the transmission is directly linked to the driving wheel, with no possibility of freewheeling. On long descents riding a high-wheeler, the rider simply took his feet off the pedals, put them on pegs sticking out of the frame, and hoped for the best. Uphill, he or she would walk.

The first hub gears—which use different sized cogs within

the hub to create different ratios—appeared in 1891. Freewheels were invented around 1897, with a clutch bearing enabling the rear wheel to run free of the gear sprocket. There were many attempts at different kinds of gears—epicyclic, bichain, multiple chainwheels, multicog, bottom bracket gears, to name just a few—but while English cyclists stuck to the hub gears patented by Sturmey Archer in 1902 and made by RALEIGH, the French went for the derailleur.

The bodies that ran cycle racing restricted technical development—led by the conservative HENRI DESGRANGE—and so the impetus for the derailleur gear came from cycle-tourists, led by the French journalist Paul de Viviès (who wrote in his magazine *Le Cycliste* under the pen name VÉLOCIO) and his close circle of friends around the central France town of St-Étienne.

Vélocio experimented with almost every kind of gear as soon as it entered the market and wrote up the experiments in his magazine. The first mention of a derailleur mechanism was in 1908 or 1909, and about this time rear gear mechanisms began to be produced that had some of the elements that still feature today: a mechanism to push the chain from one sprocket to another and a long chain running through a tension spring and pulley to take up the slack as the sprocket size changes.

In 1912, Vélocio's friend Joanny Panel, maker of the Chemineau bike, rode the TOUR DE FRANCE using a six-speed derailleur gear system that resembled designs that would stay in use for half a century: a cylinder with a short sliding shaft—the "plunger"—pushed inward by a spring, and pulled outward by a short chain on the end of a control cable. The Chemineau gear was still being produced in 1946.

The first popular derailleur was the Le Cyclo two-speed gear, made by another of Vélocio's friends, Albert Raimond, which appeared in 1924. In 1931 the

Simplex company brought out a four-speed model that looked similar, and, critically, their owner Lucien Juy won over the remaining cynics among the racing fraternity, pushing sales over 50,000 annually. Also in the 1930s, the first front derailleurs appeared; they would not become popular until after the Second World War, however.

In 1936, Henri Desgrange stepped down as Tour de France organizer, and the way was open for the use of geared bikes in the race from 1937; until then, the riders had used wheels with two sprockets on either side; to change gear they would stop, take their rear wheel out, and turn it around. "You had to do it at the right moment," the 1937 winner Roger Lapébie said. "You could lose a race if you didn't change gear at the right moment. If a good rider stopped to change gear, everyone might attack together."

Most of the yellow bikes issued to the Tourmen were fitted with Super Champion gears made by the Swiss track racer Oscar Egg,

in which the chain was "derailed" by a pushing mechanism that hung from the chainstay, with the tension pulley and spring hanging from the bottom bracket. They appeared primitive compared to the Simplex, but offered a wide range of gears. The Italians used a similar looking gear called the Vittoria.

Post-war, it was TULLIO CAMPAGNOLO who made the next breakthrough when he produced the first parallelogram derailleur, the Gran Sport, in 1950. Two other companies had produced parallelogram models, and he had bought the patent rights for one, made by Italian company Ghigghini, but his was the design that would become the industry standard. Campag' would dominate the high-end racing market for the next 35 years, as derailleur gears became lighter and slicker, mostly based on the original Gran Sport.

The next developments came in 1975 from Japan's SHIMANO, who began producing indexed gears—where the derailleur cable jumped into preset

Gear Size

◈

The system of measuring a gear dates back to the days of the high-wheeler and should be thought of in terms of a notional front wheel powered directly by the legs: a 60-inch gear (for a two-foot six-inch inside leg) would have been large for an old ordinary, but is now a climbing gear for most fit cyclists.

The imperial gear size is calculated by taking the diameter of the rear wheel in inches, multiplying it by the number of teeth on the chainwheel, and dividing it by the number of teeth on the rear cog. The lower the figure (i.e., the smaller the notional front wheel), the lower the gear. For example, on a 27-inch wheel, $48 \times 19 = 68$ inches, a medium-size gear.

Team mechanics and racers tend to think simply in terms of the teeth on the front chain ring and rear sprocket, without worrying about notional front wheels: e.g., 52×13 is a sprinting gear—108 inches for that notional imperial front wheel—while at the other end of the spectrum 30×23 is a climbing gear.

Gear size matters for various reasons. In TRACK RACING in particular, gears need to be adjusted by tiny increments to take into account air temperature, form, and the speed of the track surface. Most track racers carry a variety of fixed sprockets and chainwheels with them. In GREAT BRITAIN, young riders are limited to gears up to a certain size to avoid putting strain on developing tendons and muscles.

positions so that shifting was predictable. In 1978 Shimano made their first freehub, which replaced a single freewheel block with individual sprockets on a splined body giving total freedom of sprocket choice.

The arrival of indexed gearing in high-end road groups from 1985 meant that changing development then focused on the levers, change quality, and the number of sprockets rather than the derailleurs. 1989 saw Shimano's first prototype STI brake-lever gear changers used by the 7-Eleven team; they entered the market the following year and Campagnolo didn't catch up with their Ergopower

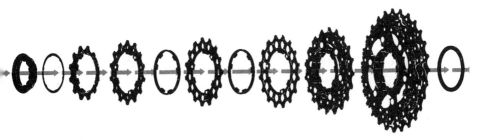

levers until 1992, giving the Japanese company a head start that enabled it to establish a dominant position in the market. Off-road, indexed top-of-the-bar thumbshifters gave way to dual levers below the bar (Rapidfire from Shimano, X-Press from SunTour) with newcomers Sram bringing out the Gripshift, based on the cylindrical handgrip at the end of the bar, from 1988.

Other developments have included tweaks in sprocket and chain ring design to make changing more rapid and reliable with thinner chains as sprocket numbers have increased from 6—the standard in the early 1980s—to 11. While Mavic was the first to experiment with electronic shifting with the 1999 Mektronic, Shimano appears to

have achieved the first reliable models with 2008's DuraAce. The smaller derailleur makers such as SunTour, Huret, and Sachs were killed off by Shimano's move to integrated transmission, where all the components are interdependent and cannot be used with those of other companies; Campagnolo followed suit.

In essence, the gear market in the early 2000s has been dominated by Shimano, thanks mainly to the STI breakthrough, with Campagnolo offering minor opposition, and Sram—who had acquired component makers such as Gripshift, Sachs, Huret, and Sedis—introducing their own brake-gear levers, Double-Tap, in 2007, thus providing proper competition for the big two.

GHOST BIKES   In some 40 countries worldwide, memorials made of white-painted bicycles can be seen on roadsides at places where cyclists have been killed by motor vehicles. The movement is strongest in the United States, where the first ghost bikes were created purely for artistic reasons by San Francisco artist Jo Slota, who in 2002 began painting the abandoned bikes and parts that littered the city white and posting photos of them on a website.

Now, however, "they serve as reminders of the tragedy that took place on an otherwise anonymous street corner, as quiet statements of cyclists' right to safe travel," according to a website that lists the memorials. Sometimes they are put up overnight so as to create a dramatic effect the following morning, as if they have appeared out of nowhere.

The bikes used are junked machines, with parts such as cables, brakes, and pedals removed so that they are less attractive to thieves and easier to paint. Sometimes they are mangled or damaged, as they would be in an accident. The Ghost Bikes website gives advice on painting the bike, creating placards, and locking it in situ, and even recommends that the bikes be carried to the site rather than wheeled to avoid wearing the paint from the tires and perhaps reducing the effect.

(SEE ALSO **MEMORIALS**)

GIANT   Taiwanese company that is the biggest bike maker in the world, shifting over five million bikes in 2007, making bikes under its own name and under contract to other producers. It is a relative newcomer. Founded in 1972 by a Japanese engineer named King Liu who needed a new venture when his eel-farming business was wiped out by a typhoon, Giant began by making bikes for other companies, primarily USA's leading mass-market bike-makers SCHWINN; eventually the American company shifted more and more of its production to Taiwan until Giant was effectively on equal terms.

Giant's first own-brand machines didn't come out until 1986 but found a ready market in the US, and the company rode the mountain-bike boom with the rest. The key change came in the mid-1990s when Giant was the first company to bring out a compact-framed machine, the TCR (see MIKE BURROWS to read about the British designer who came up with the idea), which rapidly earned a strong reputation.

In Europe deals to sponsor the Spanish ONCE team and later T-Mobile and Rabobank helped to raise Giant's profile, and earned the company credibility in the rapidly growing market for bikes to use in CYCLOSPORTIVES. Giant played a large part in popularizing off-the-rack frames, a major change in the industry that led to casualties among smaller custom frame makers (see FRAMES—MAKERS).

GIRO D'ITALIA   Like its elder brother, the TOUR DE FRANCE, the Italian equivalent was born of a circulation battle between rival newspapers. Unlike the Tour, after over a century in existence the Giro is still sponsored by its original backer, the daily *La Gazzetta dello Sport*, with a pink leader's jersey to match the pink pages of the paper.

"Absolutely essential for the paper you announce immediately the cycling Tour of Italy," read the telegram sent to the paper's cycling editor Armando Cougnet in August 1908; his boss had heard rumors that the rival *Corriere dello Sport* was about to run a Tour of Italy, and a preemptive strike was required in spite of the fact that *Gazzetta* was strapped for cash.

The first Giro began on May 13, 1909, in Italy's financial capital, Milan, and finished there 17 days later after eight stages taking in Bologna, Chieti, Naples, Rome, Florence, Genoa, and Turin. The winner was a stonemason, Luigi Ganna.

The 1920s were dominated by ALFREDO BINDA, while the 1930s began with the introduction of the pink jersey (1931) and ended with the emergence of GINO BARTALI. The year 1940, on the other hand, offered a foretaste of one of cycling's greatest RIVALRIES, when FAUSTO COPPI defeated Bartali to become the youngest winner ever, aged just 20.

After the close of the Second World War, the Giro was seen as a symbol of Italy getting back on its feet, with the first postwar edition christened the *Giro di Rinascita*: the Giro of Rebirth. The symbolism of sending cyclists from one end of the country to the other over roads ravaged by the war—in some cases they had to walk across temporary bridges—was impossible to ignore. The race proved that the country was on the move again.

The Giro has visited all Italy, including offshore islands such as Elba, and even running a time trial alongside Venice's canals to finish in Piazza San Marco (1978). From its earliest years, the race was hailed by *La Gazzetta dello Sport* as a way of uniting a country that had been a political whole for less than half a century.

The Giro has achieved that with a unique blend of heroism and skulduggery. The race is always run in late spring, when the climbs in the DOLOMITES are always vulnerable to foul weather; some of the greatest episodes (see 164) have taken place in snowstorms. The passion of the *tifosi*—Italy's crazily enthusiastic fans— means that foreign leaders have always found it hard to win; on occasions the fans have been seen to push their heroes up the great mountain passes, completely falsifying the results. At least one Giro, 1984, was decided largely because the organizer Vincenzo Torriani preferred a home

winner, FRANCESCO MOSER, to the Frenchman LAURENT FIGNON.

Particularly mountainous routes were devised in 1998 and 1999 to assist the climber MARCO PANTANI but the plan backfired in 1999 when Pantani was dominant until he was thrown off the race for failing a blood test, one of the biggest drugs scandals ever to hit cycling (see DRUGS for other major scandals in the sport and the Giro).

Even though one Italian star after another has fallen to the drugs testers, the Giro has retained its magic against the odds, helped by the passion of the *tifosi* and the arrival of foreign stars such as MARK CAVENDISH, who won a total of five stages in the race in 2008–9. The decision of LANCE ARMSTRONG to race the 2009 event simply added to the sense that the Giro was back to its old self after several difficult years.

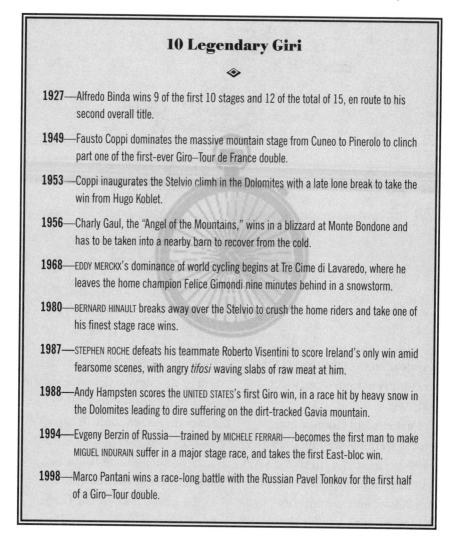

10 Legendary Giri

❖

1927—Alfredo Binda wins 9 of the first 10 stages and 12 of the total of 15, en route to his second overall title.

1949—Fausto Coppi dominates the massive mountain stage from Cuneo to Pinerolo to clinch part one of the first-ever Giro–Tour de France double.

1953—Coppi inaugurates the Stelvio climb in the Dolomites with a late lone break to take the win from Hugo Koblet.

1956—Charly Gaul, the "Angel of the Mountains," wins in a blizzard at Monte Bondone and has to be taken into a nearby barn to recover from the cold.

1968—EDDY MERCKX's dominance of world cycling begins at Tre Cime di Lavaredo, where he leaves the home champion Felice Gimondi nine minutes behind in a snowstorm.

1980—BERNARD HINAULT breaks away over the Stelvio to crush the home riders and take one of his finest stage race wins.

1987—STEPHEN ROCHE defeats his teammate Roberto Visentini to score Ireland's only win amid fearsome scenes, with angry *tifosi* waving slabs of raw meat at him.

1988—Andy Hampsten scores the UNITED STATES's first Giro win, in a race hit by heavy snow in the Dolomites leading to dire suffering on the dirt-tracked Gavia mountain.

1994—Evgeny Berzin of Russia—trained by MICHELE FERRARI—becomes the first man to make MIGUEL INDURAIN suffer in a major stage race, and takes the first East-bloc win.

1998—Marco Pantani wins a race-long battle with the Russian Pavel Tonkov for the first half of a Giro–Tour double.

GIRO DI LOMBARDIA The "race of the falling leaves" closes the professional cycle-racing year. Mellow mists and chilly rain often feature, and sometimes the first winter snow can be spotted on the ALPS. Afterward, farewells are said before the close season, and retirements quietly celebrated. Amusingly, the "falling leaves" themselves sometimes play a role: in 1992 the world champion Gianni Bugno was the big favorite, and the route had been arranged to finish in his home town, Monza, but he lost the race because he was too scared of crashing on the descents, which had been turned into skating rinks by the leaves and heavy rain.

Like the other MONUMENTS, Lombardy is a key link with cycle racing's origins. This was the first major race in Italy, although it is not the oldest (that honour goes to Milan–Turin, first run in 1876). It was founded in 1905, when Giovanni Gerbi was the winner, and run over tracks so bad that the field had to push their bikes for hundreds of meters at a time. Part of the route ran along a streetcar line.

Since then, the course has changed time and again. It has run through some of the highest passes in the Alpine foothills, and finished variously in Milan, Como, Monza, and Bergamo. It retains two constants: the mountains that border the lakes north of Milan, Lecco and Como, and the climb to the chapel at Madonna del Ghisallo (see CHAPELS for the significance of this landmark).

That ascent kick-started the career of cycling great ALFREDO BINDA, who turned professional in 1924 spurred on by the thought of a 500-lire prize awarded outside the chapel: he won it and never looked back. Lombardy was also where the Classic-winning career of SEAN KELLY took off in 1983; the Irishman also scored one of his greatest wins here in 1991.

The record winner is FAUSTO COPPI, who took four successive victories between 1946 and 1949, added another in 1954 and came agonizingly close in 1956, overtaken just two meters from the line in a defeat that summed up his painful decline. The DOUBLE of world championship victory and Lombardy in the same year is a rare feat. The only riders who have managed it are Binda (1931), TOM SIMPSON (1965), EDDY MERCKX (1971), and the Swiss Oscar Camenzind (1998).

GRASS TRACK RACING

GRASS TRACK RACING Dates back to cycling's 19th-century origins; racing on short oval circuits traced out on sports fields. The races are similar to those in conventional track racing, but usually shorter. Most popular now in Scotland, where a small group of semi-professionals make a living in summer on a circuit of events run at the Highland Games alongside caber-tossing and throwing the stone. There is also a British grass track league with a handful of weekend meetings. Tracks tend to be between 300–400 meters and are usually marked out with a painted white line and colored pegs and string. There are usually no bankings, although the Yorkshire town of Richmond boasts a very fine banked grass vélodrome, 362 meters around, at the cricket club. Racing has been going on here since 1892 when penny farthings were used, and the town's population would quadruple as spectators flocked to watch track meetings.

Bikes for grass track racing are similar to those used on paved or wooden tracks—single fixed gear, no brakes—but the gearing is lower, because grass is far harder to pedal through, no matter how short it is cut. The cranks may be slightly shorter as well, to lessen the risk of a pedal touching the ground on the curves, while wheels will be heavy-duty, with fatter tires than usual to ease out the bumps. The tires may be "tied" to the rim as well as glued, so that they will not slip off the rim when cornering. Specialists will take several sets of wheels and tires with them, then decide which to use depending on the conditions.

GOULLET, Alf (b. Australia, 1891, d. 1995)

An Australian-born, US-naturalized track racer, the record-breaking "King" of the SIX-DAY RACES held at Madison Square Gardens who earned more than Babe Ruth in his heyday. Goullet began racing in Australia, where he created his own track to train on by rolling a grass circuit using a log dragged behind a horse. He arrived in New York at the age of 19 and set a hat-trick of world records at Salt Lake City in 1912: two-thirds of a mile, three-quarters of a mile, and one mile. In 1914 he and his Australian partner, Alfred Grenda, set a record distance of 2,759.2 miles en route to victory in the Madison Square Gardens six-day, riding the final hour solo as Grenda had appendicitis. In 1916 he took American nationality; by the 1920s he was being paid $1,000 a day to race at a time when a single NFL franchise could be bought for a mere $100. He was hailed the "King of the Sixes" by the writer Damon Runyon. In 1921 firemen had to be called to the Garden to prevent gatecrashers from joining the 15,000-strong crowd; on the final night, he and the Tour de France star Maurice Brocco picked up $50,000 in prize money. By 1925 he had won the New York six-day eight times and won a total of about 400 races. He retired in 1934 and subsequently ran a skating rink. He was inducted into halls of fame in both the USA and Australia.

(SEE **MARSHALL WALTER TAYLOR** AND **A. A. ZIMMERMAN** TO READ ABOUT OTHER PIONEERING US STARS OF THE EARLY DAYS; SEE **HEROIC ERA** FOR MORE ON THE FORMATIVE YEARS OF CYCLE RACING.)

GREAT BRITAIN At the end of the naughts the nation that invented the safety bike and won the first ever road races looked set to become a world cycling superpower. The British were everywhere, thanks to MARK CAVENDISH, BRADLEY WIGGINS, Nicole Cooke, Emma Pooley, and others linked to the all-conquering Olympic team.

Cycling became popular early in Great Britain. The first recorded informal bike race took place in 1868 and Britain was at the forefront of boneshaker manufacturing. Abroad, JAMES MOORE won the first recorded road race in Paris and the first place-to-place event, Paris–Rouen. After that, it was downhill most of the way; the trouble began in the 1890s, even as cycling became massively popular. Tens of thousands were riding bikes, but racing on the road was made unlawful after a notorious incident in which a horse and cart collided with a race on the North Road (now the A1) during which cyclists were being paced by tricycles.

GREAT BRITAIN

TIME TRIALLING thus came into being, as a way cyclists could compete on British roads without attracting the attention of the police. The governing body, the NCU, became paranoid about road racing, initially refusing to recognize time trialling, and turned to supervising the track events that remained popular into the 1950s. As a result, cycle racing in Britain was in a backwater for almost a century.

There were track champions such as Leon Meredith, who won the world motorpaced title seven times between 1904 and 1913, but this was not uncommon. In 1922, the world championships were organized by the NCU, but were run as a time trial. In the 1930s, there was no road racing as such, but "massed start" races were run on circuits closed to traffic, such as the Brooklands motor racing track. In 1937, Britons Bill Burl and Charles Holland started the Tour de France; although Holland was physically up to the task, he was defeated by the lack of support for riders outside the major teams.

In 1942 Percy Stallard began organizing road races on European streets, taking advantage of the lack of traffic due to fuel rationing. Stallard was banned, opening the schism between the NCU and those who wanted racing continental style, grouped under the banner of the BLRC, British League of Racing Cyclists, who brought British cycling into the mainstream; road racing mushroomed at the grassroots level, various Tours of Britain came and went, and, suddenly, British cyclists began

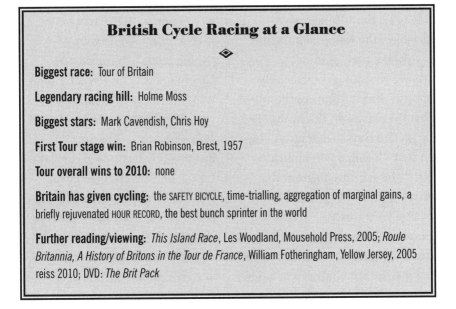

British Cycle Racing at a Glance

Biggest race: Tour of Britain

Legendary racing hill: Holme Moss

Biggest stars: Mark Cavendish, Chris Hoy

First Tour stage win: Brian Robinson, Brest, 1957

Tour overall wins to 2010: none

Britain has given cycling: the SAFETY BICYCLE, time-trialling, aggregation of marginal gains, a briefly rejuvenated HOUR RECORD, the best bunch sprinter in the world

Further reading/viewing: *This Island Race*, Les Woodland, Mousehold Press, 2005; *Roule Britannia, A History of Britons in the Tour de France*, William Fotheringham, Yellow Jersey, 2005 reiss 2010; DVD: *The Brit Pack*

competing at the European level.

From 1960, TOM SIMPSON acted as a role model by winning Classics and the world title in 1965. The presence of British teams in the Tour de France in 1960 and 1961 gave top British cyclists a point of entry to the largest race in the world. At home, the conflict between the NCU and BLRC ended in 1959 when the bodies merged to form the British Cycling Federation; in that year, the newly founded MILK RACE created a focus for the entire domestic calendar. Simultaneously, however, the rising popularity of cars resulted in all of cycling becoming increasingly marginalized. Running the world championships in the Midlands in 1970 and the Tour's first stage on British soil, at Plymouth in 1974, did nothing to stem the decline.

The 1982 world championships, run at Goodwood, made little impact on the media, but change was under way. A series of city-center races sponsored by Kellogg's in 1983 proved popular and was followed by a Tour of Britain in 1987. Critically, nightly television coverage of the Tour de France began in 1986 with commentary by PHIL LIGGETT. There was plenty to report on, with ROBERT MILLAR's ability to challenge for honors in the Tour and Vuelta, and the rise of English-speaking stars like SEAN KELLY, STEPHEN ROCHE, GREG LEMOND, and PHIL ANDERSON.

Although cycling remained marginalized at the highest level in Britain, events such as London to BRIGHTON made it clear that people wanted to ride bikes. An important turning point came when CHRIS BOARDMAN made headlines by winning the Olympic pursuit in Barcelona on a futuristic bike designed by legendary carmaker Lotus, and the Tour enjoyed two sunny days on the British south coast, in front of massive crowds, in 1994. Finally, at the end of 1996, the foundation of a British national lottery resulted in an influx of cash into

Olympic sports. Boardman's trainer Peter Keen drew up one of the first plans for how to use lottery funding, based on Boardman's Olympic and world title results, and the World Class Performance Plan began in 1997, with the aim of making Britain the world cycling champions.

By happy coincidence, a world-class facility was waiting for their use: the velodrome in Manchester had been constructed in the early 1990s and was the only tangible element of Manchester's Olympic bid, but it too was nearly bankrupt until the revamped GB team began paying to train there. Results were almost immediate with three medals, including one gold, in the 2000 Olympic Games, and the momentum didn't cease under Keen's successor as performance director, Dave Brailsford, who took over in 2003. By 2007 the team was firmly established as the number one in the world for track racing. The track racers' success led to the revival of the Tour of Britain, while in the Manchester velodrome, the long-

running Revolution events bred a track culture of their own. Meanwhile, the huge increase in cyclists riding CYCLOSPORTIVES, which were inspired by the Tour de France's spectacular Grand Depart in the capital in 2007, gave the cycle trade new buoyancy. Dominance in the 2008 world track championship and Beijing Olympics drew backing from the satellite company Sky, whose sponsorship included the running of Skyrides, group events for leisure cyclists on closed roads in major cities and a ProTour team run by Brailsford.

GREWAL, Alexi (b. Aspen, Colorado, 1960)

A talented climber from Colorado who became Olympic road race champion in the 1984 Summer Games at Los Angeles, but whose professional career never really got off the ground. Born into an Indian American family with two brothers who also raced, as did his father, a bike shop owner, Grewal dropped out of high school to train. Grewal was close to being deprived of a start in the 1984 Olympics after testing positive for the stimulant phenylethylamine. He protested the ban and was reinstated six days before the race. He has since spoken out against drug-taking in cycling. He described his 1984 L.A. win as his "smartest" victory, adding in an interview with PezCyclingNews, "I got the others working against each other and profited from that." On the 190 km course, Grewal was in the lead until he was caught by Steve Bauer with only 10 km remaining, but Grewal outsprinted the Canadian. The bicycle he rode to victory is now in the Smithsonian Institute's National Museum of American History. Grewal raced successive years in Europe for Panasonic, 7-Eleven, and RMO, all teams who were interested in his obvious climbing talents, but he had trouble coming to terms with European cycling; he was dropped by 7-Eleven after spitting at a television cameraman during the Tour de France, and he had effectively quit by mid-1987. He raced in the US until retirement in 1993, later working in construction making hand-built wooden homes; he also worked with the homeless in his hometown of Loveland. "For the last decade I've been one step away from the street," he said in a 2010 interview after announcing his comeback to racing. Grewal's brother Rishi raced successfully as a MOUNTAIN BIKING pro.

H

HAIR Leg-shaving is a rite of passage for most male cyclists, but beyond aesthetics and psychology the benefits are debatable. The most common claim is that hairless legs are more aerodynamic, but studies have shown that hair actually helps air flow over the legs. The most probable reason is that it is easier for professional team masseurs to work on smooth rather than hairy legs. Shaving probably began in the HEROIC ERA; with the amount of muck thrown up off the roads during races, the easier legs were to wash, the better, and with crashes so common, shaven legs meant bandages were simpler to put on and remove. There are exceptions: the Russian Dimitri Konyshev had a reputation for turning up to races with unshaven legs and still winning.

Moving upward, premature balding seems to be relatively common among professional cyclists, perhaps due to naturally high testosterone levels (in some cases, the male hormone may have been artificially enhanced), others maintain this is due to the heat build-up under shell helmets. Facial hair is a no-no for racing cyclists, but this is because of the amount of sweat, snot and sticky race food involved rather than aerodynamics.

Moustaches were relatively common in the Heroic Era— Eugène Christophe was nicknamed "the Gaul" and then "the Old Gaul" because of his drooping Asterix-style 'taches. Now, however, long hair, beards, and moustaches tend to be the mark of nonconformists, such as American wild man Bob Roll, who partnered his big beard with Hells Angel jackets and skull-design rings.

The same is true of the ponytails tied with elastic bands worn by LAURENT FIGNON, ROBERT MILLAR, and PHIL ANDERSON in the 1980s. Fignon said his fellow cyclists yelled at him that he looked like a girl. Millar would get a nasty crewcut every winter, he said,

so that he would not want to go to nightclubs. The goatee grown by MARCO PANTANI became a key part of his carefully nurtured "bad-boy' image as the "Pirate." The most fearsome beard cycling has ever seen was fictional, however: the terrifying facial hearthrug sported by the Russian star in the FILM *American Flyers*.

HARRIS, Reg

Born: Bury, England, March 1, 1920
Died: Macclesfield, England, June 22, 1992
Major wins: World professional sprint champion 1949, 1950, 1951, 1954; amateur world sprint champion 1947; seven British national titles; Olympic silver medallist sprint and tandem sprint, London 1948
Catchphrase: "Reg rides a Raleigh"
Further viewing: DVD: *Maestro*, 1985

In the 1950s and 1960s any cyclist seen pedaling at speed in a British town might draw the sarcastic

comment: Who do you think you are, Reg Harris? That reflected the public profile of the man who was the country's best-known cyclist in the postwar years. Harris achieved national fame for taking four world professional sprint titles between 1949 and 1954 after managing a brace of silver medals at the London Olympics in 1948 in spite of a series of injuries in the buildup.

He was voted British sportsman of the year in 1950 and was involved in one of cycling's most curious comebacks in his 50s. His notoriety at home surpassed even world road champion TOM SIMPSON, who was actually more famous in FRANCE and Belgium than in the UK. There is even a story that the sprinter himself was once stopped for running a red light and asked by police whether he thought he was Reg Harris: his reply is not recorded.

Harris began his working life at 14 as a motor mechanic in his native Lancashire and raced as an amateur in the prewar years, working in a paper mill in winter, supporting himself from prize money over the summer. In 1939 he traveled to the world track championship in Milan, only to be recalled on the outbreak of war. A tank driver in North Africa for the 10th Hussars, he was wounded in a German attack that wiped out all the rest of his tank crew and was deemed unfit to fight in 1943 due to his burns. He got back on his bike to rehabilitate after his injuries and a year later won three national championships on the track. He turned professional after the London Games and his battles with the Dutchman Arie Van Vliet on the indoor velodromes of Europe were legendary (see RIVALRIES). The late 1940s and early 1950s were one of track racing's boom times, with vast crowds flocking to venues such as the VÉLODROME D'HIVER in Paris, Fallowfield in Manchester, and Milan's Velodromo Vigorelli: Van Vliet and Harris were always at the top of the bill. He retired in 1957 but returned to racing in 1971 and took a bronze medal in the British championships. The story goes that Harris went to prepare at the Meadowbank stadium in Edinburgh and was asked by a young official "Have you ridden on a track before?" Harris replied that he had, but the blazer would not give up: "Have you ridden on a proper track like this?" Finally, someone asked Harris who he was. He followed up with gold in 1974 when he was 54 years old.

Like many successful cyclists, he was unable to match his sporting prowess in business: a bike-making venture failed, and he ended up as a salesman. He is now remembered with a fine statue in the Manchester velodrome in bronze by the sculptor James Butler.

(SEE ALSO **TRACK RACING**)

HELMETS Helmets became compulsory in professional racing from May 2003, although initially riders were allowed to remove them at the start of the final climb to a mountain top finish—where the climb was more than five kilometers long—which led to the bizarre sight of the entire field bunging their hats at team helpers as they sped onto mountains like l'Alpe d'Huez. That short-lived exception ended in 2005.

The initial resistance was partly cultural, partly macho. Helmets had been rapidly made mandatory for MOUNTAIN-BIKE racing in the late 1980s because of the risks involved and because they had been part of the sport from the beginning.

European road cyclists had used "skid-lids" made of leather strips since the early days; they were of no use whatsoever in a direct impact but might prevent abrasions. FAUSTO COPPI was ridiculed for wearing one on the orders of his wife after the death from head injuries of his brother Serse in 1951. They were

obligatory in Belgium and GREAT BRITAIN; in many other countries such as FRANCE you raced bare-headed.

Polystyrene shell helmets came from America in the 1970s. They acted as an outer "crumple zone" to protect the skull in an impact, with either a stiff outer polycarbonate layer or thin netting to protect the shell. Europeans mistrusted these initial models from companies like Bell, even though they were used by sensible types like GREG LEMOND and PHIL ANDERSON and teams such as 7-Eleven. They were seen as a cultural imposition rather than common sense.

About 1990, helmets began to use a thinner shell due to improvements in the molding process; recent years have seen improvements in straps and fitting and the introduction of carbon fiber. Thickness pads were used early on; today's helmets have cradles that can be precisely adjusted. They were made compulsory in British racing from 1992.

It seems incredible now, but in 1991 professional cyclists went on strike in protest against a new rule that stipulated they must wear shell helmets in all races. It was early March, the Paris–Nice race, and temperatures were still cool; they were worried about how it would feel wearing "big heavy things"

on their heads come the heat of summer.

There were calls for helmets to be made obligatory four years later, after the events of July 18, 1995. As the TOUR DE FRANCE peloton descended the narrow, twisting road from the Col de Portet d'Aspet in the Pyrénées, the Olympic champion Fabio Casartelli fell and hit his head on one of the concrete blocks by the roadside. He died from his injuries. His MEMORIAL now stands on the mountainside.

The final decision to make helmet use compulsory came after the Kazakh pro Andrei Kivilev had a fatal accident in March 2003. Now no one has a second thought about wearing them, partly because technology means that helmets have become lighter and better ventilated, partly because two fatal accidents in eight years of pro racing was a strong message.

Helmets have to meet national safety standards. To meet the criteria, helmets are tested by being dropped onto an anvil to imitate what would happen if a cyclist fell off and hit his or her head on the curb. The level set by the independent Snell Memorial Foundation is generally a little more strict than national standards.

Debate is ongoing over whether helmets should be made compulsory for all cyclists. A 1996 study published in the *British Journal of Sports Medicine* found that while doing this might save cyclists' lives, there was an equally strong case for making helmets obligatory for motorists and pedestrians and that there was "no justification for compelling cyclists to wear helmets without taking steps to improve the safety of all road users."

Opponents contend that compulsion would discourage cycling by overstating its dangers, and that the overall benefit to health by any reduction in head injuries would be countered by the negative impact on health of people giving up cycling due to the perception that it is dangerous.

Regardless of the law, the arguments for their use are convincing. As British Cycling Federation doctor Chris Jarvis pointed out: while they might not prevent death in the event of a direct collision with a motor vehicle, they are likely to downgrade head damage by one step in most impacts, turning what may have been concussion into a severe headache and what may have been a cracked skull into concussion, and so on.

HEROIC ERA   The term used to describe the pre–Second World War period of road racing, before improved bikes, road surfaces, and sophisticated team tactics made cycling more subtle, less purely physical, and less subject to the vagaries of fortune and the weather. Racing was strongly influenced by TOUR DE FRANCE organizer HENRI DESGRANGE, who believed the ideal race was one in which no cyclist was able to finish. One reason why the PARIS–ROUBAIX classic remains fascinating to this day is because it is professional cycling's last throwback to this time.

To create "the most courageous champions since antiquity," Desgrange banned derailleurs, slowed down technical development, and ran the Tour over inhuman distances culminating in the 5,745 km-long race of 1927. He imposed rules that now seem trivial and that outraged champions such as HENRI PÉLISSIER.

The era is only just outside living memory, but it seems remote, because few color photographs and sparse television footage remain: the image is one of mud-spattered cyclists carrying spare tires on their shoulders, gravelly roads, ill-fitting shorts, clunky-tubed bikes, stoic faces in goggles, rickety cars, and spectators who always seem to be in their Sunday best. The champion

who best epitomizes that time is Eugène Christophe of France, known as the "Old Gaul," who was the first rider to wear the yellow jersey in the Tour (see 180).

As if the demands of the roads of the time were not sufficient, there was no medical backup on the race until 1925, journalists complained about injured riders being left by the roadside after crashes, and officials were implacable. Christophe was not the only victim. The Pelissier brothers' disputes with Desgrange were typical of the frustrations felt by leading cyclists, captured in the celebrated article by Albert Londres in 1924 that led to the Tourmen being nicknamed "Convicts of the Road."

Mechanical troubles were a universal problem: in the 1919 Tour, one rider, Jean Alavoine, was estimated to have punctured 46 times. He completed his first Tour, in 1910, by carrying his broken bike six miles to the finish line, while the 1928 overall win by Nicolas

Heroes of the Heroic Era

◈

Honoré Barthélemy (France, b. 1890, d. 1964)

The Man with the Glass Eye. In the 1920 Tour de France he lost an eye after it was struck by a flint in a crash, but still finished the race eighth, half-blind and with a broken shoulder and dislocated wrist. He later rode with a glass eye, which he would take out when the roads were too dusty, filling the socket with cotton wool. On one occasion the eye fell out at the finish, and he had to go on his knees to find it.

Ottavio Bottecchia (Italy, b. 1894, d. 1927)

In 1924 Bottecchia was the first Italian to win the Tour de France and the first rider to lead the race from beginning to end. Bottecchia died in mysterious circumstances, being found dead on the roadside with head injuries: no one knew whether he fell off due to sunstroke, was murdered by the fascists, or killed by a farmer who was annoyed that he was stealing grapes. A brand of bikes bearing his name is still made today.

Eugène Christophe (France, b. 1885, d. 1970)

The "Old Gaul" won the 1910 Milan–San Remo in horrendous snow, but the incident that made him legendary happened in the 1913 Tour. Christophe was leading the race and set for victory when he was knocked off his bike and broke his forks while descending the Col du Tourmalet. Outside assistance was forbidden, so he made his way on foot to a local blacksmith's—eight miles away—and began repairing the fork himself, beginning with plain tubing. At one point, he asked a local boy to use the bellows, because his hands were occupied with the hammer. When he got back on his bike and completed the stage four hours behind the winner, he was docked a further two minutes for accepting help against the rules. A plaque now commemorates the episode. Christophe had a similar problem in the 1919 Tour when he had a 28 minute lead and appeared to be guaranteed overall victory: repairing the fork, again in a roadside forge, cost him two and a half hours.

François Faber (Luxembourg, b. 1887, d. 1915)

"The Giant," born in France but taking the nationality of his Luxembourgois father, had an imposing physique and won several CLASSICS in the years leading up to the First World War; he also took the 1909 Tour. It was a notoriously tough race: 50 of the field went home in the first week due to the appalling weather: gale-force winds and chilling rain that created deep ruts in the poorly made roads. He won five stages in a row, all the way from Roubaix on the Belgian border to Nice on the Mediterranean, and became massively popular, receiving poems and marriage offers in the mail afterward. He was killed on the Western Front early in the war.

Gustave Garrigou (France, b. 1884, d. 1963)

Finished in top five of the Tour de France eight times between 1907 and 1914, winning the 1911 race and taking a total of eight stages. One of the most consistent riders ever, finishing in the first 10 of 96 of the 117 Tour stages he rode. Later Garrigou described the roads in the mountains of the time as "just donkey tracks and I'm being polite" and recalled how he was paid five sovereigns for getting up the Tourmalet without walking.

Octave Lapize (France, b. 1887, d. 1917)

Faber's big rival in the 1910 Tour, which was the first to go through the Pyrénées or the Alps. Lapize won that year's race, but entered Tour legend after muttering the words "assassins" at the Tour organizers as he climbed the Col de l'Aubisque, fourth col of the first Pyrénean stage. Lapize was an all-rounder who won Paris–Roubaix three times; but the 1910 Tour was the only one he completed. He quit five times, complaining that the other riders ganged up on him. He became a fighter pilot in the First World War and died after being shot down in a dogfight.

Lucien Petit-Breton (France, b. 1882, d. 1917)

Christened Lucien Mazan but raced under an assumed name. Petit-Breton protested angrily when promoters referrred to him as *l'Argentin* after his country of birth. First man to win Milan–San Remo, and set an early HOUR RECORD, but is best known for winning the 1907 and 1908 Tours, the latter with five stage wins along the way. His first Tour, 1905, was truly bizarre: the race was sabotaged when nails were scattered on the route; Petit-Breton had no tires left so he quit and got the train to Paris, but he was then persuaded to return to the race where he was relegated to last place on the stage—but he still ended up fifth overall. Like other champions of the time, his life was cut short by the First World War.

Philippe Thys (Belgium, b. 1890, d. 1983)

The first man to win the Tour three times, and he would surely have won more had the First World War not intervened. He led the 1914 race from start to finish and won in spite of being fined half an hour for failing to show referees a broken wheel to prove that he had changed a wheel because of an accident. In 1919 he was never outside the first five on any Tour stage and was the first of seven Belgians in the overall standings.

Frantz of Luxembourg included 55 miles spent on a borrowed lady's bike after his own broke between Metz and Charleville. Saddle boils were common due to woolen clothing and muddy roads; raw steaks might be applied to ease the pain while as late as the 1920s the Tour's ration bags included a dose of neat spirits.

Accidents on the open road were frequent, particularly when the riders had to race at night on poorly maintained roads. The following report from *L'Auto* on the 1909 Bordeaux–Paris, sums up the spirit of the time: the race was "extremely hard: rain, snow and glacial cold. We watched a bitter battle in the middle of the night, and an accident. At La Couronne, five kilometers from Angouleme, Leon Georget hit a stone . . . performed a superb somersault, and as at that moment a [cycle] tourist was on his heels, he was brutally thrown several meters through the air. He lay stretched out, unconscious, and was taken to the nearest checkpoint in a piteous state . . . a broken collarbone and a deep wound in his head. As it froze fit to crack stone on the Poitiers road, Trousselier escaped. There was a crazy chase from the peloton and 'Trou-Trou' paid the price. The countryside was covered in a white blanket."

With cyclists trailing all over the countryside in most major races, rather than passing quickly in one compact bunch, they had more interaction with the public, who might watch a cyclist in the Tour eat a quick meal in a bar, or thaw out a hypothermic competitor in Milan–San Remo. There were numerous episodes of tacks being spread on the roads, while in the 1911 Tour it was alleged that one of the favorites, Paul Duboc, had been poisoned; so angry were the fans in his home town of Rouen that the race leader Gustave Garrigou had to be escorted through the town in disguise to avoid being lynched.

(SEE ALSO **ALFREDO BINDA, MAURICE GARIN, HUBERT OPPERMAN, HENRI PÉLISSIER**)

HERRERA, Luis (b. Colombia, 1961)

The "little gardener" was the most successful of the wave of Colombian cyclists who came to Europe after the TOUR DE FRANCE was declared "open" to amateurs in 1983. He became synonymous with their main sponsor, Café de Colombia. He earned his nickname because he spent his youth picking flowers in the fields near his birthplace, Fusagasugá.

In Herrera's first Tour, 1984, he won the prestigious mountaintop finish at l'Alpe d'Huez, riding away from BERNARD HINAULT and LAURENT FIGNON with a smooth, metronomic pedaling style, while in 1985 he won two more stages and took the mountains jersey, after reaching an agreement to help Hinault on the first mountain stage. Two years later he added the Tour of Spain to his *palmarès*.

Together with FEDERICO BAHAMONTES, Herrera is the only climber to be crowned King of the Mountains in all three major Tours. This was in spite of the fact that, like all Colombians, he had trouble adapting to European racing; he could not descend well and had trouble time-trialling and sprinting.

When he stopped racing he set up a cattle-breeding business, which was estimated to have made him $5 million, but his wealth made him a target for kidnappers. He was seized from his home in 2000 and held for 20 hours before being released; the amount paid for his ransom has never been disclosed.

(SEE ALSO **COLOMBIA, ALPS**)

HIBELL, Ian (b. England, 1934, d. 2008)

Enjoyed perhaps the longest and most strenuous sabbatical in cycling history. Given a year's leave of absence from his job in Brixham, Devon, in 1963, Hibell became one of the world's most prolific cycle-tourists until his untimely death 45 years later. He recounted his earlier exploits in his memoirs *Into the Remote Places* (Sphere, 1984). The image from that book that most perfectly sums up Hibell shows him paddling his bike across the Manurique river in South America, precariously balanced on a native-style canoe handmade of trees.

Hibell estimated he had used over 800 puncture-repair kits while touring the world, and he had ridden over 250,000 miles on conventional British touring cycles with handbuilt steel frames and drop handlebars: a Freddie Grubb carried him for over 100,000 miles, and he also used a pair of bikes made at Argos in Bristol. All were fitted with customized pannier racks, one with a brazed-on scraper to stop the frame clogging with mud.

His voyages included: Norway to the Cape of Good Hope; crossing the Sahara desert; Zeebrugge to Vladivostok; and north to south through China, this last when he was in his early 70s. Between 1971 and 1973 he became the first man to travel on land up the entire length of the American continent from Cape Horn to northwest Alaska. That tour involved crossing the Darien Gap, where the Atrato Swamp caused a supposedly impassable hiatus in the Pan-American highway. The uncharted space between the last village on either side is about 30 kilometers; for just under a month Hibell and his two companions slashed their way through the jungle, carrying their bikes over a surface of grass floating on the mud, at a rate of about one kilometer per day. In the process they ran out of food, fell out terminally with each other, and he came close to losing a foot after a misjudged blow with the machete.

Riding across Peru, he took with him a brown-haired girl from Manchester, Laura Nichols—referred to in *Into the Remote Places* as Jean—with whom he fell in love and had a son. In 1975, his escapades earned him an appearance on *Blue Peter*, where he cycled alongside presenter Peter Purves around the studio on his touring bike.

A British adventurer in the great tradition, he was caught in landslides, contracted malaria, braved spear-throwing tribesmen in Africa and murderous mobs inflamed by witch doctors, and at one point lay down under a thorn tree in the desert thinking he was going to die of dehydration.

He also had encounters with Eskimo princesses and a Dayak headman in Borneo. After all this, Hibell was mown down by a hit-and-run motorist in Greece while training for a trip to Tibet by riding from England to Athens. A collected volume of his print articles, *The Legend of Ian Hibell*, has been published posthumously.

HIGH-WHEELER Design of bike from the late 19th century with a large front wheel and small rear, with pedals driving direct to the front wheel. It is also referred to as an "ordinary" or "penny farthing." It was developed from the front-wheel driven BONESHAKER—in which both wheels were the same size— and had a heyday that lasted a quarter of a century, in which cycling became almost universal. It was superseded by the SAFETY BICYCLE.

The high-wheeler had a major advantage: if handled well the huge front wheel could absorb the ruts and potholes of poorly made 19th century roads. But it had its limitations: braking was difficult, gearing was restricted by the inside leg of the rider, and more seriously, it was intimidating to use and dangerous to ride, with head-first crashes all too frequent and fatalities not uncommon. The rider's position on top of the vast front wheel was inherently unstable—particularly in any kind of a wind— while steering was affected by the action of pedaling. It was recommended that when riding downhill, the safest position was with the legs over the handlebars so that if a "header" occurred, the cyclist could simply vault onto his feet.

Even so, high-wheelers became astonishingly popular. By the mid-1870s there were estimated to be about 50,000 on British roads. Cycling clubs and cycle races sprung up rapidly, which led to a battle between manufacturers to reduce weight. By the 1880s, the Cyclists' Touring Club had over 20,000 members and had approved almost 800 hotels for their use. By 1897 most major towns had cycling schools, teaching the skill in the same way that driving is taught today.

In America, the 1880s saw massive expansion in high-wheeler use, with the entrepreneurial Colonel Albert A. Pope as the driving force: Pope bought up all the available cycle patents, set up cycle mass production for his Columbia machine in Hartford, Connecticut, founded *The Wheelman* magazine, and set up the League of American Wheelmen to campaign for better roads for bicyclists. At the peak of bike mania, Pope was making a quarter of a million bikes per year. The volume of innovation was such that by the 1890s, the US needed a separate patent office for bicycles, while a single office could cover everything else.

The basic limitations of the high-wheeler led to further invention: to counter the gearing issue, machines such as the Coventry-made "Kangaroo" used chain drive and geared sprockets to enable a smaller front wheel to be used, while numerous more stable variants on the penny farthing design were tried, including the "star," which had the small wheel in front. The "xtraordinary" and the "facile" used lever drives to reduce the size of the front wheel. The "dicycle" had two large wheels in parallel with the rider sitting in between. These were all dubbed "safety" bikes, and eventually the high-wheeler became obsolete. Pope, naturally, was at the forefront, making his first safety bike in 1888.

HILL CLIMBS   A mass-start event up a major mountain pass, with the riders timed. Classic climbs include the Mount Evans hill-climb in Colorado, which takes in the highest paved road in the US, with a summit of 14,264 feet. It has been held since 1962. The course record for men is 1 hour 41 minutes 20 seconds by Tom Danielson (2004). JEANNIE LONGO holds the women's record with 1 hour 59 minutes 19 seconds. In New England, the Mount Washington Auto Road climb has been going for almost 40 years; the climb is 7.6 miles, the summit 6,288 feet, the steepest gradient 22 percent. The big attraction of the Mount Washington event is that apart from the three days when it is open for hill-climbs, the road is closed to cyclists.

The hill-climb in Great Britain is a time trial up a hill, from top to bottom, usually run at the end of the season as autumn sets in. The first hill-climb was run by the Catford CC in 1887, and their event on Yorks hill near Sevenoaks in Kent remains one of the classics, along with its near neighbor run by the Bec CC at Titsey in Surrey. Other classic British climbs include Monsal Head in Derbyshire, the Ramsbottom Rake in Lancashire, the Horseshoe Pass in North Wales, and Snake Pass in Derbyshire.

HINAULT, Bernard

Born: Yffiniac, France, November 14, 1954

Major wins: World road race championship 1980; Tour de France 1978–9, 1981–2, 1985, 28 stage wins; Giro d'Italia 1980, 1982, 1985, six stage wins; Vuelta a España 1978, 1983, seven stage wins; Paris–Roubaix 1981; Giro di Lombardia 1984; Liège–Bastogne–Liège 1977, 1980; Ghent–Wevelgem 1977, Flèche Wallonne 1979, 1983; Amstel Gold Race, 1981; GP des Nations 1977–9, 1982

Nickname: the Badger

Further reading: *Memories of the Peloton*, trans. Noel Henderson, 1989

During the 1992 TOUR DE FRANCE, you could buy fluffy badger toys with a picture of the five-time Tour winner, nicknamed *Le Blaireau* (the Badger), on sale for charity. It was a bizarre bit of marketing, as in real life Hinault was anything but cuddly: he remains one of the most combative cycling champions ever, earning his NICKNAME, as he said himself, "because a badger is a devil of an animal to deal with in a tight corner." It was also, he said on another occasion, because when wounded, the badger would retire to its burrow, lick its cuts, then come out fighting.

Celebrated as one of the elite club who have won five Tours de France, Hinault is stocky and outspoken, ready with a smile or a glare, aggressive on his bike and off it, most famously taking on a bunch of striking dockers who stopped the 1984 Paris–Nice race. He was not beyond throwing the odd punch in retirement, notably during the 2008 Tour de France when a demonstrator rushed on to the winner's podium at Nantes and the "Badger" gave no quarter. The clip is now a YouTube classic. Hinault said that one of his main reasons for going to school was that there might be a fight on the way there.

As a pro cyclist he was legendary as a boss or *patron* who would make the bunch race his way or suffer for their impudence. "Sometimes he would attack and the peloton would string out into a long line. Then he would sit up and start laughing, mocking us. He had a god-like aura, but I didn't like him," recalled the cyclist-turned-journalist Paul Kimmage. ROBERT MILLAR said he was so fearsome that the number 666 should be tattooed on his forehead. In 1984, having lost the Tour to LAURENT FIGNON, he took out a full-page advertisement in *L'Equipe*, proclaiming: "I shall be back next year. The badger has claws and intends to use them." True to his word he returned to win a fifth Tour in 1985.

Together with his La Vie Claire teammate GREG LEMOND he produced one of the greatest Tours ever when he finished second in 1986 after three weeks when their RIVALRY turned the event into a hotbed of intrigue and mindgames. His greatest wins came in the face of adversity, be it the crash in the 1985 Tour that left him with two black eyes and a broken nose or the ding-dong battle with Joop Zoetemelk in the 1979 race that ended with the pair sprinting out the finish together on the Champs-Elysées.

His greatest victory, perhaps, was when he dominated Liège–Bastogne–Liège in a snowstorm that forced most of the field to retire in 1980. He rode with bare legs and ended up with fingers that remained numb for three weeks afterward. He also crushed the field in the 1980 world championship to prove a point after quitting that year's Tour with a knee injury. That was a devastating race: a series of searing attacks on the Domancy hill at Sallanches that left the field in tatters. The Badger's retirement was typical: he had always said he would quit at 32, so he organized a cyclo-cross race in his village in Brittany five days before his birthday, finished 14th in front of a crowd of 15,000, and never raced again. He worked for the Tour de France organizers from 1989 onwards and remains a pungent commentator on cycling, most notably in 2009, when he had a media spat with LANCE ARMSTRONG.

HOBBY HORSE   Early bicycle with no pedals, powered by the rider pushing his feet against the ground, also known as the DRAISIENNE. See that entry for more details.

HOLLAND   The only European country where a conscious, long-term nationwide effort has been made to promote cycling as transport. It has 19,000 kilometers of bike lanes; nearly 85 percent of the population own at least one bike, and there are estimated to be 16 million bikes in the country. Cycling has been made such an attractive option that in one town, Groningen, 57 percent of all journeys are made by bike and virtually all the children cycle to school, some travelling up to 20 km.

The Dutch did not implement a national cycling policy until 1990, but as early as the 1970s there had been an increasing awareness that unrestrained road building to accommodate ever-growing car traffic was not possible; there wasn't enough space in this densely populated country. Beginning in 1974 the cycle route network was massively expanded, with investment of some $230 million; from 1990 all major cities had to implement plans for increased cycle use. The result is a massive network of traffic-free cycle paths, many of them two-way, with junctions at motor-traffic roads specially designed for cycle safety, including underpasses and bridges and clearly marked areas where cyclists can wait at traffic lights in front of cars. The aim, said one cycling policy paper, was to ensure that "all traffic participants must have equal rights."

Groningen offers a detailed view of what can be done. Proactive cycling policies began in 1969: over the years, car access to the city center has been restricted, initially in the face of opposition from businesspeople and shopkeepers. Through traffic was removed from the center, and cars directed to parking lots.

AMUSING DUTCH FACTOID

Cycle racing was banned on Sundays until the 1950s.

HOLLAND

and carriers; there are 15 at various schools. At traffic lights heavy flows of cyclists were given priority. Investment in cycle-specific facilities between 1989 and 2000 was some 23 million euros, with cycle-friendly facilities also forming part of other investment programs.

Policy documents available through the Dutch cycling information service make it clear that this has only been achieved by sustained long-term investment over several decades, with every planning decision taking into account how people are going to travel and how they can best be accommodated. Food for thought as cities grapple with congestion and climate change.

By 2000 a huge network of cycle lanes had been built (equivalent to perhaps 60 percent of the major roads); from 1980 secure, supervised cycle storage facilities were provided, roughly one a year. These provide lockers, repair facilities, rent racks,

HORSES Contests between cyclists and horses were popular in the US in the pioneering days of bike racing. The *Lordsburg Liberal* from 1888 tells of "an ugly but tough" horse that cost

$350 beating a bike over 49 miles through Colorado, while the *New York Times* published a lengthy report in 1888 of a SIX-DAY RACE in Madison Square Garden between men and horses, using an earth track for the horses outside a boarded bike track. The match pitted long-distance horse rider Charles M. Anderson against two cyclists, Irish champion William Woodside and Pennsylvania champion John Brooks; Anderson had 20 horses and could change at will, while the cyclists rode for an hour each. Racing was from 1 PM to 1 AM, to the sound of a regimental band playing tunes from *The Mikado*. The winner is not recorded.

Occasionally during the 20th century cyclists raced horses purely as stunts, including Italian CAMPIONISSIMO Costante Girardengo, Rik Van Steenbergen of Belgium, and Italian climber Claudio Chiappucci. There was also speculation about a match between Mario Cipollini and a stallion named Varenne, although it seemed that Cipo's interest in the contest was partly to invite comparison between his sexual exploits and those of the stallion. (See SEX.)

The longest-standing Man v. Horse contest took place between 1985 and 1994 in the Mid-Wales town of Llanwrtyd Wells, which hosts various bizarre events including the world bog-snorkelling championship. The Man v. Horse marathon was for runners, mountain bikes, and horses over an insanely mountainous 22-mile course that included a forest section, where the cyclists had to crawl through deep mud underneath fir tree branches that came down to a couple of feet above the track. It was sponsored by bookmakers William Hill, who invited bets on whether two legs could beat four. The first biker or runner to best the quadrupeds was mountain-bike legend Tim Gould of Yorkshire, who earned £5,000 in 1989 for beating a horse called the Doid. Gould was helped a little when the organizers ruled that vets' checks on the horses had to be included in their times.

Tougher regulations over racing mountain bikes on bridleways mean that the race is now restricted to runners against horses.

HOUR RECORD
Another influential innovation from the mind of TOUR DE FRANCE founder HENRI DESGRANGE, cycling's Blue Riband withstood the test of time almost as well as the Tour, but after more than a century it was eventually rendered meaningless by official interference.

Whereas the Tour de France created its mystique by making its participants into supermen with deeds that defied most people, the Hour is simplicity itself: how far can you go in 60 minutes? And while the Tour men performed away from public gaze, mediated by journalists and television—even if you see the Tour today on the road, it's only a fleeting glimpse—the Hour has always been a public display of just what a man can physically achieve. Circling a velodrome for 60 minutes against a schedule, any show of weakness is instantly visible: if an Hour contender has to give up, that means public humiliation.

The first man to attempt the feat was JAMES MOORE, winner of the first bike races in the late 1860s. He covered 23 km on an old ordinary in Wolverhampton in 1873, but there was no world governing body to recognize the feat. Desgrange, riding on the Buffalo track in Paris 20 years later, set the first officially sanctioned distance, then retired to work as a journalist. What he left cycling was an absolute measure of what men could achieve on two wheels with the means available to them at a certain time.

The first great Hour duel lasted seven years. Just before the First World War the Swiss Oscar Egg and the Frenchman Marcel Berthet between them put 2.7 km on the distance. Egg eventually took the record over 44 km, a distance that stood for 19 years. When it was eventually beaten, the Swiss demanded that the track in Holland used by Jan Van Hout be remeasured. Initially it was ruled that Van Hout's record was short, then it was decided that the measurement had been done too low down the track, and the record stood.

The distance set by FAUSTO COPPI in 1942 is legendary less for the distance than for another spat over measuring, with the previous holder Maurice Archambaud, and the fact that Coppi was racing in extreme conditions, with Milan under British bombardment. The attempt was timed for the early afternoon, as the bombers tended not to attack during factory lunchbreaks.

After Coppi, the Hour became obligatory for any great: JACQUES ANQUETIL succeeded in breaking the record twice, but his second attempt was not recognized, as he refused to undergo drug testing. EDDY MERCKX set what was viewed as a definitive distance in Mexico City in 1972. He virtually had to be lifted off his bike afterward, and swore he would never attempt the record again because he had suffered so much for his 49.431 km.

Merckx had used what was then cutting-edge technology, reflecting the idea that what mattered was making the bike as light as possible. His handlebars had 48 drill holes, 95 g were saved by drilling every slot in the chain, and his bike maker Ernesto Colnago made specially light tubular tires (70 g) and used titanium for spokes, stem, and bars. Merckx also attempted to replicate the high altitude of Mexico by training in a mask so that he breathed in air with reduced oxygen content as he trained.

Athlete's Hour Record:

2000	**CHRIS BOARDMAN**	Manchester	49.441 km
2005	Ondrej Sosenka	Moscow	49.700 km

However, his approach was positively primitive compared with FRANCESCO MOSER 12 years later. The Italian and his 50-strong backup team paid meticulous attention to AERODYNAMICS and diet, and the outcome was that Merckx's record was smashed not once, but twice in a few days. That feat led to aerodynamic aids such as low-profile bikes, disc wheels, and teardrop-shaped helmets becoming widely accepted.

The final, and perhaps finest, flurry of activity came between 1993 and 1996 when GRAEME OBREE and CHRIS BOARDMAN pushed the boundaries of aerodynamics and technology still further. Obree's radical tuck position proved that new thinking was possible in cycling, while Boardman—and his coach Peter Keen—took the scientific approach that was a foretaste of the British Olympic team's philosophy a few years later. That it took two of the best road racers of the 1990s, MIGUEL INDURAIN and his understudy Tony Rominger, to wrest the record from the two Britons spoke volumes about their achievements.

The Hour that stands above all the rest was also the record's last 60 minutes: Boardman's 56.375 km, set in Manchester after the 1996 Olympics using Obree's stretched out "Superman" position. Here was a man in perfect form on a machine at the limit of what was permitted at the time. "I did one minute flat for the last kilometer which is about a second off the world record," recalled Boardman. "That is how good I felt."

But the Hour's time was up. Cycling's governing body, the UCI, had been concerned by Obree's innovations and by Boardman's use of the radical Lotus bike (see MIKE BURROWS for more on that machine) and felt that technology was beginning to detract from the human side of cycling: the bikes were becoming more important than the men on them.

Their answer was to have two records. Any technology was acceptable in setting the Best Hour Performance, while gear similar to that used by Merckx was obligatory for the Athlete's Hour. Boardman's final feat before retirement was to break, narrowly, Merckx's distance, but the next beating of the hour, by the Russian Ondrej Sosenka, barely made headlines. Meanwhile, the legal niceties of what equipment could and could not be used—there was debate over pulse monitors and cycle computers, for example—made future hour attempts akin to tiptoeing through a bureaucratic minefield.

Further reading/viewing: *The Hour: Sporting Immortality the Hard Way*, Michael Hutchinson, Yellow Jersey, 2006; DVD: *The Final Hour*

Year	Rider	Location - Distance
1893	Henri Desgrange	Paris - 35.325
1894	Jules Dubois	Paris - 38.22
1897	Oscar van den Eynde	Paris - 39.24
1898	William Hamilton	Denver - 40.871
1905	Lucien Petit-Breton	Paris - 41.11
1907	Marcel Berthet	Paris - 41.52
1912	Oscar Egg	Paris - 42.36
1913	Marcel Berthet	Paris - 43.775
1914	Oscar Egg	Paris - 44.247
1933	Jan Van Hout	Holland - 44.588
1933	Maurice Richard	Belgium - 44.777
1935	Giuseppe Olmo	Milan - 45.09
1936	Maurice Richard	Milan - 45.325
1937	Frans Slaats	Milan - 45.485
1937	Maurice Archambaud	Milan - 45.767
1942	Fausto Coppi	Milan - 45.848
1956	Jacques Anquetil	Milan - 46.159
1956	Ercole Baldini	Milan - 46.393
1957	Roger Rivière	Milan - 46.923
1958	Roger Rivière	Milan - 47.346
1967	Ferdinand Bracke	Rome - 48.093
1968	Ole Ritter	Mexico City - 48.653
1972	Eddy Merckx	Mexico City - 49.431
1984	Francesco Moser	Mexico City - 50.808
1984	Francesco Moser	Mexico City - 51.151
1993	Graeme Obree	Hamar, Norway - 51.596
1993	Chris Boardman	Bordeaux - 52.27
1994	Graeme Obree	Bordeaux - 52.713
1994	Miguel Indurain	Bordeaux - 53.04
1994	Tony Rominger	Bordeaux - 53.832
1994	Tony Rominger	Bordeaux - 55.291
1996	Chris Boardman	Manchester - 56.375

KMs 30 35 40 45 50 55 60 65

Evolution of the Hour Record

HOY, Sir Chris

Born: Edinburgh, Scotland, March 23, 1976

Major wins: Olympic gold sprint, team sprint, kilometer 2008; Olympic gold kilometer 2004; Olympic silver team sprint 2000; world champion sprint 2008, Keirin 2007–8; kilometer 2002, 2004, 2006, 2007, team sprint 2002, 2005; Commonwealth champion, kilometer, 2002, team sprint 2006; MBE 2004; knighted 2008

Nickname: the Real McHoy

Further reading: *Heroes, Villains and Velodromes*, Richard Moore, Harpersport, 2008; *Chris Hoy, the Autobiography*, Chris Hoy, Harper Collins UK, 2010

The greatest cycling Olympian GREAT BRITAIN has produced, winner of three Olympic gold medals at the Beijing Games in 2008, and the first cyclist to be elected BBC Sports Personality of the Year since TOM SIMPSON in 1965. Hoy began his cycling life as a juvenile BMX star and moved to mountain-biking and road racing before becoming a track racer at the Meadowbank velodrome in Edinburgh, taking a silver medal in the British junior sprint championship in 1994. Hoy's career was transformed when national lottery funding arrived in British cycling in 1997; he was one of the early beneficiaries of the World Class Performance Plan put together by CHRIS BOARDMAN's trainer Peter Keen.

Together with Jason Queally and Craig Maclean, he made the initial breakthrough with a silver medal in the team sprint at the 1999 world championship in Berlin. The Sydney Olympic Games a year later saw Queally take kilometer gold while Hoy, Queally, and Maclean raced to silver in the team sprint. Hoy's breakthrough year was 2002, with gold medals in the kilometer and team sprint at the world championship. In 2004 he took the kilometer gold at the Athens Games, only for the UCI to drop the event from the Olympic program. Even so, Hoy then added a further six world titles in the next three years, including the world sprint championship in Manchester in 2008. No Briton had won the title since REG HARRIS in 1954.

In 2007 Hoy traveled to the Bolivian capital, La Paz, to attack the Frenchman Arnaud Tournant's standing start kilometer record. The Scot was warned before he rode that there was a risk he might collapse afterward with pulmonary edema, a buildup of fluid on the lungs. Oxygen canisters and an oxygen-filled body-bag were on standby. The velodrome there is poorly maintained: the surface is bumpy and before Hoy made his bid, the waist-high grass in the track center had to be cut with scythes.

Hoy's attempt cost tens of thousands of pounds—he made no money out of it for himself, the sponsorship cash all went into logistics—took a year's planning, and ended in relative failure when he failed, twice, to beat Tournant's time, falling short by just 0.005 seconds on his second attempt. Smashing the 500 m record was meager compensation, but record-breaking is an unforgiving business.

Beijing was the climax of his career, however. The gold rush began on day one with a blistering team sprint together with Jamie Staff and the virtually unknown Jason Kenny. The trio recorded 42.95 seconds in qualifying, the fastest time ever recorded for the three-man, three-lap effort, which broke the spirit of their main rivals, the French and Australians. The final was a formality; as was Hoy's title in the KEIRIN the following day. From the previous year's world championship in Palma, Mallorca, he had developed his own style, attacking early and relying on his strength to keep him ahead of the opposition. The silver medal went to another Scot, Ross Edgar, on a day when Great Britain landed seven medals.

The third event was the most prestigious of the series, the match sprint, and in the final Hoy was pitted against Kenny, who was no match for the older man. On taking gold number three the Scot collapsed into the arms of his father, David, and dissolved into tears prompting the headline: "The Great Bawl of China." "We try to act like robots, to keep our emotions capped throughout the whole process. That's why it all came out afterwards," Hoy later explained.

Hoy is outwardly mild-mannered and genial, but inside he is a driven man. "Bottom line, he's selfish," said performance manager Shane Sutton. "He's a gentle giant with the big Mike Tyson neck. He's a trainoholic: he loves getting up, going to work and leaving everything on the track." Hoy worked with the team psychiatrist Steve Peters in the buildup to the Athens Olympics to overcome his nerves—the kilometer is a waiting game, when you have to watch the opposition performing which can be intimidating. "There's a myth that sports people are very self-confident but I'd say a high percentage are wracked with self-doubt. Ten minutes before the start you'd rather be anywhere else." Hoy wrote his MEMOIRS in 2009 and as the London Games hove into view, he was hinting that his best days might be yet to come.

(SEE ALSO TRACK RACING, OLYMPIC GAMES)

HUMAN POWERED VEHICLES

The International Human Powered Vehicle Assocation was founded in California in 1975. HPVs are in essence any cycle with aerodynamic parts that fall outside UCI rules. These can include conventional diamond-frame bikes with fairings to enhance AERODYNAMICS, or RECUMBENT machines that offer a lower profile. The HPV HOUR RECORD is 87.123 km, set in 2008; compared with the conventional bike record of 49.7 km, the speed advantage speaks for itself.

I

INDOOR CYCLING Umbrella term for two disciplines in which the UCI recognizes world championships: cycle ball and artistic cycling. The first is similar to soccer, with the cycle wheels used to kick the ball; the second is a form of bicycle gymnastics using specially made low-gear cycles.

INDURAIN, Miguel

Born: Villava, Spain, July 16, 1964
Major wins: Olympic time trial champion 1996; world time trial champion 1995; Tour de France 1991, 1992, 1993, 1994, 1995, 12 stage wins; Giro d'Italia 1992, 1993, four stage wins; San Sebastian Classic 1990; world hour record 1994
Nicknames: Big Mig
Interests outside cycling: tractor repair, reading, sleeping

While other TOUR DE FRANCE greats such as LANCE ARMSTRONG and BERNARD HINAULT wore their hearts on their sleeves and FAUSTO COPPI and JACQUES ANQUETIL made headlines with scandal in their private lives, "Big Mig" was famously impenetrable, verging on the boring. However, he was not without his wry side, as the American journalist Dan Coyle depicted in the book *Tour de Force*. Indurain is shown a $250,000 time trial bike developed in secret by a team of technicians; asked what he thinks of it, he replies, "Very good, but don't forget about the legs."

The suspicion lingered that anyone who delved behind a façade consisting of a shy grin, understated humor, and banal statements of the obvious would find there was not a great deal hidden underneath, other than the fact that Miguel was a dab hand at tractor maintenance and was sadly missed on his family's farm when he was away racing. One Spanish sports journalist complained that "Twenty years from now, the woman of his life will not know who she has spent her life with."

Indurain's cycling career began with the tractor: one day as a child he rode to the fields to play on the machine and had his bike stolen by a pair of tramps. To console him, he was given his first racing bike, becoming a fine sprinter as a teenager. Slimmed down from his amateur days but still weighing in at 182 pounds, Indurain could have won the 1990 Tour had he not been told to assist his team leader Pedro Delgado at a critical moment. As it was, he dominated the Tour de France from 1991 to 1995, taking a "double of doubles" in 1992 and 1993 in the Giro and Tour and becoming, briefly, Spain's most popular sportsman, named the country's athlete of the 20th century: the victory that defined his career was in the Luxembourg time trial in the 1992 Tour that GREG LEMOND described as "from another planet." For the next three years, he was totally dominant in the event.

In 1994, for all his massive shoulders, he was seen riding over the Mont Ventoux in the Tour at 21 mph with his team managers pleading with him to slow down for his own good; that year he put in the definitive mountain performance of his career, burning off all the climbers such as MARCO PANTANI at Hautacam in the Pyrenées. He also broke the HOUR RECORD at the end of that year. A pragmatic, gentle giant, he dominated the Tour because his fellow cyclists liked him as well as fearing the power in his legs. "I pray to Saint Michael every time I want to stop for a pee," said ROBERT MILLAR, implying that if Indurain decided to attack he might be in serious trouble.

Indurain faced one major crisis in his five victorious Tours, when the ONCE team put him under massive pressure in a 1995 Tour stage through the Massif Central to the town of Mende; Big Mig's Banesto team cracked but he had given out so many favors in the previous four Tours that virtually every team in the race was willing to help in the chase.

Indurain was said to have lost his temper while racing only four or five times, once en route to defeat in the 1996 Tour. His implacable good nature meant he remained immune to stress as the Tour grew in size through the 1990s: his almost exclusive focus on the race—he used the Giro essentially as preparation—contributed to the Tour's transformation into the dominant event in the cycling calendar. He retired in January 1997, embittered at his team after they pushed him to start the 1996 Tour of Spain against his will, and now lives near the family home in Villava, a suburb of the northern Spanish city of Pamplona. His brother Prudencio also raced briefly as a pro. (SEE ALSO **SPAIN**)

IRELAND A "small" cycling nation that has consistently punched above its weight and has produced a fine array of international stars in spite of over half a century of political conflict between various governing bodies. More significantly, perhaps, Ireland was where the pneumatic tire was patented by John Boyd Dunlop and the first bike using those tires was advertised by one Will Edlin, of Dunlop's home city, Belfast.

Ireland had an early star in Harry Reynolds, world amateur sprint champion in 1896. Then it lay fallow as cycling became bound up in the conflict over national identity. Even so, TIME TRIALLING, British style, went on, but with one important difference: the Irish could wear shorts rather than black alpaca tights. That meant they could go faster, and the outcome was that the key time-trialling barrier for the English, 25 miles inside an hour, was actually first broken in Ireland in 1934, when Alo Donegan rode 59 minutes 5 seconds; four years later, the Englishman George Fleming visited Ireland to push the record down to 57 minutes 56 seconds.

Reflecting the politics of the island, Irish cycling was split between those who wanted it united, north and south, and those who didn't. The dispute led to violent scenes such as those in 1956 at the RÁS—an eight-day stage race which remains the linchpin of the calendar—when an Irish tricolor was carried over the border to Northern Ireland on the race lead car. The Irish flag was banned in the North, so when police tried to remove the flag, there was a fracas and the stage was abandoned. As the riders cycled to the finish, Republican songs were sung and one rider tried to remove a Union Jack from a telegraph pole. In Cookstown there was a riot involving a unionist crowd and police, and one rider was badly beaten.

There were also incidents at the 1955 world championship and the 1972 Olympic Games, where there were fights between rival Irish teams.

Amid all this, Ireland's pioneer emerged: in 1954 Shay Elliott, a quiet lad from Dublin, won a mountain stage in the Route de France amateur race; the following season he raced for ACBB in Paris (see FOREIGN

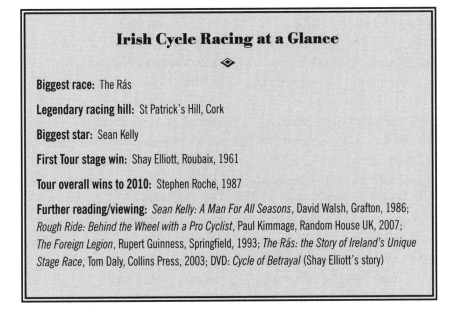

Irish Cycle Racing at a Glance

Biggest race: The Rás

Legendary racing hill: St Patrick's Hill, Cork

Biggest star: Sean Kelly

First Tour stage win: Shay Elliott, Roubaix, 1961

Tour overall wins to 2010: Stephen Roche, 1987

Further reading/viewing: *Sean Kelly: A Man For All Seasons*, David Walsh, Grafton, 1986; *Rough Ride: Behind the Wheel with a Pro Cyclist*, Paul Kimmage, Random House UK, 2007; *The Foreign Legion*, Rupert Guinness, Springfield, 1993; *The Rás: the Story of Ireland's Unique Stage Race*, Tom Daly, Collins Press, 2003; DVD: *Cycle of Betrayal* (Shay Elliott's story)

LEGION for other stars to come through this club) and in 1956 he turned professional, at a time when racers from outside the European heartland were truly the exception.

Elliott took groundbreaking wins in the Het Volk CLASSIC and stages in the Giro, Tour, and VUELTA A ESPAÑA, as well as becoming the first Irishman to lead the Tour and the Vuelta. He also took a silver medal in the 1962 world road race championship, but by the late 1960s his career was on the slide. His marriage failed, as did a hotel he owned; he returned to Ireland but never truly put his life back on the rails and in 1971 he committed suicide. He is remembered with a MEMORIAL on the pass of Glenmalure in the Wicklow Hills, and a road race is organized annually in his honor.

The political rumblings continued, and it took six years for Elliott's successor to emerge: the arrival of SEAN KELLY in pro cycling began a golden era for Irish cycling, with STEPHEN ROCHE joining him in taking the sport to new heights in the 1980s, when between them the pair won all three major Tours, the world championships, and a welter of stage races and Classics, with Kelly ranked world number one for six years. That decade also saw the foundation of the around-Ireland Nissan Classic stage race and produced other professionals: Martin Earley, who enjoyed a solid career as a *domestique*, Roche's brother Laurence, and Paul Kimmage, who went on to a controversial career as an award-winning journalist.

After Kelly and Roche retired, the Nissan ended and Irish cycling reverted to what it had been: based around the Rás, with occasional star performances at international level. The 1998 world junior champion Mark Scanlon never quite made it, but the foundation of an Irish cycling academy in 2005, and a second division pro team—both with Kelly's support—provided an injection of energy.

Most promisingly of all, in

2006–7 the sport was unified for the first time thanks to the process of political reconciliation in the North. A professional Tour of Ireland emerged again, with LANCE ARMSTRONG among the 2009 field, and that year saw three promising young riders on the pro circuit: Roche's son Nicolas—who came close to winning a stage in the Tour—his nephew Daniel Martin, and Philip Deignan, who won a stage in the 2009 Vuelta.

Ireland has given cycling the pneumatic tire, PHIL LIGGETT'S most memorable quote ("It's Roche, it's Stephen Roche"), and too many convivial evenings to count on the Nissan Classic and Rás.

ITALY   Cycle racing began early in Italy, with the first event recorded in Padua in 1869. Firenze–Pistoia, the oldest cycle race still run, began in 1870, Milan–Turin in 1876. The GIRO D'ITALIA was founded in 1909 but there was none of the conflict with the bike manufacturers that resulted in tension at the TOUR DE FRANCE. Instead, the organizers welcomed the bike makers' teams, who in turn liked an easier course that would result in more predictable racing, one result being ALFREDO BINDA's outrageous dominance. The ALPS and DOLOMITES did not figure until the 1930s—whereas in France HENRI DESGRANGE sought to make his Tour as tough as possible.

Italian cycling developed its own way of thinking, focused heavily on the *campione* or CAMPIONISSIMO, with teams constructed around helping the star. For example, just four riders—Binda, Costante Girardengo, Gaetano Belloni, and Giovanni Brunero—won virtually every major race in the 1920s, and that set a pattern that lasted until the

21st century, when *campioni* regularly fell foul of antidoping rules. The small number of stars set the stage for the RIVALRIES that marked Italian cycling— some real, many blown up by the press—while making cycling easy to read for the public.

Desgrange's decision to move to national teams prompted more of the *campioni* to appear in the Tour, with GINO BARTALI taking a dominant win in the 1938 edition with the backing of Mussolini's fascist regime, which pulled strings to make sure he did not waste his strength racing that year's Giro.

Italian Cycle Racing at a Glance

◆

Biggest race: Milan–San Remo

Legendary racing hill: Stelvio or Poggio

Biggest star: Fausto. Or is it Gino?

First Tour stage win: Vincenzo Borgarello, Perpignan, 1912

Tour overall wins to 2009: 9

Italy has given cycling: Campagnolo, Coppi, the *campione* concept, team racing, rivalries, the *tifosi*, *polemica*, but one thing above all else: passion

Great Italian Cycling Manufacturers: Where They Live and the Bits They Make

❖

Campagnolo: Vicenza. See separate section on the iconic component maker.

Pinarello: Treviso. Founded 1952, Italy's most successful frame maker of recent years, winning Tour de France nine times since 1988, notably with MIGUEL INDURAIN from 1991–5. Sponsors British Team Sky in 2010. Iconic machines: Montello SLX used by Alexi Grewal to win 1984 Olympic road race, made with Columbus steel tubing rifled inside for strength; initials GPT (Giovanni Pinarello, Treviso) stamped in various places. Paris, aluminium frame with carbon front and rear forks used by Jan Ullrich to win 1997 Tour.

Cinelli: Milan. Component maker established in 1948 by Cino Cinelli, a pro who won the 1943 Milan–San Remo, and passed to the Columbus owners in 1978; emblem is a winged C. Cino set out making bars and stems with his brother Giotto, but the company produced a limited number of frames in the 1970s, including an aerodynamic machine for Ole Ritter's HOUR RECORD attempt of 1974, and still makes bikes in the green-white-red of the Italian flag. Iconic products: Cork bicycle ribbon (1987); Spinaci handlebar extensions (1996).

Colnago: Cambiago, near Milan. Established in 1954 by Ernesto Colnago, with its emblem a clover leaf. Colnago made the super-light bike used by EDDY MERCKX to break the HOUR RECORD in 1972 and Giuseppe Saronni's world-title-winning bike in 1982, and was a partner to the Mapei team in the 1990s. Made the first front fork with straight blades, the Precisa in 1982. Now sources some of its bikes in Taiwan. Iconic designs: Master, C-40.

De Rosa: Cusano Milanino, near Milan. Founded mid-1950s by Ugo de Rosa; a small concern that began making bikes for Eddy Merckx in the late 1960s and later became official supplier to his Molteni team. Later, De Rosa advised Merckx when he started his own bike factory. Other stars to ride De Rosa include Francesco Moser, Moreno Argentin. Iconic design: Titanio, ridden by Gewiss in 1994.

Bianchi: Treviglio, east of Milan. The oldest surviving bike-making company in the world, founded 1885 by Edoardo Bianchi, now owned by CycleEurope conglomerate. Logo is a crowned eagle. Its reputation is forged by links with Fausto Coppi, Felice Gimondi, and Marco Pantani. Still makes some 15,000 high-end bikes annually, 60–70 percent painted in the light blue associated with Coppi. Iconic products: 1953 world championship winning machine ridden by Coppi, *celeste* blue on chrome, early Campagnolo Gran Sport 10-speed gears; handlebar mounted bottle cage with a spring to hold the bottle in.

Columbus: Milan. Founded early in 20th century as general producer of metal tubing, whose products also include tubular furniture, boiler tubes, ski sticks, and car chassis under the name Gilco (used by Ferrari and Maserati); made its first cycle tubing in 1931; now also makes

aluminium and carbon tubes. Iconic products: SLX, internally rifled tubing made in the 1980s; Max framesets, the first with variable sizing for increased strength, from 1987.

Gios: Turin. Frame maker founded in 1948, best known for supplying bikes in bright blue for the Brooklyn team led by ROGER DE VLAEMINCK in the early 1970s. Head badge features the Italian tricolor. Iconic machine is the original 1973 Brooklyn team bike in Columbus SL with chromed forks.

The years after the Second World War were key for Italian cycling with the rivalry between Bartali and FAUSTO COPPI giving the sport a central place in the nation's cultural fabric that is only matched in France, or in smaller heartlands such as FLANDERS or the Basque Country. While in France the focus is an event, the Tour, in Italy the two stars are the reference point for Italian cycling. No surprise then that Coppi was elected the most popular Italian sportsman of the 20th century. In France, most of the best writing and filmmaking has been about the Tour itself whereas in Italy it is Coppi's story that has given rise to novels, films, operas, plays, and eternal controversy.

The Italian cycle industry developed in the duo's wake and remains strong in the north of the country; fierce national pride meant that in the 1980s, when imports were making a huge impact on the industry across Europe, Italian manufacturers such as CAMPAGNOLO were able to adapt to the new world. The tradition is expressed in a company like Masi, still run by Alberto, son of the founder Faliero, who used to build frames for Fausto Coppi and who still keeps the original jigs used to build bikes for the *campionissimo* in his shop next to the Vigorelli velodrome in Milan.

Coppi and Bartali's lasting importance means that Italian cycling is often backward-looking, and that explains its gradual move toward the margins. All the stars since the 1950s have been compared to the big two. Vittorio Adorni, Felice Gimondi, Giuseppe Saronni, and FRANCESCO MOSER never lived up to them, and only MARCO PANTANI achieved anything like their notoriety. Italian cycling was at the center of affairs in another way, however, as the place where blood doping with EPO gained strength fastest in the early 1990s, resulting in a sudden flowering of stars before the rest of the sport caught up. But a succession of *campioni* were busted in Pantani's wake—Ivan Basso, Danilo di Luca, Davide Rebellin, Riccardo Ricco—and currently Italy is looking for new heroes.

JOURNALISTS Cycling is unique among sports in that its biggest and oldest events were founded and run by journalists. This led to an unusually close relationship between the written press and bike racing, which lasted over a century and has only changed in recent years. The first place-to-place cycle race, Paris–Rouen in 1868, was founded by Richard Lesclide, editor of the the first cycling magazine, *Le Vélocipede Illustré*. PARIS–BREST–PARIS, the TOUR DE FRANCE, and GIRO D'ITALIA began during daily newspaper circulation wars by the sports newspapers *Le Vélo*, *l'Auto*, and *Gazzetta dello Sport* respectively. The *Het Volk* Classic in Belgium was run by the paper of that name.

Early writers were often propagandists for the nascent cycling movement. Lesclide was one, as were others such as S. S. McClure of *The Wheelman* in America. In France, the writer Paul de Viviès, who wrote under the name VELOCIO, founded the "diagonals"—touring routes from one corner of France to another—and campaigned for the use of the derailleur (see Velocio's entry for his seven commandments of cycling). The director of *Le Petit Journal*, Albert Lejeune, was behind Paris–Nice, which has perhaps the most evocative name in cycling: La Course au Soleil, "the race to the sun."

While Robin Magowan was one of the first American journalists to cover the Tour de France, in 1978 (his book on that year's race, *Tour de France, the 75th Anniversary Race*, is now out of print), Samuel Abt was the first US journalist to cover the Tour regularly, producing dispatches for the *Herald Tribune* for over a quarter of a century. His books include *In High Gear: The World of Professional Bicycle Racing*; *Greg LeMond: The Incredible Comeback*; and *Off to the Races: 25 Years of Cycling Journalism*. Abt was the first American to be awarded the Tour de France medal for long service on the race. Abt said that the main challenge he faced was that he could not produce technical writing, since a newspaper audience does not have specialist knowledge of cycling, and instead he had to write about the people, the surroundings, and the strategy of the race, if it could be "explained coherently." Rupert Guinness performed a similar role in bringing the sport to the Australian public by following PHIL ANDERSON, while the British pioneer was J. B. Wadley for the *Daily Telegraph* in the 1950s and 1960s. The doyen of the press pack in cycling these days is the British writer John Wilcockson, who

edits the American magazine *Velo News* (which he founded together with Magowan's son Felix). Wilcockson, a former correspondent for the London *Times*, has covered 40 Tours since the 1960s. Jacques Augendre of *l'Equipe* was the first writer to cover 50 Tours.

As the French writer Jacques Marchand notes, the relationship between the press and the sport has changed in recent years. In the days of *l'Auto*, journalists treaded carefully around the issue of doping since the small number who covered cycling were an integrated part of the sport: their papers ran races, they stayed with the cyclists, and they traveled with the teams. Although few of them were former professional cyclists— Louison Bobet's brother Jean was an exception—but many had been keen amateurs. The sport was small in scale, and the cyclists were accessible and open. As late as 1989, it was possible to turn up at a hotel the night before the world championship and interview the Tour de

France winner off-the-cuff.

The rise of television in the 1990s and the arrival of big money in sports ended that close rapport, which has been made infinitely more complicated by a decade of doping scandals, as the *Times* writer Jeremy Whittle portrayed in his 2008 account of his career, *Bad Blood*. Cycling journalists are now divided into specialists, who cover the sport all season and have close relations with the teams, and the outsiders who turn up for the Tour de France. The riders are shielded by their agents and PR men, at races they hide in vast buses, and they are mistrustful of the press because of its coverage of drug scandals.

Most writers today are divided on the doping issue: some pretend it doesn't exist, but most admire the sport and hate doping and have an honest desire to give cyclists the benefit of the doubt unless charges are proven. There are relatively few writers who actively campaign against doping: the exceptions are *l'Equipe*'s specialist Damien Ressiot, who in August 2005 broke the news that EPO had been detected in urine samples given by LANCE ARMSTRONG during the 1999 Tour, and the London *Sunday Times* sportswriter David Walsh, who has produced a series of books detailing doping allegations against Lance Armstrong, culminating in *From Lance to Landis: Inside the American Doping Controversy at the Tour de France* (Ballantine Books, 2007).

K

KEIRIN   Probably the richest form of cycle racing on the planet, this Japanese discipline takes its name from the words for wheel and bet. This is a paced track event in which a group of nine sprinters are led up to finish speed before the pacer pulls off—usually with two or two and a half laps to go—so the sprinters can launch themselves for the line. It is the heart of a massive, intricate betting industry that is hugely popular in Japan. The sport was launched there in 1948 and is run by the Nihon Jitensha Shinkōkai (National Keirin Association).

Keirin has been part of the world track championships since 1980, and an Olympic discipline since 2000, but with two subtle differences. In the international arena the field is six riders per heat, and the pacing is done by a small motorbike with pedals to supplement the engine, known as a DERNY. In Japan the pacer who takes the sprinters up to launch speed is another cyclist.

In Japan, the riders wear motorbike helmets and body padding, with racing gear in full color depending on their rank. They bow as they enter the arena; the races typically are 2 kilometers, with a bell ringing constantly from 1.5 laps to go. The races are overseen by four judges, each one sitting in a tower on one of the four corners. The most successful keirin winner ever is Koichi Nakano, who also won the professional world sprint championship from 1977 to 1986.

"The top Japanese riders drive Ferraris and Lamborghinis and they're shocked at how penniless we are," Scotland's Olympic medalist Craig MacLean told author Richard Moore in *Heroes, Villains and Velodromes*. The top-ranked Keirin Grand Prix is worth over $1 million. A select group of foreigners—less than 10—race the circuit each year, but before competing they have to attend keirin school on a campus which has no less than four velodromes. There, the foreigners are fast-tracked but the Japanese entrants have to train and study for up to 15 hours a day. Among the entry criteria, new recruits must have no Yakuza (i.e., organized crime) connections.

As with sumo wrestling, keirin rules are arcane, devised to ensure that races cannot be fixed—the early years of keirin were marred by scandals—and cannot be affected by outside factors, so that racing conditions are perceived as fair by the betting punters. The bikes and equipment have to be made to strict guidelines by a certified builder, and have not changed for 20 years: frames are steel, and wheels have to be 36-spoked.

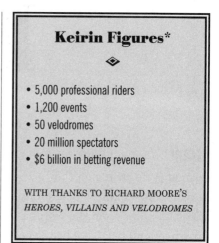

Keirin Figures*

◈

• 5,000 professional riders
• 1,200 events
• 50 velodromes
• 20 million spectators
• $6 billion in betting revenue

WITH THANKS TO RICHARD MOORE'S
HEROES, VILLAINS AND VELODROMES

All components must be approved by the NJS. Riders are responsible for their own bike maintenance, which has to be done in silence.

The hierarchy among the several thousand pros is determined by points awarded for wins and placings, with a cut taken each month: the top 50 from each category go up, the bottom 50 are "relegated." The lowest-ranked riders are eventually replaced by recruits from keirin school.

Tactics—where the rider will sit in the string behind the pacer and when he will launch his move—have to be declared

Keirin Tactics

❖

Senko:	lead-out man, attacks 800–400 m from finish
Makuri:	2nd or 3rd in line, cannot attack until 300 m from the line
Oikomi:	third or fourth, must wait until last 150 m

Keirin Offenses

❖

Shikaku:	major, offender must leave velodrome for the rest of the meeting
Juchu:	serious, fine and percentage loss of prize money
Sochu:	trivial

Keirin Ranking and Colors

❖

SS:	red shorts, black stripe, white stars—the highest ranking
S1 and S2:	black shorts, red stripe
A1, A2, A3:	black shorts, green stripe, white stars—the lowest

Keirin Betting Terms

❖

ni-sha-tan:	Exacta—first two finishers in order
ni-sha-fuku:	Quinella—first two in any order
san-ren-tan:	Trifecta—first three in exact order
san-ren-fuku:	Trio—first three in any order
uaido:	Wide—two of first three in any order

in advance and strictly adhered to on pain of fines or bans. During a three-day keirin meet, the riders have to cut off all contact with the outside world. Mobile phones, computers, and other means of communication are banned. Riders cannot make gestures that could be interpreted by illicit gamblers, such as lifting the arms to celebrate a race win.

Foreigners to race the circuit include CHRIS HOY, who went on to be Olympic champion in 2008. But outsiders rarely win. The best Japanese, on the other hand, rarely turn up at the major championships. It's more lucrative to stay at home.

(SEE **TRACK RACING** FOR OTHER INTERNATIONAL DISCIPLINES)

KELLY, Sean

Born: Carrick-on-Suir, Ireland, May 24, 1956
Major wins: Tour of Spain 1988; points jersey Tour de France 1982–3, 1985, 1989, four stage wins; Milan–San Remo 1986, 1992; Giro di Lombardia 1983, 1985, 1991; Liège–Bastogne–Liège 1984, 1989; Paris–Roubaix 1984, 1986; Ghent–Wevelgem 1988; Créteil–Chaville 1984; Tour of Switzerland 1990
Nicknames: King Kelly, the New Cannibal
Further reading: *Sean Kelly: A Man for All Seasons*, David Walsh, Grafton, 1986

"I haven't ridden with anyone who has that aura of strength," wrote a fellow cyclist of the star who was IRELAND's leading sportsman in the 1980s. "Iron man isn't enough. He's made of stainless steel." Kelly was the leader of the FOREIGN LEGION: a group of English-speaking professional cyclists who opened up the European sport during the 1980s. Other notables included STEPHEN ROCHE, ROBERT MILLAR, PHIL ANDERSON, and GREG LEMOND.

Kelly's 18-year career was one of the longest in cycling: he spanned the years from EDDY MERCKX to LANCE ARMSTRONG via BERNARD HINAULT and MIGUEL INDURAIN and topped the world rankings from

1984 to 1989. With 193 professional wins in events varying from Milan–San Remo to the Tour of Spain and GP des Nations time trial, Kelly was the last of the traditional cycling champions, capable of performing in every event of every kind from February to October, able to win time trials, bunch sprints, and stage races. His successors are specialists, to the detriment of the sport. Kelly is the last man to win both the cobbled PARIS–ROUBAIX Classic and its hilly counterpart LIÈGE–BASTOGNE–LIÈGE in the same year (1984). Today, no one aims to win both.

Kelly was born and raised on a small farm near Carrick-on-Suir, in County Waterford. As an amateur he was banned for racing in South Africa and went to France to turn professional (see POLITICS). From 1977 to 1981 he was primarily a sprinter with a reputation as a daredevil, but in 1982 his mentor Jean de Gribaldy persuaded him that he could do more. The breakthrough came in that year's Paris–Nice, which he was to win for seven years in a row; in July he won a mountain stage in the TOUR DE FRANCE and the first of four green points jerseys. In his prime, from 1984 to 1989, Kelly could win any short stage race—in other words, apart from the three major Tours—and any Classic, thanks to his sheer power and cunning. In a major Tour he would usually have one bad day in the mountains. No Irish sportsman had dominated any arena as Kelly did, and with Stephen Roche as number two on the bill, the crowds flocked to see their heroes in a newly created Tour of Ireland in the late 1980s.

If there was one major disappointment for Kelly, it was that he never won the world road-race championship. In 1982 he took the silver medal in Goodwood, England, and in 1989 he shed bitter tears at Chambéry, France, after being outsprinted by Greg LeMond. He also lost the 1987 VUELTA A ESPAÑA due to a saddle boil, which was lanced three days before the finish. He told no one, but a journalist had heard rumors of screams coming from his room in the dead of night and made sure a photographer was on hand to capture the moment when he climbed off his bike.

Kelly's absolute dedication to his sport remains legendary. In 1991 he said a little wistfully that he might break out once or twice in the winter and have a fry-up or an ice cream. He famously said that he abstained from SEX before major races. When he came back from any event, no matter how late or how dark it was, he would clean his bike; the family with whom he lived in Belgium could not work out what he was doing when he went to bed at 9 PM every night, without fail. They assumed he was writing letters or reading, but when they did peep through the door, they found him fast asleep.

Kelly's status in his home country was such that the then Irish president Mary Robinson turned up to his retirement party in 1994—as well as a host of stars including Hinault, ROGER DE VLAEMINCK, and double Tour winner LAURENT FIGNON. He still lives near Carrick, where a small "square"—in fact just a small widening in the main street—and a sports center have been named after him. He has a farm and works as a commentator for television, amusingly for a cyclist famed in his early years for being so unwilling to talk that he was said to have nodded during a radio interview.

KNOWLEDGE, the Body of tradition and received opinion "compiled" by ROBERT MILLAR in idle moments and written up by Millar in *Cycle Sport* magazine as a Tour de France survival guide. Alongside common sense items that would have a place in any coaching manual, it included the following gems:

- Learn to swear in different languages. Other riders will appreciate your efforts to communicate. They'll also know who you are talking to.
- If you need a push in the mountains, looking really sick or completely knackered is a surefire way of getting crowd sympathy. However,

should a *commissaire* spot you getting a push, shout loudly and at least your fine that night won't be for a solicited push.

- Focus on Sundays. There are four of them. The first is fairly easy to get to, the second less so, the third means you have survived the mountains, and getting to the fourth means deliverance.

- Take something nice to eat on your survival days. It'll probably be the only good moment that day.

KRAFTWERK German electronic music pioneers who were cycling mad and created the definitive tune "Tour de France" in 1983, sampling various cycling sounds—breathing, a chain running, gears changing. In 2003 the group released an entire album themed around cycling, *Tour de France Soundtracks*.

Through the 1980s the group became increasingly passionate about cycling, causing one of the classic line-up, Wolfgang Flur, to leave because, he said later, "there was too much cycling inside Kraftwerk and too little music. I didn't want to become a top-level sportsman as a side-effect."

LEMOND, Greg

Born: Lakewood, California, June 26, 1961
Major wins: World road championship 1983, 1989; Tour de France 1986, 1989, 1990, five stage wins
Interests outside cycling: wine, cross-country skiing
Further reading: *Greg LeMond, The Incredible Comeback*, by Samuel Abt (Stanley Paul, 1991)

The first American winner of the TOUR DE FRANCE, the author of one of the sport's most dramatic comebacks, the victor of perhaps the most epic Tour ever, and one of the men who did most to change professional cycling in the late 20th century, LeMond was not the first American to finish the Tour; that honor goes to Jonathan Boyer (see UNITED STATES). But he was the first American to win the professional world championship, in 1983, and the first US Tour winner when he finally triumphed in a race-long battle with his own teammate BERNARD HINAULT.

Like many American cyclists, LeMond's background was middle class; his father, Bob, was a real estate agent. Initially LeMond was a downhill skier, but he switched to cycling at 14, and by 18 he had won the world junior road race. A year later, he was a professional with the Renault-Elf team, led then by Hinault and managed by Cyrille Guimard (see TEAMS for more on Renault and other great squads); in 1982 he took the silver medal at the world road championship and won the Tour de l'Avenir—a "mini-Tour de France" for young riders—while in 1983 he rode to a solo win in the world championship at Altenrhein, Austria.

LeMond's Tour debut came in

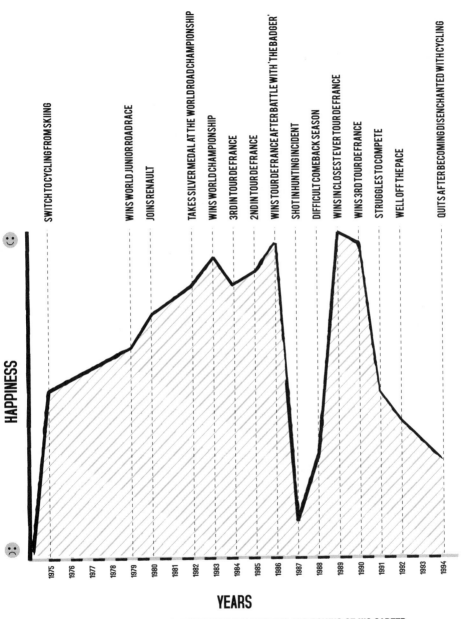

SWITCH TO CYCLING FROM SKIING

WINS WORLD JUNIOR ROAD RACE

JOINS RENAULT

TAKES SILVER MEDAL AT THE WORLD ROAD CHAMPIONSHIP

WINS WORLD CHAMPIONSHIP

3RD IN TOUR DE FRANCE

2ND IN TOUR DE FRANCE

WINS TOUR DE FRANCE AFTER BATTLE WITH 'THE BADGER'

SHOT IN HUNTING INCIDENT

DIFFICULT COMEBACK SEASON

WINS IN CLOSEST EVER TOUR DE FRANCE

WINS 3RD TOUR DE FRANCE

STRUGGLES TO COMPETE

WELL OFF THE PACE

QUITS AFTER BECOMING DISENCHANTED WITH CYCLING

HAPPINESS

1975 1976 1977 1978 1979 1980 1981 1982 1983 1984 1985 1986 1987 1988 1989 1990 1991 1992 1993 1994

YEARS

GREG LEMOND - GRADIENT PROFILE INDICTAING UPS AND DOWNS OF HIS CAREER

1984, when he finished third behind his team leader LAURENT FIGNON and Hinault, who had moved to the La Vie Claire squad. In 1985 he joined Hinault, on a three-year deal that was cycling's first million-dollar contract, with the understanding that he would help Hinault win that year's Tour and the Frenchman would assist him in 1986. In 1985 LeMond looked the strongest in the final week, at one point being told to soft-pedal when he was in a key breakaway, and had the chance of taking the yellow jersey.

The 1986 race turned into a psychological battle with Hinault, who attacked continually, insisting as he did so that he was softening up LeMond's rivals and helping his protégé become a stronger, harder cyclist. At one point, Hinault had a four-and-a-half-minute overall lead, but the Frenchman cracked in the Alps before escaping with LeMond on the climb to l'Alpe d'Huez, where they crossed the line with their arms around each other's shoulders. But Hinault still would not say the Tour was over, and there were even accusations that someone—a French fan?—

had tampered with the American's bike. To this day LeMond believes Hinault was trying to win the race for a record sixth time; "the Badger," on the other hand, still maintains he could have won the race if he had wanted, but he was helping LeMond.

The American was only 25 and seemingly set for a long reign over the Tour, but the following spring he was shot in a hunting accident in California, losing a large amount of blood, suffering a partially collapsed lung, and ending up with pellets in his intestine, liver, and diaphragm; 30 of them are still there. He was 20 minutes from death; by sheer chance a highway patrol helicopter was nearby and he was airlifted quickly to a trauma hospital.

His comeback was painful; 1988 was fallow, and he suffered in the early part of the 1989 season before returning to his best in the 1989 Tour, a three-way battle with Pedro Delgado and LeMond's former team leader Fignon. The lead oscillated between LeMond and the Frenchman while Delgado strove to recover three minutes he had lost on the opening day when he turned up late for the prologue time trial. Finally, LeMond won the race when he used new aerodynamic handlebars to overturn a 50 second deficit on Fignon in the final day's time trial to the Champs-Elysées; his 8-second advantage was the closest in Tour history.

Four weeks later, on a rainy day in the French Alps, he outsprinted Russian Dimitri Konychev and SEAN KELLY for the world championship, sealing his incredible comeback. The upshot of that was cycling's biggest-ever contract: a $5.5 million plus bonuses deal with French team Z, backed by a clothing company. That contract dragged cycling into the modern world, where at last realistic payments were given to its top performers.

In 1990 LeMond took a third Tour, matching Louison Bobet; at the time only EDDY MERCKX, Hinault, and JACQUES ANQUETIL had done better. But in 1991 and 1992 LeMond struggled, something that he now interprets as being down to the arrival of a new drug in the peloton, EPO, and he quit in 1994, disenchanted with his final years in the sport.

LeMond was one of the most innovative cyclists of the 20th century, on a par with FAUSTO COPPI in the way he pushed the sport forward. As well as being the first professional cyclist to use "triathlon" handlebars in time trials (see AERODYNAMICS), LeMond helped to popularize hard-shell cycle helmets, regarded with some suspicion when he began using them in 1990 but now universal. He also pioneered communication with the team car via mini-radios, rode titanium frames, and experimented with handlebar design in collaboration with the Scott company. He was also the first cyclist to ride the PARIS–ROUBAIX Classic using MOUNTAIN BIKE front suspension forks. Not surprisingly, he ended up with his own cycle company.

LeMond was the first star cyclist to break with the European belief that cyclists should be subservient to promoters, race organizers, and team managers, in essence an attitude that went back to the postwar years when the stars had come from blue-collar stock and reckoned they were lucky to be racing at all. He brought his family with him to races, breaking a huge taboo, raised eyebrows by getting an agent (his father) to negotiate his contracts, and insisted on doing things his way, whether that meant eating McDonald's occasionally or bringing his own portable air conditioner to hotels on the Tour de France.

He had a close-knit inner circle around him: a grumpy Belgian mechanic, Julien de Vries, who had worked with Merckx and would go on to wield a wrench for LANCE ARMSTRONG, and the distinctive figure of Mexican SOIGNEUR Otto Jacome, who had the biceps of a boxer and wore a floppy Stetson. And LeMond brought a certain eccentricity with him; in the 1991 Tour he decided to take a special carbon-fiber bike up to his hotel bedroom but neglected to tell the Z team mechanics. De Vries was in tears, convinced the machine had been stolen, and a second mechanic was dispatched to Paris—

from eastern France—to get a replacement. This was before the era of mobile phones: when the mistake was discovered, the police had to be sent to chase down the mechanic as he sped down the autoroute.

LeMond's life after retirement was as turbulent as before. He came close to divorcing his wife Kathy, he revealed that he had been abused as a child, and he made a dramatic intervention in the 2006 Tour winner Floyd Landis's doping hearing. He also became a critic of seven-time Tour winner Lance Armstrong. He attacked the Texan over his work with the controversial trainer MICHELE FERRARI, alleged that Armstrong had said LeMond could not have won the Tour without using EPO— which Armstrong denies—and raised questions about Armstrong's personal antidoping program when the seven-time Tour winner made his comeback in 2009.

LETH, Jorgen (b. Denmark, 1937)

Danish poet and film director best known in cycling for three documentaries: *Stars and Watercarriers* (1974), *The Impossible Hour* (1974), and *Sunday in Hell* (1977). His work has lent a whole new dimension to cycling and sports documentary: deeply impressionistic, epic in tone but very human, with the interplay of music and action footage playing a key role. Leth has also written 10 volumes of poetry and 8 nonfiction works, including his controversial autobiography *The Imperfect Man*. He has been chairman of the Danish film institute and commentated on some 20 Tours de France for television. He has lived in Haiti since 1991 and was honorary Danish consul on the island between 1999 and 2005.

Stars and Watercarriers tells the tale of the 1973 GIRO D'ITALIA, focusing on the conflict between EDDY MERCKX and the little climber Jose-Manuel Fuente. It is split into 10 "chapters" including "the trial of truth," centered on a time trial involving the Danish star Ole Ritter. The pursuiter/time triallist is also the key figure in *The Impossible Hour*, about his three attempts to break the HOUR RECORD in Mexico City in 1974. *Sunday in Hell* centers on the 1976 PARIS–ROUBAIX and is Leth's defining cycling work. He shot the event from all angles and included a now legendary sequence with the cyclists bouncing in slow-motion over the cobbles. Cycling also features in Leth's 1973 film *Eddy Merckx in the Vicinity of a Cup of Coffee*, a surreal mix of the director reading his poetry while subtitles deliver comment; the second half of the film includes footage from the 1970 TOUR DE FRANCE.

Leth was also involved in an abortive attempt to make a feature film about the Tour de France starring Dustin Hoffman; footage was shot on the 1986 Tour, but the film never saw the light of day.

(SEE **FILMS** FOR MORE CYCLING ON CELLULOID)

LIÈGE–BASTOGNE–LIÈGE

The oldest CLASSIC on the cycling calendar, nicknamed *la doyenne* because it dates back to 1892. The route was chosen mainly because Bastogne, 50-odd miles south of Liège through the Ardennes hills, was the farthest anyone could get to and return by train in a day, which meant that an official could be sent to manage the checkpoint there. There were several years when the race was not run, and it gained true prestige only when it began to be run the day after a neighboring race, Flèche Wallonne (see Classics), with an overall classification known as the Ardennes Weekend. The DOUBLE in the two races is a rare and coveted feat.

The race's distinctive feature is the succession of small but tough climbs through the Ardennes hills, where American and German forces fought the Battle of the Bulge in 1944. The hills start well before halfway at the town of Houffalize, where the US Army completed its encirclement of the Germans; the final phase begins with the toughest climb on the course, La Redoute—where a plaque celebrates the race and its riders—which is followed by four or five more ascents before the finish, most recently held above Liège in the suburb of Ans.

The *doyenne* is now a tactical battle, but the past has witnessed epic lone victories for EDDY MERCKX, in 1969, when he broke away with one of his *domestiques* 60 miles from the finish, and JACQUES ANQUETIL, who took his best one-day win there in 1966. The weather is often a factor as the race crosses the high hills, notably in BERNARD HINAULT's 1980 win, on a day of snow and ice that Pierre Chany described as "phantasmagoric." Only 40 of the 150-rider field were still in the race after the first 40 miles and Hinault rode the final 40 miles alone to win by nine minutes. Two joints in the fingers of his right hand remain numb to this day. The best specialist in Liège is the Italian Moreno Argentin, winner four times between 1985 and 1991.

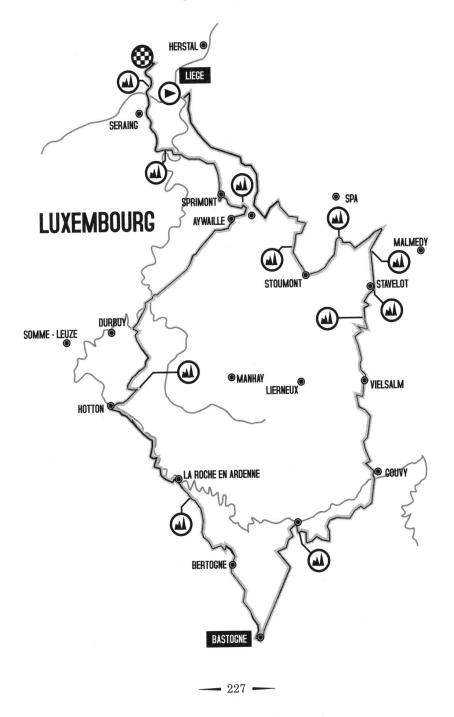

LIGGETT, Phil (b. England, 1943)

The hardworking and constantly traveling television commentator and former *Daily Telegraph* correspondent is the biggest media star in English-speaking cycling worldwide. He has a near monopoly on mainstream TV in the UK, Australia, South Africa, and the US, together with his business partner Paul Sherwen, a former professional and one of the cycling FOREIGN LEGION. By 2009 he had covered 38 Tours de France and 13 OLYMPIC GAMES.

Liggett started out as a racing cyclist in the 1960s, competing in Belgium before realizing that he wasn't going to make it. In the 1970s he went to the TOUR DE FRANCE as driver for the journalist David Saunders and took over Saunders's TV and newspaper work when the latter was killed in a car accident in 1978. Between 1972 and 1993 he was technical director of the around-Britain MILK RACE.

Liggett's career expanded in the late 1980s with the start of Channel Four's daily Tour de France coverage and its coverage of the Tour of Britain and UK city center races (see GREAT BRITAIN). His ubiquity stems from his relationship with the television production company that put together the packages for Channel Four using a mix of live images shot by Tour de France television company SFP for the organizers ASO; their material is used by almost all the English-speaking nations. Liggett has his own CYCLOSPORTIVE through the Pennines; a collection of "Liggettisms" was published in 2005.

LITERATURE

A quick freewheel through some "serious" writers for whom cycling is more than a brief reference.

Henry Miller, writer of various sexually explicit 1960s novels such as *Tropic of Cancer*, called a volume of his memoirs *My Bike and Other Friends* and devoted the final chapter to an account of his love affair with a German-made track bike bought after a SIX-DAY at Madison Square Garden. His veneration of the bike is linked to an unrequited passion for a young woman he met at high school; the bike is both substitute for the woman (he would take it to bed if he could) and a means of escape.

Another cycling fan was Ernest Hemingway, who wrote about the six-days and described the Tour of the Basque Country (see SPAIN) in *The Sun Also Rises*.

Cult Irish writer Flann O'Brien, also known as a hilarious columnist in the *Irish Times* and for producing the magical realist novel *At Swim-Two-Birds*, wrote captivatingly about bikes in *The Third Policeman*. This is a surreal murder thriller that features a pair of bike-obsessed policemen. It includes digressions on wooden rims, cycling with your mouth open, saddles, and the celebrated "atomic theory." According to this, impacts between two objects result in a transfer of atoms from one to the other. As a result, say the policemen, people who spend a lot of time on their bikes become "part-man, part-bike" while the cycles develop personalities, try to get warm, and try to eat food: "The behaviour of a bicycle that has a high content of humanity is very cunning and very remarkable. You never see them moving . . . but you meet them in the least accountable places unexpectedly." Similarly, you can tell "a man with a lot of bicycle in his veins" by his walk.

In Paris at the end of the 19th century, the surrealist writer Alfred Jarry—known for the play *Ubu Roi*—had a state-of-the-art Clément machine customized with wooden rims and caused a sensation when he turned up at the funeral of the poet Stéphane Mallarmé wearing cycling gear. He produced a calendar that includes a month called *Pédale*. Jarry wrote a short story entitled "The Crucifixion Considered as an Uphill Bicycle Race," satirizing both the Parisian obsession with all things two-wheeled and the epic imagery used to describe cycle races by writers like HENRI DESGRANGE. It includes the memorable lines "Barabbas, slated to race, was scratched" and "There are fourteen turns in the testing Golgotha course." Jarry's sarcasm has not prevented journalists using the term "a Calvary" as a metaphor for extreme suffering in a bike race time and again over the last 110 years.

Jarry also came up with a prescient picture of bike racing in his 1902 novel *The Supermale*, which has a chapter dealing with a Perpetual Motion Race. In this, five cyclists are strapped to a bike that is propelled across Europe and Asia in a race against an express train. The riders are paced by jet cars and flying machines at speeds of up to 300 km per hour and fed on Perpetual Motion Food, a blend of alcohol and strychnine. One of the cyclists dies in the saddle but continues because he has signed a contract with a massive financial penalty if he pulls out. The references to the extreme scenes in six-day racing would have been clear at the time; the satirical take on professional sports—in which the human element has been overtaken by outside interests and the participants are risking their lives to fulfil their contracts—has resonances throughout the history of professional cycling and is probably the inspiration for the race to nowhere in the critically acclaimed animated movie *Les Triplettes de Belleville* (see FILMS).

(FOR A SELECTION OF WRITING SPECIFICALLY ABOUT CYCLING, SEE **BOOKS**—SUBDIVIDED INTO FICTION, NONFICTION, MEMOIRS/AUTOBIOGRAPHY, AND TRAVEL)

LONGEVITY Cycling is not just a young man's sport, although the accepted view is that a male cyclist matures at between 27 and 29, after which his power declines with every passing year. Some examples of unusually long cycling careers:

- Reggie MacNamara of Australia was a SIX-DAY racer who competed from 1912 to 1939, retiring at 50.

- GINO BARTALI won the TOUR DE FRANCE in 1938 and 1948, by which time he was 34. He won his first Italian championships in 1935, his last in 1952, and retired in 1954 after 20 seasons as a pro.

- BERYL BURTON won 72 British national titles in a run that lasted from 1957 to 1986, by which time she was 49. When she died at the age of 59 she was still competing.

- JEANNIE LONGO was still riding the world road race championship in 2009, 23 years after her first title. She has every intention of racing in the London Olympics, by which time she will be almost 54.

- RAYMOND POULIDOR's pro career lasted 18 seasons, his first podium place in the Tour coming in 1962, his last in 1976 when he was 40.

- LANCE ARMSTRONG turned professional in 1992 and made a comeback in 2009 to finish third in the Tour aged 37.

- Joop Zoetemelk won an Olympic gold medal (as an amateur) in 1968 and the pro world road title in 1985 when he was 38. In between he finished the Tour de France 16 times, winning in 1980.

- Malcolm Elliott is currently the oldest pro on the elite men's circuit. He won a COMMONWEALTH GAMES gold medal as long ago as 1982, turned pro in 1983, and rode the Tour de France in 1987. In 2009 at the age of 48 he was still good enough to post top-10 stage placings in the Tours of Ireland and Great Britain.

LONGO, Jeannie

Born: Annecy, France, October 31, 1958

Major wins: Gold, Olympic road race 1996; world road champion 1985, 1986, 1987, 1989, 1995; world time trial champion, 1995, 1996, 1997, 2001; world pursuit champion 1986, 1988–9; world points race champion, 1989; women's Tour de France 1987, 1988, 1989; 15 French national road titles (between 1979 and 2009); world hour records 1986, 1997, 2000

Nicknames: Ma Dalton, La Cannibale

Soft-spoken, almost shy, "the grandmother of womens' cycling" does not have the abrasive attitude that might be expected of one of the most competitive cyclists to grace the sport. She certainly does not seem like a woman who is famed for falling out with teammates, officials, and suppliers, and who was described as being "the best [athlete] with the worst of personalities" (*Le Nouvel Observateur*).

In Beijing, aged 50, Longo became one of a handful of athletes to compete in seven successive OLYMPIC GAMES, and in London she can expect to move another step toward the absolute record of nine games held by the Austrian sailor Hubert Raudaschl. Initially Longo seemed cursed by the Olympics: she crashed in the road race in 1984, broke a hip a month before the Seoul Games, and made a tactical error in 1992, believing she had won, but being unaware that Kathy Watt of Australia had already crossed the line. Since then her record speaks for itself: four medals including gold in a rain-hit women's road race in Atlanta in 1996.

A superb climber and a fine time triallist but lacking a sprint, she also won 13 world titles between 1985 and 2001 on road and track, took the women's Tour de France three times (1987–9) and claimed the women's HOUR RECORD. In 2008, she took her 55th French national title since 1979, a record for longevity to compare with British great BERYL BURTON. Longo began her sporting life as a skier—she was three-time French university champion and her husband, Patrice Ciprelli, was also a French champion—and initially combined the two sports like her great rival Maria Canins. What motivates her to keep on her bike, she says, is that "cycling is her favorite means of getting around and finding new places."

She also has a degree in mathematics and is celebrated for her green lifestyle. She says she cannot stand the chemical disinfectants and cleaners used across the Western world and lives high on a mountain above Grenoble in the Alps with her flock of goats, and—although she travels to the US to prepare for major events— she rarely goes to another country without taking her own organic carrots, water filter, and deionizer.

(SEE **WOMEN** FOR A HISTORY OF WOMEN'S CYCLE RACING AND OTHER TOP WOMEN TO GRACE CYCLING)

MACMILLAN, Kirkpatrick

(b. Scotland, 1812, d. 1878)

Claimed to be the inventor of the rear-wheel-driven pedal cycle. Macmillan was a Dumfriesshire blacksmith who decided to make himself a hobby horse (see BICYCLE for the importance of this early bike). The breakthrough from earlier machines came when he realized that it would be improved if it could be propelled without one of his feet being on the ground.

His design had suspended pedals at the front with long connecting rods linking them to cranks on the rear wheel. It was heavy, but he managed a speed of about 14 mph, and in 1842 he rode it from southwest Scotland to Glasgow, a distance of 68 miles, in two days. During the trip he had an accident involving a child and was taken to court and fined five shillings the following day.

Macmillan's machine does not survive, and he never patented the design. A copy made by a cooper from Lanarkshire, Gavin Dalzell, appeared in 1847 and is in the Museum of Transport in Glasgow. Further copies were made some 20 years later by a wheelwright in Kilmarnock, Thomas McCall, inspired by the Macmillan velocipede.

MANGEAS, Daniel (b. France, 1949)

The voice of cycling in France. As the speaker of the TOUR DE FRANCE and up to 200 other races a year, the former baker introduces the riders as they sign on at the start and keeps the crowds entertained at the finish. His knowledge of even the most obscure members of the professional peloton is encyclopedic. Mangeas first worked on the Tour in 1974, and the 2010 Tour is set to be his 37th. In 2002 the race organizers gave him the ultimate accolade: his own stage start in his home village of Saint-Martin-de-Landelles on the Norman-Breton border, where he organizes the annual after-Tour criterium.

MEMORIALS

Cycle races have crisscrossed Europe for over 130 years so not surprisingly the roads of the continent are dotted with memorials to great cyclists and also race organizers and journalists, while there are also plaques to recall major events, particularly on the great mountain passes. These in turn serve as objectives for cycle-tourists, who lay flowers and souvenirs just as medieval pilgrims would have done at the shrine of a saint.

Among the most celebrated are the bleak bas-relief at the spot where TOM SIMPSON died on Mont Ventoux and the modernistic sculpture just downhill from the bend on the Col du Portet d'Aspet where the 1992 Olympic champion Fabio Casartelli had a fatal crash in the 1995 Tour de France. In other places, plaques denote notable episodes from the past: one is to be found outside the building in Sainte-Marie de Campan, France, where the Tour cyclist Eugène Christophe had to repair his forks in the 1913 race (See HEROIC ERA for more stories about "The Old Gaul").

Also in the Pyrénées, on one bend of the Col de Menté, a plaque marks the spot where an epic duel between EDDY MERCKX and the Spaniard Luis Ocana in the 1971 Tour ended when Ocana crashed in a rainstorm. Another plaque, on the Col d'Aubisque, recalls the day in 1951 when the Dutchman Wim Van Est fell 200 meters into a ravine and was rescued with a rope improvised from tires tied together. The first man to cross a mountain in the Tour in the lead, Rene Pottier, is remembered by a small memorial at the summit of the first pass covered by the race, the Ballon d'Alsace.

The graves of the greats are also frequently visited by cycling fans who leave mementoes such as racing hats and bottles. So many are left at the Simpson memorial that every now and then it has to be cleaned up.

It's not just famous racers and legendary racing episodes that are remembered, however. In Britain, a memorial at Meriden, Warwickshire, celebrates cyclists who fell in both World Wars:

an annual religious service is held there. Close to the top of l'Alpe d'Huez is a small plaque that denotes the spot where the climber LUIS HERRERA put two pieces of lava from his home country in thanks to the people of France after they sent humanitarian relief to the victims of the volcanic eruption at Armero in 1985. A plaque at the Réveil-Matin restaurant in Montgeron, near Paris, celebrates the start point of the first TOUR DE FRANCE in 1903.

On a main road outside Malaga in southern Spain, a plaque and flowers denote the spot where the Spanish professional Ricardo Oxtoa and his brother Xavier were mown down by a car in 2002. Other cyclists who have been killed in traffic accidents are now recalled worldwide by GHOST BIKES.

FAUSTO COPPI and MARCO PANTANI have between them inspired more memorials than any other cyclists—those are listed in their individual entries—but other notable names are remembered as well.

Cycling Memorials

❖

Cyclist/organizer	Location
Joaquim Agostino	Bend 14, l'Alpe d'Huez, France
Jacques Anquetil	Piste Municipale, Paris
Alfredo Binda	Cittiglio, Italy
Louison Bobet	Col d'Izoard, France
Tullio Campagnolo	Croce d'Aune pass, Italy
Fabio Casartelli	Col du Portet d'Aspet, France
Henri Desgrange	Col du Galibier, France
Shay Elliott	Glenmalure, Ireland
Maurice Garin	Armier, Italy
Jacques Goddet	Col du Tourmalet, France
Reg Harris	Manchester Velodrome, England
Hugo Koblet	Passo di Monte Ceneri, Switzerland
Octave Lapize	Col du Tourmalet, France
Eddy Merckx	Stockeu, Belgium
Luis Ocaña	Col de Menté, France
Stan Ockers	Côte des Forges, Belgium
Sir Hubert Opperman	Rochester, Australia
Ricardo Oxtoa	Malaga, Spain
Roger Rivière	Col du Perjuret, Central France
Tom Simpson	Mont Ventoux, France
Tom Simpson	Harworth, England
Jean Stablinski	Troisvilles, Northern France
James Starley	Coventry, England
Marshall "Major" Taylor	Worcester, Massachussetts
Paul de Viviès	Col de la République, France

MERCKX, Eddy

Born: Meensel, Belgium, June 17, 1945
Major wins: World pro road champion
1967, 1971, 1974; Tour de France
1969–72, 1974, 34 stage wins; Giro
d'Italia 1968, 1970, 1972–4, 34 stage
wins; Vuelta a España 1973, six stage
wins; Milan–San Remo 1966–7, 1969,
1971–2, 1975–6; Tour of Flanders 1969,
1975; Paris–Roubaix 1968, 1970, 1973;
Liège–Bastogne–Liège 1969, 1971–3,
1975; Giro di Lombardia 1971–2; Het Volk
1971–3; Ghent–Wevelgem 1967, 1969,
1972; Flèche Wallonne 1967, 1970, 1972;
Amstel Gold Race, 1973, 1975; Paris–
Brussels, 1973; GP Nations 1973; world
hour record 1972
Nicknames: Big Ted, the Cannibal

Every sport has its nonpareil and
Eddy Merckx is to cycling what Pele
is to soccer or Muhammad Ali to
boxing. While Merckx's records in
individual events may be beaten—
LANCE ARMSTRONG has outstripped
his five Tour wins—his record of
domination over half a dozen years
between 1969 and 1975 can never
be equaled. Indeed, across any
sport it's hard to find a parallel for
Merckx's unique strike rate: 54 wins

in 120 starts in 1971; 250 wins in
650 starts from 1969–73. No cyclist
as "winning" is likely to be seen
again. Merckx had looks as well: a
mop of dark hair, finely sculpted
cheekbones, sideburns worthy of the
'70s, and an expression of total self-
absorption.

The scale and volume of
Merckx's dominance was
unprecedented. For example, in just
nine weeks in 1973 he won four
major CLASSICS—Ghent–Wevelgem,
Amstel Gold Race, PARIS–ROUBAIX,
and LIÈGE–BASTOGNE–LIÈGE—
followed that with overall victory in
the three-week VUELTA A ESPAÑA,
with six stage wins en route, and,
after a brief break, added the
GIRO D'ITALIA, taking another half-
dozen stages. In winning, Merckx
would leave the opposition minutes
behind. "He always does more
than is necessary to win. He is not
content with mere glory," wrote the
Tour organizer Jacques Goddet.
He was christened "the Cannibal"
by the daughter of a French rival,
Christian Raymond, because of his
voracious appetite for victory, after
a stage in France where the bunch
trailed in half an hour behind him

(see NICKNAMES for other interesting cycling monickers).

But Merckx is not a domineering personality in the style of Lance Armstrong or BERNARD HINAULT. "I'm not a cannibal, I'm the sensitive kind," he said. He explained that his need to crush the opposition so absolutely stemmed from a lack of confidence. "When you are alone in a one-day race, you're certain to win. In a stage race, it's never certain, you can always have a bad day. The bigger your lead, the more you have [in hand] if that happens."

Two devastating events early in his career made Merckx obsessively insecure in spite of his obvious physical strength: a positive drugs test in the 1968 Giro, which he was adamant came from a spiked bottle, and a horrific crash in a motorpaced race in 1969 in which the driver was killed. The accident left Merckx with constant back pain that in turn made him worry about his position on the bike, which he would check before every race and sometimes change while riding, carrying a wrench along just in case. He would wake up in the night before major races and go to his garage to check his bikes were adjusted just right. His basement held 200 tubular tires that he would season for two years to reduce the risk of punctures. At one Giro, he travelled with 18 bikes and personally drilled out the componentry on each to save a few grams.

While Hinault played up his "grumpy badger" image and JACQUES ANQUETIL played mindgames with the opposition and press, Merckx was famed for hiding his feelings. "Merckx, a super winner, walks away without a trace of fatigue, with nothing to say, just a hint of boredom," wrote a French journalist in 1970. "He has robotised himself . . . transformed himself into a machine with the utmost meticulousness. He is half-man, half-bike." "Most of the time, there was nothing anyone could do against him," said the British pro Derek Harrison. "His legs were like pistons. The way he sat on the bike was just beautiful."

Many of Merckx's achievements have entered cycling legend. In 1972 he broke the HOUR RECORD in Mexico City in a ride that now seems poorly scheduled: he started off far too quickly, "died" for 50 minutes, and had to be lifted off his bike at the finish. During his first TOUR DE FRANCE win, in 1969, he was already in the yellow jersey and well ahead when he found himself in front on the final Pyrenean stage. He led for 85 miles and finished eight and a half minutes ahead of the next rider, on a stage when he really only needed to race defensively. In 1968, at a Giro stage finish at the Tre Cime di Lavaredo mountaintop he fought his way through a snowstorm to mop up a break that had started the climb nine minutes ahead.

Merckx had no rivals, only occasional challengers. In the Classics ROGER DE VLAEMINCK and Freddy Maertens fought him gallantly, while in the Tour de France the Spaniard Luis Ocaña threw down the gauntlet in 1971, finishing almost nine minutes ahead at the Orcières-Merlette ski resort in the ALPS. On the next stage, out of the Alps to Marseille, Merckx attacked from the start and rode so fast that the race was half an hour ahead of schedule at the finish.

The Merckx Joke

❖

The tale is told that after the death of a cyclist who tried to beat Merckx for years but was constantly frustrated, the pro went to Heaven and was greeted by St. Peter. The saint put him in a race on the smoothest velodrome he had ever seen, on the finest Italian frame. All the greats who had predeceased him were on the start line: COPPI, GARIN, and so on, but he knew he would win. As the line approached, however, he felt a wheel coming past, glanced up, and saw the face of the Cannibal; disconsolate, he went to St. Peter and said, "Eddy isn't dead yet, what's he doing here?" St. Peter replied gravely: "That wasn't Merckx. It was God. He likes to pretend he's Merckx."

Ocana summed up his rival: "It's not enough for him to win one day, he wants to win the next day and the day after that. Ayrton Senna has the same mentality, he's eaten away by the same thirst for victory. Only the very great have it. Winning for them is second nature. When they don't win any more, they come face to face with a void."

The Cannibal's career began to wane in 1975 when the Frenchman Bernard Thevenet overcame him in the Tour—Merckx crashed along the way and broke a cheekbone but still finished second—and he retired from racing in spring 1978. Until retirement in 2009 he ran a bike factory in Belgium, which was set up with the help of his former bike maker Ugo de Rosa; he also works on ASO's Tour of Qatar. His son Axel raced during the 1990s for teams such as Motorola and Telekom. Merckx grew close to Lance Armstrong when the Texan raced on his bikes while at the Motorola team, and the pair remain friends.

MILAN–SAN REMO   The longest of the one-day CLASSICS and the only one to retain a course that is virtually identical to the one first used in 1907. First come the flat plains south of Milan, then the Apennines via the Turchino pass, then it's around Genova and along the old Roman Mediterranean coast road through Imperia and Alassio to San Remo, the last substantial town before the French border.

The race was founded to publicize what was then a fading seaside resort known only for gambling; today it is the first truly major event on the cycling calendar, nicknamed "*La Primavera*" by the Italians, for whom it symbolizes the arrival of spring with the passage from fog and cold in Milan to sunshine on the Riviera. Victory here has been a rite of passage for every Italian *campione* from ALFREDO BINDA to FRANCESCO MOSER.

In its early years, Milan–San Remo was occasionally hit by hellish weather. The snowy 1910 edition remains legendary: the winner Eugène Christophe (see MEMORIALS to find out where his broken forks are remembered) might well have died of hypothermia had he not been rescued by a farmer. He warmed up in the farmhouse for half an

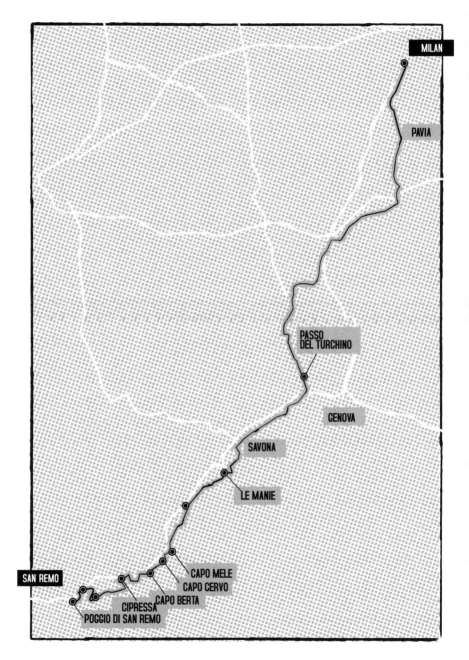

MILAN

PAVIA

PASSO
DEL TURCHINO

GENOVA

SAVONA

LE MANIE

CAPO MELE

CAPO CERVO

CAPO BERTA

CIPRESSA

SAN REMO

POGGIO DI SAN REMO

hour, then set off to complete the 12-hour trek. Only two other riders finished; Christophe then spent a month in the hospital recovering and did not race properly for another two years. Such feats were typical of the HEROIC ERA.

Today, the largely flat course means that in spite of its 190-mile length, Milan–San Remo is essentially a tactical battle that frequently ends in a mass sprint between the men strong enough to survive the series of short climbs that test their legs in the final 60 kilometers. First comes the Cipressa, a series of steep hairpins through olive groves with a dangerous descent back to the coast, next up are the Capi—

little ascents to headlands, Mele, Cervo, Berta—before the final test: the sinuous Poggio.

While FAUSTO COPPI scored several notable solo wins, including a legendary 160-kilometer escape in 1946 that began before the Turchino was crossed, the record holder in San Remo is EDDY MERCKX who won seven times in 11 years. Between 1997 and 2001 the German Erik Zabel achieved a dominance unique in any one-day event in recent years, with four wins out of five. MARK CAVENDISH gave Britain its second win in the event (after TOM SIMPSON in 1964) with his narrow sprint victory in 2009.

MILK RACE   One of the longest-lasting race sponsorships in cycling. This amateur Tour of Britain was first held in 1958 with its roots in a variety of around Britain events run during the 1940s and 1950s,

such as Brighton–Glasgow and the Circuit of Britain, backed by companies such as Quaker Oats and the *Daily Express*.

The Milk Race was sponsored by the Milk Marketing Board, a government body responsible for selling milk produced by Welsh and English farmers until the agency was abolished in 1993. It always had a down-home feel to it. The first event was flagged away by the comedian Norman Wisdom and run by the West London official Chas Messenger, who produced famously tough courses. He managed a trans-Pennine stage lasting seven hours in 1962. The Milk Race also has a place in antidoping history: soon after drugs were banned in 1965, tests carried out on the racers resulted in the first three positives in cycling.

In the 1960s and 1970s, the Milk Race became one of the biggest amateur stage races in the world, behind the Peace Race (see EASTERN EUROPE to find out more about this one) and the Tour de l'Avenir, run by the Tour de France organizers. It welcomed competitors from Russia and Poland in spite of the fact that these state-sponsored professional amateurs were usually victorious over the home cyclists who worked full-time and only raced part-time. The Russians won every year

from 1977 to 1984, apart from 1978, when a Pole won, and 1983, when the American Matt Eaton won. The era is captured in the documentary *Manpower*. The race tended to visit all areas of England and Wales—but never Scotland.

Malcolm Elliott, winner in 1987, went on to finish the Tour de France that year and briefly became a prolific winner in Europe, while the last winner, in 1993, was Chris Lillywhite riding for the Banana-Falcon pro team. There have been other Tours of Britain. The Butlin Tour was a seven-day event between Butlin's holiday camps in 1951. The Sealink Tour ran through the 1970s, usually including a transfer on the nationalized ferry company, while the Kellogg's Tour was an all-professional event that lasted from 1987 to 1994, and the PruTour, backed by the Prudential financial services company, took place in 1998 and 1999. Since 2004 the Milk Race has had a successor in the Tour of Britain, run by the Sweetspot promotions company and taking place over nine days in September.

MILLAR, Robert

Born: Glasgow, Scotland, September 13, 1958

Major wins: Three stages Tour de France; King of the Mountains Tour de France 1984; Giro d'Italia 1987; British national road titles 1978–9 (amateur), 1995 (pro); Dauphiné Libéré stage race 1990

Further reading/viewing: *In Search of Robert Millar*, Richard Moore, HarperCollins UK, 2008; documentary on DVD: *The High Life*

The Glaswegian is Britain's best ever TOUR DE FRANCE cyclist, one of cycling's greatest climbers, and one of the sport's great eccentrics. During the 1992 "Euro-Tour," where the race numbers bore the 12 stars of the European Union, Millar spent several minutes each morning scraping the stars off and carefully inscribing a Scottish saltire instead. He has an acerbic, rather black sense of humor, is a fine writer, coined various NICKNAMES for his contemporaries, and featured in a fine television documentary, *The High Life*, with soundtrack by Steve Winwood.

A double British national amateur champion, Millar was one of the FOREIGN LEGION who turned professional, which he did in 1980 with the PEUGEOT team. Initially overlooked by the management, he became the first Briton to win a major mountain stage of the Tour, at Luchon in 1983, and added a second stage and the King of the Mountains jersey in 1984. His fourth place overall remains a British record, equaled in 2009 by BRADLEY WIGGINS.

In 1985 he would have won the VUELTA A ESPAÑA if the home teams had not ganged up on him on the penultimate stage to ensure victory for one of their own, Pedro Delgado, who made a long-range attack on the Scot to overturn a deficit of more than seven minutes. Later, Millar's manager Roland Berland claimed that he had an agreement with the Panasonic team that they would help Millar during the stage if his teammates weren't up to the task; instead, they went back on the deal. Afterward, Delgado thanked the managers of the Spanish teams "for sacrificing their chances for me." Later, in February 1997, Millar analyzed the defeat in *Cycle Sport* magazine, and made the following comments. He was not informed of who was in front or what the time gap was. His Peugeot team did not have the legs to help him defend the jersey. Berland did not manage to make any deals with other teams to make up for their weakness. His conclusion was "Delgado didn't win, I lost, mainly thanks to some circumstances that shouldn't have happened."

At the time, it seemed likely Millar would go on to win a major Tour, but it did not happen: Millar added a stage win and second overall in the 1987 Giro, where he took the King of the Mountains prize; he took a third Tour stage in 1989 and won the Dauphiné Libéré stage race in 1990. A few days after he won the British national championship in 1995, his career ended abruptly when his sponsor went bust.

Millar wrote a column for the British magazine *Cycle Sport* for several years, and later wrote bike tests for *procycling* magazine. His best piece was a feature called "THE KNOWLEDGE," which detailed the dos and don'ts of professional cycling. After retirement he managed the British national road team for a year, then slipped off the radar. He emerged from obscurity in 2009 to write about the 1984 Tour for *Rouleur* magazine, offered Eurosport insights on the mountains of the Tour de France and gave the *Observer* newspaper his thoughts on Wiggins.

His younger namesake David, who won the prologue of the Tour in 2000 and a further stage in 2002, is no relation.

MONUMENTS   The five greatest one-day events in the sport are often referred to as the "monuments": Milan–San Remo, the Tour of Flanders, Paris–Roubaix, Liège–Bastogne–Liège, and the Tour of Lombardy. See their individual entries.

MOORE, James
(b. England, 1849, d. 1935)

Winner of the first road race held from city to city, Paris–Rouen, in October 1869. Moore was a vet from Bury St. Edmunds with a practice in Paris when he won what is said to be the first bike race, held over 1,200 m at Paris's Parc St. Cloud on May 31, 1868, with 10 starters. He covered the distance in 3 minutes 50 seconds; the spectators included members of the Parisian aristocracy, according to reports of the time. There were almost certainly races before this but the Parc St. Cloud event was the first for which records exist. According to the historian Benjo Maso, Moore won the second of two events; the French writer Pierre Chany mentions only one "trial of speed"

in his history of cycling, however. Moore had contacts with the Michaux family, who owned a factory where HOBBY HORSES were made. Not surprisingly, he rode one for Paris–Rouen, although it was one of the few bikes at the time fitted with a revolutionary new invention: ball bearings in the wheels. His time for the 123 km was 10 hours 40 minutes. Amusingly, an initial report in the organizing magazine gave his nationality as "French although his name is English" but Moore wrote in to correct the error.

In 1874 Moore won the McGregor Cup over one mile at Wolverhampton, which unofficially made him world champion. He also served in the French ambulance corps in the Franco-Prussian war and was awarded the Légion d'Honneur.

MOSER, Francesco (b. Italy, 1951)

"Il Cecco" is the only cyclist to have won PARIS–ROUBAIX three times in a row, but he is better known for bringing cycling into a new era by breaking EDDY MERCKX's HOUR RECORD in Mexico City on January 19, 1984, then improving his distance four days later. Moser was 32 years old and had looked a spent force, but thanks to sponsorship from the sports drinks company Enervit he assembled a team of 50 technicians to look at every area from AERODYNAMICS to diet and training. They included MICHELE FERRARI, who went on to a controversial career that included helping LANCE ARMSTRONG win seven Tours de France.

The buildup lasted three months; Moser earned £96,000 for breaking the record. Although the record was subsequently discredited when Moser confessed that he had used blood doping—not a practice banned at the time, but one forbidden in later years—it led to huge interest in aerodynamics. Moser used disc wheels, skinsuits, low-profile frame, lycra skinhat and shoe covers, and cow-horn handlebars, all of which became popular. He also gauged his training with a pulse monitor and trained specially with what amounted to weight training on his bike, riding for long periods up moderately steep climbs using high gears.

Aerodynamics, energy drinks, and scientific monitoring are ubiquitous in cycling today, thanks partly to the emphatic way in which Moser broke a record that had been assumed to be unbeatable. Following the record, Moser appeared rejuvenated and won MILAN–SAN REMO, then took a controversial win in the GIRO D'ITALIA where it was alleged that the organizers had worked behind the scenes to ensure a home winner.

As well as his record in Paris–Roubaix—which he finished 12 times between 1974 and 1986, never coming home lower than 13th—Moser was also involved in one of Italian cycling's greatest RIVALRIES, with the 1982 world champion Giuseppe Saronni. He later retired to start a bike company, came briefly out of retirement in 1995 to attempt an hour record using the tuck position invented by GRAEME OBREE, and ran a vineyard in his native Trento.

MOTORPACING Racing on the track behind full-size adapted motorbikes, known as the "big motors," is rarely seen nowadays, but was popular through the golden era of track racing, reaching a peak in the 1920s with what French historian Pierre Chany termed "the speed frenzy," when motorpace specialists would vie to become the fastest man in the world. The speeds reached were terrifying. A season-long duel in 1925 between the Belgian Leon Vanderstuyft and the Frenchman Jean Brunier, one attempt after the other, culminated with Brunier getting past 75 mph (120 kph).

They used specially adapted "stayer" bikes, with small front wheels and straight forks to enable them to get closer to the motorbike—on which the rider stood at the very rear, bolt upright (with long handlebars) to give the maximum amount of shelter. A second seat-post might be fitted between the nose of the saddle and the top tube to counter G-forces pushing the rider downward and distorting the saddle. A roller attached to the back of the motorbike meant that if the cyclist's front wheel made contact, he would stay upright. These were hugely dangerous events: in one attempt, Vanderstuyft wore seven jerseys for protection if he happened to fall.

Motorpaced was the first event on the track world-championship program in 1895, and the machines and bikes used today look like throwbacks to the 1920s; spectacular as the discipline is, it is only feasible on larger, often open-air tracks, and there was constant speculation about deals being done between the small group of drivers at the Worlds. It was removed from the championship after the 1994 Worlds in Palermo, Sicily. The last world motorpaced champion was Carsten Podlesch of Germany.

Smaller motorbikes with pedal assistance known as DERNYS are used in some track events. Some SIX-DAY RACES and track meets include Derny-paced races, and a single Derny makes the pace for the initial laps in KEIRIN races outside Japan. They are also used by track racers for training, although the Great Britain team tends to use a full-size motorbike to get greater speed.

The Bordeaux–Paris "Derby of the road" was the only CLASSIC to keep up the tradition of both motor- and cycle-pacing. It had cycle-pacing until 1930, after which the riders were paced either by commercially available motorbikes or Dernys for all or part of the distance until the race's demise in 1988. The record for the event's 580-odd kilometers was just under 30 mph (47.610 kph set by Andre Chalmel in 1979).

MOULTON, Dr. Alex, CBE
(b. England, 1920)

Designer who was the first man to make a fundamental change to cycle design since the invention of the SAFETY BICYCLE, when he launched a small-wheeled machine with full suspension in 1962. From a swinging '60s novelty to go with miniskirts and beehive hairdos, the Moulton cycle is now a design classic, although it has never ousted the large-wheeled cycle. That's because for road use conventional 27-inch or 700C wheels with pneumatic tires offer sufficient comfort and durability to make suspension an unnecessary complication.

Moulton worked initially in airplane engineering, then on car suspensions using rubber, and is best known for developing and producing the system used in another iconic 1960s design, the Mini. He took six years to produce his bike, which had a frame shaped like an F lying on its side. The critical factor was the rubber-based suspension, a version of that used on the Mini, enabling the small wheels to be used with high pressure tires so there was no compromise in ride or performance. A principal base tube connected the top of the front fork and the rear drop-out, while two extensions held the saddle and the handlebars.

To convince a sceptical, conservative market that this was a serious machine, Moulton and his marketing manager David Duffield went into sponsorship. A month after its launch, top British time triallist John Woodburn broke the Cardiff–London record on one of the bikes; a team pursuit team proved successful on them—because the small wheels enabled the team to keep closer together, reducing drag—and TOM SIMPSON became a fan when he rode one at the Herne Hill track. With help from the British Motoring Corporation, Moulton rapidly became Britain's second-largest cycle maker behind RALEIGH, selling 1,000 bikes a week by 1965. Other companies produced small-wheel bikes but never really caught up.

Initially Moulton worked with Raleigh to produce bikes aimed at the mass market; the marriage was an unhappy one and subsequently Sir Alex focused on high-quality, hand-built bikes. In 1983 the AM (Alex Moulton) 7 bike was launched, with the "space frame" made up of a lattice of small diameter tubes. A Moulton fitted with a fairing to improve AERODYNAMICS was ridden at 51 mph over 200 m, a world record.

Today, the latest Moultons incorporate suspension with rubber springs and adjustable fluid damping and offer two key features: because they are shallow in height they can be used by cyclists of all sizes, and they can be "separated"—divided into several bits—making them easy to fit in a car trunk or a suitcase. The top-of-the-range models are made in Reynolds 531 (see FRAMES—MATERIALS), with adjustable bars, stem, and brake levers. Moulton APBs (all purpose bicycles) are made under licence by bicycle and tricycle makers Pashley in Stratford-on-Avon, while Moultons are also made in Japan.

Moultons have gained a passionate worldwide following, many of whom are members of the Moulton Bicycle Club and visit the annual Moulton weekend at the company's headquarters in Bradford-on-Avon. They have been used for long-distance touring rides—their strong small wheels and low center of gravity make them well-adapted for carrying luggage—although they are best loved by commuters.

(SEE WHEELS)

MOUNTAIN-BIKING Sprang up in the US in the late 1970s from various antiestablishment off-road rides, most notably the DOWNHILL races held on the REPACK trail in California. Of the Repack crew, Charlie Kelly started the magazine *Fat Tire Flyer*, Mike Sinyard produced the groundbreaking Specialized Stumpjumper, and framebuilders Joe Breeze and Tom Ritchey and GARY FISHER all became key figures in mountain-bike mythology.

"Gary was the mechanic, the inventor, and a test rider . . . Charlie was also a test rider, constantly suggesting improvements, tracking down components, then using them until they broke. He was also the chronicler," wrote Richard Grant in his introduction to the 1988 *Richard's Mountain-bike Book*.

Repack was just one of several underground off-road rides in the US at the time. Another was the annual trek from Crested Butte to Aspen over Pearl Pass using an old mining road, while the first recorded cross-country race was held in Marin County in 1977. Many of the bikes used were "clunkers," based on the 1930s cruiser machines made by SCHWINN, scavenged from bike-shop scrap heaps and customized with motorbike brake levers, bar-mounted shift levers, fat tires, and primitive hub brakes. The term "mountain bike" was first used for a company set up by Kelly and Fisher in 1979 to market the machines.

Breeze built an early run of 10 replica "clunkers" for Kelly—with cantilever brakes and Magura motorbike brake levers—but Ritchey made the first ones to enter the market, at $1,300 each, and began using the 26-inch wheels that are now standard. In 1980 Sinyard bought some Ritchey bikes and used them as the basis for the Stumpjumper, which hit the market in 1981. A year later SHIMANO and SunTour brought out mountain-bike groupsets and by 1984, US mountain-bike sales had hit a million.

The first umbrella body, National Off-Road Bicycle Association, was founded in Kelly's house in 1983 and set the early pace for developing off-road racing. At the same time, off-road tourists such as Nicholas Crane (later to present the BBC series *Coast*) pushed the boundaries and helped boost the profile of the new bikes by taking the machines to places

like Kilimanjaro, Mont Blanc, and the Yukon. Australians Tim Gartside and Peter Murphy crossed the Sahara in 1983.

The general public might not have wanted to ride in those places, but they liked having machines that looked as if they could. Cycling off-road was not new but the notion that doing it made you part of a movement was a novelty, and it was jumped upon rapidly by well-marketed companies such as Muddy Fox, who pushed their product hard in the British market.

In 1987 there were two world championships run by rival governing bodies, one in the Alps at Villard de Lans, one in the US at Mammoth, California. The UCI sanctioned mountain-biking in 1990 and the first official WORLD CHAMPIONSHIPS took place at Durango, with Ned Overend and Juli Furtado of the US winning the cross-country events. The first UCI-sanctioned World Cup series, sponsored by Grundig, was run in 1991.

In the early 1990s, the Americans who had founded the sport began to be matched by European cyclists such as Henrik Djernis of Denmark and Thomas Frischknecht of Switzerland who had transferred from CYCLO-CROSS. Early British stars were also 'cross riders such as David Baker and Tim Gould, who formed a strong partnership for PEUGEOT.

During the 1990s stage races became popular, with the TOUR DE FRANCE organizers experimenting with a mountain-bike Tour in which the riders and caravan slept out in tents. France's Fred Moncassin became the only man to win stages in the mountain-bike and road Tours. A VUELTA A ESPAÑA was also run, and a Tour of Switzerland. In Australia, the Crocodile Trophy was born, with 17 stages averaging 150 km in length. In 1996, cross-country was accepted into the OLYMPIC GAMES with Paola Pezzo and Bart Brentjens the first champions. The blond-haired Pezzo, heavily marketed by Cannondale, gave the sport a glamour side.

By then, mountain-bike

sales had outstripped road-bike sales in the US and UK and the arrival of the fat-tire bikes had led to a complete change in the cycling marketplace, introducing vast numbers of new people to bike riding. It also radically restructured the market, bringing technical innovation in its wake that eventually transferred into road racing. Helmets were quickly made compulsory in mountain-biking and were improved rapidly as a result, making them acceptable to road racers.

There was almost constant technical development as Shimano and SunTour experimented with componentry and conditioned the market to expect annual upgrades. All the while manufacturers vied to produce the sexiest suspension bikes. Oversize aluminium became popular thanks to makers like Klein and Cannondale, while suspension came in from the early 1990s. The 1990 men's world championship was won using front suspension, and Rockshox's provision of forks to GREG LEMOND and company in PARIS–ROUBAIX from 1991 onward created a useful buzz.

Mountain-biking spawned a number of off-shoots to go with the original cross-country and downhill. Enduros are run along the same lines as CYCLOSPORTIVES, which actually drew on early mountain-bike cross-country races for inspiration. Mountain-bike orienteering has a hard-core following while trials contests are centerd on the central notion of mountain-biking—that you have to get over, around, up and down obstacles you wouldn't dare tackle on a road bike.

(SEE **CYCLO-CROSS** AND **ROUGH STUFF** FOR OTHER WAYS OF CYCLING OFF-ROAD)

MURPHY, Charles (b. New York, 1871, d. 1950)

Charles "Mile a Minute" Murphy was the first man in history to go faster than 60 mph using human muscle power. He covered a measured mile in 57.8 seconds at Maywood, Long Island, on June 30, 1899, and epitomized an era when cyclists were pushing the limits of human propulsion with whatever pacing assistance could be devised. A flamboyant track racer, Murphy would appear at events dressed in a racing suit based on the US flag, with a huge eagle on the chest. Murphy set his record behind a steam railway engine pulling a coach with a boarded enclosure at the back to shelter him; two and a half miles of planks were laid between the railway tracks to take the bike. Initially the engine could not go fast enough and, in spite of the adaptations to the coach, Murphy was constantly battered by turbulence during the minute he spent at 60 mph and weaved from side to side, almost losing control of his bike as the boards undulated due to the weight of the engine. He was splattered with dust, cinders, and burning rubber from under the carriage.

At the end of the mile, the train slowed down; Murphy couldn't. He slammed into the back of the coach and was dragged on board with his bike still attached to his feet. The sight terrified the several thousand onlookers including his wife and children.

Murphy went on to a successful professional career, claiming seven world records by 1895, and became a policeman when his racing days ended.

N

NICKNAMES   Not surprisingly in
a sport created by JOURNALISTS,
from the very earliest days it
has been the press rather than
the fans who have tended to give
cyclists their nicknames in order
to dramatize a sport in which
much of the action can be a little
monotonous. Tour founder HENRI
DESGRANGE and his sidekick Géo
Lefèvre are the founding fathers
here too: their dispatches in
L'Auto refer to cyclists as "the
Furniture Makers" champion,"
the "Prince of the Miners," or
the "White Bulldog." (For why
MAURICE GARIN, winner of the
first TOUR DE FRANCE, was
nicknamed "the Little Chimney
Sweep," see his entry.)

The most famous nickname of
all was given to EDDY MERCKX:
"the Cannibal" was coined
in 1971 by the daughter of a
frustrated Frenchman, Christian
Raymond, after the Belgian won
a stage in the Midi Libre race by
half an hour. In the 1980s, SEAN
KELLY was nicknamed "the New
Cannibal" while JEANNIE LONGO
is "the Lady Cannibal."

The lexicon of cycling beasts
is endless: the Spaniard Vicente
Trueba was "the Flea," because
of the way he jumped in the
mountains. BERNARD HINAULT
said that he was called "the
Badger" because the beast
fights hard when it is cornered.
Laurent Jalabert never really
liked being known as "the
Panda," because of the dark
circles around his eyes, while
Joop Zoetemelk was referred
to as "the Rat," because he
allegedly did not contribute in
races. Climbing "eagles" such
as FEDERICO BAHAMONTES and
Ferdi Kubler are numerous,
so too valiant "lions" such as

Fiorenzo Magni, while Jan Ullrich was known as "*Der Uhle*," the Owl, a wordplay on an abbreviation of his surname: Ulli. The British Olympic medalist Geraint Thomas has been called "the Penguin," because, said David Millar, he resembles the characters from the film *Madagascar*: cute on the outside, ruthless inside. (Millar was nicknamed "Boy Dave" until he fell foul of a DOPING scandal in 2004.) The French call any Australian cyclist "*le Kangourou*."

There have been several "eternal seconds," riders more famous for never quite managing to win: Zoetemelk was one, RAYMOND POULIDOR another. The diminutive is common—Perico for Pedro Delgado, Poupou for Poulidor—but on the other hand "Big Mig," the nickname for MIGUEL INDURAIN, was invented by British journalists when asked by an American colleague for a translation of his Spanish monicker Miguelon. The author can claim credit for the "Tashkent Terror," as the

Uzbek sprinter DJAMOLIDIN ABDUZHAPAROV was known; he was also called "the Terminator," for the way Abdu' kept falling down and getting up again.

Some nicknames just happen: no one knows who first called SEAN YATES "Tonk" or "Horse" although the sense is obvious. British journalists referred to French climber Richard Virenque as "Tricky Dicky"—when he was being evasive about the Festina drug scandal—and also "Spotted Dick," a reference to the red and white Tour climber's jersey.

Some cyclists have coined their own nicknames for marketing purposes. Tour climber Claudio Chiappucci was the first, calling himself "*il Diablo*." MARCO PANTANI was first known as "*Elefantino*"—Dumbo—because of his big ears, and also "Nosferatu" because of his emaciated face, but sold himself as "*Il Pirata*," because of his seaside roots, and created a line of bandanas, saddles, and other accessories with a skull and crossbones motif; his 1999 team launch featured a vast mock-up of a pirate ship.

With the help of a shoe company, sprinter Mario Cipollini went through many incarnations: for instance "the Sun King," "*il Magnifico*." He was also referred to as "SuperMario" and as "Moussolini," for his hair gel.

Nicknames are less prevalent in women's cycling, but the dominant force, Jeannie Longo, has been called "Ma Dalton," after the ferocious old lady created by the cartoonist Goscinny; her great rival Maria Canins was rather patronizingly known (probably by male writers) as "*La Mamma Volante*"—the flying mother.

Other great nicknames: "the Cycling Brummel" (1935 world champion Jean Aerts), "The Pious One" (GINO BARTALI), "the Mason of Friuli" (Ottavio Bottecchia, 1924–5 Tour de France winner), "*le Pedaleur de Charme*" (Hugo Koblet), and "Major Tom" (TOM SIMPSON). "The Professor" was LAURENT FIGNON, 1983–4 Tour winner; the "Gypsy" or "Beast of Eeklo" four-time Paris–Roubaix winner ROGER DE VLAEMINCK.

NUDE CYCLING   First depicted, perhaps, in an 18th-century English church window and popular in turn-of-the-century French POSTERS, cycling with nothing on has gone from a fringe activity to a way of garnering publicity and money. The rock band Queen gathered a bevy of naked models on bikes at the Crystal Palace cycling circuit to shoot the cover for their song "Bicycle Race" in 1978; 24 years later the photoshoot was recreated with 18 models on BMX bikes to promote a computer game.

LANCE ARMSTRONG brought nudity into the mainstream by posing naked—side on—on his bike for Annie Leibovitz for the magazine *Vanity Fair* in 1999. Armstrong's pose was copied by the British OLYMPIC team sprinter Victoria Pendleton—said to be wearing flesh-colored underwear—for the magazine *Observer Sport Monthly* in 2008. Apparently her dentist disapproved, but her parents were happy with the picture. Later, Pendleton's fellow Beijing gold-medalist Rebecca Romero was depicted wearing only gold body paint in a sports drink advertisement that made it into the British tabloid press.

More seriously, naked cycling is now a form of protest, with the annual world naked bike ride (www.worldnakedbikeride. org) against car culture and climate change taking place in 60 countries, including the US, Britain, Canada, Spain, and Germany. The extent of undress is up to the participants and includes various forms of body-painting but nudity is here used as a metaphor to express the vulnerability of cyclists in traffic.

In reference to the CRITICAL MASS RIDES in protest at traffic conditions, there are also naked rides called Critical Ass and Critical Tits. At the British event in Brighton one March, the temperature meant the ride had to be brief and the participants wore woolly hats and gloves. In June 2009, 700 rode in the event, then went skinny-dipping in the sea.

O

OBREE, Graeme

Born: Ayrshire, Scotland, September 11, 1965
Major wins: World pursuit champion 1993, 1995; world Hour Records 1993, 1994
Nickname: the Flying Scotsman
Further reading/viewing: *Flying Scotsman*, Graeme Obree, Velo Press, 2005; DVD *Battle of the Bikes*

In July 1993 a leading Italian journalist heard that a Scottish amateur on a homemade bike was making a largely self-financed attempt to break the fearsome HOUR RECORD held by the legendary Italian FRANCESCO MOSER. The nine-year-old record was considered definitive and cycling greats such as BERNARD HINAULT and GREG LEMOND felt it was too hard for them. The writer scoffed and said that if Graeme Obree beat Moser he would retire and return to his mamma's farm to eat pasta.

But in one of cycling's most improbable rises to fame, if not exactly fortune, Obree not only bettered Moser's distance on the velodrome at Hamar, Norway, but did so at his second attempt on the record within 48 hours. Conventional wisdom has it that it is impossible to recover from an effort such as this overnight, but Obree kept his legs from stiffening up by drinking copious amounts of water so he had to wake up to urinate. Each time he woke, he did stretching exercises to ease his muscles.

He followed that up with a world championship in the individual pursuit, beating the Olympic champion CHRIS BOARDMAN, and he added a second world title in 1995. He later wrote a detailed account of his severe depression and suicide attempts.

Obree is a policeman's son

from Ayrshire who was drawn to cycling partly to escape being bullied at school, and he has always had an unconventional approach to the sport. He turned up at his first race, a time trial, wearing Dr. Martens shoes and stopped before the finish because he assumed the race ended where it had begun. By the early 1990s, his RIVALRY with Boardman had become intense, as much due to the contrast between the pair as what happened on the road. It was captured in a television documentary, *Battle of the Bikes*. Obree built his own bikes and lived off a diet of sliced white bread, marmelade, and cornflakes. At one point in his life, when his phone was cut off, he could only be reached by calling the pay phone on the street where he lived.

The key to Obree's success was his hunch that a radical "tucked-in" aerodynamic position would make him faster (see AERODYNAMICS). "I got the hacksaw out, turned the bars up, cut the extra off and that was me. I hadn't been riding much, but I did a personal best." In 1989 he won 26 time trials and took the British hour record. Much of his training was done on an adapted home trainer with a leather belt—"like for round your waist"—to control resistance.

The machine he designed to beat Moser's hour record had an F-shaped frame like a MOULTON folding bike, a narrow bottom bracket to keep his feet close together, and high handlebars so that his arms could be bent up underneath his chest. To get the bike narrow, he incorporated a washing-machine bearing, not because it was all he could afford, but because it was the perfect size. Riding on the Bordeaux velodrome, Boardman bettered Obree's distance a week after the Scot beat Moser's distance, but Obree returned the following April to regain the record. Five months later, the quintuple

Tour winner MIGUEL INDURAIN went even faster.

Obree's sporting success and easygoing manner hid the fact that he was mentally ill. His successes, he said, came from a terror of failing. He was driven, he said, by "a need to win to feel worthwhile enough to go about the daily business of life." Obree made several attempts to kill himself before he was eventually diagnosed as manic depressive with a personality disorder. His record and world championship had been "a life shock" he said later, taking him from hunting for pennies down the back of his sofa to contracts worth thousands of dollars. "I was just swept along. Cycling was a party trick and I liked the reaction."

The radical position adopted by Obree challenged conventional thinking, which was that the diamond frame adopted in the late 19th century was the most efficient form for cyclists: other cyclists tried the tuck, including Moser, who made a comeback in order to prove that only the position had

enabled Obree to beat his distance. The cycling authorities felt that too much attention was being paid to aerodynamics and banned the tuck a few minutes before Obree defended his pursuit title in 1994.

After being prevented from riding that year, Obree responded by creating a new position nicknamed "Superman," in which his arms pointed straight forward, and he used it to win the 1995 world pursuit title. Superman was used by the Italian team to dominate the 1996 Olympic Games track events, while Boardman set a definitive Hour Record using it later that year. The position was ruled illegal at the end of 1996, and Obree retired from cycling, although he returned in 2006 to take the team prize in the Scottish 10-mile time trial championship. A FILM entitled the *Flying Scotsman* was made of his life story starring Johnny Lee Miller. In February 2011 Obree again made headlines with his revelation that he is homosexual, which made him the first high-profile male cyclist to come out.

OCHOWICZ, Jim (b. Milwaukee, Wisconsin, 1951)

A mainstay of US road racing for 30 years, and a legendary team manager, Ochowicz began his cycling career as a track racer, competing in the team pursuit at the 1972 and 1976 summer Olympics. He was one of the founders of the 7-Eleven cycling team in 1981 and managed the squad when it successfully transferred to European racing in 1985, becoming the first US team to start the Tour the following year. The squad included stars of US cycling such as Davis Phinney and Andy Hampsten, who gave the United States their first victory in the 1988 Giro d'Italia. In 1990, Ochowicz's team led the TOUR DE FRANCE for nine stages with the Canadian STEVE BAUER. When 7-Eleven ceased sponsorship at the end of 1990, Ochowicz obtained backing from the Motorola corporation. The team initially relied on the Australian veteran Phil Anderson and was then built around a rising star: Lance Armstrong. Motorola ceased sponsorship at the end of 1996, and Ochowicz became a stockbroker working with Thomas Weisl, owner of the US Postal Service team. He maintained his links with professional cycling by managing the US national team at the world road race championships and served as president of US Cycling from 2002 to 2006. In 2007 he began working with the Swiss squad BMC, the connection being that Ochowicz helped secure sponsorship for the team's precursor Phonak with the iShares company, only for the deal to fall through when Phonak leader Floyd Landis tested positive. Ochowicz helped guide BMC to ProTour status in 2010. He is married to the former track cyclist and Olympic speed skater Sheila Young.

OLYMPIC GAMES Cycling was included in the Olympics when they were founded in 1896 by Baron de Coubertin and has been in every Games since, apart from 1904 when there were no official events. For 100 years, however, the Olympics carried less weight in the cycling world than the TOUR DE FRANCE or road-race WORLD CHAMPIONSHIP. The professional elite were unable to compete so the Games were seen as, at best, a stepping stone to a pro career. As a result, prior to 1996, very few of cycling's top names figured in the results: for example, the only "amateur" Games medalist to win a Tour de France is Joop Zoetemelk of Holland.

The program has undergone numerous changes. Women's cycling was a disgracefully late inclusion in the Games, given that women were brought into the world road-race championships in 1958. It was another 26 years before the Games recognized women's cyclists, with Connie Carpenter winning the inaugural road race in Los Angeles. In track racing, the women's sprint did not figure until 1988, and the pursuit in 1992, and women remained hard done by well into the 21st century, with only one event for female sprinters compared to three for the men.

The most significant recent change occurred in 1996 in Atlanta, when "open" cycling events were held, with the best professionals permitted to compete. That was achieved by removing the distinction between the amateur and pro sides of the sport; in that year, the road time trial was also introduced, and MIGUEL INDURAIN's victory symbolized the arrival at the Games of the biggest names in cycling. In the same year, the MOUNTAIN-BIKE cross-country was brought in.

BMX was made an Olympic sport in 2008, but this happened amid huge controversy, as the kilometer time trial—an event dating back to the 1896 Games— was dropped in spite of intense opposition. More hot debate looked to be in store running up

United States Olympic Medals

❖

Paris, 1900　　　　bronze: John Henry Lake, sprint

St. Louis, 1904　　only US cyclists competed in all seven cycling events, thus winning 21
medals. Marcus Hurley won four gold medals and a bronze; Burton Downing won
two golds, three silvers, and a bronze.

Stockholm, 1912　bronze: road-race team; Carl Schutte, road race

Los Angeles, 1984　gold: Mark Gorski, sprint; Steve Hegg, pursuit; Alexi Grewal, road race; Connie
Carpenter, women's road race

silver: Nelson Vails, sprint; Rebecca Twigg, women's road race

bronze: Leonard Harvey Nitz, pursuit; time-trial team

Seoul, 1988　　　bronze: Connie Young, women's sprint

Barcelona, 1992　bronze: Erin Hartwell, kilometer; Rebecca Twigg, women's pursuit

Atlanta, 1996　　silver: Marty Nothstein, sprint; Erin Hartwell, kilometer; Susan DeMattei, women's
cross-country

Sydney, 2000　　gold: Marty Nothstein, sprint

silver: Mari Holden, women's individual time trial

bronze: Lance Armstrong, individual time trial

Athens, 2004　　gold: Tyler Hamilton, individual time trial

silver: Deirdre Demet-Barry, women's individual time trial

bronze: Bobby Julich, individual time trial

Beijing, 2008　　gold: Kristin Armstrong, women's individual time trail

silver: Mike Day, BMX

bronze: Levi Leipheimer, individual time trial; Donny Robinson, BMX; Jill
Kintner, women's BMX

to 2012, as radical alterations were made to the track program to achieve parity for men and women Olympians.

Three events with long-standing traditions, the pursuit, points race, and Madison, were removed. They were replaced by a new event, the omnium, a six-event "pentathlon" style event combining a kilometer time trial, 250 m flying start time trial, points, scratch, "devil take the hindmost," and pursuit. The women sprinters were set to gain two events, the team sprint and KEIRIN, gaining parity with their male counterparts.

(SEE **TRACK RACING** FOR MORE ON THESE DISCIPLINES.)

OPPERMAN, Sir Hubert

Born: Rochester, Australia, May 29, 1904
Died: Knox, Australia, April 24, 1996
Major wins: Australian champion 1924, 1926–7, 1929; Paris–Brest–Paris 1931; OBE 1952, knighted 1980
Nickname: Oppy

One of AUSTRALIA's greatest sportsmen in any arena, "Oppy" was a pioneer who won hearts and minds in Europe in the 1920s then went on to a successful career in POLITICS after the Second World War. Opperman was a butcher's son who delivered telegrams on his bike, played Australian Rules Football and cricket at school, and was picked up at the age of 17 by Malvern Star Cycles. Opperman won four Australian road championships for the bike company, and his name was always to be associated with them. Through Malvern boss Bruce Small, who would remain his manager throughout his cycling career, he was introduced to Don Kirkham, one of two Australians to finish the 1914 TOUR DE FRANCE (the other being Iddo "Snowy" Munro). The 18-year-old Oppy soaked up Kirkham's tales of racing in Europe and set off in 1928 for his own campaign that would include the Tour de France, paid for in part by a fundraising campaign in three newspapers in Australia and New Zealand. In the Tour, Opperman and his three teammates were at a huge disadvantage: most of the stages were TEAM TIME TRIALS in which they would struggle against 10-man squads while having to finish within each day's time limit. They also faced language difficulties: their manager was French and the race organizers would not permit him to talk to their translator, the journalist Rene de Latour, who wrote of "poor lonely Opperman being caught day after day by the various teams of ten super athletes, swopping their pace beautifully." Even so, Opperman rode into Paris 18th overall, over eight and a half hours behind the winner Nicolas Frantz of Luxembourg. He was immediately invited to ride the Bol d'Or 24-hour race at the Buffalo velodrome in Paris, a nonstop event in which the stars were assisted by teams of pacers. There were two attempts to sabotage his bike by sawing through the chain, but his team manager found a heavy substitute machine to enable Oppy to win. He was warmly applauded

for his ability to urinate while riding. He completed 909 km (565 miles) and was persuaded to keep going for another 79 minutes to add the world 1,000-kilometer record. So popular were his feats in France that he was voted athlete of the year by the readers of *L'Auto*, the paper that ran the Tour.

In 1931, he returned for a second attempt at the Tour, finishing 12th, but, more significantly, he managed to win PARIS–BREST–PARIS, the first victory by a non-European in the toughest CLASSIC of the time. The race was run in rain and headwinds, but the biggest obstacle was simply staying awake through two nights on the road. Here Opperman admitted that he was helped by his experiences racing massive distances in Australian events such as Sydney– Melbourne: he banged his head with his hands, sang tunelessly every few minutes, and swallowed the coffee, tea, soup, and chops provided by Small. Incredibly, the 49-hour race came down to a five-man sprint on the Versailles velodrome, where Opperman won by 10 lengths.

In 1934, Opperman moved to Britain for a road-record campaign, sponsored by BSA, who were linked to Malvern. He broke five distance records in a fortnight, including the END TO END from Land's End–John O'Groats in 1934. He broke virtually every record on the books in Australia, setting a Freemantle–Sydney time of 13 days, 11 hours, 52 minutes, and closing his career by smashing 100 records in a 24-hour attempt in Sydney.

After serving in the war in the Royal Australian Air Force, he entered the Australian Parliament and was, variously, minister for transport, minister for immigration, and high commissioner to Malta. He continued cycling until the age of 90, and was actually on an exercise bike when he died.

PANTANI, Marco

Born: Cesena, Italy, January 13, 1970

Died: Rimini, Italy, February 14, 2004

Major wins: Tour de France and Giro d'Italia 1998, eight stage wins in each; second, 1997 Tour; third, 1994 Tour; second, 1994 Giro; bronze medal, 1995 world road championships

Nicknames: Dumbo, the Little Elephant, Nosferatu, the Pirate, and Pac-man—because of the way he would gobble up rivals one by one en route to a mountaintop finish

Reading: *The Death of Marco Pantani*, Matt Rendell, Phoenix, 2007

The charismatic and deeply troubled Italian was one of professional cycling's most celebrated climbing talents and one of its most distinctive stars thanks to his shaven head and big ears. He was one of a small minority to achieve the DOUBLE of wins in the GIRO D'ITALIA and TOUR DE FRANCE in the same year, but died a tragic death and came to epitomize the drug problems of the sport in the 1990s and beyond.

Pantani emerged as a professional in the 1994 Giro, taking second to Evgeni Berzin and showing MIGUEL INDURAIN a clean pair of heels in the mountains. In the 1994 Tour de France it was impossible to ignore him: he made dramatic attacks, fell off every now and then, and finished third. Every mountain inspired the same thought: when would Pantani make his move, and what would happen?

In 1995 he won two Tour stages, but suffered a horrific collision with a 4 × 4 while descending in the Milan–Turin; it was widely assumed that the compound fracture of his right shin had ended his career.

In April 1996 it had healed to a massive lump, with livid scars where the pins had been put in to stabilize the fracture. At that point he could only pedal a low gear, to avoid putting pressure on the leg.

By July 1997 he had recovered sufficiently to win two mountain stages of the Tour and take second overall. His wins in the 1998 Giro d'Italia and Tour were inspiring after the DOPING scandal that hit the 1998 Tour. The legendary double put him on a level with the greats of cycling; overnight he became Italy's biggest sports star, with earnings estimated at £2 million a year. But his downfall came suddenly in June 1999 when he was thrown off the Giro d'Italia, at a point where a crushing victory was seemingly assured, for failing a blood test that indicated possible use of EPO. He was embittered for the rest of his life by the incident; he was convinced he had been unfairly targeted and could not believe the way that the cycling milieu turned its back on him.

Subsequently, officials found evidence he had used EPO; he was later banned for the use of insulin, found in a syringe when police raided the Giro. In 2000 he returned to cycling to complete the Giro—after a papal reception in the Vatican—and won the Mont Ventoux stage of the Tour, but during his spell in limbo he had acquired a cocaine habit that dogged him to his retirement in 2003 and beyond. "I'm fighting simply to get back my peace of mind and my love of the bike," he said early that year. When he was found dead of a heart attack in a hotel in Rimini on Valentine's Day 2004 he was an addict whose friends had made numerous, fruitless attempts to clean him up.

Pantani's death has inspired a charitable foundation and an elaborate mausoleum in his home town, where his statue stands on the main square. There are also roadside MEMORIALS to recall some of his greatest exploits: on the Mortirolo and Fauniera passes in Italy and at the Deux Alpes ski resort in France. Two major CYCLOSPORTIVES, the Nove Colli and the Marco Pantani, go over climbs associated with him.

(SEE ALSO **ITALY**, **DRUGS**)

PARALYMPIC CYCLING Brought in as an Olympic sport in Seoul in 1988—for road events only—with the first track events in Atlanta in 1996. The UCI recognizes three categories of event in Disability Cycling: Blind and Partially Sighted (VI or B/VI), Cerebral Palsy (CP), and Locomotor (LC). Riders are assessed before their category is allotted. VI riders race on the back of a tandem with a fully sighted pilot. Races include flying 200 m, match sprint, kilometer time trial, and pursuit.

CP is a condition occurring at birth that interferes with the development of the brain, affecting muscle tone and spinal reflexes. Brain injuries later in life can lead to the same symptoms, and these athletes compete with congenital CP cyclists. Locomotor athletes are divided into four categories depending on the level of limb disability; they can and often do compete on handcycles.

The GREAT BRITAIN cycling team has a dedicated paralympic section that dominated its events in Beijing in 2008, winning 17 gold medals and 3 silvers. Britain's leading cycling Paralympian is Darren Kenny from Dorset, a double gold medal winner in Athens and a triple gold medalist in Beijing in 2008. Kenny injured his neck in the RÁS Tour of Ireland aged 19 and returned to racing 11 years later merely in order to get fit.

PARIS–BREST–PARIS Every few years strange sights are to be seen on back roads between Paris and Brittany: vast groups of cyclists with their bikes festooned with panniers riding through the night in great streams of cycle lights, bedraggled cyclists lining up outside school cafeterias and village *salles de fêtes* to fill up on carbohydrate-rich food, and, oddest of all, men and women clad in lycra sleeping wherever they can by the roadside: in haystacks, hedges, doorways.

Such is Paris–Brest–Paris, one of the great pioneering races when it was founded in 1891, now two different mass events run in four- and five-year cycles for several thousand cycle-tourists who don't mind a little sleep deprivation. In villages and towns along the 1,200 km route, the population turns out to watch the cyclists, who try to complete the event within the 90-hour limit. That means riding through the night, three times, with a few short naps along the way: sometimes in market halls, with labels at their feet to tell helpers when they want to be woken up. In parts of Brittany, local people still turn out to place candles in jam jars and tins to light the way into their villages at the dead of night.

PBP was founded in 1891 by the newspaper *Le Petit Journal*, as a test of bicycle reliability at a time when penny farthings were being supplanted by diamond frames. Charles Terront won the first race in 71 hours 22 minutes, with the aid of the 10 pacers placed along the route to help the riders. The race's distance, straight down Route Nationale 12 and back, was such that it was decided to organize it only once every 10 years. The great publicity line was that as the turn point was in the French *département* of Finistère, it could be billed as a race "to the ends of the earth." The second edition, 1901, was won by MAURICE GARIN in just over 52 hours. *Le Petit Journal* was joined as sponsor by *L'Auto*; such was the paper's increase in sales that its editor HENRI DESGRANGE began looking for ideas for an annual event that would last even longer and be an even greater test of stamina: he and his colleague Géo Lefèvre came up with the TOUR DE FRANCE.

The last pro PBP race was in 1951 and was won by Frenchman Maurice Diot in a record 38 hours 55 minutes, a time that still stands today. Randonneur and AUDAX events had begun

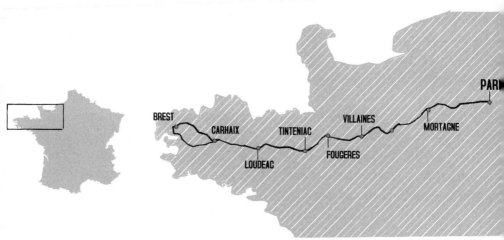

in 1931, and while the pro race could not draw enough entrants, the *touristes* kept turning up. The *randonneur* and audax events were run by different organizations until 1991 when the events were combined.

In 2003 some of the first male finishers were excluded from the closing ceremony and penalized two hours after finishing with the fastest times in the event's history. They had contravened various rules but more importantly were felt to have behaved in a way that contravened the spirit of the event, including "pushing the controllers at a control, urinating in a built-up area, not respecting red lights and stop signs on numerous occasions, using the lights of a following car illegally and not letting a controller's car pass." In essence, those penalized had crossed the intangible line between a "tourist event," in which a time may be taken but the spirit of the event is amicable, and a race, in which anything goes in order to be quickest from A to B.

(SEE **CAPE TOWN**, **CYCLOSPORTIVES**, AND **ÉTAPE DU TOUR** FOR OTHER LONG-DISTANCE CHALLENGES)

PARIS–ROUBAIX The "Queen of Classics," *La Pascale*, or simply the "Hell of the North," this is the most coveted one-day CLASSIC of them all. All the MONUMENTS of cycling are founded on tradition: the inclusion of over 30 miles of COBBLES means that Paris–Roubaix is simply a throwback to the HEROIC ERA, when road surfaces played a key role in every cycle race. The event is not universally popular among professionals because of the risks involved: every year there are crashes on the cobblestones and a cyclist's entire season can be compromised. *"Une cochonnerie,"* was the verdict of BERNARD HINAULT. "A man's race," said SEAN YATES, the best Briton in the event. "Cycling's last bit of madness," according to the TOUR DE FRANCE organizer Jacques Goddet.

The event was immortalized in one of the finest cycling FILMS ever: JORGEN LETH's masterpiece *A Sunday in Hell*. Today, it is a key event on the roster of Tour de France organizers AMAURY SPORT ORGANISATION, and French television devotes vast resources to covering it, including specially adapted motorcross bikes to get in-race footage and fixed cameras on the main cobbled sections.

Paris–Roubaix goes back to 1896 and was originally run to publicize a newly built velodrome in an industrial suburb of the city of Lille. It was run on Easter Sunday in the face of opposition from the Church; to placate them, a mass was held at 4 AM before the start. The event still finishes on the velodrome although there have been brief flirtations with other finishes within Roubaix. The riders collapse on to the grass in the middle of the track after the finish; they are doing exactly what the first winner, the German Josef Fischer, would have done. Uniquely for a modern race, the riders shower off the mud and blood in an archaic washroom, where the press can interview them. No other Classic has stayed so close to its past.

Initially the cobbles were just

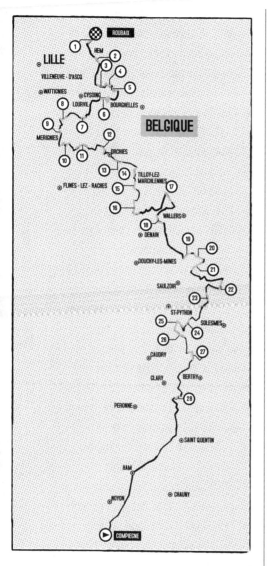

LILLE
ROUBAIX
HEM
VILLENEUVE - D'ASCQ
WATTIGNIES
CYSOING
LOURVIL
BOURGHELLES
MERIGNIES
BELGIQUE
ORCHIES
TILLOY-LEZ
MARCHIENNES
FLINES - LEZ - RACHES
WALLERS
DENAIN
DOUCHY-LES-MINES
SAULZOIR
ST-PYTHON
SOLESMES
CAUDRY
CLARY
BERTRY
PERONNE
SAINT QUENTIN
HAM
NOYON
CHAUNY
COMPIEGNE

part of the route as they were in other races, but by the 1960s the organizers were actively

seeking out cobbled sections to liven up the event. The turning point came in 1968 with the discovery of a horribly deformed, undulating track through the Wallers-Arenberg forest—close to the coalmines that featured in Émile Zola's *Germinal*—that has been the centerpoint of the race since then.

Now the cobbles are threatened by development and restricted to back roads through the fields, with bucolic names such as Prayers' Lane and Sugar Mill Lane. The Amis de Paris–Roubaix exist to maintain them, investing a lot of labor and about €15,000 a year. There are about 30 sections, all subtly different depending on whether the cobbles are slate (slippery) or granite (bad for punctures), uphill, downhill, well maintained, or badly drained and full of water. The decisive point today is about 20 km from the finish, the long, dragging section that leads to a lonely café at Carrefour de l'Arbre: the Crossroads of the Tree.

Racing on the cobbles is a

unique skill, based on pushing a big gear, for as long as your strength lasts, while trying to avoid the potholes and keeping an eye open for crashes. "You can't make any abrupt movements. If it's wet and you make a last-minute movement, you're down," said Yates. "It's like off-piste skiing through trees: you have to have wide vision, all the time." A single rider losing control can result in an instant pile-up; if a rider punctures, it can take several minutes to get a wheel change because team cars get left way behind as the

The Four- and Five-Star Sections

◆

The cobbled sections are numbered, in descending order to the finish, and given star ratings for difficulty by the organizers according to how long they are and the condition of the cobbles. Four and five stars are the hardest.

No. 26 Quiévy–Saint Python: 3.7 km long, including a 2-kilometer uphill drag, which makes it one of the toughest parts of the course. 4*

No. 19 Wallers–Haveluy: 2.5 km long; cobbles are good but often muddy. 4*

No. 18 Trouée d'Arenberg: 2.4 km long, used since 1968, dead straight with irregular, large cobbles, with many potholes. 5* (See COBBLES for more detail)

No. 10 Mons en Pévèle–Mérignies: 3 km long, including two right-angle bends that are often muddy. Particularly bad in the wet. 5*

No. 6 Cysoing–Wannehain: 2.5 km in two sections either side of the village of Bourghelles, with the second particularly rough. 4*

No. 5 Camphin-en-Pévèle: 1.8 km; includes a muddy 90-degree bend, with the roughest cobbles towards the end. 4*

No. 4 Camphin-en-Pévèle–Carrefour de l'Arbre: the key section comes just before the finish, initially flat then rising slightly toward the café on the worst cobbles. 5*

race strings out through the cobbled lanes.

And then there is the continual bumping: "Like sitting on a pneumatic drill," was the verdict of the 1990 runner-up Steve Bauer. The mechanics try various tricks to reduce the pain: at one point in the 1990s, Rockshox MOUNTAIN-BIKE forks became popular, but the usual tweaks are thicker handlebar tape and fatter tires, run at a slightly lower pressure than usual. Winning Paris–Roubaix is the mark of the true cycling great: FAUSTO COPPI and EDDY MERCKX both managed it, but Hinault is the last Tour winner to triumph in cycling's hell. The record winner is ROGER DE VLAEMINCK, with four victories, while FRANCESCO MOSER is the only man to win three times in a row (1978–80). No American has won the race, but George Hincapie placed second in 2005 and was in the top 10 seven times.

Other races have tried to follow Paris–Roubaix's unique format. One of the most successful is the Eroica, which is held on dirt roads—*strade bianche*—in Tuscany. The Tro Bro Léon is a Breton race that includes unsurfaced lanes in the far west of France, while in Britain the East Midlands Cyclassic takes in a raft of mucky farm tracks.

The Paris–Roubaix CYCLOSPORTIVE is held every other June so that amateur cyclists can get the full cobbled experience: the bumps, the velodrome, and the showers. All finishers receive a cobblestone mounted on a base. A mountain-bike event was organized briefly in the 1990s and there are junior and under-23 races on shorter courses.

PATERSON, Banjo (b. Australia, 1864, d. 1941)

Australian poet who produced the ballad "Mulga Bill's Bicycle" in 1896; probably the best-known cycling poem, it is contemporary with H. G. Wells's novel about early cycling *The Wheels of Chance* (see BOOKS). The poem has been in print since 1973 and is among Paterson's most popular works. It deals with Mulga Bill's purchase of a bike, his pride in his riding skill, and his downfall when—of course—he crashes. The poem is celebrated today in the Mulga Bill Bicycle Trail at Eaglehawk, the Victoria town where it is set. Mulga is a species of shrub that grows in the bush; the implication being that Mulga Bill is a yokel with ideas above his station.

The poem begins:

Twas Mulga Bill, from Eaglehawk, that caught the
    cycling craze;
He turned away the good old horse that served
    him many days;
He dressed himself in cycling clothes,
    resplendent to be seen;
He hurried off to town and bought a shining new
    machine;
And as he wheeled it through the door, with air of
    lordly pride,
The grinning shop assistant said "Excuse me,
    can you ride?"

The joke is that Bill cannot ride, and after ending up in "Dead Man's Creek," swears to stick to his horse in future.

(SEE POETRY FOR OTHER CYCLING POEMS)

PATTERSON, Frank   See ART

PAVÉ   French word for COBBLES.

(SEE ALSO FLANDERS, PARIS–ROUBAIX, CLASSICS)

PEDERSEN, Mikael (b. Denmark, 1855, d. 1929)

Danish inventor who produced an iconic early "safety" type machine launched in 1897: the frame was built using cantilevered tubes set in 21 triangles, giving greater strength and enabling the frame diameter and gauge to be cut to the minimum. One early machine weighed only 13 lb at a time when over 30 was the norm. The Dursley-Pedersen was made by Lister and Company at Dursley in Gloucestershire and also featured a hammock-type saddle made of cord—the first models used 45 yards of woven silk—and "tied" between the top of the seat tube and the head tube. About 8,000 were made between 1900 and 1915; not surprisingly they are now collectors' items.

Pedersen built up a thriving business in Britain but lost the company due to poor business practices. He was reduced to selling matches and was buried in a pauper's grave. His body has since been repatriated to Gloucestershire.

PÉLISSIER, Jean "Henri"

Born: Paris, France, January 22, 1889
Died: Dampierre, France, March 1, 1935
Major wins: Tour de France 1923, 10 stage wins; Milan–San Remo 1912; Paris–Roubaix 1919, 1921; Giro di Lombardia 1911, 1913, 1920; Bordeaux–Paris 1919; Paris-Brussels 1920; Paris–Tours 1922
Nickname: the Iron Wire (*La Ficelle de Fer*)

One of the stars of the HEROIC ERA, Jean "Henri" Pélissier was capable of winning on any terrain. His disputes with HENRI DESGRANGE highlight the demands race organizers imposed at the time. In 1919 the TOUR DE FRANCE boss forbade him from getting help from other riders and Pélissier walked out, and he did so again in 1920 after he was docked two minutes for throwing away a punctured tire.

In 1923, Pélissier won the Tour, prompting Desgrange to compare his victory to "a work by Racine, a perfect statue, a faultless painting or a piece of music you never forget." Late in his career, Pélissier and his brother Francis founded an early riders' trade union.

During the 1924 Tour, Pélissier put on two jerseys for a stage that started in Le Havre in the middle of the night: one issued by the Tour organizers, one of his own. He threw the latter away when the sun came up, which was against the rules; Desgranges got wind of it and the pair had a row in public. Pélissier abandoned the next day after a judge counted his jerseys at the start and in a fine example of early media management made sure that the leading journalist of the day, Albert Londres, knew about it. Londres found Henri, his brother Francis, and another rider in the Café de la Gare in Coutances in Normandy; the ensuing interview was originally entitled "Les Martyrs de la Route" but later was known as "Les Forcats de la Route"—"the Convicts of the Road," a term that became synonymous with the outrageous demands made on the cyclists of the time.

Pélissier told Londres that he and his brother used DRUGS, opening his pillbox and showing the journalist "cocaine for the eyes, chloroform for the gums . . . and do you want to see the pills? We ride on dynamite. When the mud is washed off us, we are as white as sheets. We are drained by diarrhoea. We dance jigs in our bedroom instead of sleeping. Our calves are leather, and sometimes they break." Francis added: "And as for my toenails, I've lost six out of ten."

"One day," concluded his brother, "they will put lead in our jerseys because God didn't make us heavy enough."

Pélissier had a tragic end: his wife Leonie committed suicide in 1933, and two years later his girlfriend Camille shot him with five bullets from the same pistol during a violent argument.

PEUGEOT Celebrated French cycle company that had the longest unbroken sponsorship in cycling until its demise in 1987. Its motif, the Lion, goes back to the company's days as a steelmaker in the mid-19th century; it was founded in the 18th century to make watermills. Peugeot began sponsorship in 1896, won their first TOUR DE FRANCE in 1905 with Louis Trousselier, and went on to win La Grande Boucle 10 times.

Peugeot was a family affair that began manufacturing in 1882 with a high-wheeler known as the Grand Bi and was making 20,000 bikes a year by 1900; by 1892 it had expanded into car making, and this is now the main activity. In the First World War, the company made plane engines and shells as well as cars, trucks, and bikes. The cycle company's peak came in 1955, when its factory at Beaulieu turned out 220,000 machines, employing some 3,500 workers. In the 1970s it produced the definitive Peugeot, the PX-10 racer, with componentry from French producers such as Mafac (brakes), Simplex (gears), and Stronglight (chainsets).

While car output continued to be strong, the bike-making side declined in the 1980s and 1990s, with the name eventually sold to licence-holder CycleEurope. The Peugeot car company still sells bikes, but none of them are racing machines.

Peugeot was the last cycling squad to survive as a purely factory team without a main extra-sportif sponsor—although it had backing from petrol companies such as Shell and BP—and thanks to its massive sponsorship of club teams as well, its checkerboard design jerseys were ubiquitous in French amateur racing in the 1970s and 1980s. In the 1960s its riders included a young EDDY MERCKX and TOM SIMPSON, while in the 1970s the team featured the 1975 and 1977 Tour winner Bernard Thévenet.

From its amateur "feeder" club ACBB in Paris, Peugeot took on members of the FOREIGN LEGION such as STEPHEN ROCHE, PHIL

ANDERSON, and ROBERT MILLAR in the 1980s. Its last great Tour was 1983, when Pascal Simon looked a likely winner until he broke his shoulderblade in a crash while wearing the yellow jersey. In 1987, the factory team was discontinued due to rising costs, although it continued as Z-Peugeot, and the bikes were later ridden by the Festina team.

(SEE **GIANT** AND **RALEIGH** FOR OTHER ICONIC CYCLE MAKERS; **TEAMS** FOR OTHER NOTABLE CYCLING SQUADS)

POETRY The only anthology on the market is *The Art of Bicycling* (Breakaway Books, 2005, ed. Justin Daniel Belmont). This includes poems by major names such as Walt Whitman, Dylan Thomas (who rhymes penny farthing with Camarthen), Seamus Heaney, Pablo Neruda, and Yevgeni Yevtushenko. The only professional cyclist represented is the late MARCO PANTANI. Also included is the work of the British poet Jeff Cloves, who has kindly allowed me to reproduce two of his poems here. The first was written after the death of TOM SIMPSON, the second 20 years after the death of FAUSTO COPPI.

Un petit Tour de France

Henry Miller
buys a French racer
sells it and regrets
for ever

A photo of a woman
she rides a bike
Paris is liberated
her smile is a flag

Sartre and Simone de B
seated on a tandem
they quarrel when
she demands to steer

Le Café de Copains
champions on the wall
the arthritic patron
up there too

Alfred Jarry poses
astride his dear machine
everyman his own bicycle
dit Pere Ubu

In the Parc des Princes
sashes and bouquets
the winner smiles
I did it for France

Alone on the Alps
Tommy Simpson is dying
christ it's hard
he takes a little help

(FOR THE DEFINITIVE AUSTRALIAN CYCLING POEM, "MULGA BILL'S BIKE" SEE **BANJO PATERSON**; SEE ALSO CYCLING IN ART AND **LITERATURE**, AND **BOOKS**.)

Il Campionissimo

When you were king of the mountains
Fausto
the kilometres hissed by
like busy moments
beneath your tyres
and the pavé was no more
than grit on your tongue
young Italian girls
threw wayside flowers
as you ticked past
spokes flashing in the sun
and in the Tour de France
peasants in the Alps
leaned from windows and shouted
allez Coppi!
and forgot their own man

I remember how
you never seemed to lose
and how
you pushed your goggles
on to the brow
of your thin face
and smiled
as you crossed the line
and how
the photographers hounded
your lady in white
as she waited
for her lean brown prince to race
to her embrace

And when that dread disease
did for you as
for any mortal
I thought again of the pain
that might have been
behind the goggles
and the tight grin
behind the private smile
for the waiting lady
the quiet lady in white
who waited at the line
to give the greatest prize of all

But it's long gone now
Fausto
the flash pop picture press
the gossip column glare
has switched to another scene
you can relax
it's time to sit up in the saddle
ride on the tops
freewheel a little
you're out in front
and they'll never catch you
now

POLITICS Cycling and cycle racing have always been closely linked to political developments in the wider world. For example, the newspaper circulation war that led to the Tour de France's foundation was born of the political controversy involving Alfred Dreyfus, while the invention of the bike was important in women's rights. In Ireland, the national tour caused political controversy in its early years (see RÁS).

Both the GIRO D'ITALIA and TOUR DE FRANCE have had political undertones, the Giro more so than its French counterpart. In 1911 the race celebrated 50 years of Italian unification, while the 1946 event was seen as an expression of the nation rising from the ashes of war. That race visited disputed territories such as the city of Trieste and the newly integrated Alto Adige, where the freshly elected president of the reborn republic, Alcide de Gasperi, made a point of visiting the race.

Politicians have always loved to get involved with cycling.

It was a similar story in Nazi Germany, where cycle rallies were run, bike accessories bore swastikas, and tires were marketed with swastika imprints. In fascist Italy, Benito Mussolini was not a massive cycling fan—he preferred motor racing because of its modernity—but he still made overtures to the young GINO BARTALI. The 1938 Tour de France winner was unwilling to be used for propaganda purposes but still succumbed to pressure from the sport's minister to ride the 1937 Tour as well as the Giro; unfortunately he crashed. After the war, Bartali was close to Italy's new prime minister Alcide de Gasperi, who represented the pro-Catholic Christian Democrats; he campaigned on their behalf and responded to De Gasperi's call to win the 1948 Tour as Italy came close to a communist revolution. (See Bartali's entry for whether or not he actually saved the nation.)

The first VUELTA A ESPAÑA was explicitly political. It was an incarnation of the country's sense of patriotism, according to an editorial in the promoting paper: as Spain's Civil War loomed, such words were a call to arms for the fascists. Before the start of the 1941 Vuelta, the peloton lined up at Madrid's Puerta del Sol, considered the spiritual center of the Spanish state, put out their right arms, and sang "Cara al Sol," the Falange anthem. Later, the race was sponsored partly by the Spanish Ministry of Education, and politically aware stage winners often saluted the military from the podium.

After FEDERICO BAHAMONTES won his Tour de France on July 18, 1959—the anniversary of the military uprising that spawned the 40-year dictatorship of General Franco—he was greeted by el caudillo upon his return as 14 military brass bands played in his honor. When the pair met, Bahamontes recalled that Franco wanted to discuss soccer, but the dictator was a Real Madrid fan, while the cyclist supported Barcelona. "I couldn't really help him," recalled the "Eagle of Toledo."

The Franco legacy lingers on in the fact that even today, the Vuelta never visits the heart of the Basque Country. During the dictatorship, the race often started and finished there, to make the point that the fiercely independent nation was part of the mother country. This tradition was poorly received as Basque nationalism gained pace. In 1968 a bomb was exploded on the race route, while 10 years later the separatists scattered tin tacks and timber beams on the road before the two final stages, both of which were thus canceled.

The nationalists bombed that year's Tour de France as well and were in action again when the Tour started in San Sebastian, setting fire to two cars, one of which contained a month's worth of clothes belonging to the TV commentator PHIL LIGGETT. Whenever the Tour visits the Pyrenees, the Basques are prominent, brandishing banners calling for the release of political prisoners;

when the race enters the Basque country, the signs are in Basque as well as French to appease the locals.

There have also been specifically political cycling movements. In the early 20th century the German Workers Cycling Federation boasted 150,000 members while socialists across Great Britain formed an entire network of Clarion cycle clubs in the 1890s. At one time the Clarion clubs numbered over 100, running houses where the members could socialize in between holding rallies and distributing Socialist literature from their bikes. There are still 24 Clarion cycle clubs in Britain, but they are not politically affiliated.

Politicians still like to be seen with successful cyclists. Various French presidents, including Nicolas Sarkozy, have visited the Tour de France. Greg LeMond and Lance Armstrong were both invited to the White House after their respective Tour de France victories. George Bush senior

was photographed with his wife Barbara on bikes in China in the 1970s. After the British Olympic cycling team's success in Beijing in 2008, Prime Minister Gordon Brown invited the team head, Dave Brailsford, to speak at the Labour party conference. But jumping onto the bike bandwagon doesn't always work out. Brailsford made a point of telling Labour about the virtues of a team sticking together, at a time when the government was riven by infighting.

On the other side of the spectrum, the current British prime minister David Cameron will always remain the politician who rode his bike to work—with a car following behind him carrying his bag and his shoes. George W. Bush fell off his bike, funnily enough, but perhaps the ultimate letdown came when former French president Jacques Chirac invited the Tour de France to his fiefdom in the Dordogne in 1998 only for one of the biggest drugs scandals in the race's history to ruin the party.

POLO Bicycle polo was a demonstration sport at the London OLYMPIC GAMES in 1908. The gold went to IRELAND, which was the nation where the sport was founded in 1891 by one Richard J. Mecredy.

Bicycle polo is exactly what it sounds like—a version of the horseback game on two wheels, with steeds that don't eat and can be bought by the common man. Field dimensions vary from 150 by 100 meters to 100 by 80 meters (for some reason the French prefer a smaller field). The ball is 12 to 15 inches around, the mallets three feet long. Six or seven players make up a team, with four or five on the field at once. (Similarly, the French like a different number of players.) Internationals last 30 minutes broken up into four seven-and-a-half minute chukkas. If a match runs to extra time, the goals may be widened. The rules are simple: a sliding scale of extra hits or goals for fouls, yellow and red cards. The UCI recognizes cycle polo and there is an annual world championship. India, USA, and Canada are among the strongest nations.

POSTERS The rapid expansion in bicycle production at the end of the 19th century (see BICYCLE for background) produced intense competition between bike makers who vied to produce the most attractive posters to sell their products. In Paris, where decorative poster art had begun in the mid-19th century with the lithographic printing work of Jules Chéret, there was a brief period when art and cycling came together. Artists such as

HENRI DE TOULOUSE-LAUTREC and Pal—the nom de plume of Jean de Paleologue—glamorized cycling with the same talent that had been used to advertise the exoticism of Paris's demi-monde with its revues such as those at the Moulin Rouge.

Many of the images were risqué for the time: a naked woman with the wings of Mercury publicized Gladiator cycles; a bare-breasted Amazon (by Pal) the appropriately named Liberator Cycles; cycling lessons at the Palais-Sport in Paris were advertised by a young lady in suspenders. The British firm Humber used a more staid gentleman in regulation Cyclists' Touring Club gear but also a coquettish ad with a young gentleman stealing a kiss from his riding partner.

Most distinctive of all, however, was Toulouse-Lautrec's depiction of an early race at London's Catford Velodrome to publicize the Simpson chain sold by Spoke's bike shop. *La Chaîne Simpson* includes the early champion Constant Huret amid a variety of multiple pacing bikes and raffish onlookers. (See ART to read about other greats who have used cycling for inspiration.)

To give some idea of what these posters are worth, an original of Pal's native American chief advertising Cleveland cycles can be bought for under $10,000 while an original of *La Chaîne Simpson* has been valued at nudging $100,000.

Aficionados could also seek out posters used to advertise the Peace Race (see EASTERN EUROPE), in the distinctive heroic style of Socialist Realist art.

POULIDOR, Raymond

(b. France, 1936)

The most popular cyclist FRANCE has ever produced was still a fixture at the Tour more than 40 years after his heyday in the 1960s when he went head-to-head with JACQUES ANQUETIL in one of the greatest RIVALRIES cycling has seen. "Poupou" never won the Tour and never wore the yellow jersey, but he did win hearts for his shy smile, constant misfortune, and the courage he showed in attacking first Anquetil—his equal in the mountains and far superior in the time trials—and later EDDY MERCKX, who was simply better in every domain.

At the peak of his celebrity it was estimated that he would be first choice as a dinner guest for almost half the French population. It was said that while French men admired Anquetil for his success, their wives all wanted to mother his great rival. His nickname gave rise to the headline *Poupoularité*, while politicians refer to

Poulidor syndrome: France's perceived tendency to accept being a worthy loser rather than a clinical winner. His memoirs summed up his career: *La Gloire sans le Maillot Jaune* (1977).

Born of farming stock in the Massif Central, Poulidor seemed the country boy alongside the more sophisticated Anquetil and he raced in an agricultural way, more reliant on brute strength than tactics. He still won the VUELTA A ESPAÑA and Milan–San Remo but is better remembered for his incredible record in the Tour: 14 starts and 12 finishes, with 11 top 10 overall placings and 8 finishes in second or third overall. The moment when he captivated France came in the 1964 race when he and Anquetil fought out an elbow-to-elbow battle on the Puy-de-Dôme, with Poulidor gaining the upper hand on that occasion but narrowly missing out on the yellow jersey. His career was a model of LONGEVITY, with third-place Tour finishes in 1962 and in 1976 when he was 40 years old. Since retirement that year, Poulidor has returned to the race every year, and is the undisputed star of the publicity caravan promoting products as diverse as banks and coffee.

POWER The question of how many lightbulbs a cyclist can power has been kicked around for over a century and gained new resonance in the 1990s as it became possible to make an accurate measurement of the wattage produced by a bike rider using POWER CRANKS. Generating stations powered by bikes were used in England in the early 20th century, while BSA produced a cycle generator for the army to power lights and communication devices in the field during the Second World War.

In a sprint, a top cyclist can put out about 2,500 watts for about 5 seconds; over a more sustained effort, say 10 seconds, it would be about 1,800 watts; in a 4-minute track pursuit, about 500 watts; in a time trial, a cyclist with BRADLEY WIGGINS's physique, for example, could sustain about 430 watts for an hour; on an easy training ride where it's possible to talk to your neighbor, the average cyclist would be putting out around 200 watts.

An investigation by the BBC's *Focus* magazine in October 2009 concluded that if the average "reasonably fit" cyclist's

> **POWER FACTOID**
>
> A sprint cyclist making a starting effort produces, briefly, more torque than a Formula One car. Team GB's team sprint Man One Jamie Staff can put out 600 newton meters in the first half of his first pedal revolution.

HOW MANY CYCLISTS DOES IT TAKE TO POWER...

A LOAD OF WASHING TO DRY IN A TUMBLE DRYER (4850 WATTS), 32-49 CYCLISTS.

LIGHTING A ROOM, WITH ENERGY SAVING LIGHTBULBS, 1 CYCLIST.

AN AVERAGE LCD TELEVISION (130 WATTS), 1 CYCLIST.

A PLASMA TV (320 WATTS), 3-4 CYCLISTS.

KEEPING DEVICES ON STANDBY AND A FRIDGE GOING, TWO CYCLISTS PEDALLING CONSTANTLY.

sustained power output was between 100 and 150 watts of energy, a family home would need about 100 cyclists on permanent standby to keep all its electrical devices functioning. The Human Power Station came up with the following: A load of washing to dry in a tumble dryer would require 32 to 49 cyclists pedaling for an hour (4,850 watts). Lighting a room with energy-saving lightbulbs could be dealt with by just one bike rider. An average LCD television (130 watts) would need one cyclist; a plasma TV (320 watts), three or four cyclists. And merely keeping devices on standby and a fridge going would need two cyclists pedaling constantly. And making your morning coffee (800 watts), that would call for 8 to 10 cyclists, depending on how many cups you need.

POWER CRANKS

There are several ways of measuring POWER output—sensors in the chain, sensors on the roller of a stationary home trainer—but the SRM (Schoberer Rad Messtechnik) German-made crankset is the best. It has eight strain gauges that measure the deflection in the chain ring as a cyclist pushes down on the pedals. The information is translated into a measure of the power output in watts, which can in turn be downloaded into a computer.

The cranks first appeared in the mid-1990s and had a large, crude handlebar computer; this has now been shrunk to the extent that pro cyclists carry the devices in races. The cranks are integral to most serious training programs as they offer the best objective measure of how hard a cyclist is able to work. Heart-rate monitors appeared at the end of the 1980s, and are accurate, but pulse rate is subject to factors such as heat and fatigue, which make training to a set rate difficult: on the other hand, you can either reach a set power output or you can't.

Information from the cranks is one of the keys to the success of the GREAT BRITAIN cycling team (see CHRIS HOY, BRADLEY WIGGINS). "We can understand the physics of what is going on, so we can tell where best to spend our time and energy," the team's then performance scientist Scott Gardner explained in 2008.

The team has over 100 of the cranks—costing about £2,000 each—and employs a technologist in the Manchester Velodrome whose principal task is to ensure they are always perfectly calibrated.

They use the data to tweak training programs and to devise strategies for track races—for example, the graphs showing the riders' power output for a team pursuit can be compared with their speed to see how the formation can be changed to be most efficient. SRM information can also be used to model performance on a treadmill: the precise power outputs on an SRM file for a mountain-bike race, say a rehearsal on the Beijing course, could be replicated in training.

PYRÉNÉES The inclusion of France's southern mountain range in the TOUR DE FRANCE route in 1910 was a turning point for cycling. The race organizer HENRI DESGRANGE sent the riders over four climbs that have acquired legendary status: the Peyresourde, Aspin, Tourmalet, and Aubisque. It was on the latter that the key episode occurred: the eventual race winner Octave Lapize (see HEROIC ERA) went past a group of organizers and spat out the word "assassins." Desgrange was absent: uncertain whether the first mountain stage would be a success he decided to stay away. Nonetheless, he was instantly aware of the headlines that could be made by sending Tour cyclists where mere mortals dared not venture, so next year he sent the Tour into the ALPS.

The climbs of the Pyrenées have a different character compared to those in the other

CLIMB	LENGTH	ALTITUDE	HEIGHT GAIN	NOTED FOR
Tourmalet (from Saint-Marie-de-Campan)	17.1 km	2,115 m	1,275 m	Tunnels and a huge statue, the giant of the Tour, on a bleak "up and over" summit
Aspin (from Arreau)	11.9 km	1,489 m	670 m	Verdant slopes with wandering cows and the biggest slugs in France
Aubisque (from Argelès-Gazost)	29.1 km	1,709 m	1,365 m	Vertiginous section after Col du Soulor where the road is cut into a mountainside
Peyresourde (from Bagnères-de-Luchon)	14.3 km	1,569 m	944 m	Steady gradient, majestic sweeping hairpins through meadows to a v-shaped pass
Hautacam (from Argelès-Gazost)	15.5 km	1,616 m	1,136 m	Tight, steep hairpins and constant gradient changes en route to a bleak ski station
Marie-Blanque (from Escot)	19.6 km	1,035 m	700 m	Steep and dead straight "wall" in last 3.5 km on west side; vultures and bears on the slopes
Port de Pailhères (from Usson-les-Bains)	16.8 km	2,001 m	1,300 m	Narrow roads and a scenic summit where the road twists around a vast rock outcrop

major Massif. They tend to be shorter than in the Alps and do not climb so high. The only pass over 2,000 m in the Pyrenées that is regularly climbed in the Tour is the Tourmalet, a mere 2,115 m compared to over 2,600 m for the Galibier and Iseran in the Alps.

On the other hand, the Pyrenées offer steeper climbing, and roads that have been less well engineered: evenly graded hairpins and wide carriageways are relatively rare. "Walls" such as the Col de Marie-Blanque and the Col de Bagargui—around 13 percent—are typical, as are narrow, tightly hairpinned climbs such as the Col d'Agnès.

The slopes of the mountains around the climbs tend to be gentler and greener, less spoilt by ski resorts and industry.

As in the Alps, numerous CYCLOSPORTIVE events take in the great climbs. They include the Hubert Arbes, run by one of BERNARD HINAULT's old teammates, which takes in the Tourmalet and the Soulor/Aubisque; from the Spanish side, the Quebrantahuesos sportif includes the Marie-Blanque.

Further reading: *Tour Climbs*, Chris Sidwells, Collins, 2008

(SEE **RAID PYRENEAN** FOR AN INFORMAL IF PAINFUL WAY TO TACKLE THE GREAT CLIMBS IN ONE GO)

Q

QUOTES

Tour de France

"Riding up a mountain in the Tour if you are bad is like being sick."—ROBERT MILLAR

"Do they not have wings, those men who have today managed to climb to heights where eagles dare not go?"—Tour founder HENRI DESGRANGE on climbers

"Getting married is not like the Tour de France. You can't just climb off if it goes badly."—SEAN KELLY

"Ride like you just stole something."—LANCE ARMSTRONG to his teammate Floyd Landis in the 2004 Tour

"The Tour de France produces in me such persistent satisfaction that my saliva flows in imperceptible but stubborn streams."—Salvador Dalí (see ART)

"The Tour is the nearest thing to life outside life itself. You're born and you set out. For some, things go wrong from the start . . . sometimes the deserving win. Those with connections have every advantage . . . sometimes justice puts the boot in and upsets things."—Terry Davenport in Ralph Hurne's *The Yellow Jersey* (see BOOKS—FICTION)

Personalities

"The bike comes first."—Sean Kelly after his wife Linda said he cared about his car and his bike more than about her

"Anything beats working for a living and I've been delaying the inevitable as long as possible." —SEAN YATES on why he has never stopped cycling

"The thing is not where you finished, but how much [money] did you make."—TOM SIMPSON

"People like watching me on television because they never know if I'll still be in the bunch when they come back from having a quick leak."—The gloriously unpredictable Pedro Delgado of SPAIN

"Some cyclists race to give people a thrill, some race to win. I belong to the second group." —Five-times Tour winner and quiet man MIGUEL INDURAIN

"If you put a cup of milk between his shoulders at the foot of a mountain he would cross the summit without spilling a drop."—René Vietto on the super-stylish campionissimo ALFREDO BINDA

"If I had to make the perfect cyclist I would give him ANQUETIL's legs, Armstrong's brain, the power and authority of HINAULT, Indurain's heart and one of my bikes."—EDDY MERCKX

Cycling and the bike

"God created the bicycle as a tool for men to show effort and exaltation on the hard road of life."—Motto of the cycling CHAPEL at Madonna del Ghisallo

"There are many times when physically I would welcome a car hitting me and cutting it all short there and then, I hurt so much."—Alf Engers (see TIME TRIALLING)

"A perfect expression of the machine aesthetic."—designer Stephen Bayley

"You would be surprised at the number of people in these parts who nearly are half men and half bicycles."—Flann O'Brien (*The Third Policeman*, see BOOKS— FICTION)

"[The velocipede] replaces collective brutish unintelligent speed with collective speed, obeying man's will."—Richard Lesclide, *Le Vélocipede Illustré*, 1869

"To ride a bicycle properly is very like a love affair—chiefly it is a matter of faith. Believe you can do it, and the thing is done; doubt and for the life of you, you cannot."—H. G. Wells (*The Wheels of Chance*, see BOOKS— FICTION)

"'There is a lot of uphill about a bicycle tour,' said George, 'and the wind is against you.' 'So there is downhill, and the wind behind you,' said Harris."
—Jerome K. Jerome, *Three Men on the Bummel*

RACE ACROSS AMERICA Iconic long-distance event run from the West Coast of the UNITED STATES to the East, founded in 1982 as the Great American Bike Race. That event was run from Santa Monica to the Empire State Building, had just four entrants, and was won by Lon Haldeman in 9 days, 20 hours, 2 minutes, at an average of 12.57 mph, a far cry from the first crossing of the US in 1887, when the journalist George Nellis took just under 80 days on a HIGH-WHEELER.

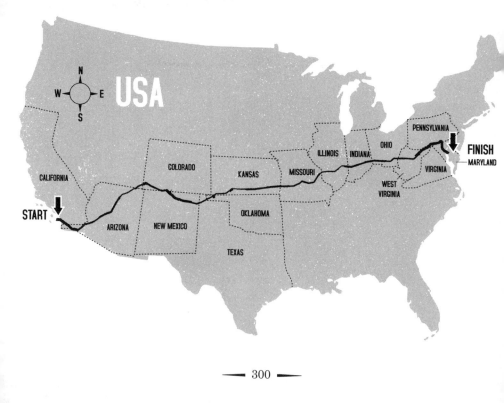

The RAAM is not run in stages, but instead the clock runs continuously as on a RECORD attempt such as the END TO END, making it a battle against sleep deprivation as well as a test of cycling stamina. Sometimes up to half the solo racers pull out due to exhaustion. As in record attempts, the cyclists have support teams traveling with them; at night they must be accompanied by a vehicle with flashing lights for safety reasons.

The race is divided into solo and team categories, with teams of up to eight riders permitted, each man racing a separate leg while the others rest. The relay teams average over 500 miles per day and have gotten the record down to six or seven days although the solo category remains the most prestigious. In 1989 teams of RECUMBENT cycles entered. Entrants must be members of the Ultra Marathon Cycling Association and must have ridden a set number of qualifying events.

Because the course varies from year to year—although it is always run west to east—RAAM records are measured in average speed, not time. The fastest average is by Pete Penseyres in 1986, 15.4 mph for 3,107 miles; the women's record was set by Seana Hogan (1995), 13.23 mph for 2,912 miles.

(SEE **PARIS–BREST–PARIS** AND **RAID PYRENEAN** FOR THE MOST LEGENDARY LONG-DISTANCE EVENTS IN EUROPE)

RADIOS Since the late 1990s, team managers and riders in professional races have used small radios for communication; the rider carries a transmitter/receiver in the back pocket of his jersey connected to an earpiece/microphone while the manager has a microphone and receiver in the car. If the race is being televised live, the manager or mechanic will have a small-screen TV in the car so that he can observe the race in real time and issue instructions—time gaps on a break, when to chase a break or get across to an attack—as the action happens. The radios are also used to warn riders of obstacles such as traffic islands and dangerous corners, while a sprinter such as MARK CAVENDISH will be advised on conditions close to the finish; riders will use the system to tell the manager if they need service, for example after a crash or puncture.

The system originated in the US and was brought to Europe by GREG LEMOND in 1991. The Motorola team of SEAN YATES, PHIL ANDERSON, and LANCE ARMSTRONG was the first squad to use it from 1994 onwards. Previously, communication between riders and team staff was minimal. The managers would rely on Radio Tour—the internal radio system used by most major races—while the riders would watch for a blackboard carried by a motorcycle marshal, on which was written information such

as a break's time gap and the numbers of the riders in a move. To give instructions to his riders, the manager would have to wait for one of them to call him to the back of the bunch—for example to collect bottles—or he would have to drive up to the bunch and find them.

There is some debate about the use of the radios, as opponents claim it gives the managers too much influence over tactics and the riders are mere pawns. In particular, it is said that attacking racing is impossible, because teams can react so quickly to threatening moves. To encourage riders to use their initiative, the UCI banned radios in under-23 races. At the 2009 TOUR DE FRANCE, the organizers attempted to run two stages without radios being used, but were stymied when riders did not race, apparently in protest. The UCI decided at the end of 2009 that it would phase out the devices' use, but did not give a timescale and it seems that a battle with the teams might well be in prospect.

RAID PYRENEAN An informal challenge for the fit cyclist that takes in all the major passes in the PYRENÉES and has been going since 1952. The 713 km route from Hendaye on the Atlantic to Cerbère on the Mediterranean is pre-set, includes 11,000 m of climbing and has to be covered within a time limit of 100 hours. There is a window when it can be done, between June and September, when the highest passes are free of snow.

Cyclists wishing to tackle the Raid have to acquire pass books (*brevets*) from the organizing club, CC Béarnais, in the town of Pau. They supply accommodation info and numbered bike tags, as well as medals for those completing the course. The books are stamped at overnight stops, while there may be informal checkpoints along the way. The Raid can be tackled independently, although there are also package companies that will arrange the trip.

The Alpine equivalents, the Raids Alpine (see ALPS) are longer, tougher, and less

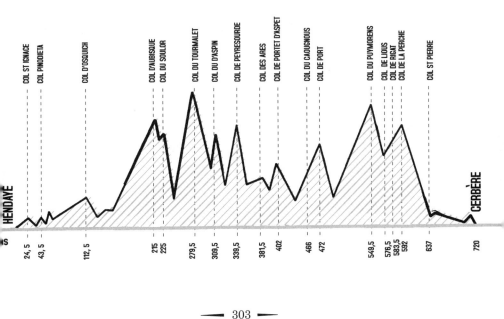

popular. Other less well-known raids include Calais–Brindisi and Paris–Gibraltar while France has nine "diagonals" connecting the extremes of the country, starting or finishing in Brest, Strasbourg, Perpignan, Dunkirk, Menton, and Hendaye.

RALEIGH   One of the world's most celebrated bike makers, once the biggest in the world. Its world-famous "heron" frame badge once graced an industry leader, sturdy roadsters ridden worldwide, and a TOUR DE FRANCE winner.

The company began in 1886 on Raleigh Street in Nottingham, England, in a small workshop that made three safety bicycles a week; local lawyer Frank Bowden bought the operation and founded the Raleigh Cycle Company in 1888. One of Raleigh's earliest stars was the great American track cyclist A. A. ZIMMERMAN.

Apart from a brief spell as a public company it remained in the Bowden family until 1934, making cycles, Sturmey Archer hub gears—patented in 1902—motorcycles, and motorbike gear boxes. By the 1920s the company was making 3,000 cycles per week.

It flirted with making a three-wheel car but by 1938 was solely a bike company turning out half a million bikes a year. Production was over a million in 1951, at the zenith of the British cycle industry, but business went rapidly downhill in the 1950s as the car gained in popularity. A series of mergers, including Raleigh's own takeover by the Tube Investments Group, brought other famous British cycle and motorcycle names such as BSA, Triumph, Sunbeam, and Hercules under the Raleigh banner.

The 1960s saw attempts at

collaboration with SIR ALEX MOULTON to produce small-wheel bikes, after Moulton's invention had revitalized the market. From 1965 Raleigh competed with its own small-wheeler, the RSW16, with a massively expensive publicity campaign. The war with Moulton ended when Raleigh bought its competitor out. With two hugely successful models, the Chopper, an iconic kids' bike, and the Twenty, a small-wheel shopping bike, the 1970s saw the company boom again. Raleigh profited from a massive increase in the market in the UNITED STATES and had other overseas operations including the Gazelle company in Holland and large sales of classic old roadsters across the former British empire. By 1975 its site in Nottingham covered 75 acres.

In Europe, Raleigh sponsored the most successful professional team of the late 1970s and early 1980s, managed by the Dutchman Peter Post but barely ever including more than one British cyclist in its lineup. Post brought the company world titles in 1978 and 1979 and the Tour de France title with Joop Zoetemelk in 1980, with 77 stage wins in the Tour between 1976 and 1983.

Raleigh had largely abandoned high-end racing bikes at the end of the 1950s, producing them in the 1960s through the Carlton brand then changing tack to its own lightweight department, which never truly flourished. Along with much of British manufacturing, Raleigh suffered in the 1980s when the British cycle market expanded but mainly on the back of imported machines and the sudden craze for BMX; Raleigh was hit by imports—its image simply wasn't glamorous, and its products seemed backward—while the BMX boom was shortlived. Market share plummeted, component manufacture gradually ceased, jobs were slashed, and the company was sold in 1987 to Derby International, a specially created parent company. Initially, Raleigh flourished

The Raleigh Team Song

◈

One of the more forgettable Raleigh products was a record made by the TI-Raleigh squad in the late 1970s. *"Wie zijn de vedettes"* translates roughly as "Who are the stars?" and was described by Tim Clifford in *Cycle Sport* magazine as "as unholy a slab of pre-techno Europop as you could ever hope to encounter. Imagine a ditty that crosses oompah band with can-can and throws in a bit of banjo along the way and you will have the drift. Wisely the team's singing chores are restricted to the chorus—an unfortunate affair that has them singing 'O wie o wie o wie' rather a lot—and adding inexplicable 'ha-ha-ha-ha' laughing descants at random during the verses."

The final verse, roughly translated, runs like this:

We want the glory
Ours is the victory
Up the Champs-Elysées
Our first prize awaits
We don't care
We just want the yellow
And Holland will sing along

Another piece of less-than-tasteful Eurotrash was produced by HOUR RECORD breaker FRANCESCO MOSER but fortunately this has sunk without trace.

again, as the market grew after the arrival of the MOUNTAIN BIKE, thanks in part to a highly successful off-road team led by stars such as the glamorous Caroline Alexander and a high-end range of mountain-bikes under the M-Trax label. Derby expanded to buy a string of cycle makers, most notably US mountain-bike company Diamondback.

In the early 1990s, Raleigh devised the first hybrid bike, the Pioneer, which used mountain-bike technology adapted for solely on-road use, to get away from the exclusive image of racing bikes. The company also experimented with suspension at the inexpensive end of the market, something that is ubiquitous today, and produced an early electric bike, the Select, in 1997.

In 1999, however, globalization hit the UK operation. First the company stopped making frames in Nottingham, retaining painting and assembly. Losses increased, one financial restructure followed another, and a proposed move to a site outside Nottingham was aborted when planning permission was contested. Assembly of bikes in the UK ended in 2002, but the company relaunched a UK-based road racing team for 2010. There are hopes that if this squad flourishes the name Raleigh may eventually return to the Tour.

Cycling names who "rode a Raleigh"

- A. A. ZIMMERMAN: sprinter of the Victorian era who was America's first cycling star.

- REG HARRIS: iconic sprinter of the 1950s who was the first British cyclist to have a national profile. The slogan was "Reg rides a Raleigh."

- **Paul Sherwen:** *domestique* of the late 1970s/early 1980s who was among the first members of the FOREIGN LEGION.

- **Joop Zoetemelk:** Dutch star known as "the Rat" who was the winner of the 1980 Tour de France.

- **Hennie Kuiper:** quiet cuddly Dutchman who was an Olympic and world road champion.

- **Jan Raas:** bespectacled Dutchman who was a prolific winner in the late 1970s, world champion in 1978.

- LAURENT FIGNON: bespectacled Frenchman who could have

won the 1989 Tour de France but didn't (though he did win in 1983 and 1984).

- **Caroline Alexander:** English mountain-bike star of Scottish parentage who was first British woman to make it on the international stage.

- **Rod Ellingworth:** never quite made it as a pro with Raleigh but went on to be mentor to MARK CAVENDISH.

RÁS Irish term for cycle race, pronounced Rohsss, but usually referring to one Rás in particular. The Rás is an around-IRELAND stage race run in late May, dating back to 1953, and is unique because it offers amateur cyclists their only chance to participate in a full-length national tour alongside professional squads. It should not be confused with the professional Tour of Ireland, a shorter event for pros only.

Attempting to survive the Rás is a highlight of any amateur cyclist's career. As well as being a tough race in itself, with daily 100-mile stages, the "night" stages are legendary: the music and drinking among the caravan

(and some of the tougher riders) can last until the next day's stage start.

The first Rás was a two-day event named the Rás Tailteann, setting the tone for an event in which sport and politics rubbed shoulders. The Tailteann Games were a legendary Celtic sports festival that had particular significance for the Irish independence movement; the first trophy was a wreath of laurels picked at the site of the original Tailteann Games. The link was explicit when the first race started from in front of the General Post Office in Dublin, the focus of the Easter Uprising. The field were all members of the National Cycling Association, a body which did not recognize Irish partition and was thus banned from international competition.

Irish cycling was divided at the time between a body that recognized partition, the CRE (Cumann Rothaiochta na hEireann, which translates as the Cycling Association of Ireland), and the NCA. The Rás was born mainly to create an alternative Irish tour to rival events run by the CRE; an article in the 1961 race program described CRE members as "traitors," "scabs," "a brood of vipers," and "reprobates." An early Rás organizer, Joe Christle, was also editor of *An Phoblacht*, the Republican newspaper; it was, says the Rás's official history, understood that "a core of individuals" within one club that contributed heavily to the Rás organization "were active within the IRA at that time."

In the early years of the Rás, Christle explicitly linked the race to the struggle for Irish nationhood, but there were other characteristics that made for long-term success. The race visited rural parts of Ireland, stages finished in the early evening so that locals could finish work and then watch, the distances were at the limit of what the riders could manage, and the field included teams from the Irish counties to maintain local interest. There was also an emphasis on Irish culture.

The first around-Ireland Rás, in 1954, was billed as "the greatest cycle race ever," in spite of widespread doubts that anyone would be able to complete the 900 miles and a lack of sponsorship; the budget was raised by raffles, dances, stories sold to newspapers by one organizer, Kerry Sloane, and a large unofficial donation from the Gaelic Athletic Association. A field of 60 started the race, which had stages to Wexford, Cork, Tralee, Ennis, Athlone, Armagh, and Newry—the latter symbolically important, being over the border in Northern Ireland.

The Rás rapidly established

itself as the centerpiece of Ireland's cycling calendar, the one event all amateur cyclists aspired to finish. To be a "Man of the Ràs" meant braving bad weather, ill fortune, and poor roads. "Let's hear it for the Men of the Rás," booms the race public address half a century on.

The Rás created its own cycling culture, populated by heroes barely known outside Ireland such as the 1955 winner Gene Mangan and, half a century later, the "Godfather" of the event, Philip Cassidy, who figured prominently from 1980 to 2001. There were legendary episodes such as the "Cookstown incident" of 1956 (see IRELAND) and the Italian affair of 1992, when Irish cyclists ganged up to intimidate the Italian national team and there were scuffles on the bike, and there were legendary families such as the MacQuaids, four of whom won a dozen stages between 1974 and 1988, and one of whom, Pat, is the president of the UCI. The spirit is typified by the greatest Man of the Rás, Shay O'Hanlon,

a multiple stage winner between 1960 and 1975, who is still working as a volunteer on the race 30 years later.

The weather is always unpredictable and so too the racing. The term "Rás break" refers to a move that looks insignificant but ends up expanding in numbers and is decisive. If the night stages are legendary, so too is the camaraderie among the caravan, where the men who run the broom wagon consider it an affront if a rider climbs in who is not utterly spent. Incredibly, thanks to long-term sponsorship from FBD insurance and the Irish National Dairy Council, plus a sympathetic organizer in Dermot Dignam, the race retained its unique character into the 21st century.

Further reading: *The Rás: The Story of Ireland's Unique Stage Race,* Tom Daly, Collins Press, 2004

(SEE **IRELAND** FOR OTHER MAJOR IRISH RACES AND STARS; **POLITICS** FOR OTHER CYCLING EVENTS THAT HAD MORE THAN A PURELY SPORTING IMPACT)

RECORDS When humans first put their legs over bikes in the mid-19th century, the question was obvious: how far can I get under my own steam on this thing, and how long will it take me? That Victorian spirit of self-discovery lives on in the sport's various records: place to place, speed records, and distance records—the longest distance in a set time—of which the HOUR RECORD has carried the greatest prestige since its inception in 1895.

In GREAT BRITAIN, the Road Records Association (founded 1888) administers place to place and distance record attempts such as the END TO END, and in British TIME TRIALLING there are "competition records" set in official races over their standard distances.

Some famous records:

- CHARLES MURPHY's breaking of the 60 mph barrier behind a train in 1899.
- Dutchman Fred Rompelberg reached 166.9 mph on Bonneville Salt Flats paced by an adapted dragster in 1995.
- The British paced record of 98.21 mph was set by Dave le Grys behind a Rover car on an unopened stretch of the M42 motorway near Birmingham, England, in 1985.
- For the around-the-world record, land circumnavigations have to be at least 18,000 miles and include 8,000 miles by sea or air, and pass through two antipodal points. A 25-year-old Scotsman, Mark Beaumont, managed to do the distance in 195 days in July 2008, averaging around 100 miles a day through 20 countries for more than six months.
- The most demanding track record after the Hour is the standing start kilometer, set in La Paz, Bolivia, by the Frenchman Arnaud Tournant, at 58.875 seconds. La Paz is the venue of choice because it has the highest velodrome in the world, at 3,408 m above sea level. That altitude means that

with 33 percent less oxygen in the air, air resistance is as low as it can be for a cyclist.

- The world endurance record for spinning on a stationary bike was set in 2009 by Mehrzad Shirvani, who rode for 192 hours at Kortrijk in Belgium, napping for between 45 seconds and 3 minutes each hour. Not surprisingly, he entered a state he describes as "supraconsciousness," akin to a coma.

- Today's fastest men on two wheels are the tiny number who compete in extreme MOUNTAIN-BIKE downhill speed trials, in which the riders race on ski slopes. The current production bike record is held by Markus Stoeckl of Austria with 210 kph, while the prototype bike record is held by Frenchman Eric Barone with 222 kph.

RECUMBENTS Bicycles or tricycles where the rider sits in a bucket seat close to the ground, with the pedals in front of him and a long chain connecting to the rear wheel. They come in two kinds: long wheelbase, in which the front wheel is in front of the pedals, and short, in which the chainset and pedals are at the front. Drive is usually to the rear wheel.

They first appeared in the late 19th century amid fevered experimentation with bike position; the first one is said to have been the Normal Bicyclette built in Ghent in the early 1890s. Racing recumbents known as Velocars were commercially available in France in the 1930s and were used to win pursuit matches and set RECORDS. In 1934, Francois Faure used one to set a new HOUR RECORD.

The UCI reacted by banning recumbents from organized events. Restrictions on cycle length and AERODYNAMIC aids had been brought in in 1914, while UCI Article 49 of 1934 effectively limited bike design to safety-type machines. Further development was delayed for 40 years, until the inception of HUMAN POWERED VEHICLE championships in California.

The principle benefit is aerodynamic; by being lower down, the overall profile of the bike is reduced. Their adherents also maintain that they are more comfortable and safer because having a low center of gravity, they are more stable. However, recumbents have never caught on. Opponents would claim this is because they are less safe to ride, because the low profile means the rider is less visible to traffic and also because less power can be put out from a relatively upright sitting position; enthusiasts claim the aerodynamic benefits outweigh any inefficiencies.

Particularly when a smoothed-out fairing is fitted, in some cases completely enclosing the rider, a recumbent can travel considerably faster than a road bike, although enclosed machines create a new problem; the rider is not cooled down by air flow. The most popular version is MIKE BURROWS' Windcheetah. To prove its road-going potential, one version was used by long-distance specialist Andy Wilkinson to set an END TO END record; the time was almost four hours faster than a normal cycle and speeds close to 80 mph were reached on descents.

RELIABILITY TRIALS   Cycling club events in which the participants have to complete a set course within a certain time. There may also be a set minimum time to discourage racing. Unlike CYCLOSPORTIVES, which operate on the same principle, reliability trials do not usually have direction arrows as part of the challenge is finding your own way.

(SEE **PARIS–BREST–PARIS**, **RAID PYRENEAN**, AND **ÉTAPE DU TOUR** FOR OTHER LONG-DISTANCE CHALLENGES)

REPACK   Celebrated downhill MOUNTAIN-BIKING course on Pine Mountain, near Fairfax in California's Marin county, just north of San Francisco, where the fat-tired sport was born thanks to a series of informal

MARIN COUNTY

events using customized bikes run between 1976 and 1979. The events were not organized, but "spontaneously called together when the sun and moon assumed

appropriate aspects." Early racers on the course included GARY FISHER, the "father of mountain-biking"; no more than 200 ever joined him.

Two miles long and dropping 1,300 feet, the course earned its name because the series of tortuous turns meant that the primitive hub brakes of the time would burn out and had to be repacked with grease after each run. "In addition to its incredible steepness it features off-camber blind corners, deep erosion ruts and a liberal sprinkling of fist-sized rocks," wrote the race organizer Charlie Kelly in an article for *Bicycling* magazine in 1979. Kelly's website contains all the results from his original

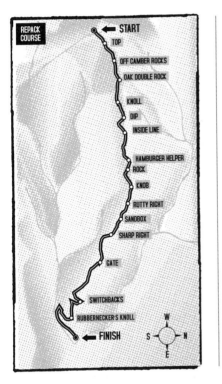

notebooks, apart from the first race, which was held on October 21, 1976.

Fisher set the course record of 4 minutes 22 seconds in the seventh race on November 20, 1976. By 1977 prizes were being awarded courtesy of local bike shops, timing was on digital watches, and an endurance event was run that was a precursor of today's cross-country races. The events ended in 1979 after a racer sued a television company when he broke his wrist; the course was resurrected in 1983 and 1984 for officially sanctioned races.

RIVALRIES Cycling's great conflicts can run deep. In 1992 a journalist visited FRANCESCO MOSER and happened to mention his great rival Giuseppe Saronni; Cecco's tirade against *"il Beppe"* lasted almost half an hour. Ask BERNARD HINAULT about GREG LEMOND and the response is terse, and whatever you do, don't ask LeMond about Hinault, and in particular, don't ask about the way the Frenchman behaved during the 1986 TOUR DE FRANCE. LeMond is still not happy, even though he won.

There are two definitive rivalries in cycling, against which all others have to be judged: GINO BARTALI and

FAUSTO COPPI in the 1940s and JACQUES ANQUETIL and RAYMOND POULIDOR in the 1960s. Both relationships remain permanently etched on the national consciousness in Italy and France.

Bartali and Coppi started out as teammates in the 1940 GIRO D'ITALIA, where the younger Coppi upstaged his older boss to win the event. Their rivalry was at its most intense after the war and reached its nadir at the 1948 world championship in Holland, where the pair watched each other like hawks, eventually getting fed up with it and heading to the changing rooms. It took elaborate negotiation by the Italian national team manager ALFREDO BINDA merely to get them to start the Tour de France in 1949 in the national team; on the road there were constant accusations of double-dealing from both men and their backers. Time and again, Binda had to bang their heads together; by the 1952 Tour, Bartali had finally accepted Coppi's superiority.

Most of the time the pair had a good relationship off their bikes, but the rivalry was massively important to the press. Every time either said anything about the other man, it was headline news; as for their fans, they would argue bitterly in bars and still do so today. On the road it only needed one to have the slightest problem—a puncture, an unshipped chain—for the other to attack. They devised elaborate strategies against each other: Bartali detailed a teammate to watch Coppi's legs and warn him the moment the vein behind his knee began pulsating, as that was a sign he was weakening. Coppi asked his teammates to take Bartali out on the town before the 1948 MILAN–SAN REMO, in the hope that they would have a long night out and the "old man" would be tired the next day. They sent spies to spread disinformation, Bartali would get a teammate to search his rival's hotel room for drugs.

ANQUETIL and POULIDOR had a different relationship: there was no bitterness, at least on Poulidor's side, and the rivalry clearly served as an extra form of motivation for "Master Jacques." In 1967, the night before the Critérium National one-day race, he was quaffing whisky at 3 AM with his manager Raphael Geminiani when "Gem" suggested they drink to Poulidor's win the next day—Anquetil was not planning to ride—but the joke backfired. Anquetil told his wife Janine to set his alarm clock for 7 AM, and duly won the race.

Poulidor and Anquetil's rivalry did not last as long as the 15-year conflict between Bartali and Coppi, but made as big an impression: 30 years later, French politicians were still being asked who they supported. Anquetil could never quite understand why, for all his success, the French public always preferred the underdog, Poulidor. "Of course I would like to see Poulidor win the Tour in my absence. I have beaten him so often that his victory would merely add to my reputation."

While Moser's rivalry with Saronni was essentially a parody of the Coppi/Bartali conflict, largely the product of the Italian press, REG HARRIS and the Dutch sprinter Arie van Vliet were bitter enemies for a short while. They were initially friends, but fell out after Harris told his fellow Englishman Cyril Bardsley to appeal to the judges after Van Vliet put a pedal in his wheel in the 1958 world championship. To fan the flames, Harris accused Van Vliet of being soft, saying "he's never been out in a cape and sou'wester and ridden in the rain for eight hours." After that, Van Vliet would recruit other riders to help him against Harris and the pair had occasional shoving matches in races. "An enormous bloody war," Harris termed it. "Every time Arie said 'Look isn't it time this was over?' I'd say 'It'll never be over as far as I'm concerned.'"

Some of the bitterest episodes have involved cyclists on the same team. The Coppi/Bartali dispute had its origins when the pair raced together at the start of Coppi's career. Hinault and LeMond fell out because they both wanted to win the 1986 Tour, in which the Frenchman had promised to help LeMond but appeared to go back on the deal. The 1987 GIRO D'ITALIA saw an epic conflict between STEPHEN ROCHE and his nominal leader Roberto Visentini.

There were echoes of the Roche/Visentini battle in the 2009 Tour, when LANCE ARMSTRONG contested team leadership with the Spaniard Alberto Contador, who was isolated within the Astana team. Armstrong briefed against the Spaniard, attacked him early in the race, and in the final week Contador was to be seen hitching lifts with rival teams and his brother to get to his hotel after stage finishes.

In track racing GREAT BRITAIN and AUSTRALIA were bitter rivals in the early 21st century. In racing component manufacture, SHIMANO and CAMPAGNOLO compete intensely and had a stranglehold on the sport that has only recently been threatened. But the last word on rivalries should go to Anquetil, who had a thought for Poulidor even on his deathbed, where he said a final goodbye to him with the words: "Sorry, Raymond, you're going to finish second again."

ROAD RACING Began on November 7, 1869, with the running of Paris–Rouen, organized by the magazine *Le Vélocipede Illustré*, which published the rules on October 20. The course was 135 km beginning at the Arc de Triomphe with five checkpoints en route. The race was open to "all velocipedes, all mechanical devices powered by the force of a man, by weight, foot and hand action, monocycles, bicycles, tricycles, quadricycles or polycycles. They may only convey one person, who will drive and direct the machine, which he may not change during the race." Walking by the machine was permitted, as were repairs en route. The riders were banned, however, from taking dogs with them or entering under false names. They were permitted to eat and drink, to wear what they wanted, but they were banned from giving each other any assistance such as "pulling each other by cords or chains." Entry was free, and a time limit of 24 hours was set. First prize was 1,000 francs, second prize a "double suspension" velocipede.

The start list was published on October 20, with 203 names, including six women, three Belgians, and a German—and six Britons, including the eventual winner, JAMES MOORE, who took 10 hours 40 minutes for a course later worked out to be 123 kilometers. *Le Vélocipede*'s editor Richard Lesclide wrote: "the attitude of the people in the villages along the way was excellent. The velocipedists were greeted with bravos, congratulations and encouragements. Guns were fired as they went through to add to the jollity."

Initially, however, it was in ITALY that racing on the open road gained popularity most rapidly, with a proliferation of events in the early 1870s, including Milan–Turin, first run in 1876 and the oldest major road race still in existence. In Britain, meanwhile, track events were popular, and so too long-distance road events such as the North Road 24-hour TIME TRIAL won by G. P. Mills in the early 1880s, with a distance of 365 km on a HIGH-WHEELER. The fashion for marathon events went back across the Channel to France, where the circulation war between a host of French cycling magazines led to the creation of Bordeaux–Paris by *Véloce-Sport* magazine in 1891. Mills won that event, thanks to a cunning attack at the main feed station in Angoulême, where his best pacemaker was waiting; he covered the distance in 26 hours

34 minutes, stopping only to "satisfy natural needs."

Later that year, the first Paris–Brest–Paris was run by a rival publication, *Le Petit Journal*—and the HEROIC ERA had begun, with newspapers competing to run longer and harder events; the creation of the TOUR DE FRANCE in 1903 was the logical outcome.

Early on there was little structure: pacing in the great events was common, be it with tricycles, cars, or just bicyclists carefully selected for their speed, meaning that the best pacemakers were in great demand; without them, it was impossible to win. There were arcane registration procedures to ensure that cyclists started and finished the race on the same bike; for example, early Tour machines were marked in secret by the organizers so the riders couldn't change them. But by the First World War, the main elements of today's road racing season were in place: the five one-day MONUMENTS, the GIRO D'ITALIA and Tour, and a wealth of other CLASSICS and lesser stage races.

The 1930s saw a gradual increase in race speeds as road surfaces improved while team tactics and equipment improved gradually as well, but HENRI DESGRANGE's conservatism held back development in areas such as GEARS.

The years after the Second World War saw rapid changes. The introduction in 1948 of the season-long Desgrange–Colombo prize, awarded for performances across the great races, led to a rapid internationalization of road racing, with the great champions coming out of their home countries more readily, and public support booming. Agents became powerful figures, creaming off percentages from the appearance fees they charged for stars in circuit races and track meetings.

At the same time, with his Bianchi team, FAUSTO COPPI refined team tactics; his squad was highly structured and well equipped, with the star at the center, serviced by *domestiques*—

gregari in Italian—who catered to his every need, pushing him early on to save his strength and making the pace to set up the race-winning attack. Finally, Fiorenzo Magni and Raphael Geminiani were the prime movers behind the arrival of *extra-sportif* sponsors to back up the constructors in the 1950s (see TEAMS).

The 1960s saw the system refined with the demise of the independent category, which had provided a stepping stone between the amateur and professional ranks; the beginning of proper drug testing, and the last Tours run under the national team system. The next 30 years were stable, almost backward: professional road racing was largely dominated by riders from the European heartland, sponsors were mainly interested in their own domestic markets, the calendar changed little, and a small number of major stars raced most of the big events taking their teams with them.

That all began to change in the 1980s, as first the English-speaking nations arrived led by the FOREIGN LEGION, followed after the fall of the Berlin Wall by waves of former "amateurs" from EASTERN EUROPE. At the same time, the Tour de France began to dominate the calendar thanks to a massive expansion in television rights and coverage. Sponsors with world interests such as T-Mobile and Panasonic appeared, and the last constructors' teams, RALEIGH and PEUGEOT, went under. Prize money and salaries mushroomed: in 1983 LAURENT FIGNON received £20,000 from his first Tour win, while 16 years later LANCE ARMSTRONG made over $7 million from his first Tour win.*

The sport remains in a state of flux. Since 1998, a series of DRUG scandals have created permanent instability and made a true hierarchy hard to establish as stars are unmasked as cheats. The governing body, the UCI, has tinkered continually

*Figures from Benjo Maso, *Sweat of the Gods*, trans. Michael Horn, Mousehold Press, 2005

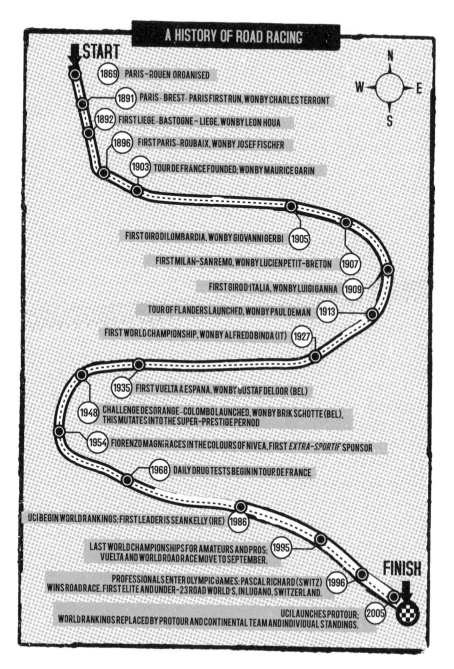

A HISTORY OF ROAD RACING

START

(1869) PARIS–ROUEN ORGANISED

(1891) PARIS–BREST–PARIS FIRST RUN, WON BY CHARLES TERRONT

(1892) FIRST LIEGE–BASTOGNE–LIEGE, WON BY LEON HOUA

(1896) FIRST PARIS–ROUBAIX, WON BY JOSEF FISCHER

(1903) TOUR DE FRANCE FOUNDED: WON BY MAURICE GARIN

FIRST GIRO DI LOMBARDIA, WON BY GIOVANNI GERBI (1905)

FIRST MILAN–SAN REMO, WON BY LUCIEN PETIT-BRETON (1907)

FIRST GIRO D'ITALIA, WON BY LUIGI GANNA (1909)

TOUR OF FLANDERS LAUNCHED, WON BY PAUL DEMAN (1913)

FIRST WORLD CHAMPIONSHIP, WON BY ALFREDO BINDA (IT) (1927)

(1935) FIRST VUELTA A ESPANA, WON BY GUSTAF DELOOR (BEL)

(1948) CHALLENGE DESGRANGE–COLOMBO LAUNCHED, WON BY BRIK SCHOTTE (BEL). THIS MUTATES INTO THE SUPER-PRESTIGE PERIOD

(1954) FIORENZO MAGNI RACES IN THE COLOURS OF NIVEA, FIRST *EXTRA-SPORTIF* SPONSOR

(1968) DAILY DRUG TESTS BEGIN IN TOUR DE FRANCE

UCI BEGIN WORLD RANKINGS: FIRST LEADER IS SEAN KELLY (IRE) (1986)

LAST WORLD CHAMPIONSHIPS FOR AMATEURS AND PROS: VUELTA AND WORLD ROAD RACE MOVE TO SEPTEMBER. (1995)

PROFESSIONALS ENTER OLYMPIC GAMES: PASCAL RICHARD (SWITZ) WINS ROAD RACE. FIRST ELITE AND UNDER-23 ROAD WORLD'S. IN LUGANO, SWITZERLAND. (1996)

FINISH

UCI LAUNCHES PROTOUR; WORLD RANKINGS REPLACED BY PROTOUR AND CONTINENTAL TEAM AND INDIVIDUAL STANDINGS. (2005)

N
W   E
S

with the professional side of the sport since the inception of the world rankings.

The World Cup was created in 1988 and died a lingering death, Classics were created and died, others lost their value, the calendar was restructured in 1995, while 2005 saw the foundation of the ProTour, splitting pro racing into an elite of ProTeams with feeder systems in each continent to provide a coherent structure. The UCI's three-year feud with ASO led to speculation that the sport might split to form two rival pro calendars. There is still debate over the use of helmet RADIOS.

Thanks primarily to the worldwide impact of LANCE ARMSTRONG, the sport has become globalized. Although the WORLD CHAMPIONSHIPS have been devalued by their end-of-season date, and major races in FRANCE, Italy, and SPAIN have disappeared, a wave of new events has emerged, led by the Tour of California and the Tour DownUnder.

Further reading: *A Century of Cycling, the Classic Races and Legendary Champions*, William Fotheringham, Mitchell-Beazley, 2003

ROCHE, Stephen (b. Ireland, 1959)

Together with SEAN KELLY, the cherubic Dubliner took Irish cycling to a brief position of world dominance in the 1980s. Roche has a place in cycling history shared only by EDDY MERCKX as a winner of the GIRO D'ITALIA, TOUR DE FRANCE, and world title in a single year.

He managed the feat in 1987, taking the Giro after a dramatic attack en route to the Sappada ski station. The victim was his teammate Roberto Visentini—who was wearing the pink jersey—and Roche's "treachery" made him, briefly, a hate figure among the Italian *tifosi*.

The Carrera Jeans team was split, with one *domestique*

allocated to Roche, the Belgian Eddy Schepers, and the rest working for Visentini. Visentini accused Roche, Schepers, and one of the mechanics, Patrick Valcke, of "holding séances" in their hotel room and said he had bought up all the foreigners in the race to work against him. At one stage finish, Schepers had to threaten Visentini's fans to keep them away from Roche; as the Irishman rode up the mountains the livid *tifosi* spat at him, threw rolled-up newspapers at him, and waved slabs of raw meat under his nose. Roche had the last laugh as he won the race—with some help from ROBERT MILLAR—and took the Giro and world championship that year.

The Tour followed, after a race-long battle with Pedro Delgado that included an episode at La Plagne in the ALPS where he blacked out briefly after the finish. Roche eventually took the yellow jersey from Delgado on the penultimate day to win by just 40 seconds. That year's world title in Villach, Austria, looked destined for Kelly, but it was Roche who attacked a late break to win.

However, his career went downhill from there, in a classic case of the CURSE of the rainbow jersey. He barely raced as world champion following a serious knee injury and operation, pulled out of the 1989 Tour, and was bizarrely eliminated from the 1991 race after his team started without him in a team time trial stage. He achieved one more major win, a stage in the 1992 Tour, before retirement in 1993. He now runs a hotel in the south of France. Both his son Nicolas and his nephew Daniel Martin are successful professional cyclists.

ROUGH STUFF Cycling off-road using road bikes that are often adapted with fatter tires and cyclo-cross brakes. In Britain rough-stuff routes include green lanes, old Roman roads, and roughly surfaced bridleways, while in Scotland the network of military roads built by General Wade is used. Rough Stuff predates the invention of the MOUNTAIN BIKE by many years, dating back to the late 19th century.

The Rough Stuff Fellowship publishes ride details and a newsletter.

(SEE **CYCLO-CROSS** AND **MOUNTAIN-BIKING** FOR OTHER WAYS OF GETTING AWAY FROM ASPHALT)

SADDLES From the late 19th century until the 1970s, most saddles were made the same way: from a teardrop-shaped leather strip strung on a metal frame. Now, however, the

principal volume producer of leather saddles is the British firm Brooks, and most models are a hybrid of plastic or carbon-fiber base, foam or gel padding, with a slim covering of either fine leather or synthetic fiber. The center of the cycle saddle industry is in the Veneto region of Northern Italy, home to Selle Royal, Selle Italia, and Selle San Marco.

Leather saddles such as the iconic Brooks B17 look distinguished but are heavier than composite ones and sag if they get wet; they also have to be "broken-in," a process in

which they are ridden for several hundred miles until their shape matches that of the rider's behind. While this is going on they have to be dressed with some kind of oil such as neatsfoot, seal oil, or in extreme cases motor oil. Some aficionados go so far as to soak them in oil. Not everyone goes as far as TOM SIMPSON, who made his own saddle using a plastic sports saddle, some foam, and his wife's handbag; mostly, cyclists find a ready-made one which suits and stick with it.

SADDLE SORES A perennial issue, but less common today. Professional cyclists of the HEROIC ERA suffered almost constantly from saddle boils, when the skin of the crotch becomes abraded, enabling dirt from the road to get in and infection to develop. In the 1950s and 1960s, the TOUR DE FRANCE doctor Pierre Dumas describes seeing riders with a massive swelling in the perineum nicknamed the "third testicle." LOUISON BOBET's career was cut short after he heroically rode on with a saddle boil to win the 1955 Tour, and an uncomfortable sore probably contributed to LAURENT FIGNON's narrow defeat in the 1989 Tour.

Geoffrey Nicholson, in *The Great Bike Race*, recalled the 1976 Tour runner-up Joop Zoetemelk pulling down his shorts to show journalists a boil "the size of an egg" on his inner thigh to explain why he wasn't able to challenge the winner Lucien Van Impe. LANCE ARMSTRONG's teammate Frankie Andreu finished one Tour with a vast hole cut in his saddle to accommodate a sore.

Some cyclists swear by the use of cream on the insert in their shorts, others prefer to pedal dry; none now resort to the 1930s remedy of putting a raw steak down below. All are agreed, however, that nothing apart from a little cream should come between a cyclist and his insert, once made of soft chamois leather (which would harden uncomfortably with washing and had to be treated before use), now more likely to be an artificial padded fabric. Repeated cycling seems to harden the skin in the crotch for male cyclists, who should not have to resort to the remedies recommended by TOM SIMPSON: ice water baths or cocaine lotions to deaden the nerves.

SAFETY BICYCLES

A type of bike born of a spate of inventions in the 1870s and 1880s as designers attempted to improve on the HIGH-WHEELER by making the bike more stable and introducing rear-wheel drive. The definitive safety bicycle was produced in 1885 with the launch of the Rover designed by JAMES STARLEY.

Starley's third model for the Rover had the diamond frame, rear chain drive—the bush-roller chain as we know it today had been invented in 1880—and direct front-wheel steering that now define most bikes. The size of the Rover could be altered for cyclists of various heights; the gears were also changeable by varying the size of chain rings and sprockets. An 1869 machine made by Frenchmen Meyer and Guilmet had included similar features but had never been marketed due to the Franco-Prussian war.

The only issue with safety-type bicycles was that the smaller wheels were less forgiving than the larger ones used on the high-wheeler, but that was solved in 1888 when John Boyd Dunlop, a vet in Belfast, patented the

pneumatic tire (see TIRES for the development of this vital item). Initially the tires were glued and bound to the wheel-rim but later in the decade Michelin of France patented a wired-on tire.

Fundamentally, the modern bicycle was born. What remained was perfecting the various areas: the development of gearing, lighter and stronger components, mass production to drive down prices and make the machines ever more popular. Key developments in WHEELS, FRAMES (materials and design), BRAKES, tires, and GEARS are covered in their individual sections.

SCHUERMANN, Clemens (b. 1888, d. 1957), Herbert (b. 1925, d. 1994), and Ralph (b. 1953)

The German family of architects who between them have built many of the world's velodromes: 122 at the last count, including the Olympic tracks in Beijing, Barcelona, Seoul, Mexico City, and Rome; the Hamar track in Norway; the Meadowbank velodrome in Edinburgh; the UCI's World Cycling Center track in l'Aigle, Switzerland; and the Vigorelli velodrome in Milan.

Clemens Schuermann was a track cyclist who invented an early cycling helmet and later became an architect who began constructing velodromes in 1926. He experimented with velodrome construction with a temporary track in his home town of Muenster, which he built and rebuilt each year, continually altering the transitions—the point where the rider exits the banking and enters the straight. He discovered that at this point, centrifugal forces mean a properly designed track can guide the rider around the curve so that he or she does not have to turn the handlebars.

The Vigorelli was Clemens's masterpiece; his son Herbert continued the tradition, working around the globe on 55 tracks and helping the UCI with track design, reducing standard length to 250 m. He handed the business down in turn to his son Ralph, who designed the velodrome at Hamar, Norway, in a radically shaped building resembling a Viking longship, and, most recently, the futuristic track used at the Beijing OLYMPIC GAMES.

(SEE ALSO **HOUR RECORD**, **TRACK RACING**)

SCHWINN America's best-known cycle maker, which was founded in Chicago by two German émigrés, Ignaz Schwinn and Adolph Arnold, started production in 1895 and was responsible for two classic designs. Under Ignaz's son Frank W. Schwinn, the Aerocycle was based on motorcycle design with 2.125-inch balloon tires—specially produced by the American Rubber Company at Schwinn's request— vast mudguards, a chrome-plated headlight, and push-button bell. It was later known as the cruiser. The Stingray of 1963, designed by Al Fritz, was another motorcycle-based design. Fritz was inspired by a Californian youth trend for fitting bikes with motorbike parts, and produced a machine that featured high-rise handlebars known as apehangers, a banana-shaped seat, and 20-inch wheels, which was adapted by RALEIGH and marketed successfully in the UK as the Chopper.

Schwinn's Paramount was its most successful road bike brand, introduced in 1938 under Frank W. Schwinn and made in low numbers in a small unit that was separate from the main factory, but after that the company never seemed truly at ease with road bike manufacturing, possibly because it never sponsored a team that raced in the European hotbed. The Paramount was updated in the 1950s with Reynolds tubing, and the multi-geared Varsity and Continental brands sold well in the 1960s. But Schwinn missed out on the surge in road racing interest in the US in the 1970s: the bikes they offered were not light or responsive enough compared to what was offered from Europe. Similarly the company failed to truly capitalize on the later BMX and MOUNTAIN-BIKE booms—although ironically enough the Schwinn cruisers were an inspiration for the earliest mountain bikes, and Schwinn briefly produced a mountain bike named the Klunker 5. Schwinn outsourced manufacturing to GIANT, which launched its own brands and overtook it in the late 1980s. The name has been bought, sold, and relaunched over the last 15 years. In 1993, during one difficult spell, Richard Schwinn, great-grandson of Ignaz Schwinn, founded Waterford Precision Cycles, an offshoot based in the former Paramount production plant in Waterford, Wisconsin, which makes lightweight machines in limited numbers.

SERCU, Patrick (b. Belgium, 1944)

The greatest SIX-DAY rider ever, Sercu was born into a family that epitomized the cycling tradition of FLANDERS. His father Albert came close to winning CLASSICS such as the Tour of Flanders and Paris–Tours in the 1940s and was a world-championship silver medalist. To give his son the best possible start in cycling, he restored the velodrome in the little town of Rumbeke so that he could train on it.

Patrick was an amateur and professional world sprint champion, and set world records over one kilometer, but he also had sufficient stamina to race well in the longest stage races. His sprint gave him 14 stage wins in the GIRO D'ITALIA and the green points jersey in the 1974 TOUR DE FRANCE, where he had a fair bit of help from EDDY MERCKX, with whom he formed a winning team in several sixes.

His high cheekbones meant he looked a little like the Cannibal and on the winter velodromes between 1966 and 1983 he was as dominant as Merckx was on the road, winning 88 six-days out of the 224 he contested. How did he do it? To start with, Sercu had the perfect blend of speed and stamina for the Madison relay races that are at the heart of sixes: few could outsprint him for points, not many were stronger when it came to making lap gains. And his status meant that promoters would almost always give Sercu the strongest partners: he would sometimes be given a local hero—for example, he won the London six with Tony Gowland in 1972—but often he teamed up with another record winner, the Dutchman Peter Post (see RALEIGH for information on Post's career as a team manager). He continued winning when Post retired in 1972. He is now director of the Ghent Six-Day race.

(SEE ALSO TRACK RACING)

SEX Medical opinion is divided over whether cycling is good for sexual health. Studies that indicate that pressure in the genital area from bicycle saddles can lead to male impotence and female genital soreness tend to be countered by evidence of the physical and mental well-being that comes from cycling. Early on, there was speculation that cycling after intercourse might be damaging for men and that the very act of cycling might turn women into nymphomaniacs. No research exists to support either theory.

There are claims that the invention of the bicycle in the 19th century resulted in an expansion of the human gene pool because the mating range of adult humans expanded among all social classes, simply because people could travel further and faster to find partners.

The issue of sex and racing is a vexed one: testosterone is rampant in the sport (and not merely the injected drug) while popular wisdom held for many years that professionals should be celibate. A chick-lit novel based on the Tour, *Cat* by Freya North (see BOOKS—FICTION), implies that there is plenty of bedhopping on the race, and LAURENT FIGNON recalled inventing an alibi for a teammate who wanted a rendezvous with "an unofficial Miss France." Teams have varying policies on wives and girlfriends attending races. "Nobody has the wife with them when they are working," said one manager in the 1990s.

At a lecture in the 1980s, however, the great all-rounder SEAN KELLY was asked whether he had a personal policy when it came to the bedroom; he replied that he would abstain for a week before a one-day CLASSIC and three weeks before a stage race; one onlooker speculated whether

Kelly's wife Linda was still a virgin. ALFREDO BINDA, manager of the Italian team in the 1940s and 1950s, said that in his racing days he permitted himself sex once a year.

In the 1930s, the SOIGNEUR Biagio Cavanna felt that the issue was not having sex but the time cyclists might spend going out to pick up girls, so he recommended his riders visit a brothel instead. His protégé FAUSTO COPPI was found in his hotel room in bed with his mistress, the White Lady Giulia Occhini, before a pursuit match in 1953: he told the soigneur that he could make love and then win and was proved right.

Prolific sprint winner Mario Cipollini made much of his macho reputation, cycling with a picture of Pamela Anderson on his handlebars and commenting that "ejaculating costs only as many calories as a bar of chocolate so it's not a worry for me. I've won plenty of races after having sex." Cipollini once broke away in a race with a fellow sprinter, and then disappeared off the road for a rendezvous with two girls, and marketed himself as a sex god: his shoe sponsor distributed postcards that showed him being fed grapes by a harem of topless beauties.

The stresses of their profession mean that cyclists often have tangled private lives: the 1920s French great HENRI PELISSIER was shot dead by his mistress, while Coppi's messy divorce provoked anger among fans and the Catholic church. The domestic arrangements of JACQUES ANQUETIL verged on the incestuous: he set up a *ménage à trois* with his wife Janine and her daughter from her first marriage, Annie, with whom he had a daughter, Sophie, then became involved with Janine's daughter-in law, Dominique, with whom he had a son. It was, says Sophie in her memoirs, *For the Love of Jacques*, partly due to his desperate need to produce an heir, partly also because he was the undisputed ruler of their Norman household.

SHIMANO Together with Italians CAMPAGNOLO, the Japanese company is one of two world leaders in cycle-component manufacture, although recently their dominance has been shaken by newcomer SRAM. Unlike Campag', however, Shimano is a diverse enterprise and a world leader in fishing tackle and also makes snowboarding equipment, although bike bits account for about 75 percent of its income (2005 figure). Shimano also has far greater market reach, covering mountain-biking and leisure cycling. Shimano is a public company in Japan and also manufactures in Czechoslovakia, China, Malaysia, and Singapore; the American arm is privately owned.

Established in the 1920s, the company emerged as a serious contender in cycling during the 1970s, when it rode the surge in the industry in the US to become, so it claimed, the world's largest DERAILLEUR makers. Next they moved into Europe, where top cyclists who raced on Shimano gear included Freddy Maertens; their first attempt to take on Campagnolo was the Dura-Ace groupset in 1974.

The key innovation came in 1984, with the introduction of Shimano Index System, in which the gear lever "clicked" into preset positions to provide quicker and more accurate gear shifting; crucially, the levers, cable, cable housing, derailleur, chain, and sprockets were all considered to be parts of a unit dedicated to producing the best possible gear shift.

Another landmark was the introduction of the Freehub system, in which separate sprockets slid directly onto a hub that incorporated the freewheel, rather than hub and freewheel being separate. Critically, that meant that gear ratios could be rapidly changed by switching individual sprockets, something pro-team mechanics rapidly appreciated.

The improvements to Dura-Ace meant the company was beginning to threaten Campagnolo's hegemony in pro cycling component making, and the breakthrough came in 1989, when the American 7-Eleven team started using a prototype gear shifter, incorporated into the brake lever—STI, or Shimano Total Integration. It took Campagnolo several years to catch up, and by then Shimano had moved to the top of the market.

Thanks to early innovations such as thumbshifting gear levers, and SPD clipless off-road pedals—double sided, with small, sturdy plates that did not clog up with mud, brought out in 1991— Shimano was already dominant in the burgeoning mountain-bike market, with the road-oriented Campagnolo never producing anything that challenged their inventive Deore and XTR groupsets.

Shimano did not win a major Tour until 1988, when Andy Hampsten won the GIRO D'ITALIA, and their first TOUR DE

FRANCE win came in 1999 with LANCE ARMSTRONG, whose seven successive Tour wins cemented their position in the road market. In 2002, Shimano-equipped bikes won all three Grand Tours. By 2009, their range included electric gears on the range-topping Dura-Ace group, using a battery about the size of a mobile phone power unit, and biodynamic chain rings, reshaped so they were not exactly oval, but almost diamond-shaped with rounded corners.

○■○■○■○■○■○■○■○■○■○■○■○■○■○■○■○■○■○■

SIMPSON, Tom,
(b. England, 1937, d. 1967)

Dapper, daring, and charismatic, Simpson was the first cyclist from GREAT BRITAIN to make a major impact on European professional racing. A coal miner's son whose early hero was FAUSTO COPPI he won a bronze medal in the Melbourne Olympics of 1956 then moved from his home in Nottinghamshire in 1959 to the town of Saint-Brieuc in Brittany to avoid national service.

He rapidly became one of the stars of the pro circuit thanks to victories in CLASSICS such as the Tour of FLANDERS in 1961, Bordeaux–Paris in 1963, MILAN–SAN REMO in 1964, and the GIRO DI LOMBARDIA in 1965, the year

Watching and Reading Tom Simpson:

❖

Major Tom, (Chris Sidwells, Mousehold Press 2000), retells the story from his nephew's perspective

Cycling Is My Life (Tom Simpson, Yellow Jersey, 2009) is the re-issue of Simpson's ghosted 1966 autobiography

Put Me Back on My Bike (William Fotheringham, reissued Yellow Jersey, 2007) is the best-selling Simpson book

Death on the Mountain is an award-winning BBC documentary from 2007

Something to Aim At is a personal collection of interviews and archive material by the film-buff Ray Pascoe, as is *The World of Tom Simpson*

Wheels Within Wheels is a more recent DVD of Simpson-related interviews

(SEE ALSO **POETRY** FOR A SIMPSON-INSPIRED WORK)

he became the first—and to date the only—Briton to win the world road-race championship. Simpson was also the first Briton to wear the yellow jersey of the TOUR DE FRANCE, for a single day in the 1962 race. Those wins earned him the BBC Sports Personality of the Year in 1965.

Simpson won hearts for his "all or nothing" racing style and his showmanship, be it posing in silly hats or performing stunts for the crowds on his bike. He was celebrated for posing for photographs wearing a sharp suit and bowler hat and carrying an umbrella in the style of Major Thompson, an "Englishman abroad" created by French writer Pierre Daninos.

He was also a dreamer whose ambitions included owning a train and who was determined to create the best living he could for his wife, Helen, and their two children. He died on July 13, 1967, in the Tour de France after collapsing on Mont Ventoux (see ALPS) in baking heat while under the influence of amphetamines and alcohol. His MEMORIAL still stands near the top of the mountain, bearing the words "Olympic medallist, world champion and British sporting ambassador."

SIX-DAY RACING   Born of the 19th-century vogue for marathon events, and once hugely popular in America, these track races now exist on the margins.

The first six-day cycling race was held at the Islington Agricultural Hall in November 1878: the riders simply rode for as long as they could within the six days and the fastest of the dozen men in the field was one Bill Cann from Sheffield, who covered 1,060 miles, losing seven pounds in the process.

The concept was exported to America where the crowds took ghoulish pleasure in watching the riders' suffering: the final sessions, when the riders were in a zombielike state, would often sell out. The events were exercises in sleep deprivation, with SOIGNEURS providing stimulants to keep their charges awake for as long as possible.

The *New York Times* of December 10, 1897, described the winner of a Madison Square Garden Six, Charles W. Miller, as "drawn and haggard, his eyes sunk and inflamed . . . the cruel chafing of the saddle had sunk deep into his flesh." Major TAYLOR, the legendary African American sprinter, scheduled one hour's sleep in eight in his first six. The helpers would cook food for the riders in a small enclosure in the track center; their charges would eat from the pot as they rode and throw it back when it was empty. At one point at the end of the race, a hallucinating Taylor was convinced he was being chased by a man with a knife.

By the end of the 1890s, rules were put in place to limit the riders to 12–18 hours a day on the track; to get round this, organizers brought in two-man teams. The result was the invention of the "Madison"—named after the arena at Madison Square Garden, purpose-built for cycle racing—in which one rider would circle the track resting while the other raced for a short while before grabbing his partner's hand and "throwing" him up to racing speed. The introduction of points for intermediate sprints counting toward the final standings made the races more lively and resulted in the typical team composition being a sprinter and a stayer. That remains the case today, typified by the GREAT BRITAIN world championship winners in 2008, MARK CAVENDISH and BRADLEY WIGGINS (see their separate entries and GREAT BRITAIN and OLYMPIC GAMES for more on both of them).

In the early years of the 20th century, six-day racing was a lucrative business in the US and Europe, with fees of up to $1,000 a day going to top performers such as the Canadian William "Torchy" Peden and Reggie "the Iron-Man" MacNamara of Australia, famed for having cut off his own finger with a hatchet when he was bitten by a poisonous snake in the bush.

The events attracted celebrities such as Bing Crosby, who was rumored to pay the hospital bills of cyclists who crashed, actors like Douglas Fairbanks, the opera singer Enrico Caruso, and the actress Peggy Joyce. Al Capone might turn up to offer $100 primes.

Six-day racing in the US began to die off in the Depression of the 1930s; in Europe sixes continue, mainly in Germany. They consist of a series of evening sessions over six days, usually lasting into the wee hours, with an overall classification based on the Madison sessions and a variety

of other events (see TRACK RACING) that keep the crowds happy and count for points toward the overall standings.

The biggest winner in six-day racing is the Belgian PATRICK SERCU, who formed a dominant team together with Holland's Peter Post through the late 1960s to the early 1970s. Only one British cyclist has been a consistent six-day winner in recent years: the pursuiter Tony Doyle, who made up a strong team with Australia's Danny Clark for 19 of his 23 wins. The events now exist on the margins, as the UCI prefers to see World Cup meets that act as buildup toward the WORLD CHAMPIONSHIPS and Olympic Games, and it's uncertain how long they will survive now that the Madison has lost its status as an Olympic event in 2012.

SLANG

- **Abdu':** any sprinter who crashes because they won't look where they're going or who throws

his bike from side to side in an exaggerated way. (See ABDUZHAPAROV to learn the origin of this term.)

- **Baked:** over-trained.

- **Ben Hur:** a crash caused, unintentionally or otherwise, by a part of one riders bike jamming the spokes of another rider's wheel.
- **Big meat:** large gear, large chainring.
- **Bonk:** running out of energy and fuel during a race or ride, which causes a severe reductions in one's ability to produce power. Also known as *knock* or *hungerknock*.
- **Broomwagon:** vehicle that travels last in a race convoy to gather up riders who drop out.
- **Bunny-hop:** jumping the bike over an obstacle by lifting the front wheel and using upward force in the pedals to pull up the rear wheel. Road racers do it to avoid potholes and (in Belgium) to switch between pavement and asphalt; mountain bikers do it over most obstacles.
- **Cat. 5 tattoo:** a grease mark left on a rider's leg by a chainring or chain. Also known as a *rookie mark*.
- **Convoy:** the cavalcade of team vehicles behind a major race ("use the convoy").
- **Diesel:** a racing cyclist who rides mainly at a steady pace and finds sudden sprints hard to handle.
- **Feathering:** braking technique where rapid, frequent application of the brakes avoids skidding.
- **Flick:** make a sudden movement to one side to discourage opponent in a sprint. Also used as a general term for deceiving, tricking an opponent or teammate, or being ripped off by a sponsor (he flicked me, I got flicked).
- **Fred:** a disparaging term used by racers for a cyclist who they regard as being beneath them in status or ability. A Fred can be a novice rider with no obvious skill but costly clothing and equipment. More commonly it is someone with profoundly unfashionable or dated gear, often a bicycle commuter. May well have a *Cat. 5 tattoo*.
- **Granny gear:** derogatory term for a very low gear, often

attained by the use of a...

- **Granny Ring:** the smallest chainring of a triple chainset.
- **Hairnet:** crash hat made of leather strips used before shell helmets became vogue.
- **Hammerhead:** a rider who maintains a relentlessly high pace.
- **Hand-sling:** maneuver in TRACK RACING where one rider "throws" the other into the action.
- **Honk:** to ride out of the saddle on a climb.
- **Juice:** dope (juicer: a rider who dopes).
- **Lead-out, lead-out man:** in a sprint, two cyclists from the team will organize themselves so the slower man sets the pace in the final kilometer until the sprinter can make his effort. In major races, a team will all work to keep the pace high until the last lead-out man can launch the sprinter.
- **Lunched:** an irreparably broken component, particularly an expensive one.
- **Mafia:** When riders from several different teams combine their efforts in order to control a race, then share the prize money.
- **Meet the man with the hammer:** blow up, or get the *bonk*.
- **Pretzeled:** severe damage to a frame or wheel.
- **Retrogrouch:** a rider who eschews the latest in equipment.
- **Ride on mineral water:** to race without using drugs.
- **Road rash:** skin abrasions caused by a fall (also known as *gravel rash*).
- **Sandbag:** Not giving as much effort as you are capable of when you are supposed to be pulling on the front for your team in order to save energy and seek individual glory in the final stage of the race.
- **Shelled, spat out, shat out:** all terms used for getting left behind by the pack, usually due to *bonk* or *meeting the man with the hammer.*
- **Sitting in:** getting shelter in the pack or behind the break as a *wheelsucker* might.
- **Snake bite:** a flat usually caused by an underinflated tire.
- **Squirrel:** an erratic bike handler

whose twitchy riding can cause crashes.

- **Swag or schwag:** merchandise offered as prizes, items given to riders by sponsors free of charge. Pro and sometimes even amateur riders get swag bags from sponsors at the start of each season.
- **Swanny:** English variant on SOIGNEUR, French, team helper or carer.
- **Switch:** a sideways move like a flick but more sustained, preventing opponent from coming past.
- **Tacoed:** see *pretzeled*.
- **Time bonus:** used in stage racing, when seconds may be deducted from the overall time of riders who place in the first three in the stage, or at intermediate sprints.
- **Track stand:** holding the bike motionless by balancing the force of the pedals against gravity or the brakes. Most often seen in track sprinting, where one rider may stand still to force the other to take the lead. Skilled road cyclists can do this at traffic lights.
- **Unobtanium:** what any obscenely expensive bike part is made of.
- **Water-carrier:** team rider (French *domestique*).
- **Weight weenie:** cyclist who is obsessed with getting his bike as light as possible without sparing his cash.
- **Wheelsucker:** a rider who doesn't contribute to a break or who "sits in" in the pack all day, only emerging for the final sprint.

(FOR A GLOSSARY OF RACING-SPECIFIC TERMS, SEE **FRENCH**, THE LINGUA FRANCA OF EUROPEAN RACING)

SOIGNEUR For a century, these men were the *éminences grises* of professional cycling, providing massage, magic remedies, and advice to the riders. There were no qualifications other than who a soigneur had worked with. They began working life as gravediggers, fishmongers, and bus drivers. Knowledge was handed down through the generations.

The breed was declared extinct early in the 21st century after the most notorious, Willy Voet, published his scandalous *Massacre à la Chaîne* in 1999 (*Breaking the Chain*, Yellow Jersey, 2000), detailing the various nefarious practices these dastards got up to in order to enhance the performance of professional cyclists, some of whom had no idea what was going on. The term "carers" is now used.

The first was "Choppy" Warburton, the only Briton to figure in their ranks. It almost doesn't matter what Warburton did, his nickname alone means he qualifies, but he was also banned and had a client or two (famously the Briton Arthur Linton) who died. He was immortalized, rifling through his drugs bag, by the artist TOULOUSE-LAUTREC.

Early soigneurs had multi-sport backgrounds; FAUSTO COPPI's mentor Biagio Cavanna came through soccer, boxing, and six-day racing and had underworld connections. Cavanna was blind, which helped when it came to cultivating mystique. It was Cavanna who gave Coppi much of his reputation for being unpredictable and fussy: massaging in the dark, using white not red wine vinegar, having total silence in the hotel. It all added to the reputation of the blind man—his hands worked better when it was quiet—who was not popular with the team management, partly because of Coppi's dependence, partly because of the percentage of Coppi's winnings that he took.

Cavanna is one of the founding fathers of the profession, because of the breadth of his brief: masseur, talent scout, confessor, moral adviser, trainer, provider of early DRUGS and drinks made

Magic Remedies

❖

Xooee v ochkax

Transliteration of Russian for "penis in the eyes": this is what an ex-Soviet masseur at the Italian Carrera team used to say when his charges got on the massage table, reflecting their relative positions. It's called cultural exchange.

The blind man's hands

The notion that blind men give better massage goes back to Fausto Coppi's guru Biagio Cavanna, who used the mystique to great effect. His charges still swore his touch was superior 60 years later. To enhance his mystique, "Biasu" himself made a point of knowing precisely where they had been and what they had been doing, in spite of his being sightless. The Spanish team ONCE, sponsored by a blind charity, had a sightless masseur on their staff.

Get thee to a brothel

The Cavanna special: sex per se is not harmful, but going out in the evening and looking for partners detracts from cyclists' rest periods and exposes them to stuff like colds, at best (something team officials have noted in more modern times). His answer (not theirs): pay for it.

Gus Naessens's porridge

Naessens was the miracle worker who looked after TOM SIMPSON. One of his specials was boiling up cattle feed into porridge and putting it into the cyclists' feed bottles. The theory was it would sit in the stomach and prevent the muscles from using energy better directed to the legs. These days, he'd be selling crystals as a mental health aid.

Condom up the bum

Willy Voet's proudest moment was when he was initiated into this old Belgian method of getting clean urine into a dope-control bottle: clean urine in the condom, which is concealed up the anus, small rubber tube to the penis, bit of hair on the tube so it is camouflaged (a "refinement" of which our Willy was particularly proud). It's fine as long as the urine provider hasn't been on the gear on the quiet, as happened on one famous occasion.

Tail of newt and eye of frog

GINO BARTALI didn't have a legendary healer, but he had plenty of his own wacky peasant ideas: vinegar compresses, tobacco from cigarette butts applied locally, grape juice rubs. He was a firm believer in the power of magnetic fields and aligned his hotel room bed north–south. Other potions of the time included extracts of bee and toad venom, ether, pure cola, egg yolks in port, and cigarettes.

It's all for me, honest

JACQUES ANQUETIL's soigneur Julien Schramm and Voet both came up with the same answer when caught with large amounts of dodgy substances. It was not for the cyclists, they said, but for their "own consumption." Schramm changed his mind when asked to inject himself with the amphetamines he was carrying, while Voet realised he was going to carry the can on his own and squealed to the police.

Not positive but pregnant

No one knows whether this really happened: it's the old tale in which the rider swaps urine with that of his wife with unforeseen results. But urine substitution is an old one, with soigneurs pissing in pots while the dope-testers backs are turned, tubes hidden in funny places, and even catheters being used to flush out the bladder with clean wee. Ouch.

of orange juice, fruit pulp, and grain. He was known variously as *maestro*—which also means teacher—the "Miracle Worker" and the "Muscle Wizard."

The TOUR DE FRANCE doctor Pierre Dumas described the soigneurs as witchdoctors, whose "value was in their valise"—in other words, in the remedies they carried. Sometimes their maxims were simply perverse, such as the long-standing belief that cyclists shouldn't drink much in hot weather and that they should eat salt fish when training to harden them up. They would buy patent medicines, scratch the labels off, and sell them at 100 times the price.

Their clients were often credulous characters who would pay through the nose for magic potions such as Cavanna's *la bomba*—a mix of cola and mild amphetamine—and the go-faster mixes known in France as *la topette*. The effect was in large part psychological, because placebos worked as well: Voet describes one rival soigneur who had a "time trial special," which

one rider in his charge simply had to have; Voet switched it for glucose solution, and the cyclist still flew.

There were straight soigneurs, but Voet's book changed the way all were seen. He described the little deals, the drug-carrying, the elaborate ruses handed down through generations to get around urine tests, the devotion to duty that was not reciprocated by their charges. When Voet was arrested, his main charge, Richard Virenque, was more worried about how he would get his drugs.

The rise of the sports doctor and the entry of women into the profession in the late 1980s was what sounded the death knell for the old-fashioned soigneurs, rather than the name change. Women soigneurs such as LANCE ARMSTRONG's Irish leg rubber Emma O'Reilly didn't do the mystique thing, although they might wrap the day's race food in *Penthouse* pages to cheer up their charges, as O'Reilly's consoeur Shelley Verses once did; sports drinks took over from magic remedies.

SPAIN A relative latecomer to international cycling, partly down to poverty, partly also due to the political turmoil of the 1920s and 1930s. The national Tour in the cycling heartland of the Basque Country didn't begin until 1924, and the VUELTA A ESPAÑA itself didn't get properly established until the 1950s. Early stars included the "Torrelavega Flea," Vicente Trueba, who weighed a mere 112 pounds and had a disabled left hand, while Julian Berrendero was King of the Mountains in the 1935 TOUR DE FRANCE, and

double Vuelta winner in spite of having spent several stints in concentration camps during the

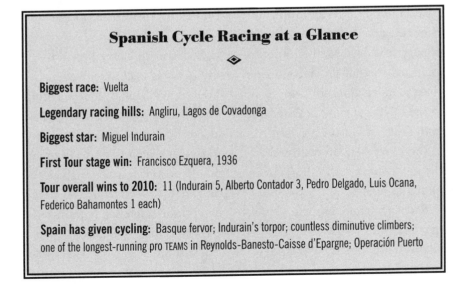

Spanish Cycle Racing at a Glance

◆

Biggest race: Vuelta

Legendary racing hills: Angliru, Lagos de Covadonga

Biggest star: Miguel Indurain

First Tour stage win: Francisco Ezquera, 1936

Tour overall wins to 2010: 11 (Indurain 5, Alberto Contador 3, Pedro Delgado, Luis Ocana, Federico Bahamontes 1 each)

Spain has given cycling: Basque fervor; Indurain's torpor; countless diminutive climbers; one of the longest-running pro TEAMS in Reynolds-Banesto-Caisse d'Epargne; Operación Puerto

Civil War.

It was not until the emergence in the postwar years of Miguel Poblet—the first Spaniard to win Milan–San Remo—Bernardo Ruiz (third in the 1952 Tour) and above all of FEDERICO BAHAMONTES that Spanish cycling truly emerged. The "Eagle of Toledo" was a child of the civil war who recalled riding his bike and racing purely in order to get food in the hungry 1940s.

Bahamontes was the first Spanish Tour de France winner and was followed by two equally mercurial climbers, the "Watchmaker of Avila" Julio Jimenez, and EDDY MERCKX's great rivals Jose-Manuel Fuente and Luis Ocaña. The latter came close to defeating the "Cannibal" in the 1972 Tour but crashed out of the race on a rain-hit descent in the Pyrenées. He returned the next year to take the Tour in Merckx's absence.

Pedro Delgado was the next star; his victories in the 1985 Vuelta and 1988 Tour de France led to an expansion in teams and races—in 1988 the Federation had to put a cap on the number of teams to calm things down—while the period 1991–96 saw an economic boom in cycling. That was partly due to an unprecedented period of dominance in the Tour for MIGUEL INDURAIN but the ONCE team led by the Swiss Alex Zülle and France's Laurent Jalabert were also a force to be reckoned with, as were Clas, for whom the Swiss Tony Rominger took the Vuelta in 1992, 1993, and 1994.

Spain began to cool down after the Vuelta's move to a September date in 1995 and Indurain's retirement at the start of 1997. Now, the sport in Spain is an object lesson in the ravages DOPING can cause. There have been numerous high-profile positives, and a massive blood-doping scandal, revealed in the Operación Puerto inquiry, made matters worse. Sponsors have fled, and there is now only one Spanish-backed team in the ProTour, the Basque squad Euskaltel.

The Basque Country remains

the heartland. Its fans have put up much of the money by subscription to finance the Euskaltel team—which is Basque backed and only hires Basque cyclists. The Atlantic coast is the home of the San Sebastian CLASSIC and the week-long Vuelta a Pais Vasco, which dwarfs the Vuelta in terms of popular support. Boasting Orbea and BH bike makers and Exte-Ondo clothing, it is also a center of the bike industry.

SPONSORS

Your check's in the mail: a litany of bizarre backers of cycling.

- **Saville Stainless:** a Sheffield firm who made toilets. Don't make jokes to their ex-leader Mark Walsham about pulling the chain.
- **Chris Barber:** honky tonk tonk, wah wah wah. The jazz group headed by the iconic trumpet player backed a British team briefly back in the 1960s.
- **Banana:** sounded weirder than it was. A consortium of fruit importers that backed a very winning team headed by, inter alia, current GB coach Shane Sutton.
- **Brooklyn:** chewing gum.

That was strange. As was the incident when the firm owner's daughter got kidnapped in New York and the team ran out of money.
- **Sauna Diana:** a bar close to the Belgian–Dutch border where you could go and discuss "business" with the lady of your choice. Possibly the least politically correct team bus decoration ever.
- **Astana:** a consortium of Kazakh businesses including steel and railways with a casual attitude to paying wages. Led by LANCE ARMSTRONG in 2009 but still known informally as Team Borat.
- **Zero Boys:** a group of unemployed pros in the late

1980s who sold their jerseys on a freelance race-by-race basis. It didn't catch on.

- **Silence:** anti-snoring remedy that sponsored a leading Belgium team during the late noughts, including Cadel Evans (see AUSTRALIA) in its line-up. The team was also backed by a pregnancy test, Predictor.
- **Linda McCartney:** a company producing vegetarian food under the name of the ex-Beatle's late wife was a curious one. Curiouser still was when the manager put together a team with money that wasn't there from three major companies and it went bust after three weeks.
- **Lotteries:** what is it about national lotteries and two wheels? They have backed cycling in Belgium (Lotto), Spain (ONCE), and France (Francaise des Jeux/FDJ. com). It can't be coincidence, just pure chance no doubt.

***

STAGE RACES   As well as the Big Three of GIRO D'ITALIA, TOUR DE FRANCE, and VUELTA A ESPAÑA, there are a host of other smaller multi-day events run on similar lines. The longest-standing ones include:

- **Tour of Switzerland:** run in June, longest after the big three, and famously well-endowed with prize money.
- **Dauphiné Libéré:** also in June and a key Tour warm-up event that takes in the climbs that will figure in the July race.
- **Paris–Nice:** the "race to the sun" is the main season-opener in France, symbolically taking the field from the wintry north to the sunny Riviera.
- **Tirreno–Adriatico:** race of the two seas through central Italy that is the main preparation event for MILAN–SAN REMO.
- **Tour of Catalonia:** long and tough

but run in June, which means it clashes with Switzerland and Dauphiné.

- **Tour of Basque Country:** Spain's biggest event after the Vuelta, famously tough as it is run on the hilly north coast.
- **Tour de l'Avenir:** mini Tour de France run for under-25s.

Newcomers include:

- **Tour Down Under:** based in Adelaide and now a way for pro teams to start the season somewhere sunny.
- **Tour of California:** main pro race in America, famously sponsored by Amgen, which makes EPO.
- **Tour of Britain:** growing in popularity on the back of the OLYMPIC team's success and now seems to have resolved early safety problems.
- **Tour of Qatar:** it's early season, it's sunny, and there is no shortage of prize money. EDDY MERCKX is race director.

⚬▬

STARLEY, James (b. England, 1830, d. 1881) and **John Kemp** (b. England, 1854, d. 1901)

Respectively the "father of the cycle industry" and his nephew, the bike maker behind the Rover safety machine.

James Starley started out working on sewing machines and was one of 19th-century cycling's most inventive minds, responsible for tangential spoking, as used in most spoked wheels today, and various radical TRICYCLES. The Ariel HIGH-WHEELER he produced with William Hillman in 1870 is viewed as a defining moment. The machine was relatively light and had wheels with spokes that could be adjusted; it was Britain's first metal bike produced in any quantity. His most important invention, however, was the differential gear, used on his tricycles, which enabled cyclists to sit side by side and pedal without the imbalance in force turning the machine in a circle: it became standard on the motorcar. James Starley's tricycles—most notably the Coventry rotary and Royal Salvo—established a form for the three-wheeler of today and foreshadowed the modern bicycle, with chain drive and front wheel connected directly to the handlebars.

John Kemp Starley worked with his uncle making Ariel cycles before founding his own company making tricycles that were branded Rover from 1883. Their "safety" bicycle appeared in 1885; the third variant had a diamond frame, rear-wheel chain drive, and two wheels virtually the same size, establishing the template for the modern bike. After Starley's death, the Rover company began making motorbikes and cars, and it would eventually become a key name in British car manufacture.

STELVIO   The greatest mountain pass in the Eastern Alps and probably the most legendary climb tackled by the GIRO D'ITALIA. The Giro only visits every few years though, giving the Stelvio similar cachet to Mont Ventoux in France (see ALPS). The race went up the Stelvio for the first time in 1953 when FAUSTO COPPI used the pass to make an audacious attack on the race leader Hugo Koblet and won the last Giro of his career. As he climbed through the snowdrifts on the second-highest pass in the Alps, he was cheered on by his mistress, the White Lady Giulia Occhini; after the stage they had an assignation in his hotel. One of the greatest moves of BERNARD HINAULT's career came on the mountain in 1980, when he won his first Giro there.

Over 15 miles long and rising to 2,758 m, the Stelvio has a unique history. It was built in 1825 to connect the Austro-Hungarian empire with its

Italian province of Lombardy, and was fiercely fought over during the First World War. Its hairpins are the "greatest driving road in the world" according to the gear-head

television show *Top Gear*. CYCLOSPORTIVES that take in the Stelvio include StelvioBike in August and the Dreiländergiro; there is also a one-off mass ride up the pass, the Cima Coppi,

---

STRADA, Alfonsina
(b. Italy, 1891, d. 1959)

The only woman to compete in any of the three major men's Tours, Strada was born Alfonsina Morin. She won numerous races and was invited to pre-Revolutionary Russia to meet Czar Nicholas II before riding the men's Tour of Lombardy in 1917 and 1918. She entered the 1924 Giro as "Strada, Alfonsin"—deliberately deleting the *a* from her first name to keep the organizers in the dark regarding her gender— and remained in the race for four days. On day five she broke her handlebars and finished

outside the time limit, with the end of a broomstick where part of her bars should have been. She was eliminated but invited to continue by the organizers because the public had gotten wind that a woman was in the race and she had novelty value. Strada started each morning with the race and was timed in in the evening but did not figure on the official listings. She finished 28 hours behind the winner, Giuseppe Enrici, after the 3,613 km and went home with 50,000 lire.

(SEE **WOMEN** FOR MORE ON WOMEN'S RACING; **BERYL BURTON, NICOLE COOKE,** AND **JEANNIE LONGO** FOR GREAT WOMEN RACERS)

T

TANDEMS Bicycles built for two date back to the early days of cycling innovation, and travel quicker than "singles" for obvious reasons: pedaling power is doubled, the actual weight of a racing tandem can be less than twice that of a road bike, friction is the same apart from some loss in the complex drive train, while wind resistance does not increase drastically. In Britain, the Tandem Club (founded 1971) offers its members advice, racing calendars, and regular meets.

Most tandems have a second "timing" chain connecting the front rider's chainset with that of the "stoker" at the back, with the chain rings for the timing chain having an identical number of teeth to keep the pedaling in sync. There are variants that can allow the riders to select different chain ring sizes, or one to freewheel while the other pedals.

There is some uncertainty over the advantages of having the secondary chain rings in phase (where both riders' pedals are at the same part of the pedal stroke at the same time)—the consensus appears to be that with the cranks in phase, the riders can coordinate their efforts better; out of phase

enables a better performance to be got out of a pairing of widely differing leg strengths.

Tandem wheels and brakes have to be more substantial than on a single, with the rear wheel—which has more strain put on it than the front—often having a wider hub to reduce the dish (distance between the rim and the flange of the hub where the spokes are located). That in turn means the spokes are slightly longer and more gently angled, and less likely to snap. The hubs may well be adapted for hub brakes, which avoid heating the rims and risking a tire blow-out on long descents; mountain-bike-style disc brakes are also used.

A tandem at full tilt on a velodrome is a spectacular sight, but a rare one. The last tandem sprint world championships were run in Palermo, Italy, in 1994, after which the event was deleted from the program. The champions were Fabrice Colas and Frederic Magne of France. Tandems are still used, however, for PARALYMPIC CYCLING.

TAYLOR, Marshall Walter

Born: Indianapolis, Indiana, November 8, 1878
Died: Chicago, Illinois, June 20, 1932
Major wins: World sprint champion 1899; 8 world records including paced flying start mile 1 minute 32 seconds (Philadelphia, November 15, 1898), and standing start paced mile 1 minute 33.4 seconds (Paris, 1908)
Nickname: Major

Further reading: *Major Taylor: The Fastest Bicycle Rider in the World*, Andrew Ritchie, Van der Plas/Cycle Publishing, 2009

"The earliest, most extraordinary, pioneering black athlete in the history of American sports," runs part of the introduction to Andrew Ritchie's biography of the lightning-fast sprinter from the turn of the last century. Taylor overcame racial prejudice to rise to the top of his profession, yet died in poverty and was buried in an unmarked grave.

Born into rural poverty just outside Indianapolis, Taylor was enlisted as a companion to the son of the white family who employed his father as a coachman, learning early on that color need not be a barrier. He earned his nickname when a teenager because, to earn money, he performed stunts on a bike while wearing a soldier's uniform outside the cycle shop where he worked. By the age of 16 he was winning local races and was adopted by a trainer, "Birdie" Munger.

As cycling expanded in the US, however, color became an issue: white amateurs, particularly from the South, were against blacks racing with them. In 1894, blacks were excluded from the League of American Wheelmen, reflecting the power of segregation; they were still permitted to race but their status was ambiguous and open to individual interpretation. Fearing that Taylor's success would lead to trouble, Munger persuaded him to move to Worcester, Massachussetts, where racism was less of an issue, and where he worked in Munger's bike factory. Late in 1896, Taylor managed to break—unofficially—the world fifth of a mile record and turned professional to race at the legendary Madison Square Garden track (see SIX-DAY RACING). He became a star of the American professional track circuit, arousing constant curiosity—and some animosity—as a black athlete earning big money at a time when, as Ritchie writes, "his brothers were expected to doff their hats and step aside for any white man in the street."

Taylor began receiving threats against his life as he raced, and at one meeting was pulled off his bike and strangled into unconsciousness. On other occasions he received threatening letters and had nails scattered in front of him. Racial politics continued to dog Taylor's career. He was a massive draw for promoters and sponsors, but as the only black professional at the time he faced resentment from, for example, hoteliers who refused him accommodation, as well as judges at races, and other competitors. "The uncompromising deviousness of his white rivals deprived him for two consecutive years of the possibility of becoming champion of America," wrote Ritchie. Even so, by the end of 1898 he was beating world records on a regular basis—he held seven including the paced mile, which denoted the "fastest man in the world." In 1899 he took the world paced mile close to 44 mph with the help of a steam-powered pacing engine, and later that year he took the world one-mile championship, becoming only the second African American world champion. But at first he was unable to buy a house because of his color, and when he did so, in Worcester, Massachusetts, without revealing his identity, he was not made welcome.

In 1901 his career reached its zenith with a three-month trip to Europe in which he defeated the leading European sprinter, Edmond Jacquelin of France, and won over crowds and media across the continent, the first African American athlete to do so. Between 1902 and 1904 he traveled and raced continuously in Europe, the US, and Australia. But at home, he still faced constant hostility, even in cities such as San Francisco, where the color line was drawn in restaurants and hotels.

Taylor spent 1904 and 1905 out of racing due to physical and mental exhaustion and finally retired in 1910. Afterward his fortunes declined, the wealth he had earned on the velodromes dissipated—despite the publication of his MEMOIRS in 1929—and he died in Chicago in 1932. The body was unclaimed, and he was buried in a pauper's grave.

TEAMS Cycling has always been among the most commercial of sports: when JAMES MOORE won the first road race in 1869 he was supported by a bike maker while major races were all run by newspapers in order to increase sales.

The earliest serious sponsors were the cycle companies La Française—who supported MAURICE GARIN, the first Tour winner—and PEUGEOT, who were the longest-standing sponsors in the sport. The cycle maker Alcyon backed the most powerful team in the HEROIC ERA, claiming the first five places in the 1909 Tour and taking overall victory four years running. This led to a problem: the biggest manufacturers wanted victory so much that they would buy every star they could. The budgets to run a team became so large that only a few teams had enough money to be competitive, which made the racing dull.

The domination of teams such as Alcyon—or the "sky-blues" as they were known— and La Sportive in the 1920s prompted the Tour organizer HENRI DESGRANGE to bring in national teams starting in 1930, to make the racing more open and more exciting. In an attempt to counter the power of the manufacturers, the Tour organizers issued standard bikes to the riders.

That began a conflict between the national and trade team concepts that lasted until the 1960s, by which time the bike industry was struggling and an Italian named Fiorenzo Magni had brought in the first proper "extra-sportif" sponsor, the face-cream makers Nivea. "I rode for a team named 'Ganna,' and at the end of 1953 they told me they were pulling out," he recalled. "I said 'Why should I ride for a bike maker? Who has said it has to be like that?'"

Magni's team was GS Nivea-Fuchs, with the bike-maker's name on the jersey as per the rules. Other early sponsors included chewing-gum makers Brooklyn, the Quinquina aperitif company—who marketed their St. Raphael drink through

JACQUES ANQUETIL and his appropriately named teammate Raphael Geminiani—and Italian fridge makers Ignis. Initially extra-sportifs were banned in France, but eventually they persuaded the Tour organizers to include trade teams in the race; national teams last figured in 1968.

Initially, sponsorship was a flexible concept: riders might race for different sponsors in different countries. The better teams were highly organized, though, with the Bianchi squad of FAUSTO COPPI leading the way in the 1940s and 1950s. By then the principles were long-established: a team would have one or more leaders, and the rest would organize themselves in his support, assisting in chasing down threatening rivals, making the pace before the time came for the leader to attack, and helping the number-one get back to the bunch if he had mechanical problems.

Cycling took a long time to become fully professional, however. In the 1950s even the

better riders had contracts only for eight or nine months of the year; teams were sometimes simply cobbled together for major races on an ad-hoc basis. In the 1960s there were plenty of cases of hopeful amateurs turning "professional" for a jersey and a bike, often losing money in the process. There was also an intermediate category: "independents," who could ride certain pro races and top amateur events. That served as a stepping stone and a fallback if things went wrong, until the category was abolished in the 1960s.

Although most pros gradually became full-time, salaries remained relatively small for all apart from the most senior riders until the 1990s. By then, the hierarchy had begun to change, with teams like TI-Raleigh showing that strong groups of talented riders could be more potent than squads with just one star. The arrival in the sport of new blood with the FOREIGN LEGION changed the structure in another way as GREG LEMOND,

Great Teams

◈

A subjective selection of the world's greatest teams, based on longevity, race results, management, and stylishness of their gear. For some reason, the greatest teams seem to have the best outfits—or is it that the outfits become iconic by association with the greats?

Bianchi: Began sponsoring in 1899 and became one of the first complete "racing machines" built around FAUSTO COPPI, a legacy that then included the later greats of Italian cycling, from Felice Gimondi to Moreno Argentin, all in iconic eggshell blue jerseys.

Faema/Faemino: EDDY MERCKX was just the greatest name to wear the red jersey, in a tradition that ran back through the '60s with RIK VAN LOOY, Charly Gaul, and FEDERICO BAHAMONTES.

Gitane/Renault/Castorama: Under Cyrille Guimard, a talent-spotting, Tour-winning machine that took the 1976 race with Lucien Van Impe and followed up with BERNARD HINAULT, GREG LEMOND, and LAURENT FIGNON. The Renault stripes remain one of the great jersey designs, while Castorama's "carpenters overalls" were imaginative if not pretty.

TI-Raleigh/Panasonic: Under Peter Post's dictatorial management one of the "winningest" teams of the 1970s and 1980s built around a Dutch core that included Jan Raas, Gerrie Knetemann, and Joop Zoetemelk, and later featured PHIL ANDERSON and ROBERT MILLAR.

Telekom/T-Mobile/Columbia/HTC: Like the penknife with many blades and loads of handles, the squad led by MARK CAVENDISH in 2010 bore little resemblance to the German team that won the 1996 Tour with a drug-fueled Bjarne Riis. But Telekom/T-Mobile changed German cycling for ever—for good and bad— thanks to Riis, Jan Ullrich, and company, and their pink strip remains instantly recognizable.

Peugeot/Z/Gan/Credit Agricole: The granddaddy of teams, dating back to the HEROIC ERA, and producing probably the most distinctive jersey design, the checkerboard worn by TOM SIMPSON, EDDY MERCKX, Bernard Thévenet, ROBERT MILLAR, STEPHEN ROCHE, and many others, as well as almost every amateur in France. The checkerboard went in 1988, but under Roger Legeay the personnel and team structure remained largely unchanged and the historic link was retained until the end of 2008 with leaders including GREG LEMOND and CHRIS BOARDMAN.

Reynolds/Banesto/Baleares/Caisse d'Epargne: Longstanding Spanish team under the aegis of Jose-Miguel Echavarri that changed sponsors every few years and brought cycling Pedro Delgado and MIGUEL INDURAIN, winning six Tours between 1988 and 1995.

Mapei: Eyewatering multicolored shorts, mouthwatering results in the 1990s. The first truly international superteam included stars like Johan Museeuw and Tony Rominger and launched the careers of riders like 2009 world champion Cadel Evans. The clean sweep of the first three in 1996 Paris–Roubaix was the defining moment.

PHIL ANDERSON, and STEPHEN ROCHE in particular took salaries to a new level, dragging up the base level.

The advent of a world ranking system in the mid-1980s (see HEIN VERBRUGGEN to read about the man who brought this in) and qualifying for major races decided through team standings led to a massive hike in the value of middle-ranking cyclists who didn't necessarily win much but had earned points by riding consistently. That at least raised salaries and there was an all-around increase in budgets—tens of thousands of dollars in the 1970s, many millions for teams such as Sky three decades later—as the TOUR DE FRANCE captured an increasingly large worldwide audience through the 1990s.

At the same time, teams remained poorly organized in many cases—although there were notable exceptions such as Bjarne Riis's CSC—and there was insufficient regulation. Smaller teams went bust at a rate of almost one a year, because there were no strict checks to see if they had any financial stability. The advent of another Verbruggen baby, the ProTour in 2005, resulted in tighter financial scrutiny, while the early years of the 21st century saw teams become increasingly concerned about the impact of DRUGS. Several major sponsors—most notably T-Mobile in Germany—pulled out because of negative publicity after drug scandals while some of those who stayed in the sport brought in their own internal antidoping programs. Standards were pushed higher, however, by the arrival of new backers such as Columbia Sportswear and Team Sky, run by outsiders who worked on business principles rather than on tradition.

TEAM TIME TRIAL

Exactly what it says, and varies from "two-up" races run in Britain for two-man teams, to the stages of the TOUR DE FRANCE that are contested by full squads of nine. There was a team time-trial world championship over 100 km from 1962 until 1993. A non-medal race for professional teams will return to the WORLD CHAMPIONSHIPS from 2012. The UK championship ran from 1970 to 1999 and was reinstituted in 2004.

Choice of formation is key in team time-trialling: some teams adopt a "two-line" formation, with the riders rotating continuously, taking short turns at the front.

A higher speed results, but because weaker members do the same amount of work as the stronger men, they tire more quickly. In the "one-line" formation, the riders stay at the front of the string for as long as they feel is appropriate; the weaker elements do shorter turns.

In team time trials in the Tour de France, teams have to have a minimum number of finishers; the rules of team time trials in stage races vary, sometimes with the actual time of each squad counting toward his or her overall time, while sometimes a system of bonuses is put in place to ensure that losses are capped.

TELEVISION

"Newspapers created the Tour de France, radio made it popular, television made it magnificent," said the TOUR DE FRANCE organizer Christian Prudhomme as he launched the 2010 race. Prudhomme, it should be noted, is a former television presenter, but he is broadly right.

The modern-day Tour is a televisual product, and that has an impact right through the sport. First, the way the sport is depicted is completely different. The historian Benjo Maso made the point that the victories of

EDDY MERCKX made less impact on public consciousness than those of FAUSTO COPPI because television pictures could not hide how weak Merckx's rivals were; much of the time Coppi was equally dominant, but the written press could big up his opponents.

The search for televisual novelty means that the Tour organizers seek out new, dramatic backdrops—in 2010 the vast North Sea dykes of Holland were the novelty—and they try to construct a route that may provide a last-ditch denouement. The dream scenario was that of 1989, where the race was decided in the final meters of the final stage (see LAURENT FIGNON, GREG LEMOND). Television finances the race; sponsors enter cycling in order to get in the Tour and "show the jersey," and ever-greater resources are devoted to getting the pictures and showing them.

The Tour has massive airtime, growing from 38 hours in 1986 to 112 hours in 1996. Live stage coverage picks up about 50 percent of the available audience. The great increase in worldwide audience came in the 1980s as new nations figured in the action: 50 million in 1980, a billion six years later. The Tour is now covered by 65 stations transmitting to 110 countries. The television rights grew accordingly, going from 12 million francs in 1990 to 85 million francs eight years later. By then, television was the biggest contributor to the event's income.

Television money has enabled the sport to survive because it trickles down in various ways, but it has also created the massive imbalance within the sport, where the Tour dominates the entire year and lesser events struggle to get screen time because of production costs. The outcome has been that ASO, who run the Tour, have become the dominant force because they can use the Tour's revenues to subsidize smaller events, and its prestige to find sponsors and venues (see ASO entry for how far their tentacles stretch).

This is all relatively new.

The Tour was not shown live on TV until 1958; stage finishes in Paris were not even shown on the same day until the following year, while it was 1960 when images began to be shown using motorcycle cameras. Now it is televised in 186 countries.

○═○

THIEVES The most prolific bike thief is believed to be Igor Kenk, a 50-year-old retired police officer in Canada, who in July 2008 was found to have 2,285 bikes stored in warehouses and garages across Toronto after a sting operation in which police planted bikes in various locations in the city and watched to see who stole them. Police raided a shop run by Kenk and found so many bikes inside that they could not be moved out of the upper floor. He was sentenced to two and a half years in jail—about three days per bike. In 2010, his story was made into an acclaimed graphic novel by Richard Poplak and Nick Marinkovich.

○═○

THREE PEAKS The longest and hardest CYCLO-CROSS race in the world has been run annually over Whernside, Ingleborough, and Pen-y-Ghent in the English Peak District since 1961. Whereas most cyclo-cross races are on short park circuits, the Peaks consists of a single large loop with over 5,000 feet of climbing. The cyclo-cross was inspired by the classic fell run over the three mountains, and at the end of 1959 the first cyclist to complete the course was a 14-year-old schoolboy, Kevin Watson, who took almost seven hours.

The cyclo-cross was founded two years later and now draws such a large field that in places riders have to line up to get over stiles. Since its inception, course changes have extended the distance to almost 40 miles, of which about 34 can be ridden. Part of the course is on private land, meaning that the race offers the only chance to ride the complete circuit. Mountain bikes were permitted for a few years in the 1990s, but the rule now is that only cyclo-cross bikes can be used.

TIME TRIALLING Yet another English eccentricity in European eyes, this branch of the sport is the most popular racing discipline in Great Britain, yet it exists in almost total isolation. It was not until 1994 that a regular time trial world championship was inaugurated—the first winner was CHRIS BOARDMAN—and time trialling in Europe is limited to a few one-off events held in autumn and individual stages in stage races. But in Britain, thousands of cyclists test themselves against the watch most weeks from February to October, and an informal local time trial is where most British bike racers compete for the first time.

The growth of time trialling can be traced back to cycling's formative years, when racing was banned on British roads after a legendary episode on the North Road—the main road from London to Edinburgh, now the A1—in which a horse collided with a cycle race. The British governing body, the National Cyclists' Union, forbade racing on the roads and refused to recognize RECORDS set on the roads.

The NCU's hope was that racers would compete on tracks, but that was impractical as not every town had one. Time trialling was the way competitive cyclists got around the ban: running timed events over fixed distances in which the racers rode "alone and unpaced," separated by intervals of one or two minutes. Because the competitors rode solo, with no numbers (although they had to have bells), who was to know if

— 365 —

they were racing? There were no prizes, and the racers had to wear black. If they wore white socks, for example, they would be disqualified, and were, as late as 1945. Courses were referred to by CODES so that no one outside cycling clubs knew where the start and finish would be.

There had been time trials before—the NCU had run a championship in 1878—but the first time trial over one of today's set distances was run over 50 miles on October 5, 1895, by the North Road Cycling Club. In 1930 the sport was given further impetus with the creation of the BRITISH BEST ALL ROUNDER by *Cycling* magazine.

The most popular distances today are 10, 25, 50, and 100 miles, and for most club cyclists the key targets are those that equal a 25 mph average—24 minutes for 10 miles, "under the hour" for 25, and so on. A handful of 12-hour contests are also run as they enable cyclists to qualify for the BBAR, and there are also events over 24 hours and 15 miles, as well as over hilly courses of any distance from 10 to 60 miles. Hilly events on nonstandard circuits have become more popular since the first world championships were held in 1994, as they replicate the sort of course used at the World's. They are also easier to organize as traffic has become heavier on Britain's main roads. The end of season HILL CLIMBS are as atmospheric and popular as ever.

The joy of time trialling for the average cyclist is that even if you do not win, you always come away from a race with a result: your personal time. This can be compared with your times on other courses and those of your rivals—and national stars as well—and progression can be noted. Being low-key—usually just a few people with a watch in a parking lot—they are easily organized, which is why most British cycling clubs run mid-week evening time trials on local courses. The best-known time triallist to go on to bigger things was CHRIS BOARDMAN, a national champion at 25 miles, who used skills honed in British time trialling to win the yellow jersey three times in the Tour de France prologue time trial. However, he felt that a lack of bunched racing in his early years meant he did not have perfect bike handling skills: he quit three Tours due to crashes. Another time triallist to make it on the world stage was BERYL BURTON, who used her ability to ride solo to win several world titles, but lacked a sprint. SEAN YATES went from British time trialling to become one of the most respected pros on the European circuit and returned to "testing" after retirement. Boardman and more recently BRADLEY WIGGINS used time trials as part of their preparation for the Tour de France and Olympics. Time trialling has produced its own list of purely British greats such as Ray "The Boot" Booty, who was the first man to break four hours for 100 miles in 1956, and Alf Engers, a flamboyant baker from the East End who took the 25-mile record from 55 minutes 11 seconds in 1959 to 49 minutes 24 seconds in 1978.

Some Great British Time Trials

◆

"25" championship: The most competitive and the most prestigious national title, but it is currently being challenged by the national "10." Changes course every year.

National hill-climb championship: See HILL CLIMBS for more details

Anfield "100": First run in 1889 and still organized on quiet Shropshire roads by the club that boasted early Bordeaux–Paris winner G. P. Mills among its members.

SCCU "100": Run since 1908, by a grouping of clubs; the team winners receive an Edwardian shield measuring more than three feet by two and embossed in silver with a time-trialling scene.

Nelson Wheelers Circuit of the Dales: A hilly springtime 50-miler over a course that includes towns such as Kirkby Lonsdale, Sedburgh, Hawes, and Ingleton and climbs such as Garsdale.

North Road Hardriders: Classic early season event in Hertfordshire including steep hills and descents (sometimes icy).

TIRES

Pioneered by John Boyd Dunlop, who wanted to improve his son's tricycle. He used a "sausage" on the wheel rim, which was first a water-filled hosepipe, then a tube of rubber wrapped in canvas. Dunlop then put on a rubber tread and a one-way valve that only let air in, not out, and patented the design in 1888. Initially there was scepticism, but in May 1889 his tires were tested in competition in Belfast by W. Hume, who won four events out of four.

Also in the 1880s, another household name, Hutchinson, began making tires at their factory in France.

In about 1887 the concentric bead principle or "clincher" that held the tire on to the rim was patented by A. C. Welch. Dunlop bought the patent in 1892. This was to be the basis of their fortune, being the only practical way to make a clincher tire that could be easily detached from the rim to enable punctures to be repaired.

In 1892, Michelin ran a race from Paris to their base in Clermont-Ferrand, open only to riders using pneumatic tires; they arranged for 25 kg of nails to be scattered on the road, to demonstrate how good their products were. Ironically the first finisher, Auguste Stéphane, was using Dunlops; he was disqualified.

Tires divide into conventional high-pressures, in essence a refinement of the 1890s Michelin design, and tubulars or "sew-ups," in which the inner tube is held inside a cylindrical casing made by sewing both sides of the carcass together. Tubulars were

TIRE

RIM

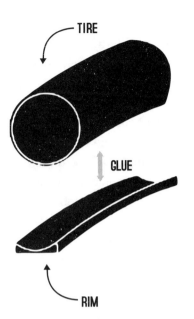

TIRE

GLUE

RIM

the racer's choice for a century after the Wolber company offered a prize for the first Tourman to finish on its "removable" tire; the Tourman with a spare or two strung round his neck epitomized the HEROIC ERA. The only downside was the fact that they had to be glued securely onto the rim, meaning that the casing had to be unstitched if the inner tube needed repair. Once restitched after repair, a "tub" was never quite the same again.

In the late 1970s and early 1980s, Michelin began producing the first high-performance "clincher" tires with a narrower, lighter casing and a flexible bead so the tire could be folded, and since then clincher performance has improved virtually year on year, to the extent that now the difference between high-grade clincher and medium-weight tubular is a matter of tiny degree: the best tubulars offer about a 50 g saving, which is significant in high-performance terms, but their cost and the risk of puncturing makes them second choice for most road racers.

Tubulars remain the first-choice for velodrome racing, however, because punctures are less likely, and for safety reasons: they should not come off the rim in the event of a puncture. Sticking them on remains an art, however: the new rim has to be abraded to give the glue purchase, and then it has to be given several coats. Top tubular makers include Vittoria of Italy, and Clément of France, while generations of CYCLO-CROSS riders swore by custom-made studded fat "tubs" from Parisian firm Dugast. Aficionados emulate top racers such as EDDY MERCKX and keep tubulars for years in dark places to season them like fine wine, and pro-team service courses sometimes have a locked tubular room in which—the Motorola mechanics used to claim in the early 1990s—the head wrench-man can go and savor the rubber and glue fumes.

Tire covers have been made of various materials including hemp and nylon, while silk-woven tubular tires were once the ultimate choice for track racing, with heavier cottons used for training and road racing. The bullet-proof fiber kevlar is a recent development but is now common to most high-end tires to give an extra puncture-proof edge.

Punctures were once the cyclist's bane. Generations have sought remedies for this thorny problem, including thin tape underneath high-pressure covers, foam injected tires, semi-solid tires made up of multiple rubber balls and a pump (the Skinner Automatic) located inside the wheel that made a single pedal stroke with every revolution of the wheel. The modern generation of tires makes riding generally flat-free.

Tire-savers were popular for many years: lightly sprung strips of wire with a plastic strip on them that would be fixed to the brake bolts so they brushed the surface of the tire, to whip off any thorns or flints before they were pushed through the cover. (They had one nasty side-effect, which was to spray water all over the rider in the wet.) Few cyclists, however have gone as far as the British Tour de France star ROBERT MILLAR, who in winter would put a tubular tire inside a high-pressure cover in place of the inner-tube.

TOULOUSE-LAUTREC, Henri de
(b. France, 1864, d. 1901)

The French impressionist was an illustrator of early cycling in Paris, a racing fan who went regularly to the Buffalo and Seine velodromes through his friendship with the track's technical director Tristan Bernard. The results, wrote Bernard, did not interest the artist, but the atmosphere and the people did. Toulouse-Lautrec's poster for the Simpson chain company, *La Chaîne Simpson*, is an iconic example of the genre (see POSTERS for others; ART for what draws artists to cycling).

The version seen most often depicts the French champion Constant Huret, watched by the raffish Bernard and the French importer who gave himself the English name Spoke. It shows one of what became known as the Chain Matches from 1896, when the Simpson company pitted top cyclists of the time such as the Welsh stars Jimmy

Michael and Arthur Linton against all-comers to publicize the product. Toulouse-Lautrec traveled with the team from Paris to London to attend the matches.

This is actually Toulouse-Lautrec's second attempt. The first, showing Michael training—complete with his trademark toothpick in his mouth—was rejected because the chain company was not happy with the artist's depiction of the triangular links. Intriguingly, the picture also shows the *soigneur* Choppy Warburton looking for something—a pick-me-up presumably—in a Gladstone bag (see SOIGNEURS for more on these witchdoctors and their magic remedies).

The artist also drew his friend, the singer Aristide Bruant, on his bike and produced a notable lithograph of the American sprinter A. A. ZIMMERMAN (*Zimmerman et Sa Machine*) to go with a magazine article written by Bernard.

TOUR DE FRANCE   After the finish of the first Tour de France in 1903, the winner MAURICE GARIN gave the organizer HENRI DESGRANGE a handwritten account of the race to be printed in Desgrange's newspaper *L'Auto*. "You have revolutionised the sport of cycling," he wrote, "and the Tour de France will remain a key date in the history of road racing." His words still

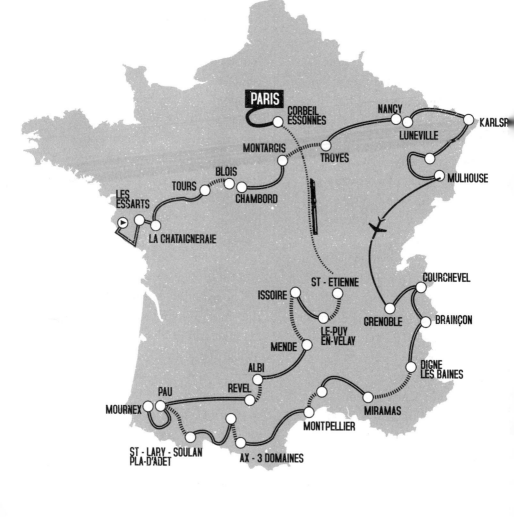

ring true. Approaching its 110th birthday, the Tour is cycling's flagship race, the only event in the racing calendar that has significance in every country, and the biggest annual sports event in the world.

The Tour's enduring fascination lies in the fact that its core principles have not changed. It began life as an outlandish, mammoth publicity stunt, and still is. It still circumnavigates France on public roads and remains free for the public to watch. Unlike every other great sports event in the world, it goes out to its public rather than being confined to a stadium. People travel to watch the race, but virtually every village in France has been visited at some point. As the late Geoffrey Nicholson wrote, it is the only form of international conflict that takes place on the doorstep other than war itself. It is also now an integral part of the French summer, "the fete of all our countryside" as the writer Louis Aragon put it.

The man who dreamed up the Tour was Géo Lefèvre, rugby and cycling writer at *L'Auto*, but

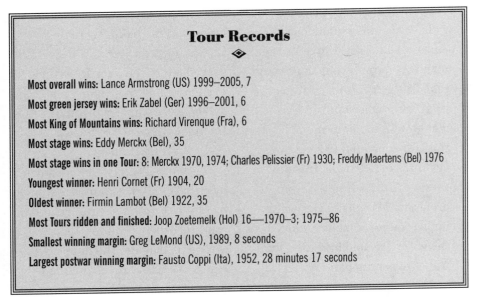

Tour Records

Most overall wins: Lance Armstrong (US) 1999–2005, 7

Most green jersey wins: Erik Zabel (Ger) 1996–2001, 6

Most King of Mountains wins: Richard Virenque (Fra), 6

Most stage wins: Eddy Merckx (Bel), 35

Most stage wins in one Tour: 8: Merckx 1970, 1974; Charles Pelissier (Fr) 1930; Freddy Maertens (Bel) 1976

Youngest winner: Henri Cornet (Fr) 1904, 20

Oldest winner: Firmin Lambot (Bel) 1922, 35

Most Tours ridden and finished: Joop Zoetemelk (Hol) 16—1970–3; 1975–86

Smallest winning margin: Greg LeMond (US), 1989, 8 seconds

Largest postwar winning margin: Fausto Coppi (Ita), 1952, 28 minutes 17 seconds the editor Desgrange coined the name. At a meeting to discuss ways to boost circulation, which was flagging, Lefèvre suggested "a race that lasts several days, longer than anything else. Like the SIX-DAYS on the track but on the road." Desgrange answered "If I understand you right, *petit* Géo, you're proposing a Tour de France?" The term was not a new one: the *Compagnons du Tour de France* were apprentice craftsmen who took three years to go around the country. France had been circumnavigated several times by bike and the French daily *Le Matin* had run a Tour de France car race in 1899.

The race was announced in the paper on January 19, 1903; the plan was for an event that would take 35 days, but after protests from the professional cyclists who would make up the field this was amended to a six-stage event taking 19 days. Initially there was little interest from professional cyclists: Desgrange upped the prize money, halved the entry fee, and allocated five francs expenses per day. There were 78 entries.

Desgrange was not confident of the race's success and stayed away from the first Tour when it began on July 1, 1903, at the Réveil-Matin Café in the Paris suburb of Montgéron (the first road stage of the centenary Tour of 2003 began from the Réveil-Matin, still in situ but now a Wild West themed restaurant).

It was Lefèvre who followed the race from start to finish, traveling by train and bike, and providing a page of reports every day. His son described his role like this: "lost all alone in the night, he would stand on the edge of the road, a storm lantern in his hand, searching the shadows for riders who surged out of the dark from time to time, yelled their name and disappeared into the distance. He alone was the 'organisation' of the Tour de France."

The early Tours were marred by cheating: in the first race won by Maurice Garin several riders were thrown out, and in the second, Garin and the next three riders overall were disqualified

Tour Landmarks

◈

1903—first Tour won by Maurice Garin

1910—race passes through Pyrenées for first time

1911—the race goes over Col du Galibier in the Alps

1919—first yellow jersey, worn by Eugène Christophe

1920—Philippe Thys is first man to win the Tour three times

1930—publicity caravan appears

1933—first King of the Mountains prize awarded to Vicente Trueba (Spain)

1937—derailleur GEARS permitted

1947—first stage finish outside France (Brussels)

1949—Fausto Coppi is first man to win Tour and Giro in same year

1950—elimination for finishing outside stage time limit brought in

1952—first mountain top stage finish: l'Alpe d'Huez

1953—green jersey for points prize introduced, won by Fritz Schaer (Switz)

1954—first Tour start outside France, Amsterdam

1964—JACQUES ANQUETIL is first man to win the Tour five times

1967—first time-trial prologue

1968—regular drug tests introduced, last Tour contested by national teams

1971—first air transfer between stages

1974—first cross-Channel transfer for stage in Plymouth

1975—Tour finishes on Champs-Elysées for first time

1983—Tour goes "open," including Colombian amateurs

1984—women's Tour de France begins, won by Marianne Martin (US); it ends in 1989

1995—MIGUEL INDURAIN is first man to win Tour five times in a row

1998—Festina doping scandal

2005—Lance Armstrong takes seventh win in a row

(for more details, see GARIN). The winner was the man placed fifth, Henri Cornet, who at 20 remains the Tour's youngest winner. It was estimated, however, that 125 kg of tacks were strewn on the route the following year, and the same thing happened in 1906, when only 14 riders finished.

The Tours of the HEROIC ERA were slogs that called for superhuman levels of willpower and endurance, along appalling roads that made massive demands on poorly built bikes. In the first Tour, some participants took up to 35 hours to complete the stages. There were countless episodes in which cyclists broke frames or wheels and had to carry out roadside repairs; most celebrated is the episode in 1913 when Eugène Christophe broke his forks and had to repair them in a blacksmith's.

Early on, the Tour flirted with various formats. Initially there was a rest day after each stage, and it was decided on points from 1906 to 1911. Later, team time trials became a main feature as Desgrange tried to prevent the riders forming alliances on the road. But it gradually moved to a format similar to that of today's race: daily stages with the occasional rest day. Desgrange took the race outside France's borders in 1905, when it visited Alsace-Lorraine. He held time trials, both individual and for teams. There have been modifications, but only relatively minor ones.

The biggest innovation came in 1910, when the race was taken into the PYRENÉES. The move was proposed to Desgrange by his assistant, Alphonse Steinès, who reconnoitred the Col du Tourmalet in January, when it was blocked by snow. He walked over the pass and telegrammed his boss to say the road was perfectly usable, although he had barely seen it. The Tour's first major mountain stage, from Luchon to Bayonne, included the four legendary passes of the Peyresourde, Aspin, Tourmalet, and Aubisque. As he pushed his bike up the Aubisque, the eventual race winner Octave

Lapize looked at Lefèvre and company—Desgrange was absent—and spat out the word "assassins." The ALPS were included in the route a year later. On the Col du Galibier, that year's winner Gustave Garrigou shoved his bike through massive snowdrifts on a road that was little more than a mud track.

For many years, the Tour's appeal lay in the fact that the public could relate to the effort involved in bike racing, as pretty much everyone could ride a bike. They could admire the Tourmen's ability to achieve feats beyond mere mortals, be it winning a sprint at 50 kph, climbing a mountain, or whizzing downhill at 100 kph: "industry mixed with heroism" as Aragon put it.

Today, that has changed a little. Few people ride bikes to work any more, but cycling enthusiasts can ride the race's great mountains in any number of leisure events, and many ride up and down before the race comes. It's rare in any sport for

spectators to be able to emulate their heroes in this way. The inception of the ÉTAPE DU TOUR in 1993 enabled ordinary mortals to ride one leg of the race under the same conditions as the Tourmen, assuming they were fit enough, and led to a huge increase in semi-competitive endurance events.

The Tour is more than a mere sports event. Fans of GINO BARTALI claim that his 1948 win saved Italy from revolution. Desgrange believed that the sacrifice embodied by the Tour riders could serve as a moral example, and Jean-Marie Leblanc, who ran the race from 1989 to 2004, believed the event had a social mission: bringing good cheer to forsaken parts of France. It was under Leblanc that the race began traveling to the center of the country rather than keeping to the periphery.

Leblanc also followed the example of his predecessor Jacques Goddet in his attempts to keep the race "of its time" by including modernistic engineering works such as the

The 10 Greatest Postwar Tours

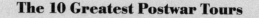

1989—Greg LeMond overcomes a 50 second deficit on the final time trial stage to win by 8 seconds from Laurent Fignon after the pair swap the lead five times.

1964—a tense battle between Jacques Anquetil and RAYMOND POULIDOR reaches a climax on the Puy-de-Dôme hilltop where Anquetil hangs on, just.

1969—EDDY MERCKX is never threatened in his first Tour but turns the race into a personal battle, winning stage after stage. The "Cannibal" is born.

1986—three weeks of intrigue and drama as LeMond and Bernard Hinault do battle. They are in the same team, but is "the Badger" out to win for himself?

1949—Fausto Coppi overcomes a 32-minute deficit to win the race by 20 minutes in a style that is compared to the perfection of Dante's *Divine Comedy*.

1979—the defining Tour of the Hinault years, in which the Badger loses time early on to Joop Zoetemelk and hunts the Dutchman down with consummate ruthlessness.

1998—MARCO PANTANI snipes away at the German Jan Ullrich then wins the race on a rainswept day in the Alps to clinch a great comeback in a race torn apart by scandal.

1971—Merckx and the Spaniard Luis Ocana take each other apart until Ocana over-reaches himself in the Pyrenées and crashes on the Col de Menté.

1987—Stephen Roche and Pedro Delgado attack and defend in the final week, with the outcome in doubt until Roche takes the lead on the penultimate day.

2003—Lance Armstrong is in poor form in the centenary Tour but digs deep in the Pyrenées to overcome Jan Ullrich for the toughest of his seven wins.

Channel Tunnel, the Pont de Normandie, and Norman Foster's colossal viaduct at Millau. Leblanc also recognized political events such as the anniversary of the Normandy landings, and, more controversially, the European Union in 1992, when the Tour missed the Pyrenées in order to visit every EU country that had a land border with France—Spain, Belgium, Luxembourg, Germany, and Italy—and included stages finishing in both EU capitals, Strasbourg and Brussels.

The early Tours had another effect: they gave the French a sense of the geography of their own country, according to one study (Boeuf and Leonard, 2003): "By the cartography of France that it helped make known, the Tour acted as a teacher in showing a map printed with the contours of the country—which was rare until the Great War— and very quickly popularised the notion of France as more or less hexagonal." And the Tour has inspired some fine writing, most notably the essays of Antoine Blondin in the 1950s and 1960s and the structuralist Roland Barthes.

The Tour became more tactical after the Second World War. Road surfaces and bike manufacture improved, teams became more sophisticated, and

cyclists became fitter. Standards are now so high that the race has become "chess on wheels": a subtle tactical game where for much of the time not a great deal looks to be happening. FAUSTO COPPI was the first Tour winner to truly structure his team so that they raced solely in his interests and the first to plan his race around certain key stages, which is the strategy of every Tour favorite today.

Nowadays, the race usually follows an implacable physical logic: all the riders weaken gradually, but the strongest deteriorate more slowly. Usually the best man in the field at half-distance will win. The greatest Tours are those where this does not apply. The best examples include 1989's three-way battle between LAURENT FIGNON, GREG LEMOND, and Pedro Delgado that culminated in the closest ever finish; STEPHEN ROCHE's narrow win over Delgado in 1987; or BERNARD HINAULT and Joop Zoetemelk's tense fight in 1979.

Since 1998, the Tour has been afflicted by almost annual

DOPING scandals but cheating has always played a part in the race. Garin was banned for two years for taking a train in 1904 and there have been episodes when favorites have been pushed up mountains, bikes have been sabotaged, waterbottles spiked. But the drugs issue has proved more intractable. In 2005 there were allegations against the seven-times winner LANCE ARMSTRONG, in 2006 the first man to Paris, Floyd Landis, was disqualified, and in 2007 the likely winner, Denmark's Michael Rasmussen, was thrown out of the race.

While other cycle races struggle to get space on the roads and fight for television time, the Tour's biggest problem has been growth, on a massive scale since the mid-1980s. The Tour has always been as much a commercial as a sports event. It never had an era of "pure" amateurism, although at one point cyclists with no commercial backer (*touristes-routiers*) were allowed in the field.

Gradually, too, after the war, the Tour changed from an event intended to increase the circulation of the organizing newspaper to one that paid its own way through sponsorship and television rights. The big changes came in the 1980s after French broadcasting was deregulated, leading to a massive increase in coverage of the Tour as the nationalized stations fought for market share.

The viewing audience increased from 50 million in 1980 to a billion by 1986. The Tour generated 12 million francs of rights in 1990, 85 million in 1998, over a third of the budget. The race's income shot up: according to French author Pierre Ballester, the Tour now has an annual budget of around 100 million euros, of which 45 million comes from television rights (about half of these in France), 47 million in sponsorship, about 4 million from stage towns, and about 1.5 million in marketing spin-offs.

To bring in a new worldwide audience, the race went from being largely French teams and

French riders with a smattering of foreigners, to being largely international with enough Frenchmen to ensure the home crowds kept interested. There were more teams and bigger, multinational sponsors. The Tour went from being watched mainly by local crowds, to being an event fans travel to, perhaps building an entire vacation around watching the race and being bussed in by a travel company.

Such growth is not without danger, and the Tour is now threatened by its own massive scale, what the French term *le gigantisme*. Doping is part of that, as the vast amounts of money on offer mean it's worth a cyclist paying for sophisticated practices, if he feels he can live with the risk to his reputation. There is now so much media coverage of the race that any scandal creates its own momentum, but the size of the race has brought other problems as well.

With 4,000 people and some 1,500 vehicles, the Tour caravan is now so massive that it causes vast traffic jams in stage towns, and it can take hours to get down from mountain top finishes in the Alps and Pyrenées. So many people travel with the race that hotel rooms are solidly booked for 60 miles around many finishes; the huge convoy of race vehicles has caused a series of deaths among spectators, and the event is vulnerable to political protests of any kind. But in 1904 Desgrange lamented that his Tour had been a victim of massive public interest: the race's success has been founded on excess and that will always be the case.

Recommended further reading: *The Great Bike Race*, Geoffrey Nicholson, Magnum, 1977; *The Yellow Jersey Companion to the Tour de France*, Les Woodland, Yellow Jersey, 2003; *Le Tour, A History of the Tour de France*, Geoffrey Wheatcroft, Simon and Schuster UK, 2007

TRACK RACING

Initially, cyclists competed on the same asphalt and grass running tracks used for athletics, or on the oval circuits used for horse racing, but the quest for speed and spectacle led to an early generation of banked cycle tracks built in the late 19th century: in the US, most early professional races were contested on tracks, typically wooden, between 200 and 500 yards, with banked turns at either end. It is estimated that by 1895 there were 100 velodromes across the United States, with a "Grand Circuit" drawing together the country's best cyclists between May and November. A. A. ZIMMERMAN and Major TAYLOR were the two biggest stars of the early years.

Paris boasted the Buffalo velodrome, built in 1893 on the site of Buffalo Bill's Wild West show near Porte Maillot and promoted by the owner of the Folies Bergère; it was here that the tradition of ringing the bell on the final lap of a race began. In a brief stint of track mania, velodromes sprang up in many provincial towns, and races such as PARIS–ROUBAIX were organized to promote them. It was in France that the first use of the banking to gain speed was recorded, in a six-man sprint that decided the French one-kilometer title in 1894. Henri Farman, recorded *La Bicyclette*, "left the string and went obliquely across the track to the outside, as if inviting his rivals to go to the front. He had gained a little speed and seeing that the others were almost at a halt, he used the momentum to attack suddenly and using the slope of the track he arrived at the middle of the bend with 20 m lead."

In Europe there were events such as the Cuca Coca Cup, a 24-hour race behind pacemakers held at London's Herne Hill and the Bol d'Or, held at the Buffalo. In the United States, the early SIX-DAY races earned a fearsome reputation and were to be a mainstay of the calendar until the 1930s. Massive prizes were earned by the biggest stars such

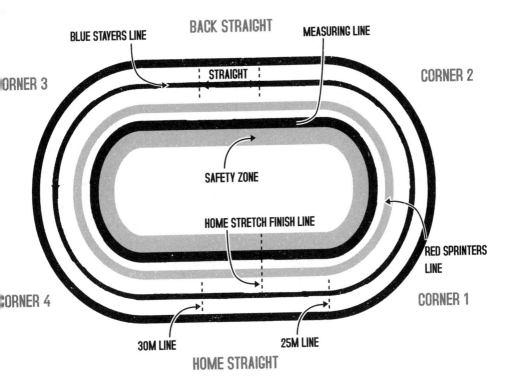

BLUE STAYERS LINE

BACK STRAIGHT

MEASURING LINE

CORNER 3

STRAIGHT

CORNER 2

SAFETY ZONE

HOME STRETCH FINISH LINE

RED SPRINTERS LINE

CORNER 4

CORNER 1

30M LINE

25M LINE

HOME STRAIGHT

as ALF GOULLET, Frank Kramer, and Reggie MacNamara. In spite of efforts of promoters like John M. Chapman, who set up a franchised circuit in the northeast and ran six-day races in New York, track cycling died a slow death in the United States between World War I and II as the emphasis shifted to baseball and football. The final event was held at Madison Square Gardens in 1939.

Paced riding was initially the norm in record attempts and long-distance track races: riders would shelter themselves behind multicycles with five or six riders, nicknamed "pedaling artillery." There might be an additional team riding alongside the solo rider to shelter him from sidewinds. Demi-fond, as it was known, became popular in the 1890s, particularly in Germany, where purpose-built tracks were constructed, and the first world title was won by the Welshman Jimmy Michael in Cologne in 1895.

These were spectacular and dangerous events, and they were succeeded by motorpaced races just after the turn of the century, which were even riskier. The death toll early on was high; if anything broke at speeds between 50 and 60 mph, the rider stood little chance, as in the 1918 accident at the VELODROME D'HIVER (Vel d'Hiv) that killed the French champion Louis Darragon, who broke a pedal while at full speed, hit the balustrade around the track with his head, and died instantly. Today's roadsize motorbike events are a spectacular throwback to this very dodgy past.

As stadium sports gained popularity, track suffered in the early years of the 20th century; the golden era in Europe was between World War I and II, with the arrival of sprinters such as Britain's Bill Bailey, France's Lucien Michard, and Australia's Bob Spears, and later Belgium's Jeff Scherens and Louis "Toto" Gerardin. In Europe, even after World War II, vast crowds would flock to venues such as the Vigorelli velodrome in Milan, the Vel d'Hiv in Paris, and the Palais des Sports in Brussels. The French journalist Pierre Chany described the spectacle in Milan, with scalpers selling tickets for five times their value, crowds six deep on the pavement stopping traffic, and a crowd of 20,000 inside rising as one to applaud their heroes and jeer at the "villains." An open-sprint competition at the Vel d'Hiv could readily attract 400 starters.

The key to track racing's survival after its death in the United States was the presence of stars of road racing such as Fausto Coppi alongside established track racers such as the sprinters Antonio Maspes, Arie Van Vliet, and Reg Harris. The Vel d'Hiv drew crowds that might have included the millionaire Henri de Rothschild and the writer Ernest

Hemingway, who wrote of the "smoky light of the afternoon, the high banked wooden track, the whirring sound the tires made on the wood as the riders passed, the effort and tactics as the riders climbed and plunged, each one a part of his machine."

Road racing was a gritty, grimy occupation, but evening track meetings were the glamour side of cycling. Road champions would ride into town on the overnight train, then stage a dramatic entrance to the velodrome in sunglasses—to hide the bags under their eyes—wearing tailored suits, with Brylcreemed hair. Afterward, they might dine on oysters, steak, and champagne.

In one winter, Coppi rode 21 such meets, either invitation pursuit matches or international omniums. What mattered was performance and pleasing the crowd: TOM SIMPSON, for example, would ride, wall-of-death style, up the vertical advertising boards at the top of the track, or take one hand off the bars in a finish sprint and "pretend" to take a tow by grabbing a rival's saddle.

In Europe track racing gradually declined with the advent of television: the road stars lost their mystique, so there was no reason for the crowds to come and watch them on the track. Sponsors realized they would get more exposure from having their men race on the road. Most of the great velodromes, like the Vel d'Hiv, are gone or they are dying, like the Vigorelli. The sixes cling on, mainly as late-evening entertainment for German drinkers, but are threatened by the removal of the Madison from the Olympic program.

If there is a flicker of hope, it has come from Britain's creation of a new style of track racing: the Revolution meetings, which have taken advantage of GREAT BRITAIN's success at successive OLYMPIC GAMES, and have also been run in Australia. America may well be next. The format is accessible and lively, entry prices are low, and it boasts celebrities as well as Olympic champions to draw in the crowds; a championship format of the Revolution meetings was adopted in 2009, with big names leading teams that included youth riders to create a narrative over the winter.

TRACK RACING—DISCIPLINES

The Olympic track disciplines are as follows:

- **Sprint:** two riders compete in a series of knockout races over three laps. Seeding is determined by a time trial over 200 m; fastest meeting slowest and so on. The early knockout rounds are sudden-death; the later rounds are best of three. Riders who exit early have a chance to re-enter the contest via the *repêchages*, a second chance, which offer losers a chance to fight their way back in.

- **Individual pursuit:** two riders start from opposite sides of the track and are timed over their distance. The objective is to "pursue" the opponent and overtake them; if that does not happen, the fastest wins. First round is a time trial to determine seeding for the medal ride-offs; first v. second, third v. fourth. Women race over 3 km, men over 4 km.

- **Team pursuit:** for men, run on the same basis as the individual, over 4 km. Riders do half-lap or one-lap turns at the front.

- **Team sprint:** for men, two teams of three riders timed over three laps. Qualifying through a time trial round to determine seeding for the ride-offs.

- **Points race:** a bunched race over 160 laps (40 km) for men, 100 laps (25 km) for women, decided on points awarded every ten laps—5, 3, 2, 1— with a 20-point bonus for any rider who can lap the field. If riders tie on points their final positions when they take the checkered flag determines their place.

- **Madison:** a relay bunch race for men held over 200 laps (50 km) for teams of two riders, one of whom is racing while the other circles at the top of the track waiting to be put in the race. This is done by a hand-sling, in which the faster rider grabs the other's outstretched hand and "throws" him into the race. There are two objectives: to lap the field, and to earn points in sprints every 20 laps. If teams finish on the same lap, points total determines their placings.

- **Keirin:** Japanese discipline for men and women in which six riders follow a pacing motorbike which accelerates to 50 kph for men, 40 kph for women before pulling off the track with two and a half laps to go, after which it is a sprint for the line. Run through a series of qualifying rounds in which the lineups are determined by a draw

(see KEIRIN for details of the intricate ceremonial the sport involves in Japan, and the massive betting scene).

The same disciplines are included in the world championship program, plus the following:

- **Women's team pursuit:** over three kilometers for three riders.
- **Women's team sprint:** over two laps, for two riders.
- **Time trials:** over one kilometer for men, 500 m for women. These events were dropped from the Olympic program after 2004.
- **Scratch:** a bunch race over 15 kilometers for men, 10 kilometers for women. First over the line wins.
- **Omnium (men and women):** a test of all-round skills held over a single day: 250 m time trial, scratch, pursuit, points race, kilometer time trial, devil (see below).

Other track events include: **Devil Take the Hindmost**, a crowd-pleasing event in which the last rider over the line each time is eliminated until three are left to contest the final sprint; **Win and Out**, the opposite, held over five laps in which the winner is the first rider over the line on lap one; he or she has to pull out, then the second is the first over the line on lap two and so on; **Danish pursuit**, which is a points race followed by a Devil with rankings decided over the two events; **Course des Primes**, a race with prizes awarded every lap; **Motor-paced**, in which the riders race in the slipstream of motorbikes, usually low-powered machines known as DERNYS, although on outdoor tracks full-size bikes may be used.

TRICYCLE The pioneering days of bicycle design between 1870 and 1900 gave rise to a huge variety of multi-wheeled machines—primarily tricycles and quadricycles—with different seating configurations and wheel arrangements. By 1884, over 120 different models were being made in 20 factories in just one English manufacturing center, Coventry.

JAMES STARLEY's Coventry Lever Tricycle of 1876, with a large central wheel, and smaller ones at either end, was the first lightweight tricycle to enter mass production. Starley also designed the Salvo quad, which was sold to Queen Victoria and renamed the Royal Salvo.

There were rear-drive tricycles with dual steering wheels at the front, quads in which the drivers sat side by side, and the Hen and Chickens, a HIGH-WHEEL bike in the middle of four small wheels, the idea being to make the machine as stable as possible for cargo carrying.

The classic upright tricycle as we know it today, with one steering wheel at the front and two driving wheels at the back, began to appear in the mid-1880s, at the same time as the SAFETY BICYCLE. Early examples

were the Humber Cripper—
named after a professional
racer, Robert Cripps—and the
curiously named Psycho from
Starley.

The stability of the tricycle
makes it suitable for carrying
heavy loads over short distances:
the design is used for rickshaws
in Asia and in some cities in
the UK, Europe, and the US.
Delta tricycles have a recumbent
design, while Tadpole trikes are
RECUMBENTS with two steered
wheels at the front and one
driving wheel at the rear.

The largest British tricycle
maker today is Pashley,
founded in 1926 and based in

Stratford-Upon-Avon. In the
UK, the Tricycle Association
was founded in 1929 to cater for
trike enthusiasts, and the Road
Records Association recognizes
tricycle place-to-place records.
There are a small number of
tricycle criteriums, and a tricycle
world championship, on a time-
trial format.

U

UCI see UNION CYCLISTE
INTERNATIONALE

UNION CYCLISTE
INTERNATIONALE   Also known
in English as International
Cycling Union.

Cycling's worldwide governing
body, founded in 1900, split
into two arms in 1965, one
governing pro racing (FICP)
and one for amateur federations
(FIAC), with the UCI as an
umbrella body. In 1992 all
three were merged; in 1996 the
distinction between amateur and
professional racers was ended.

The UCI inhabits a purpose-
built center in the Swiss town
of Aigle, near Lausanne, that
includes offices, a library, a
200-meter velodrome, and the
world cycling center, where

Competitions Run
by the UCI:

◆

World championships
UCI ProTour
UCI Continental Tours
Women's world road cup
CYCLO-CROSS world cup
MOUNTAIN DIKING world cup
BMX world cup
INDOOR CYCLING championships, for artistic
cycling and cycle ball

cyclists from outside the
European heartland can come to
train.

The UCI is no stranger to
controversy: questions were asked
about a major contribution to its
antidoping program from seven-
time TOUR DE FRANCE winner
LANCE ARMSTRONG. The ProTour
circuit was controversial (see
HEIN VERBRUGGEN), so too various

restructurings of the professional ROAD RACING calendar, and recent decisions to drop some of the most traditional events from the OLYMPIC GAMES track racing program.

The UCI owns the rights to the WORLD CHAMPIONSHIPS, which are sold to various towns or regions each year. It also runs antidoping, in tandem with national antidoping bodies, and provides race referees (*commissaires*) who levy fines in Swiss francs. The current president is Pat MacQuaid of Ireland, who was reelected unopposed in 2009.

UNITED STATES OF AMERICA

Whereas Europe has always been seen as the heartland of cycle racing and China is the nation that goes to work on its collective bike, cycling in the United States has known fluctuating fortunes. Having once been as popular as baseball is today, it hit the doldrums as the automobile took over but has enjoyed a strong renaissance over the last quarter of a century: the Tour de France has entered public consciousness and LANCE ARMSTRONG has become a national celebrity.

In the HEROIC ERA following the invention of the safety bicycle, cycle racing was as popular in the United States as in Europe, if not more so. There were 600 professionals competing in track races at the end of the 19th century, and as A. A. ZIMMERMAN, America's first cycling star, explained, "the racing in those days extended over a greater part of the country. Nearly every state and county fair had bicycle racing as an attraction. We rode principally on dirt tracks and we made a regular circuit, going from one town to another and riding practically every day." Crowds of up to 20,000 attended track races to watch stars such as Major TAYLOR, and SIX-DAY RACING was a lucrative, glamorous little industry in its own right.

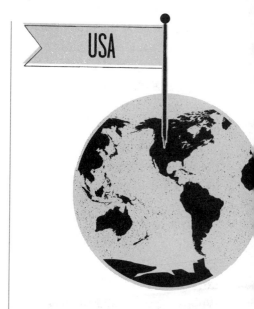

As the sixes died out during the Depression, there was no homegrown tradition of road cycling to replace them. Unlike in Europe, where cycling became the mode of transport of the working class and road racing expressed that cultural tie, in the United States the automobile was king. That only began to change in the 1970s, as the middle class discovered cycling's health and environmental benefits. The early part of the decade saw a 40-fold increase in demand for lightweight bikes. Even so, in FILMS such as *American Flyers* (1985) and *Breaking Away* (1979) cycle racing is depicted as a strange activity performed by marginalized young men.

The revival in the United States was spearheaded in women's track racing through the 1970s, with Sheila Young, Sue Novara, and Connie Paraskevin winning sprint world titles, while men's amateur teams gradually improved on the road, and the first professional pioneer, JONATHAN BOYER, traveled to France to ride for the ACBB club in Paris (see FOREIGN LEGION for how ACBB played host to numerous English-speakers), then rode the 1981 Tour de France for BERNARD HINAULT's Renault team.

A key factor was the rise of a major stage race: the Red Zinger Classic, later the Coors Classic, held in Colorado during the 1970s and 1980s. Organized by charismatic marketing professional Michael Aisner, the race was responsible for turning Boulder, Colorado, into the center of American cycling. The town hosted the world road championship in 1986, and now more US pros live in and around Boulder than anywhere else.

The Coors Classic broke new ground by launching a women's stage race alongside the men's event. It was watched by President Gerald Ford and is credited with sparking comedian Robin Williams's obsession with bike racing. Aisner eventually took his event to California and Hawaii, brought in top European teams, and even got the best Soviet racers to turn up for the 1981 event, less than a year after the US had boycotted the Moscow Olympics (see EASTERN EUROPE for more on the Russians).

The Russians, led by Olympic champion Sergei Soukhoroutchenkov, met fearless opposition in a new American star: junior world champion GREG LEMOND, then only 20 years old. LeMond fought off the Soviets, drawing a crowd of 40,000 to the race finale in Boulder. He followed Boyer to Renault, and the pair finished

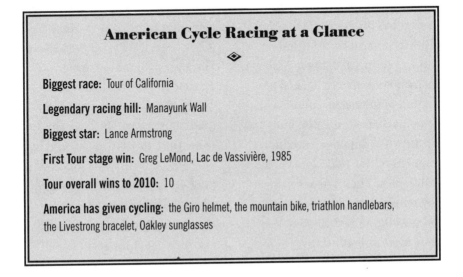

American Cycle Racing at a Glance

Biggest race: Tour of California

Legendary racing hill: Manayunk Wall

Biggest star: Lance Armstrong

First Tour stage win: Greg LeMond, Lac de Vassivière, 1985

Tour overall wins to 2010: 10

America has given cycling: the Giro helmet, the mountain bike, triathlon handlebars, the Livestrong bracelet, Oakley sunglasses

2nd and 10th in the world road championship in 1982. The 1984 Olympic Games in Los Angeles gave cycling more momentum, with America taking nine medals. The RACE ACROSS AMERICA helped raise the profile of cycling as well. So too did the first US stage win in the Tour, LeMond's time trial victory at Lac de Vassivière in 1985. Later that year, LeMond raced the Coors Classic with Hinault. When the pair posed in Stetsons with their legendary manager, Cyrille Guimard, for *l'Equipe*, America's return to the cycling mainstream seemed complete.

On the road, the next step was a US pro team racing the European circuit, and that appeared in 1985 when 7-Eleven convenience stores backed a squad managed by Mike Neel, who had raced in Italy, and JIM OCHOWICZ, who had raced for the US in the 1972 and 1976 Olympics. They broke taboos by employing a blonde female SOIGNEUR named Shelley Verses, but more substantially, their bucktoothed climber named

AMERICAN FACTOID

Coors Classic organizer Michael Aisner also masterminded Brigitte Bardot's campaign against the slaughter of fur seals in the Arctic.

Andy Hampsten took a stage in the Giro, and the team won more stages at the Tour in 1986. Under Jim Ochowicz, the squad would go on to a successful run backed by the Motorola phone company from 1991 to 1996. After that, US Postal Service and Discovery Channel moved in as European pro team sponsors.

The Coors Classic ceased in 1988, but a new US Tour ran from 1991 to 1996 sponsored by DuPont, and this was followed in 2006 by the Tour of California, which has drawn professionals of ever-higher quality. The US can also boast its own CLASSIC: the Philadelphia International

Stars of US Racing

◆

Frank Kramer: Along with Major Taylor and A. A. Zimmerman, a hero of the halcyon era of US track racing. Kramer was persuaded to turn pro in 1900 by Taylor, and his career outlasted that of the Major: he won the US sprint title 18 times, with his last title coming in 1921, when he was 41 years old. He raced mainly in the United States, but had two successful seasons in Europe, 1905 and 1906, and also took the world sprint title in the only year he entered, 1912, when it was held in Newark. He retired in 1922.

Andy Hampsten: Bucktoothed, slender climbing specialist from Ohio who turned pro for 7-Eleven in 1985, won a stage in the Giro d'Italia, and was signed by Bernard Hinault's La Vie Claire team for 1986, when he won the first of two back-to-back wins in the Tour of Switzerland. In 1988, back with 7-Eleven, Hampsten won the Giro d'Italia, a victory forged in a snowstorm on the Gavia Pass. His final major win was the l'Alpe d'Huez stage in the 1992 Tour de France, the year he finished fourth overall in the Tour, a repeat of his placing of 1986.

Sheila Young: One of a bunch of US cyclists who doubled up successfully with speed skating, Young achieved a rare double in 1973 when she took the world sprint title on the velodrome and the rink. She went on to win the sprint title twice more, and won gold, silver, and bronze medals in skating at the winter Olympics in Innsbruck in 1976, becoming the first US athlete to win three medals at a winter Games. In that year she married JIM OCHOWICZ, who would go on to manage the 7-Eleven and Motorola pro road teams. She retired, then returned to competition in 1981 to take another track sprint world title. Young's big rival was another speed skater turned sprinter, Sue Novara, who won a total of seven world championship medals. Other speed skaters who were also successful cyclists are Beth Heiden, winner of the world road title in 1980, and her brother Eric, regarded as the greatest speedskater ever but also capable of finishing the Giro d'Italia for 7-Eleven in 1985.

Championship dates back to 1985 and is the final leg of the Triple Crown that includes the Lancaster Classic and the Reading Classic, all held in the same week. Until 1985, the best American in Philadelphia was crowned US champion. The race includes its own legendary cobbled climb, the Manayunk

Landmarks in US Cycle Racing

◈

1866—Pierre Lallement files the first US patent application for a pedal cycle

1878—Albert August Pope begins producing Columbia high-wheelers

1880—League of American Wheelmen founded in Newport, Rhode Island

1891—First six-day races held in Madison Square Gardens

1893—A. A. Zimmerman takes gold medal at first world championship

1899—Major Taylor becomes world sprint champion

1912—Frank Kramer wins world sprint title at Madison Square Garden

1950—Final six-day race in New York

1973—Sheila Young wins gold medal in women's world sprint championship

1975—First Red Zinger Classic stage race held in Colorado; from 1980 it is known as the Coors Classic

1975—Sue Novara follows Young to women's sprint gold

1980—Beth Heiden wins women's world road championship

1981—Eric Boyer becomes the first American to finish the Tour de France

1983—Greg LeMond becomes first American to win world pro road championship

1984—Marianne Martin wins first women's Tour de France

1985—7-Eleven begins racing in Europe; Andy Hampsten and Ron Keifel win stages at the Giro d'Italia; Greg LeMond, riding for La Vie Claire, is first US stage winner in the Tour de France

1986—7-Eleven is the first US team to compete in Tour de France; Alex Stieda wears the yellow jersey; LeMond wins the Tour, becoming first American to wear yellow; World road and track championships held in Colorado Springs

1988—Last Coors Classic held; Hampsten wins Giro d'Italia

1989—LeMond wins his comeback Tour after near-fatal injury and adds the world road championship

1991—First Tour DuPont held; it continues until 1996

1993—Lance Armstrong wins world road title in Oslo, Norway

1994—LeMond retires

1996—Armstrong wins Fleche Wallonne; is diagnosed with testicular cancer in September

1999—Armstrong wins his comeback Tour

2003—Armstrong joins Jacques Anquetil, Eddy Merckx, Miguel Indurain, and Bernard Hinault as a five-time winner of the Tour de France

2005—Armstrong retires for the first time after winning seventh Tour

2006—First professional Tour of California held, won by Floyd Landis who is disqualified later that season from winning Tour de France after testing positive for testosterone

2009—Armstrong makes his second comeback to racing

2011—Armstrong rides his final race as a pro. Maybe.

2011—US city of Richmond, Virginia, among the favorites to host 2015 world road championship

"Wall," two streets where the gradient reaches one in six.

In 1986 the Canadian Alex Stieda, riding for the US team 7-Eleven, briefly wore the yellow jersey in the Tour de France, and LeMond began an extraordinary run of US successes in the great race. Since then, LeMond and Armstrong have between them won the Tour 10 times.

Between the LeMond and Armstrong eras, the cycling world discovered two purely American disciplines: BMX and MOUNTAIN BIKING. Both introduced whole new generations of cyclists to the sport, while the mountain bike brought in its wake a raft of technical innovations and spawned a crop of manufacturers who now enjoy strong reputations on the road. Trek started out as a small frame builder in Wisconsin in the late 1970s, Specialized were producers of the first mass produced mountain bikes, while Cannondale began as a cycle-bag maker and began making its characteristic oversized aluminum frames in 1983.

Armstrong's run of successes drew major sponsors into a sport that had been hit by doping problems: in 2010 Columbia Sportswear, Garmin, and Radioshack were all backing teams in the UCI ProTour, while BMC, run by Ochowicz, is a fourth major US team. In Armstrong's protégé, Taylor Phinney, now a pro with BMC, America may just have a new LeMond in the making.

VAN LOOY, Rik

Born: Grobbendonk, Belgium, December 20, 1933

Major wins: World road race champion 1960–1; Milan–San Remo 1958; Tour of Flanders 1959, 1962; Paris–Roubaix 1961–2, 1965; Liège–Bastogne–Liège 1961; Giro di Lombardia 1959; Ghent–Wevelgem 1956–7, 1962; Paris-Brussels 1956, 1958; Paris–Tours, 1959, 1967; Flèche Wallonne, 1968; points winner Tour de France 1963; 7 Tour stage wins; 12 Giro stage wins; 18 Vuelta stage wins

Nicknames: the Emperor of Herentals, Rik II, the Wheelbreaker

One of the great figures of postwar cycling, with between 400 and 500 wins and a record in the one-day CLASSICS surpassed only by EDDY MERCKX, and one of many stars to emerge from FLANDERS.

Unlike Merckx, Van Looy was never a good enough time triallist or climber to win a major Tour but he managed to take every Classic at least once, apart from the Amstel Gold Race, which was founded as his career came to an end. He was a dominant force between 1956 and 1968; he ran his team, the "Red Guard" with an iron hand (see TEAMS for other iconic squads). He selected devoted riders with specific skills—sprinting, working on windy days, stamina, climbing—and decided what gears they used, when they would go to bed, and how much they were paid. One *domestique* had to carry a wrench in case "the Emperor" wanted to adjust his saddle or handlebars in a race.

⚙ INTRIGUING VÉLIB FACTOIDS

The bikes are washed using pure rainwater so no polluting detergent is necessary.

The bikes are 99 percent recyclable including the tires. The service teams use vehicles powered by biofuel and electric bikes.

The estimated distance each machine travels each year is 18,250 km. They were used 42 million times in the first 18 months.

There is a glut of bikes that have been dropped off at the bottom of France's two hilly districts, Belleville and Montmartre, with few left at the top, for obvious reasons.

Videos have been posted on the Internet showing the bikes being ridden on BMX tracks, down the steps of Montmartre, and in Metro stations: Vélib Extreme.

Not all the bikes are roughed up. One repairman found a bike that had been customized with fur-covered tires.

❋

VÉLIB Groundbreaking scheme set up in Paris where a vast fleet of rather heavy bikes are rented to anyone for a nominal fee. Lyon was the pioneer, while schemes had been established in Amsterdam, Copenhagen, and Oslo, but Paris was the first to be established on a truly massive scale in a national capital city with no history of bike use. Other cities have followed suit including London.

Paris has some 20,000 bikes distributed between 1,500 automated rental stations, approximately one station every 300 m. The bikes are gray, made in Hungary by the Lapierre company, which also supplies high-end bikes to the La Française des Jeux pro team. They weigh 22.5 kg (a top racing bike is around 8 kg), have three-speed gears, lighting by LEDs that are always on and are powered by dynamo, a basket, and a locking system.

Use is by subscription, allowing an unlimited number of trips up to 30 minutes; longer rental periods cost from one euro, on a sliding scale that increases with the length of rental to 151 euros for 20 hours. The idea is to encourage people to use the bikes for short, frequent trips rather than hanging on to them.

The system has proved massively popular but has not been without its pitfalls. Three people were killed in traffic accidents in the first year, and estimates vary as to the number of bikes that were stolen and recovered in various states of distress or taken to EASTERN EUROPE and AFRICA to be sold on. It seems to be several thousand at least. The company that runs the scheme, JC Decaux, complained initially that it was simply too tough and expensive to make any profit.

Getting the subscription is not totally straightforward: "Like all good things French, getting out a one-day Vélib ticket at a roadside machine involves a Kafkaesque bureaucratic nightmare of special codes, endless button pressing and loud swearing," was the verdict of one British writer, Angelique Chrysafis, in the *Guardian*. Computer crashes are not uncommon, while the bikes have to be shipped around the city to compensate for the uneven flow of journeys.

However, in a city that previously barely had a bike on its streets, cycling is now ubiquitous. Vélib has also introduced a whole new social element to the capital as people help each other use the bikes—another chance for the French to initiate romances—while convention demands that if a bike has mechanical trouble, its saddle be pointed in the air to alert other users and maintenance teams.

VÉLOCIO   Pen name of the JOURNALIST Paul de Viviès, the man who invented the term "*cyclotourisme*" and edited the magazine *Le Cyclisme* in which he described his tours in glowing detail. Is credited with inventing the derailleur, although this is not strictly accurate (see GEARS); he was, however, a tireless campaigner on behalf of multiple gearing and at the center of a group in Saint-Etienne that developed the gears. He is best known for:

The seven commandments of cycling:

1 Make your stops few and brief, so that you never let up.

2 Take small and frequent refreshments: eat before you get hungry, drink before you get thirsty.

3 Never ride until you are abnormally tired, when you lose your appetite and cannot sleep.

4 Put on more clothes before you feel cold, and take them off before you feel hot; don't be afraid to expose your skin to sun, air, and rain.

5 Eliminate wine, meat, and tobacco from your diet, at least during a ride.

6 Never push too hard; remain within your limits above all early in a ride when you are tempted to expend too much energy because you feel full of strength.

7 Never ride because your pride tells you to.

VELOCIPEDE   Term loosely used to describe early bicycles prior to the arrival of the penny farthing in the 1870s; see BICYCLE, BONESHAKER, and DRAISIENNE for more details.

VÉLODROME D'HIVER (Vél d'Hiv)

The name of Paris's most celebrated indoor track has come to stand for French complicity in the deportation of Jews to Nazi death camps during the Second World War. The track is known mainly now for the Rafle du Vél d'Hiv (the Vél d'Hiv roundup) in which thousands of Jews were detained in the track before deportation. A memorial now stands near the site of the track at Quai de Grenelle, close to the Eiffel Tower.

The Vél d'Hiv was built by HENRI DESGRANGE after an earlier track owned by his paper *L'Auto* was demolished during construction of the Eiffel Tower. It hosted various sports but was best known for cycling, with Ernest Hemingway among those who watched racing there. It could hold 14,000 people and its super-steep bankings were known as "the cliffs." It was the scene of a memorable near-riot in 1947 when the crowd protested a judging decision by throwing anything they could lay hands on: food, cushions, crutches, and even a chamberpot.

By then the track had a gruesome past. During World War II it was used for rallies by France's largest fascist party and was first used as a prison in summer 1941. The Rafle du Vél d'Hiv occurred the following year, when police and gendarmes rounded up 13,000 Jews and imprisoned an estimated 7,500 in the track for five days, in appalling conditions due to the heat—the glass in the massive roof had been painted blue to deter bombing and the windows were kept closed. There were only five lavatories and one water tap, and a little food and water brought in by Quakers and the Red Cross. There were many suicides, and any escapees were shot. From there prisoners were taken to camps outside Paris and thence to Nazi death camps.

There is still debate about the complicity of the man in charge of the track, Jacques Goddet, who went on to run the Tour for 40 years after the war. It is known that he handed over the keys to the Germans although his supporters claim that he had no choice.

The track was demolished in 1959 after a fire, and the site is now occupied by flats. The memorial stands on a curved base, representing the track, and depicts deportees including children, a pregnant woman, and a sick man. It was inaugurated in 1994; a year later the French president Jacques Chirac opened the debate about France's past by acknowledging that French gendarmerie had collaborated with the occupying forces. It is the site of an annual holocaust memorial ceremony.

VERBRUGGEN, Hein (b. Netherlands, 1941)

A combative, articulate Dutchman who ran the UNION CYCLISTE INTERNATIONAL from 1991 to 2005, introducing a number of innovations to cycling—some successful, some less so—before moving on to become a prominent figure in the Olympic movement.

Verbruggen began his cycling career in marketing, working for the Mars chocolate bar company when they sponsored a professional team in the early 1970s. By 1990 he had risen up the hierarchy of cycling to head the professional arm of the sport, the FICP, and in 1991 he became UCI president.

Under Verbruggen professional world rankings were brought in along the lines of the ATP ranking in tennis—these were actually invented by the French cycling magazine *Vélo*—a year-long World Cup was inaugurated and attempts were made to export cycling beyond its European heartland, with major events in Canada and the UK. The UCI was moved to its present base in Aigle, Switzerland, and a world cycling center set up, including a velodrome designed by the SCHUERMANN family. Moves were made to bring in nations such as AFRICA.

The cycling calendar was radically altered, with the VUELTA A ESPAÑA moving from April to September and the WORLD CHAMPIONSHIP from August to September. The Vuelta has never seemed to work so late in the year and the World Cup concept did not take off as the TOUR DE FRANCE came to dominate the cycling season in the 1990s. Once Perrier pulled out, the event never found a sponsor and was eventually dropped.

In 1996 Verbruggen achieved his masterstroke, gaining professionals access to the OLYMPIC GAMES. To enable that, the sport had to be brought under one banner. The amateur and professional categories were abolished and replaced by Elite and Under-23. Under Verbruggen both MOUNTAIN-BIKING and BMX were brought into the Olympics, but there was controversy when the long-established kilometer time trial was dropped.

The DRUGS problem became increasingly high-profile in the 1990s and in an attempt to limit the use of EPO, the UCI under Verbruggen brought in blood testing in 1997, initially to monitor professional cyclists' health. The tests were counterproductive, actually encouraging the use of EPO within a certain limit, but they paved the way for more radical blood profiling as well as tests for blood transfusions.

When Verbruggen moved on in 2005, his final initiative was to devise the ProTour structure, which guaranteed entry to major races for teams who paid a registration fee to the PT—run by the UCI. It had a stuttering start. The two organizers who run the bulk of professional events, Italy's RCS and France's AMAURY SPORT ORGANISATION, wished to retain the right to choose who rode their events and were worried that the UCI's agenda was to strip them of lucrative broadcasting rights.

The outcome was a four-year standoff with the governing body during which the Tour was sometimes run outside UCI rules and antidoping regulations, with bitter exchanges of words that took the Tour organizers to the brink of breaking away to set up a "rebel" movement within the sport. Peace broke out in 2008, but the ProTour epitomized Verbruggen's legacy: radical and controversial.

❊❊❊❊❊❊❊❊❊❊❊❊❊❊❊❊❊❊❊❊❊❊❊❊❊

VUELTA A ESPAÑA   The third of cycling's great Tours along with the GIRO D'ITALIA and TOUR DE FRANCE, the Vuelta is also the youngest, founded in 1935, initially with the support of General Franco's military dictatorship (see POLITICS). Not surprisingly in a country hit by a dire civil war, the Spanish Tour took two decades to become established; the second edition in 1936, held shortly before the conflict began, was close to being canceled.

The Vuelta was not a regular fixture on the calendar until the mid-1950s and suffered for many years from a calendar date (mid-April to early May) that put off Italians preparing for the Giro, which began a few days after the Vuelta finish, and was too early for stars building to the Tour de France, but it has not been improved by a switch from April to September masterminded by HEIN VERBRUGGEN.

A showpiece finish on the Paseo de la Castellana avenue in the capital Madrid is traditional, but the heartland of the Basque Country is never visited, for political reasons (see POLITICS again). Sometimes the Vuelta seeks out Tour climbs in the Pyrenées but more often it heads for its own legendary ascents: the Puertos de Serranillos and de Navalmoral in the Sierra de Gredos west of Madrid, or the climb to Lagos de Covadonga in the lonely Cantabrian mountains on the Atlantic coast, home to some of the last wolves in Europe. The Sierra Nevada is another fixture.

Founded in 1935 by the

newspaper *Informaciones*, the
Vuelta was shamelessly political,
vaunting its "patriotism" at a
time when that meant support
for the right wing headed by
General Franco; it was firmly
linked with the regime. At first
foreign stars had to be brought
in for cash: FAUSTO COPPI was
well past his best when he
accepted 11,000 pesetas a day to
ride the 1959 race while JACQUES
ANQUETIL at least gave value for
money in 1963 by winning.

The Vuelta hosted occasional
visits from the likes of EDDY
MERCKX, who missed the 1973
Tour de France so he could win
it while Hinault took a legendary
victory in 1983, whipping the
home stars but having to push so
hard he damaged a tendon close
to his knee and could not race for
a year. The Vuelta truly began
to feel like an integral part of the
international cycling calendar
only after Franco's death led
to Spain's reintegration with
the wider world, helped by the
arrival in the 1980s of Spain's
biggest star since FEDERICO
BAHAMONTES, the charismatic,

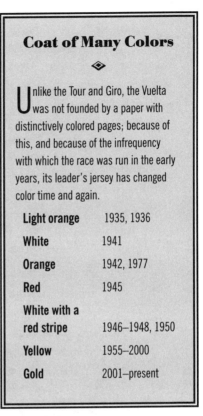

Coat of Many Colors

Unlike the Tour and Giro, the Vuelta was not founded by a paper with distinctively colored pages; because of this, and because of the infrequency with which the race was run in the early years, its leader's jersey has changed color time and again.

Light orange	1935, 1936
White	1941
Orange	1942, 1977
Red	1945
White with a red stripe	1946–1948, 1950
Yellow	1955–2000
Gold	2001–present

unpredictable Pedro Delgado.

"Everyone has forgotten what
it was like back then," wrote
LAURENT FIGNON, who rode the
race in 1983. "Spain had only
just emerged from the Franco
era. It was like the third world;
anyone who went over there
at the start of the 1980s would
know what I mean. For cyclists
like us, the accommodation

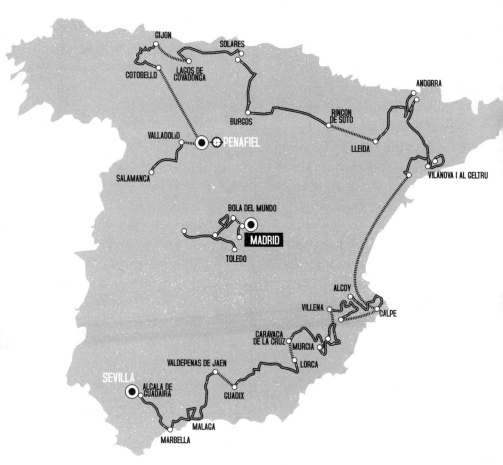

and the way we were looked after were not easy to deal with. Sometimes it was barely acceptable. Professional cyclists of today cannot imagine what it was like in the 1980s in a hotel at the backside of beyond in Asturias or the Pyrenées. The food was rubbish and sometimes there was no hot water, morning or evening."

Delgado's first Vuelta win in 1985 was hugely popular at home, even though to a non-Spaniard it was clearly a setup, with ROBERT MILLAR the victim. The arrival of "Perico" coincided with an economic boom in

Spain, and the beginning of live television coverage of the Vuelta. The number of Spanish teams blossomed and with MIGUEL INDURAIN dominant in the Tour de France from 1991–1995 Spanish cycling boomed briefly, even though Indurain never rode the Vuelta in his best years. Instead, the dominant forces in the 1990s were Swiss: Tony Rominger, who rode for a team sponsored by the Asturian dairy cooperative Clas, won from 1992–1994, while Alex Zülle, backed by the Spanish lottery ONCE, took the 1996 and 1997 races.

As the 21st century dawned, the Vuelta appeared fragile yet again. There were rumors that the format might be tweaked and that it might revert to its old, popular spring date. It is now seen as a consolation race for those who have slipped up in the Tour de France, while some stars simply turn up to get a fortnight's preparation for the WORLD CHAMPIONSHIPS and then go home to rest. The Tour organizers AMAURY SPORT ORGANISATION bought a 49 percent stake in the organizing company Unipublic, but of the big three, the Vuelta looked to have the least certain future.

W

WAR An army cycling unit manual issued at the end of the 19th century recommended that when fighting cavalry its members should turn their bikes upside down and spin the wheels to spook the horses. It is not recorded whether or not this strategy was ever used in anger, but it reflects the reality of the day: the bicycle was more than a means for people to get about: its impact on personal mobility meant it was seen by the government as a key instrument in war.

Simply put, if you could get your foot soldiers into action quickly, that could change the outcome of a battle. Moreover, unlike conventional cavalry mounts, the bicycle did not need feeding and could be easily transported overseas. There were early proposals to put together fighting battalions mounted on HIGH-WHEELERS, but it was the advent of the SAFETY BICYCLE in the late 1880s that led to the formation of bicycle detachments.

The 26th Middlesex (Cyclist) Volunteer Rifle Corps, formed in 1888, was the first, with cyclists divided up according to their mounts: safeties, high-wheelers, TRICYCLISTS. The Middlesex numbered nearly 400. In 1906, cycling maneuvres involved 50 cyclist companies. There were experiments with defensive tactics against cavalry such as putting the cyclists inside a "fence" of cycles and trials with various tricycle-borne machine guns. Armed cyclists feature in "The Land Ironclads," a short story written by H. G. Wells just before the First World War. In that conflict, the

British army included 14 cycle battalions, totalling 7,000 men, with folding bicycles made by the Birmingham Small Arms company (BSA) most commonly used.

The British were not the only ones using two-wheeled soldiers. Cycle maker Bianchi produced a folding bike in 1915 for the "*bersaglieri*," the Italian light infantry, in 1915, which had fat tires and suspension for off-road use; it is claimed to be the precursor of the MOUNTAIN BIKE. The future double TOUR DE FRANCE winner Ottavio Bottecchia was part of a cycling squadron on the Austro-Italian front while the Tour de France founder HENRI DESGRANGE oversaw the training of 50,000 French cycling soldiers during the conflict.

World War I cut short the careers of several greats: the 1907 and 1908 Tour winner Lucien Petit-Breton was killed near the front at Troyes in 1917, while other Tour winners to lose their lives were Octave Lapize, shot down in 1917 close

to Verdun, and Francois Faber, killed in 1915 while carrying a comrade back to his lines through no-man's-land (see HEROIC ERA for more on these champions).

More fortunate was Paul Deman, first winner of the Tour of FLANDERS, who was a spy working for the Belgian secret service, smuggling documents into Holland on his bike. He was decorated for bravery by the English and French as well as his homeland; shortly before the war closed he was arrested by the Germans and sentenced to death, with the armistice happening just in time to save him.

There are other tales, such as that of the 1938 Tour winner GINO BARTALI: along the lines of Paul Deman, the "Pious One" pretended to go out training each day in occupied Italy but in fact he was a courier working for a resistance network riding between Florence and Assisi: he advised on train movements, but most important, hidden in his frame were forged documents that were used to make fake passports enabling Jewish refugees to escape. The network is said to have saved some 800 lives.

Bartali's great rival FAUSTO COPPI spent much of his war in a prison camp in North Africa; their teammate in the 1949 Tour de France Alfredo Martini, on the other hand, used his bike to ferry Molotov cocktails for the Italian partisans, a risky business on the rocky roads of the time. On a more sinister note, the VÉLODROME D'HIVER in Paris earned a grim reputation after it was used as a transit camp when the Nazis and French collaborators rounded up thousands of French Jews for transportation in 1942.

Numerous troops of cyclists also figured in combat in the Second World War; at the Normany landings, for example, paratroops were dropped with folding bikes, again made by BSA. The Germans used cyclist battalions in their invasion of Norway, and 20,000 cycles were vital in the Japanese attack on Singapore through supposedly impassable jungle. The cycle was the vehicle of choice for guerrilla groups—booby-trapped by Italians in Rome and by the Vietcong—while in the Vietnam war thousands of bicycles and porters were used to ferry supplies for the Vietcong. One senator remarked, only partly in jest, that it would be better to bomb their bikes than their bridges.

Switzerland maintained bike-borne troops into the 21st century while the Swedes kept them going into the 1980s. Both used heavyweight machines; the final Swiss bike, the MO-93, had seven-speed gears and carry-racks front and rear. The Swedish bike was sold under the Kronanbike label after Swedish army bikes kept finding their way onto the secondhand market.

The end of the First World War was marked, in spring 1919, by the running of the Circuit des Champs de Bataille, a seven-day stage race starting and finishing in Strasbourg along the Western Front. The roads were barely recognizable, the riders ill-trained, and outside the major cities there was no food to be found. A truck followed the race carrying potatoes, meat, and butter. PARIS–ROUBAIX was also run that spring, through the devastated cities and ravaged countryside of Northern France.

"It's hell," wrote HENRI DESGRANGE. "Shell-holes one after the other, with no gaps, outlines of trenches, barbed wire cut into 1,000 pieces; unexploded shells on the roadside, here and there, graves. Crosses bearing a jaunty tricolor are the only light relief." That year's race was christened "Hell of the North" by another writer, and the name has stuck.

Bike racing across Europe never quite stopped during World War II, although the major Tours were not organized.

The Tour de France organizer Jacques Goddet was always proud of the fact that he had refused to put on his race under occupation in spite of coming under pressure; the Giro, for its part, was replaced by a series of one-day races with an overall title, the Giro di Guerra. The Tour of Flanders was the only major event to be run in an occupied country, and did so with German police help; this led to controversy after the conflict. In France, races were run virtually up to Liberation in both the occupied and non-occupied zones, as Jean Bobet relates in his detailed *Le Vélo a l'Heure Allemande* (*Cycling in German Time*, La Table Ronde, 2007). In Great Britain, the near-absence of traffic on wartime roads enabled Percy Stallard to bring in road racing, European style.

WATSON, Graham (b. England, 1956)

The first Anglophone photographer to break into the tightly knit group of snappers who shoot European cycle racing and who consequently has done much to popularize the sport in English-speaking nations over the last 30 years. Like TV commentator PHIL LIGGETT, Watson started as a bike racer; he spent time working in a London photo studio and began his photography career shooting for *Cycling* magazine. He moved to *Winning* in the 1980s where he made his name thanks to his work with breakthrough stars such as SEAN KELLY and GREG LEMOND, and thanks to one sequence of pictures in particular showing Jesper Skibby being run down by the organizers' car in the Tour of FLANDERS.

He has been a fixture at leading US magazine *VeloNews* for many years and has been close to LANCE ARMSTRONG since the Texan turned pro in 1992. As well as selling pictures and annual calendars and working for many of the top teams, Watson has produced over 20 books, including inside accounts of his life in bike racing. These offer a different perspective to that of most writers, because motorbike-borne photographers have unique access to the decisive moments of the greatest races.

WEIGHT   An obsession for professional cyclists. The story goes that when the Italian trainer Luigi Cecchini began working with the Dane Bjarne Riis, he handed him two kilogram bags of sugar and said: imagine riding with that lot under your saddle. Riis lost a few kilos and won the 1996 Tour, albeit, he later confessed, with the help of EPO as well. There are also tales of riders training with weights under their saddle, although none now go as far as Jean Robic, the 1947 Tour winner, a featherweight who would collect a *bidon* containing 10 kg of lead at the top of a mountain to help him keep up on the descent.

The importance of weight loss when climbing is clearly illustrated, although the precise effects vary from rider to rider, because of factors such as the steepness of the hill, the rider's power output, and the percentage of a rider's weight that is lost. One estimate (MICHELE FERRARI's) is that a kilo adds 1.25 percent to a rider's time up a hill. That means, in essence, that for each kilo a rider is heavier, he is having to work 1.25 percent harder.

The ratio between the power a cyclist can produce without "blowing up"—sustainable power—and his weight is the key figure: Ferrari estimated that the figure a Tour winner needs to produce is 6.7 watts per kilo (quoted in Dan Coyle, *Tour de Force*). In 2009, weight loss was one of the keys to BRADLEY WIGGINS's transformation into a TOUR DE FRANCE contender: the Briton went from 77 kg at his track racing weight to 73 kg. Critically, he lost weight while minimizing his loss of power. His trainer estimated that even at his Tour weight, he would still be able to ride a 4,000 m pursuit at 4 minutes 15 seconds pace, only slightly slower than he was doing in training in the run-up to the Beijing OLYMPIC GAMES.

WHEELS   Relative to its weight, the bicycle wheel is one of the strongest man-made constructions, having to take loads in various planes: up and down (radial—the rider's weight, bumps in the road, braking), side to side (lateral—particularly where the rider is standing on the pedals to climb a hill), and twisting (torsional—the circular motion from the chain and sprockets that drives the bike forward). An experiment with a conventional wheel built by Condor Cycles estimated its working load-to-weight ratio at about 400-1.

Early BONESHAKERS featured wheels of "West Indian hardwood, amaranth, makrussa, hickory or lemon tree"; wood continued to be used for rims, particularly for track racing, up to the Second World War. They were made either by turning a single strip into a hoop and biscuit-jointing the ends, or by lamination.

The development of the HIGH-WHEELER led to a focus on wheel design and a gradual evolution from the cart-type wood spoked wheels used by early cycles such as the DRAISIENNE. The key development came in 1870 when JAMES STARLEY patented the Ariel high-wheel cycle. This had wheels on which the spokes were tensioned so that the riders' weight was suspended; four years later, Starley introduced tangential spoking, in which the spokes ran at opposing angles, crossing over each other.

Steel rims were initially ubiquitous, with wood used for racing, but aluminium gradually took over, with the main market

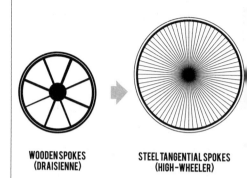

**WOODEN SPOKES
(DRAISIENNE)**   **STEEL TANGENTIAL SPOKES
(HIGH-WHEELER)**

difference whether the rim was single walled—one layer of metal—or double walled, with two, for greater strength. Over 130 years later, specialist rim-makers such as France's Mavic, makers of the legendary SSC black-anodized tubular rim (Special Service des Courses) still supply this kind of rim.

But at the racing end of the market, there have been other developments in recent years. The first disc wheel design appeared in 1892. The idea was that it would be more AERODYNAMIC than spoked wheels, but there were already questions about how it would perform in side winds. It was not until FRANCESCO MOSER smashed

SAME-SIZED WHEELS (SAFETY BIKE)   **DISC WHEEL**   **CARBON-FIBRE ONE-PIECE**   **MODERN WHEEL**

the HOUR RECORD in 1982 that disc wheels came back into the picture. The breakthrough was in the idea that on the flat at least aerodynamics mattered more than weight. Moser's use of the wheels was challenged but his lawyers won the case by arguing that the wheels actually had one single spoke.

Carbon-fiber discs are now ubiquitous wherever pure speed matters: time trials on road and track and track endurance races. Rear discs are always used, with the choice of a front disc depending on wind conditions, as wind from the side can affect the bike's stability. Variants on the disc include one-piece carbon wheels with three or four vast

flattened spokes.

From 1994 when CAMPAGNOLO brought out the Shamal, the top end of the racing and then the CYCLOSPORTIVE market was gradually taken over by deep-rimmed wheels, which had a V section rather than the traditional shallow U. These are put together in the manfacturer's factory, rather than lovingly crafted from individual spokes, rims, and hubs in a wheelbuilder's shop. "Factory-built" wheels, carbon-fiber for racing, aluminium for training, are now the gear of choice, and in a time trial, one will be used at the front end rather than a disc. Virtually every cycle component maker has gotten in on the act.

WIGGINS, Bradley

Born: Ghent, Belgium, April 28, 1980

Major wins: Olympic pursuit champion 2004, 2008; Olympic team pursuit champion 2008; world pursuit champion 2003, 2007, 2008; world team pursuit champion 2007, 2008; world Madison champion (with Mark Cavendish) 2008; world junior pursuit champion 1998

Nicknames: the Twig, Wiggo

Further reading: *In Pursuit of Glory*, Bradley Wiggins, Orion, 2010

A mainstay of the GREAT BRITAIN Olympic TRACK RACING team who won two gold medals in Beijing and then equaled the British record set by ROBERT MILLAR when he finished fourth in the 2009 TOUR DE FRANCE. Wiggins is a gangling Londoner—although born in Ghent—with a penchant for the Mod culture of the 1960s, the music of punk rockers the Jam, and a collection of electric guitars. He is also one of the finest impersonators in professional cycling: his imitation of fellow 2009 Tour star MARK CAVENDISH is particularly hilarious.

Wiggins's estranged Australian father Garry was a top professional on the SIX-DAY RACING scene in the 1980s; by 1998, Bradley had surpassed his father by taking the junior world pursuit title, and in 2000 at the age of 20 he won an Olympic bronze medal in the team pursuit. The world pursuit title followed in 2003, and in 2004 he took three medals in the Athens Olympics: gold in the individual pursuit, silver in the team event, and bronze in the Madison. No Briton had achieved anything to match this since the 1960s, but Wiggins received little recognition at home; his sense of deflation was such that he turned to drink for several months, getting through his entire collection of Belgian beer and spending much time in the pub.

He made his Tour de France debut in 2006 and rode strongly in the 2007 race, coming close to winning a time-trial stage, but had his sights fixed on defending his Olympic title in Beijing. He took three gold medals (individual and team pursuits, Madison) in the 2008 world championships and followed up with two golds in the pursuits in China despite suffering from a severe virus shortly before departure.

The following year, having got the Games out of his system, he astonished most of European cycling by riding an almost perfect Tour, struggling only on the penultimate day's mountaintop finish at Mont Ventoux and finishing just 32 seconds behind third-placed LANCE ARMSTRONG, who tipped him as a possible future winner. It was an improvement that hinged on two things: weight loss and his need to find new goals after his Olympic triumphs.

By the end of the season he was the object of one of cycling's biggest transfer battles between Team Sky and his 2009 backer Garmin, eventually moving to the fledgling British squad.

In 2008 he published his MEMOIRS, *In Pursuit of Glory*. The title was thought up by Brad and his wife, Cath, and the book delves deep into his relations with his father and his problems post-Athens.

WOMEN   At the start of the cycling era, the new pastime played a key role in getting women out of the kitchen, away from chaperones, and out of constraining multiple petticoats and corsets into "rational" dress. Surprizing as it may seem now, the CYCLISTS' TOURING CLUB was involved in at least one case in the 1890s where a female member was refused entry to the women's bar in a hotel because she was wearing "rational" dress—in essence baggy long trousers—rather than a skirt.

"For women, the bicycle became a vehicle of liberation from domesticity and isolation," wrote the historian Jim McGurn in *On Your Bicycle* (John Murray, 1980). There were disputes over the pros and cons of rational dress and long skirts, and public resistance in remote parts to the former; it remained an issue until the 1920s.

Women began racing soon

Six Great Women's Champions

◈

Hélène Dutrieu (b. Belguim, 1877, d. 1961) First women's HOUR RECORD holder, setting a distance of 39.190 km in 1895. Dutrieu was one of a group of professionals who used the Simpson lever chain immortalized by HENRI DE TOULOUSE-LAUTREC. She won world track titles in 1897 and 1898, and in November 1898 she won a 12-day race in London. She was awarded the Cross of Saint André by King Leopold of Belgium and went on from racing to stunt cycling (for example, looping the loop), motor sport, and then aviation. In 1910 she became the fourth woman in the world to be licensed as an airplane pilot, causing a minor scandal when it was revealed that she did not wear a corset in the cockpit. She was the first woman pilot to stay airborne for more than an hour. She later took French nationality and was awarded the Légion d'Honneur.

Eileen Sheridan (b. 1942) was British cycling's second woman star after Marguerite Wilson, a double winner of the British Best All Rounder (1949 and 1950). Sheridan set records at most of the set time-trial distances before turning professional for the Hercules bike company to break place-to-place records. Her best was Land's End to John O'Groats (1954) in 2 days 11 hours 7 minutes. She featured in a documentary made by Dunlop entitled *Spinning Wheels: Cycle Sport 50s Style,* which also included REG HARRIS, and did publicity for Player's cigarettes.

Maria Canins (b. 1949) Italian who combined cross-country skiing and road racing at the highest level, becoming JEANNIE LONGO's greatest rival in the late 1980s. Canins was a great climber but a weak time triallist, so her best wins were in races where she could use her climbing skills. She twice won the women's Grande Boucle, won four medals in world road titles (two bronze, two silver), and took stage races such as the Giro d'Italia and Tour of Norway. She went on to take two mountain-bike world titles as a veteran and 15 Italian cross-country skiing championships in various categories.

Connie Carpenter-Phinney (b. 1957) American who came to cycling from speed skating, in which she won a national title in 1976. That year she won the US road and pursuit titles, repeating the double in 1977 and 1979. In 1984 she became the first women's Olympic road race champion in Los Angeles, narrowly outsprinting her teammate Rebecca Twigg. Carpenter was also a national collegiate standard rower. She is married to Davis Phinney, a stage winner in the Tour de France in 1987, and their son Taylor is tipped to be the next big name in US cycling.

Yvonne McGregor (b. England, 1961) was one of the first wave of British track cyclists to succeed after the beginning of lottery funding in 1997. Like CHRIS BOARDMAN, McGregor was a time triallist, hour record breaker, and pursuiter who was trained by Peter Keen from the early 1990s. The Yorkshirewoman took a surprise win in the points race in the 1994 Commonwealth Games, then was part of the British track riders' breakthrough in Sydney, taking bronze in the individual pursuit. She added the world title that year and was made an MBE in 2002.

Leontien Van Moorsel (b. Netherlands, 1970) Triple Olympic champion in Sydney in 2000, where she won the road race, the time trial, and the 3 km pursuit. She defended her road title in Athens in 2004 in spite of a crash on the penultimate lap, after which she retired as one of Holland's most successful Olympians. Van Moorsel traded on a glamorous image, wearing bright lipstick and long painted fingernails, but took time out of the sport between 1994 and 1998 to recover from anorexia and depression. On her return she won the world time trial title and took silver in the road race on home soil.

after the first men's race in 1869 but the cycling authorities have consistently failed to keep up with their progress. There were early records set by the American Jan Lindsey and Germany's Marguerite Gast, while the best early women's track racer was Hélène Dutrieu of France (see opposite), who set an hour record of 39.190 km; the infamous "Choppy" Warburton (see also SOIGNEUR) had female protégés such as "Lisette"—Amélie le Gall—who won an early world championship in 1896.

In GREAT BRITAIN, the Rosslyn Ladies' Cycling Club was founded in 1922. Marguerite Wilson was British cycling's first woman star, a record-breaker who rode as a professional in the 1930s, breaking every women's record on the books including the END TO END and 1,000 miles. It was not until the 1950s that women's racing took off again; the Women's Cycle Racing Association was founded in 1956 and began running a national road race championship. Eileen Sheridan won the first women's BBAR and 100 title in 1950. (The first women's national TIME TRIAL championship was the 25 held in 1944).

While the UCI began holding a women's road race world title in 1958 (the first held in Reims, France, won by Elsy Jacobs of Luxembourg) under pressure from Eileen Gray, one of the first women to race in British national colors in 1946, they did so against a certain amount of opposition, and women's racing truly began to gather pace only in the 1970s and 1980s. That was thanks partly to an upsurge in interest in the US after the foundation of the Coors Classic, and by the end of the 1980s most of the best women's races were in North America.

The women's TOUR DE FRANCE started in 1984 and was run concurrently with the men's race but that came to an end in 1989 and a similar event known as La Grande Boucle Féminine is run by a different company, but lasts less than a week. The toughest races on the women's calendar are the Tour de l'Aude and GIRO D'ITALIA, while the women's World Cup includes scaled down CLASSICS such as Flèche Wallonne and the Tour of FLANDERS. The money available in women's road racing is minimal compared to what is on offer for men; the disparity is far greater than, say, in tennis.

MOUNTAIN-BIKING has played a key role, because women competed on equal terms from the sport's beginnings in the 1970s and the sport did not have road racing's tradition of discrimination. That meant that when mountain-biking took off in the early 1990s women such as Britain's Caroline Alexander and the Americans Juli Furtado and Missy Giove were able to make a far better living than if they had been racing on the road.

On the other hand, questions about women's cycling were still being raised in the early 1990s, when there was debate about the length and toughness of women's road racing—the UCI felt distances should be restrained, while some races such as the Ore–Ida Classic in the US deliberately went outside the rules.

Women's racing in the OLYMPIC GAMES began only in 1984 and in the Commonwealth Games as late as 1990. At the time of the Beijing Olympics the British sprinter Victoria Pendleton rightly complained that women were discriminated against in track racing, with only three events to the men's seven. This will be put right in 2012, but is many years overdue.

(SEE ALSO **BERYL BURTON, NICOLE COOKE, JEANNIE LONGO, ALFONSINA STRADA**)

WORLD CHAMPIONSHIPS

Cycling as a world sport was not unified in the 19th century but the dominant organization was Britain's National Cycle Union, strictly an amateur body. Their national title races were considered unofficial world championships. The first was a mile race at Wolverhampton in 1874, won by JAMES MOORE, while in 1879 a long-distance race was organized, lasting 26 hours and won by Charles Terront of France. When the NCU helped to found the International Cycling Association, that body ran the first official world championships, held in Chicago in 1893 to coincide with a world exposition. There was limited participation from outside the US, which took two of the three gold medals.

The Italians began campaigning for a world road-race championship after the First World War, and an amateur title was inaugurated in 1921. The French Grand Prix Wolber was considered an unofficial professional world title until the UCI ran its first professional road race title in 1927, with pros and amateurs riding together on the Nurburgring in Germany. The winner was ALFREDO BINDA of Italy. The UCI has been slow to promote women's racing and there was no world title for women until 1958, when

Defending the world professional/elite title is a rare feat. Only five men have managed it:

Georges Ronsse (Belgium) 1928–9
Rik Van Steenbergen (Belgium) 1956–7
RIK VAN LOOY (Belgium) 1960–1
Gianni Bugno (Italy) 1991–2
Paolo Bettini (Italy) 2006–7

the winner was Elsy Jacobs of Luxembourg.

The Worlds has always been contested by national teams and are run at a different venue each year, always on a circuit. This gives the racing a completely different tenor to most professional events. The great issue is whether national trainers can pull together a disparate group of pros, most of whom race in competing teams for the rest of the season, and turn them into a unit even though it may be in their interests to work for a pro teammate who has a different national jersey on.

The issue is particularly acute in Italy, where the world championship has massive significance, with a tradition going back to Alfredo Binda and FAUSTO COPPI and the *azzurri* are always under colossal pressure. Italian fans still hark back to an episode in Holland in 1948 where Coppi and his great rival GINO BARTALI refused to cooperate and disappeared lamely to the changing rooms.

There are often claims that riders have betrayed their national teammates and notorious cases where this has clearly happened. GREAT BRITAIN was rocked by a scandal at the 2004 world championship in Madrid when two British riders who race for Italian pro teams were seen to work for the Italians. The coach resigned and the cyclists were told they would never wear the national jersey again.

All world championship winners are awarded a rainbow jersey, which can be seen in pictures going back to 1924, and is subtly different depending on the discipline—the time-trial jersey, for example, incorporates a stopwatch. From the top down the stripes are blue, red, black, yellow, and green. A world champion has the right to wear the jersey when competing in his or her discipline. For example, in a time-trial stage of the TOUR DE FRANCE the world time-trial champion can wear his rainbow jersey, while the road champion can wear his in the road race stages.

Once the cyclist's year as world champion has ended, he or she retains the right to wear the rainbow stripes on the collar or cuff of their racing jersey. There is some debate about whether the professional road race jersey carries a CURSE, due to the fact that world champions have frequently failed to live up to

---

Magnificent Seven: Classic World Road Titles

❖

1953—Fausto Coppi takes a solo victory at Lugano, the last truly dominant win of his career, and is seen in the company of his mistress "the White Lady" on the podium. Scandal ensues.

1954—At Solingen, LOUISON BOBET chases down the Swiss Fritz Schaer then wins alone. The "Marseillaise" is heard on German soil for the first time since the war.

1967—EDDY MERCKX enters the big time by winning the pro title at Heerlen, Holland. Britain takes the amateur and women's titles with Graham Webb and BERYL BURTON.

1980—BERNARD HINAULT completely crushes the field on the tough circuit at Sallanches, salvaging a year ruined by a knee injury and ignominious withdrawal from the Tour de France.

1989—LAURENT FIGNON and GREG LEMOND reprise their battle from that year's Tour de France in a rain-hit race at Chambéry. LeMond adds the rainbow jersey to his Tour title.

1993—In Oslo, LANCE ARMSTRONG solos to the pro title ahead of MIGUEL INDURAIN; Jan Ullrich takes the amateur crown. Both men will go on to win the Tour, Armstrong will dominate the event.

2002—A rare example of a pure sprinter taking the title: Mario Cipollini crowns a seamless piece of team racing by the Italians to achieve the crowning glory of his career.

their titles, and there have been one or two cases of bizarre injury and even death.

Traditionally the world championships were held in late August, enabling the winner of the Tour de France to carry his form through to the title races. The TEAM TIME TRIAL title was held alongside the road races, contested by amateur teams of four riders. In 1994 the team time trial championship was replaced with a solo TIME-TRIALLING title; the first winner was CHRIS BOARDMAN.

In 1996, the format was radically altered to coincide with the category changes under HEIN VERBRUGGEN that enabled professional cyclists to enter the OLYMPIC GAMES. The professional and amateur categories were abolished and replaced with Elite—top-ranked senior riders from the various continents and those riding for UCI-listed teams—and Under-23. The road events were separated from the track, and the road races moved to late September, after the VUELTA A ESPAÑA. For several years the junior men and women's events were run alongside the seniors'.

From 2012 the Worlds format will be extended, with the junior men's and women's races integrated once again with the senior events, and the racing taking place over a full seven days. The UCI has also introduced a team time trial for men's and women's trade teams on the preceding Sunday, while the Worlds will include a CYCLOSPORTIVE for amateur riders.

Other world championships include: track, held in late March; BMX, held in summer; MOUNTAIN BIKING cross-country and DOWNHILL, held in September; INDOOR CYCLING, held by November; CYCLO-CROSS, held in late February; PARALYMPIC cycling, held in November; masters (40–70-year olds) held in October.

YATES, Sean (b. England, 1960)

The most popular cyclist in Britain since TOM SIMPSON, a legendary hard nut nicknamed "Horse" or "Tonk" for his ability to ride for long spells at high speed in any weather while seemingly unaware of any physical pain. Yates is a devotee of extreme sports—skiing, ice-climbing, motorcycling, bodybuilding—who found his metier in cycling, where he was a British national champion at TIME TRIALLING.

After a spell racing as an amateur in Paris at the ACBB club, he turned professional in 1982 as one of PEUGEOT's FOREIGN LEGION but did not break through until 1988 when he won stages in the VUELTA A ESPAÑA and TOUR DE FRANCE, the latter a time trial at what was then a record speed. A distinctive figure, who rode with his handlebars drooping, his shorts pulled halfway up the thigh, and had a mass of varicose veins on his right calf, Yates became a mainstay of the 7-Eleven and Motorola teams (see USA). He was a hero of LANCE ARMSTRONG when the future seven-time Tour winner turned professional in 1992, while BRADLEY WIGGINS talks fondly of watching his fine ride in the 1994 PARIS–ROUBAIX Classic.

That year Yates also wore the Tour's yellow jersey for a day; he was ready to retire but Armstrong persuaded him to keep going for two more years. After retirement, he managed the British team sponsored by Linda McCartney Foods, then became a *directeur sportif* at CSC before moving to

Armstrong's Discovery Channel and Astana squads, all the time riding his beloved time trials when back home in Britain. His 2010 move to Sky as a *directeur sportif* saw him complete the circle by returning to a British team.

ZIMMERMAN, Arthur Augustus
"A. A." (b. Camden, New Jersey, 1869, d. 1936)

Nicknamed "the Flying Yankee," or "the Jersey Skeeter" because of his pedaling speed, Zimmerman was the first real world star of cycling, the fastest track sprinter of cycling's early years, a prolific record-breaker, and the winner of over 1,400 races. He was the first man to get inside 12 seconds for the flying 200 m (a good time currently is around 10 seconds) while his kilometer world record of 1 minute 9.2 seconds set in 1894 lasted more than 20 years. In 1893 he was the first man to be crowned world sprint champion.

Zimmerman was famed for his rapid pedaling style, estimated at up to 190 revolutions per minute. Together with Frank Bowden of his sponsor RALEIGH he produced an early training manual: *Points for Cyclists with Training.*

Like Major TAYLOR—who he met just as the Major was beginning his rise in the early 1890s—Zimmerman was a product of American track racing, then at its zenith; like Taylor he was sensationally popular when he raced in Europe. He won gold in the first WORLD CHAMPIONSHIPS in 1893 but subsequently his amateur status was called into question. His prizes included bicycles, horses and carriages, pianos, a house, land, silver plates, coffins, jewelery, clocks, and diamonds, and he used his name to market products such as shoes, toe-clips, and clothes. In 1893 the NCU banned him after he struck a deal to ride RALEIGH bikes, so Zimmerman turned professional, asking that his contracts in Paris be paid in gold.

After dismaying the French due to his lean frame—"he looks as if he eats nothing but string" wrote one journalist—Zimmerman won his first races at the Buffalo stadium in Paris from the front with such ease that he was asked to make it look harder; instead, he won from behind. He followed up his French tour with a trip to Australia, drawing a crowd of 27,000 in Sydney. But as with Taylor, the strain of travel and racing caught up with him and he was burned out by his late 20s. He stopped racing in 1905 and ran a hotel until his death in 1936. The Swiss Urs Zimmerman, who finished third in the 1986 Tour de France, is no relation.

(SEE ALSO **TRACK RACING, UNITED STATES**)

All the books mentioned in the text were of use at one time or another, but so too were the following throughout:

Alderson, Frederick, *Bicycling, a History* (David & Charles, 1972).

Augendre, Jacques, et al., *Portraits Legendaires du Cyclisme, compilation*, (Tana, 2007).

Berto, Frank J, *The Dancing Chain* (Van der Plas Publications, 2009).

Chany, Pierre, *La Fabuleuse Histoire du Cyclisme* (La Martinière, 1997).

Ejnès, Gérard and Schaller, Gérard (eds.), *Cent Ans du Tour de France*, (SNC L'Equipe, 2002).

Jacobs, Rene, and van den Bremt, Harry, *Gotha* (Presses de Belgique, 1984).

McGurn, Jim, *On Your Bicycle* (John Murrary, 1987).

Perry, David B, *Bike Cult*, (Four Walls Eight Windows, 1995).

Woodforde, John, *The Story of the Bicycle* (Routledge, 1970).

ACKNOWLEDGMENTS

This book required input from many sources, but specific thanks are due to Ian Austen for providing advice and criticism, to Jo Burt for information on Mint Sauce, to Mark Cavendish for reminding me about "hairnets," to Tim Clifford for giving me the run of his library and showing me his Victorian dog pistol, to Jeff Cloves for advice on poetry and for kindly allowing me to print two of his works, to Luke Edwardes-Evans for the loan of his dissertation on the National Clarion movement, to Richard Hallett for advice on equipment, to Peg Jarvis for agreeing to be interviewed about art and cycling, to Matt Parker for reminding me about soigneurs, to Heiko Salzwedel for providing information on East German cycling, to movingtargetzine for answering questions about cycle couriers, and to Jim Varnish for additional information on cycle speedway.

At Yellow Jersey I remain indebted to Matt Phillips for his patience in overseeing a large, complex project of this kind, and thanks are also due to my sports editor at the *Guardian*, Ian Prior, and my agent, John Pawsey, for their continuing support. Further thanks are due to Christopher Gove at Telegramme Studio for his superb illustrations and Rich Carr for his immaculate text design.

As with previous books, however, the biggest debt is due to Caroline, Patrick, and Miranda for their tolerance in the face of my obsession with life on two wheels.